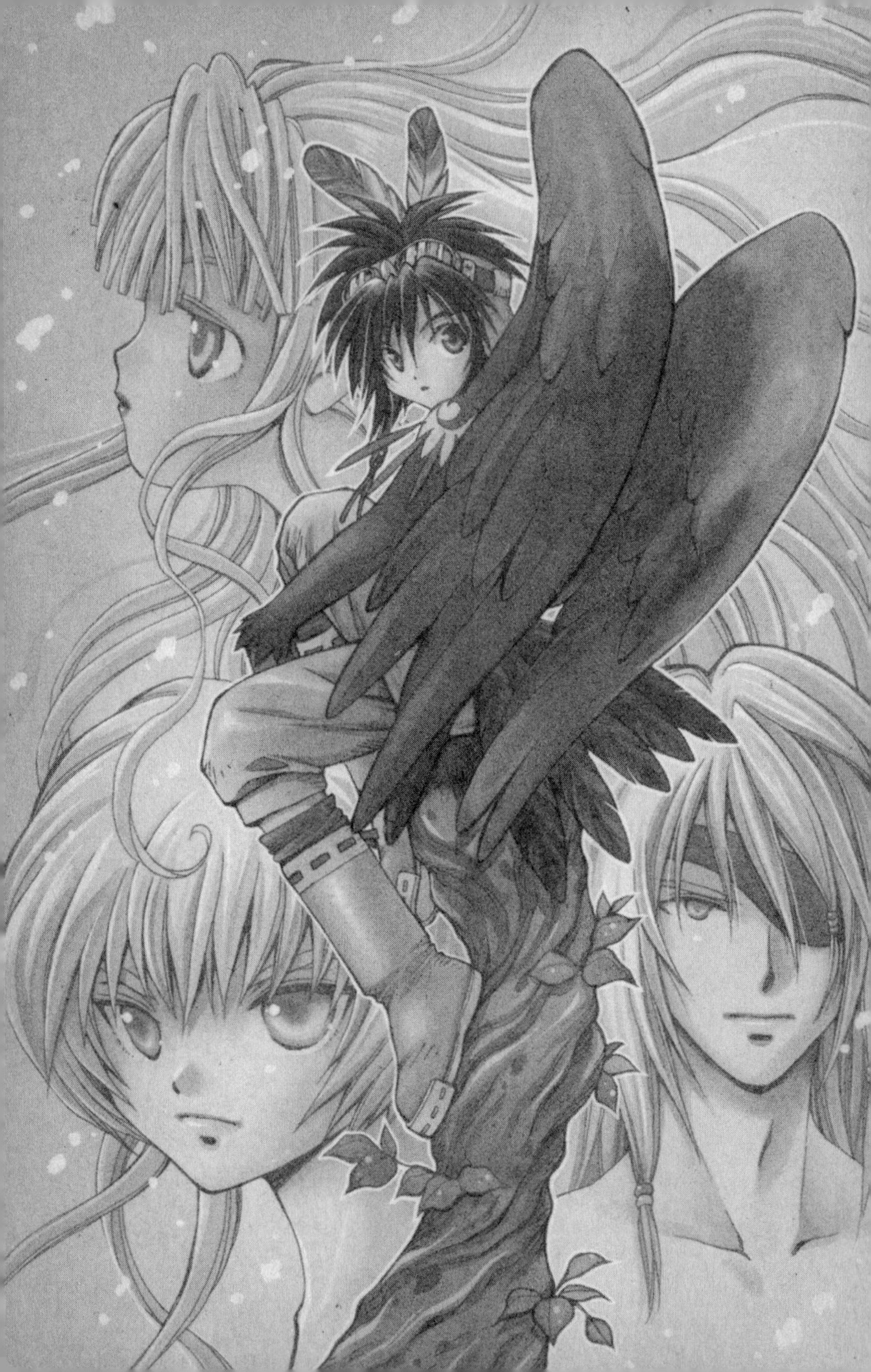

+Anima Vol. 1
Created by Natsumi Mukai

Translation - Alethea Nibley
English Adaptation - Karen S. Ahlstrom
Copy Editors - Peter Ahlstrom and Hope Donovan
Retouch and Lettering - Jennifer Carbajal
Production Artist - Jennifer Carbajal
Cover Design - James Lee

Editor - Troy Lewter
Digital Imaging Manager - Chris Buford
Managing Editor - Lindsey Johnston
Editor-in-Chief - Rob Tokar
VP of Production - Ron Klamert
Publisher - Mike Kiley
President and C.O.O. - John Parker
C.E.O. and Chief Creative Officer - Stuart Levy

A **TOKYOPOP** Manga

TOKYOPOP Inc.
5900 Wilshire Blvd. Suite 2000
Los Angeles, CA 90036

E-mail: info@TOKYOPOP.com
Come visit us online at www.TOKYOPOP.com

ISBN: 1-59816-347-7

First TOKYOPOP printing: May 2006
10 9 8 7 6
Printed in the USA

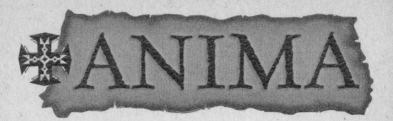

Volume 1
by Natsumi Mukai

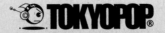

HAMBURG // LONDON // LOS ANGELES // TOKYO

+ A N I M A

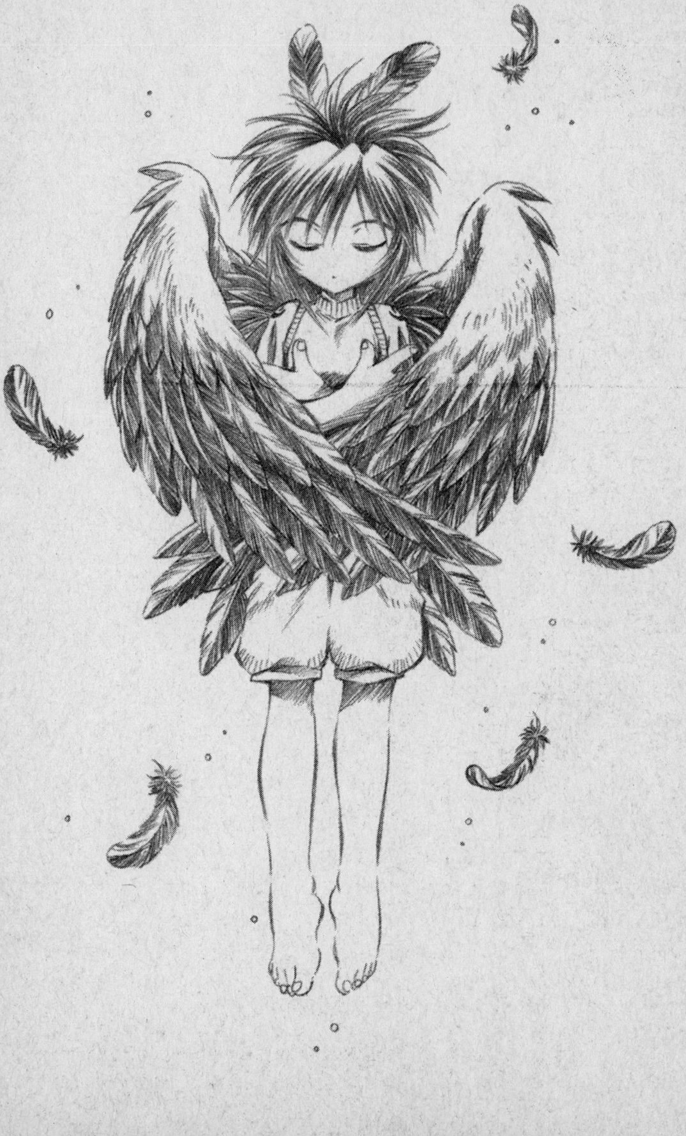

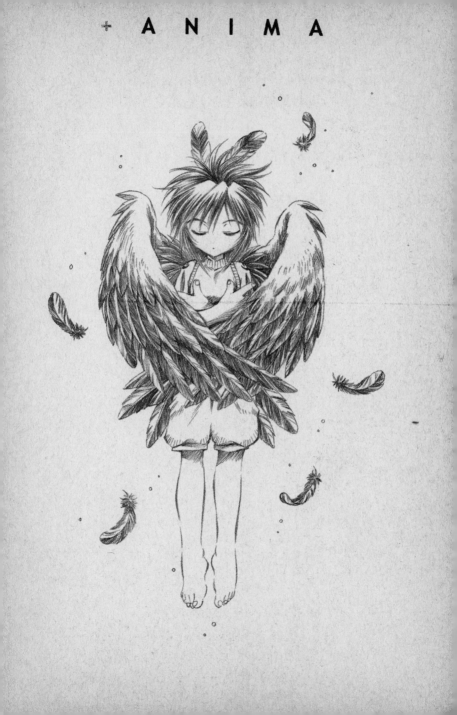

+ANIMA

プラスアニマ

迎夏生

NATSUMI MUKAI

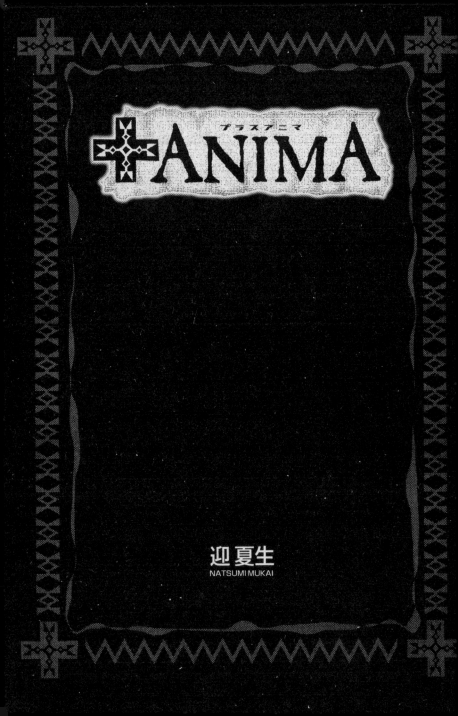

CONTENTS

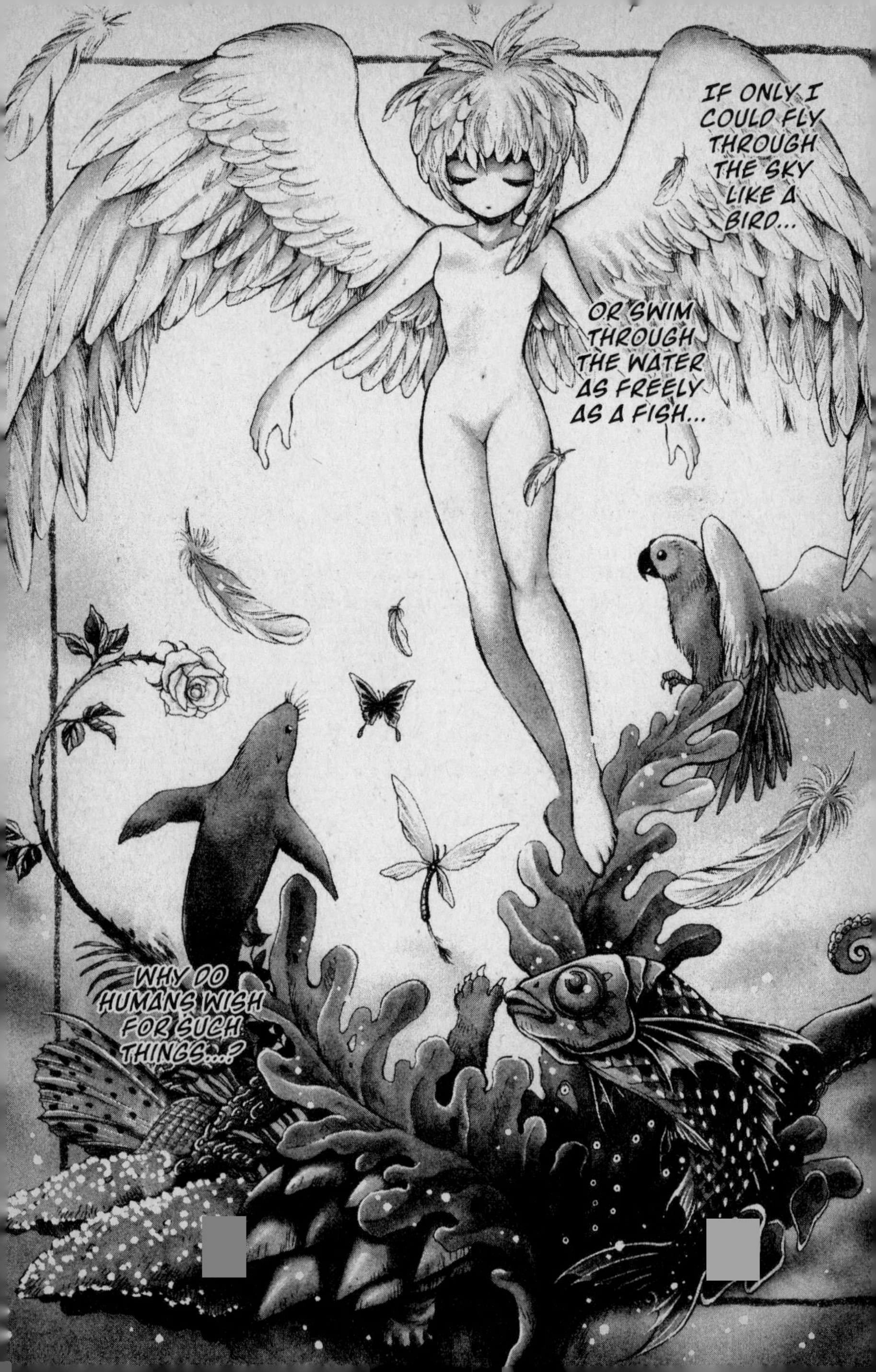
IF ONLY I COULD FLY THROUGH THE SKY LIKE A BIRD...
OR SWIM THROUGH THE WATER AS FREELY AS A FISH...
WHY DO HUMANS WISH FOR SUCH THINGS...?

Chapter 1
The Black Angel and the Silver Princess

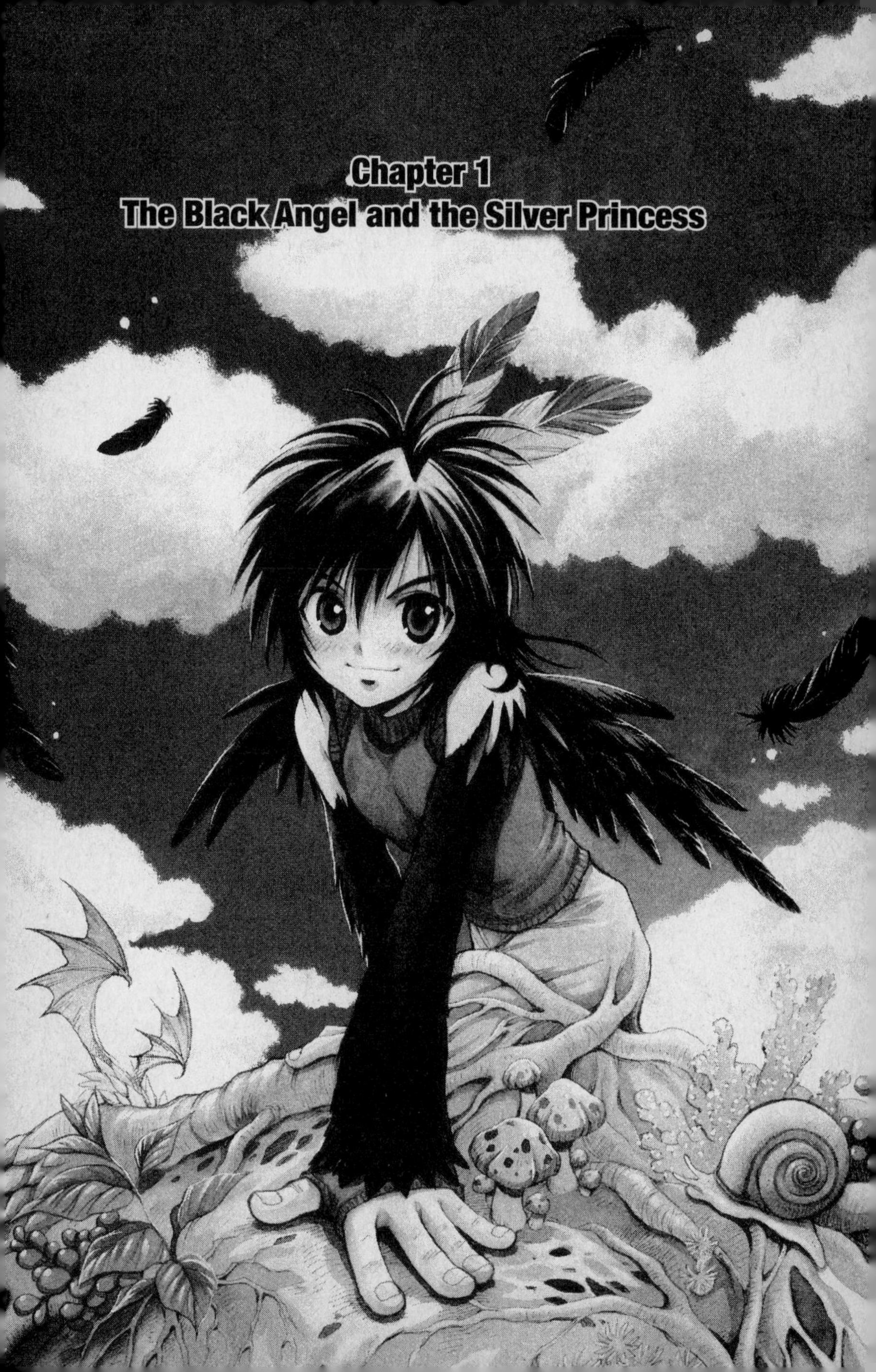

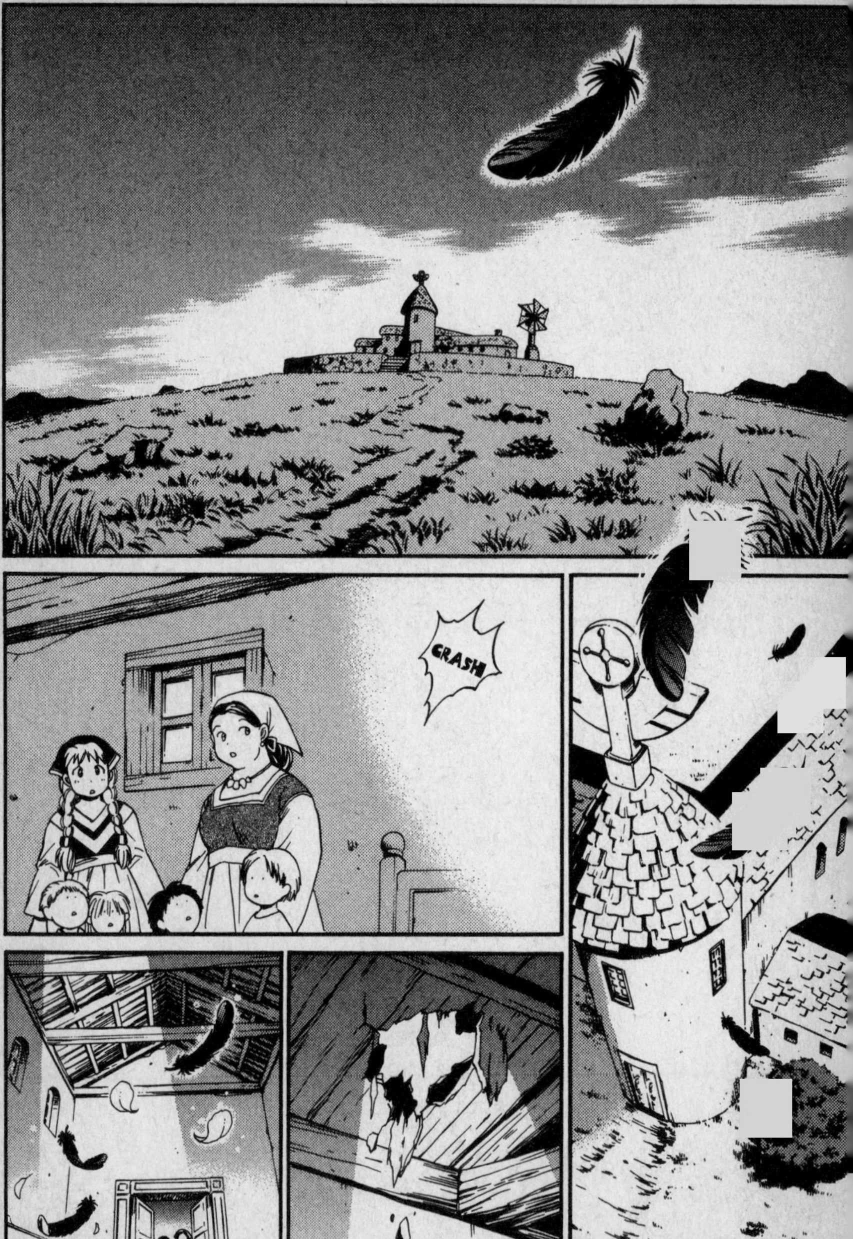
CRASH

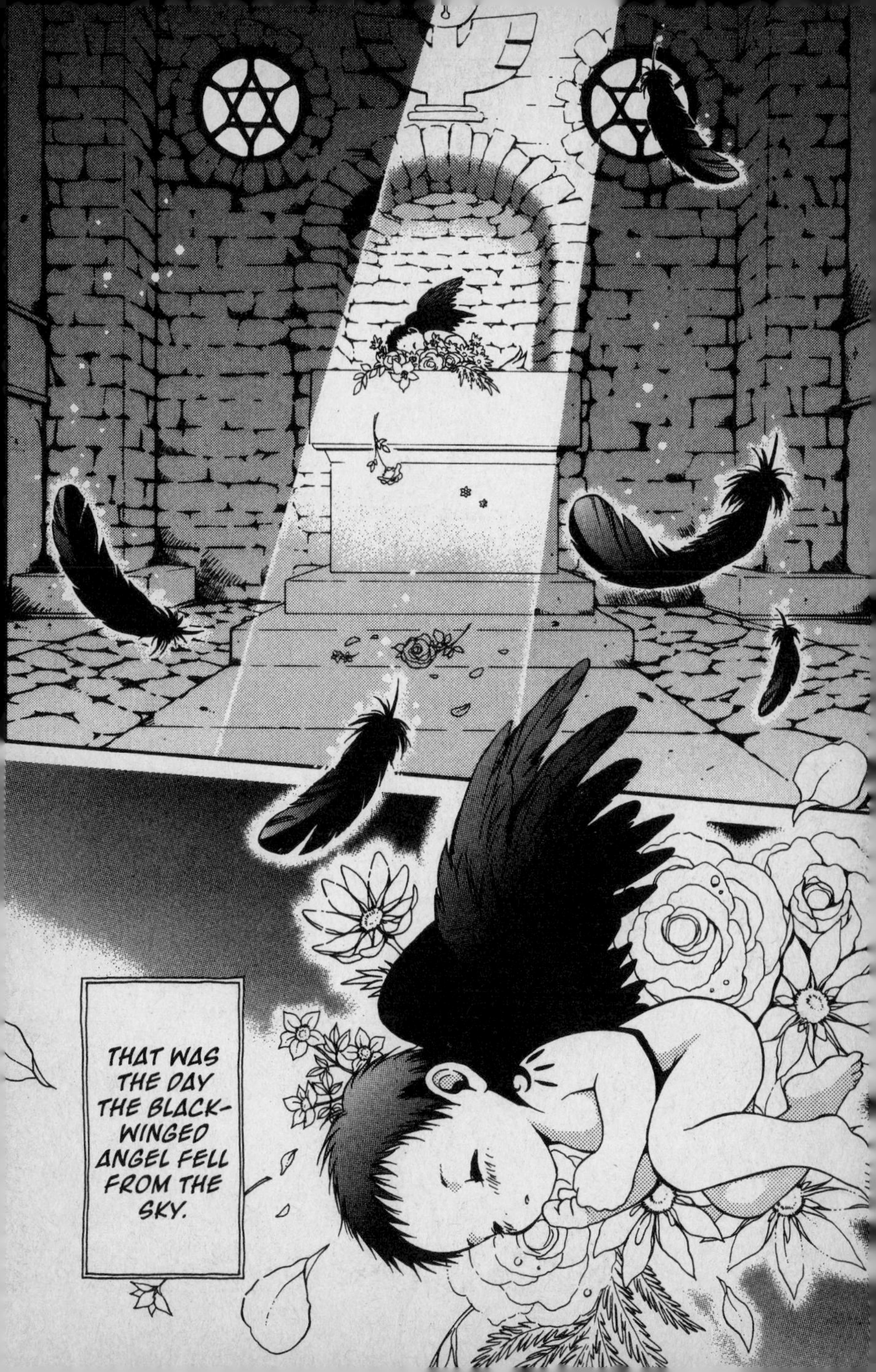
THAT WAS THE DAY THE BLACK-WINGED ANGEL FELL FROM THE SKY.

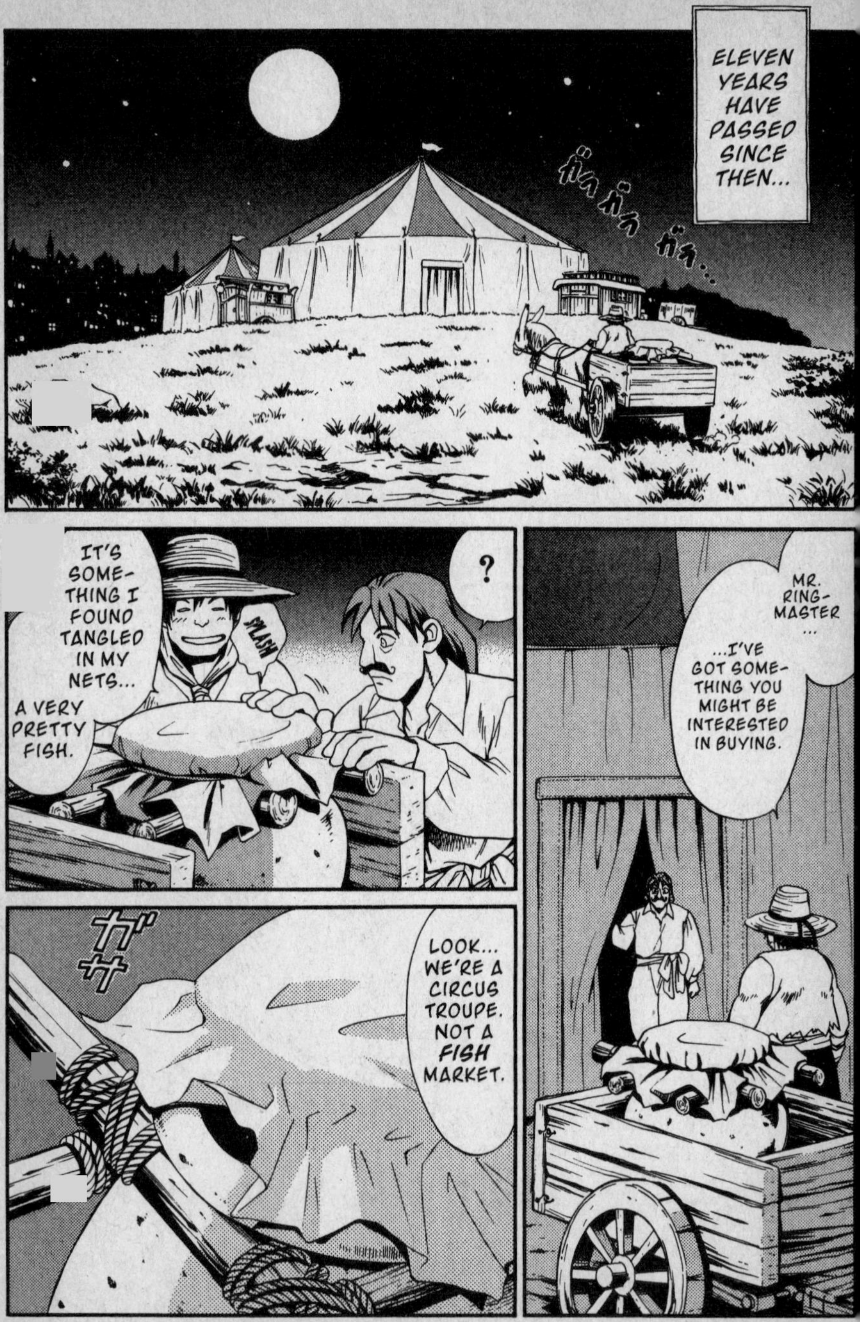
ELEVEN YEARS HAVE PASSED SINCE THEN...
ガラ ガラ ガラ...
MR. RING-MASTER...
...I'VE GOT SOME-THING YOU MIGHT BE INTERESTED IN BUYING.
?
SPLASH
IT'S SOME-THING I FOUND TANGLED IN MY NETS...
A VERY PRETTY FISH.
LOOK... WE'RE A CIRCUS TROUPE. NOT A *FISH* MARKET.
ガサ

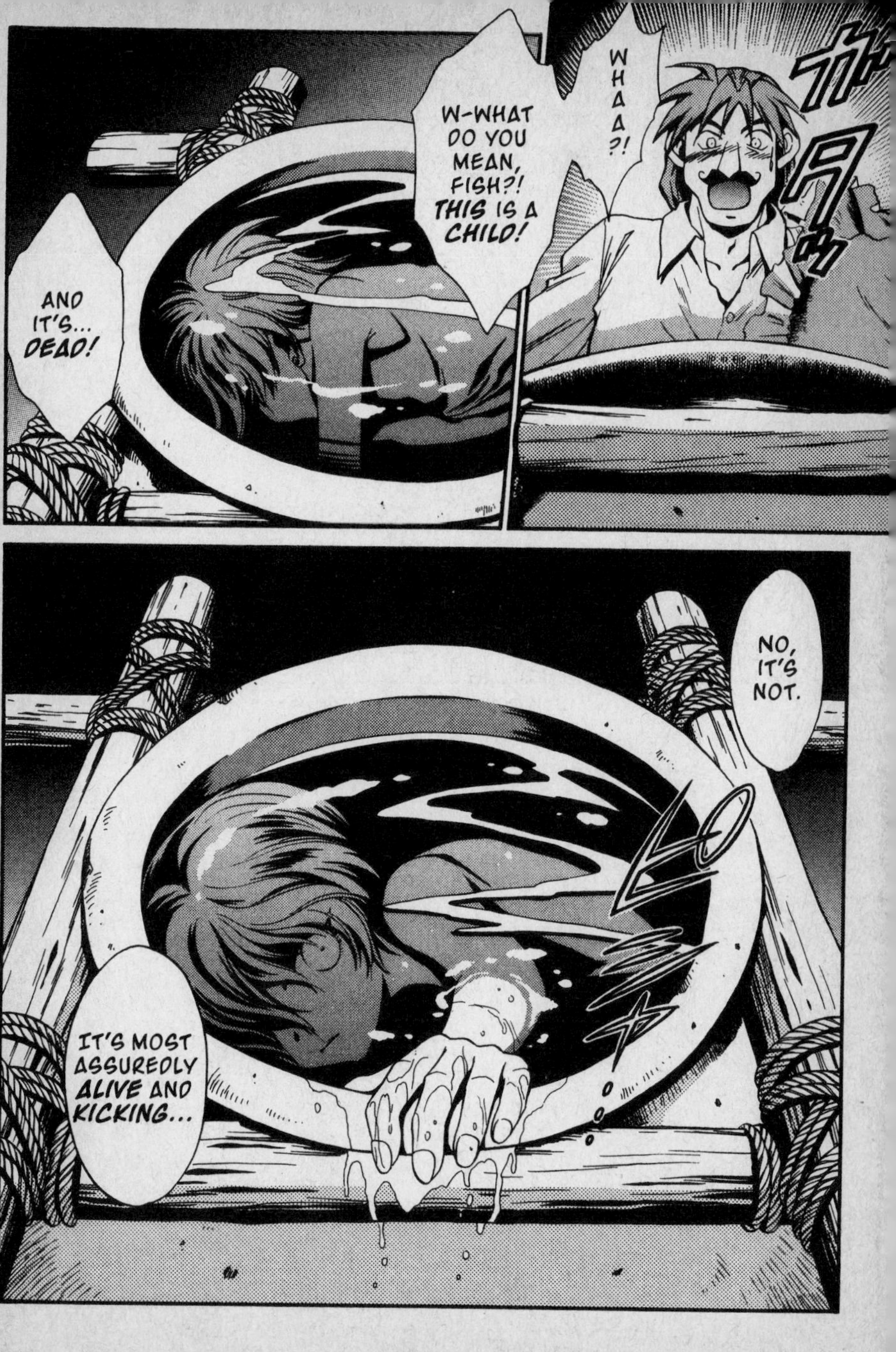
WHAAA?!
W-WHAT DO YOU MEAN, FISH?! THIS IS A CHILD!
AND IT'S... DEAD!
NO, IT'S NOT.
IT'S MOST ASSUREDLY ALIVE AND KICKING...

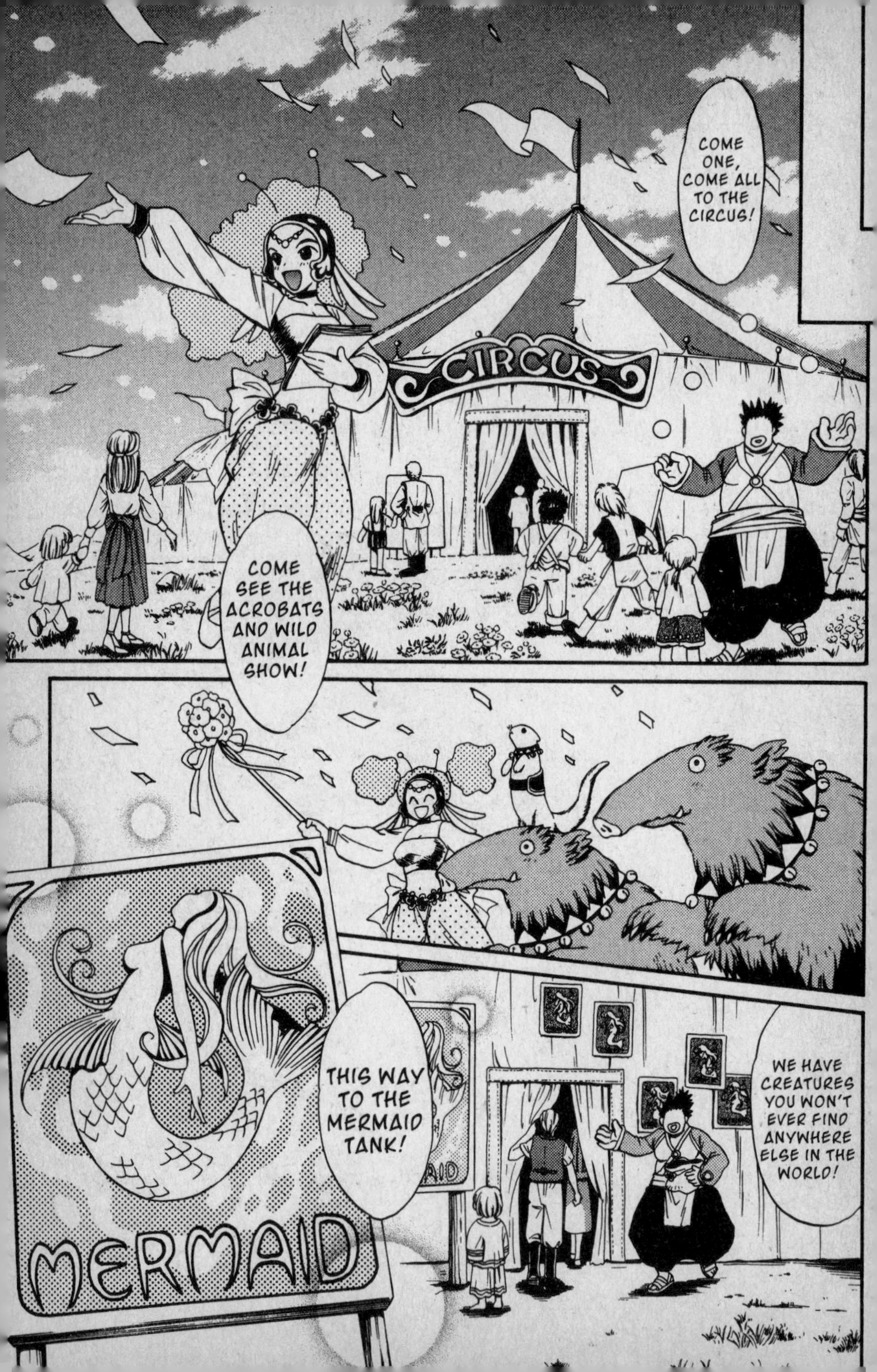

COME ONE, COME ALL TO THE CIRCUS!
CIRCUS
COME SEE THE ACROBATS AND WILD ANIMAL SHOW!
WE HAVE CREATURES YOU WON'T EVER FIND ANYWHERE ELSE IN THE WORLD!
THIS WAY TO THE MERMAID TANK!
MERMAID

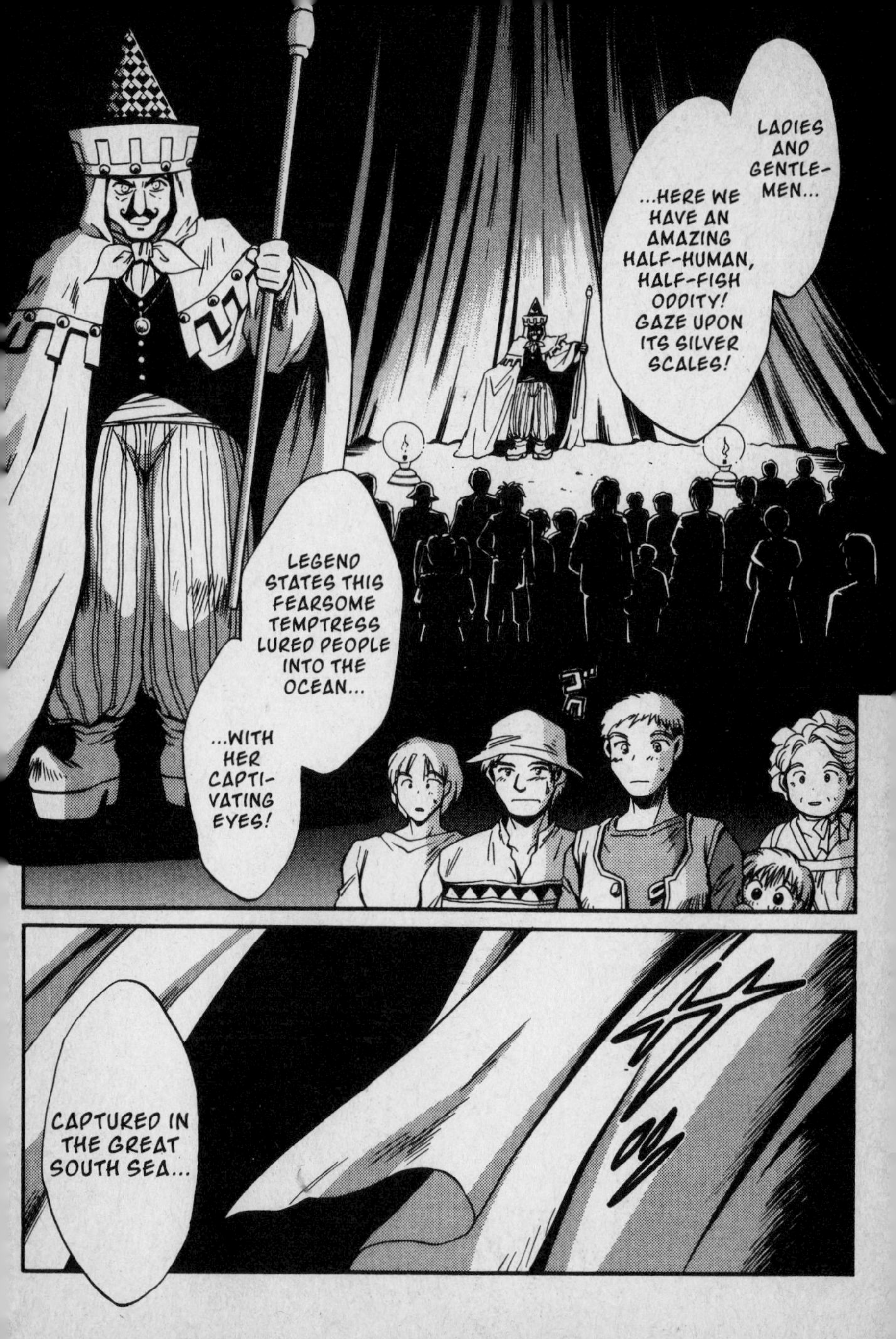
LADIES AND GENTLEMEN...
...HERE WE HAVE AN AMAZING HALF-HUMAN, HALF-FISH ODDITY! GAZE UPON ITS SILVER SCALES!
LEGEND STATES THIS FEARSOME TEMPTRESS LURED PEOPLE INTO THE OCEAN...
...WITH HER CAPTIVATING EYES!
CAPTURED IN THE GREAT SOUTH SEA...

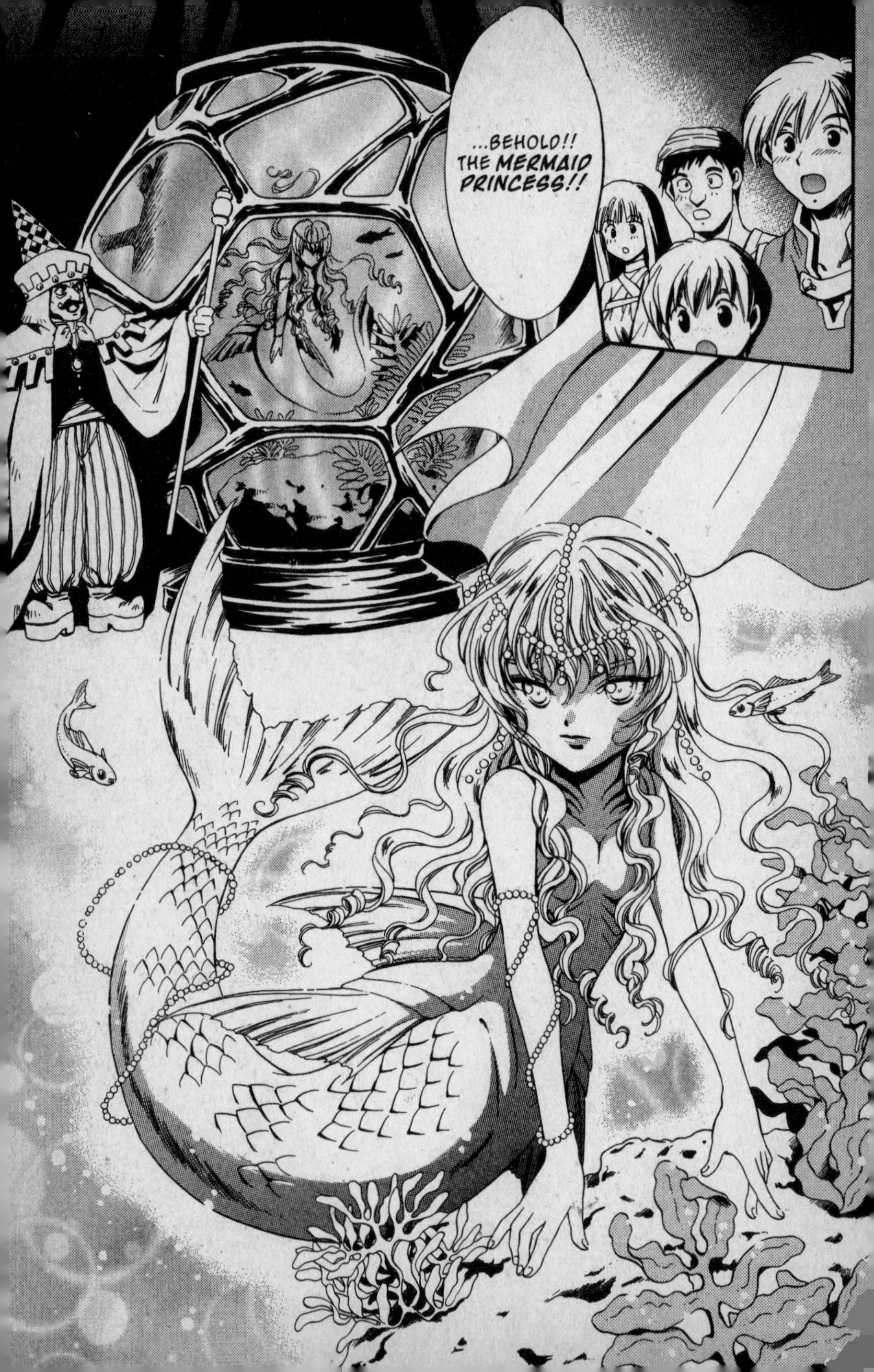
...BEHOLD!! THE MERMAID PRINCESS!!

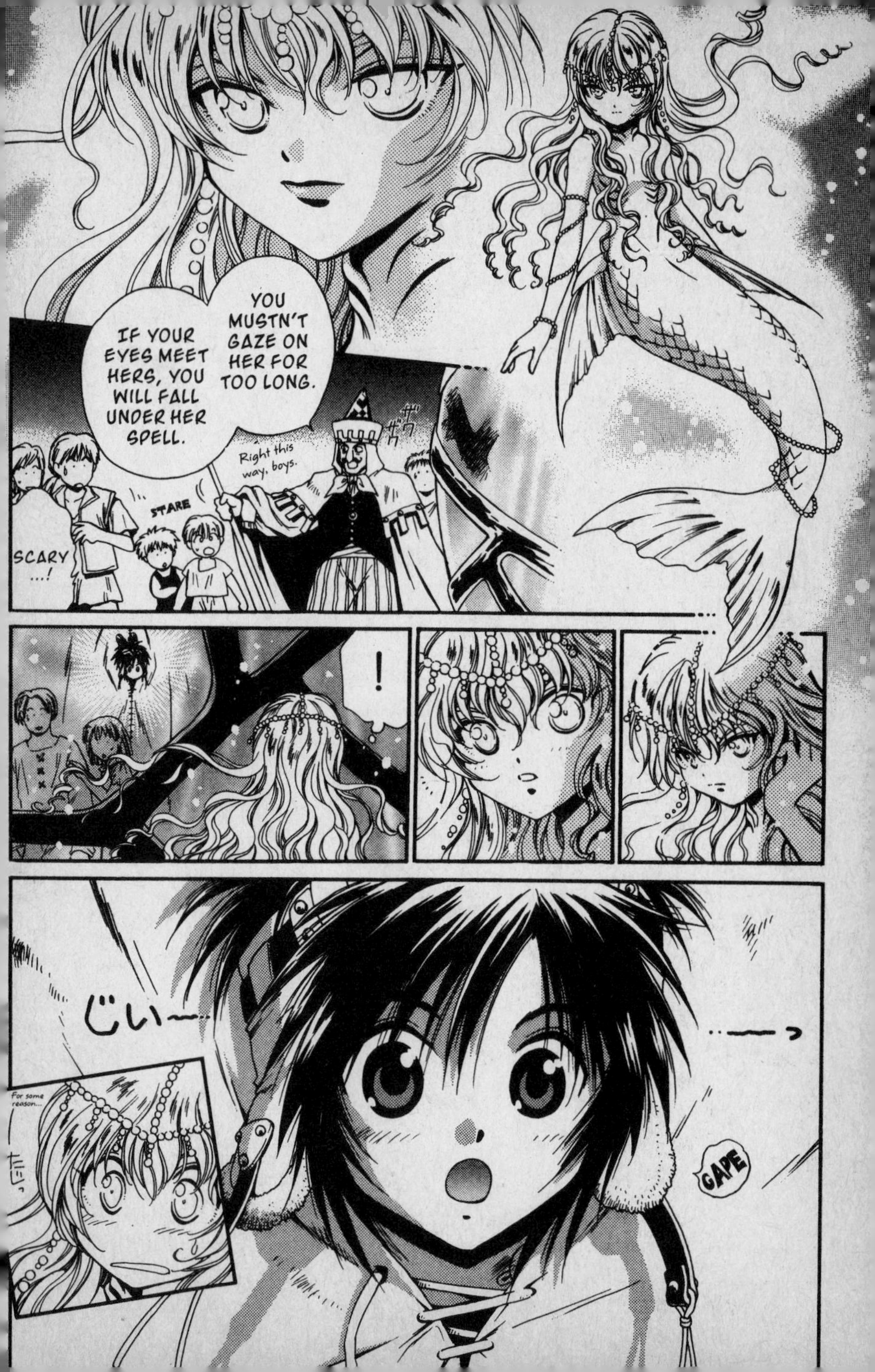
YOU MUSTN'T GAZE ON HER FOR TOO LONG.
IF YOUR EYES MEET HERS, YOU WILL FALL UNDER HER SPELL.
ザワ ザワ
Right this way, boys.
STARE
SCARY ...!
!
...—っ
じぃ—...
GAPE
For some reason...

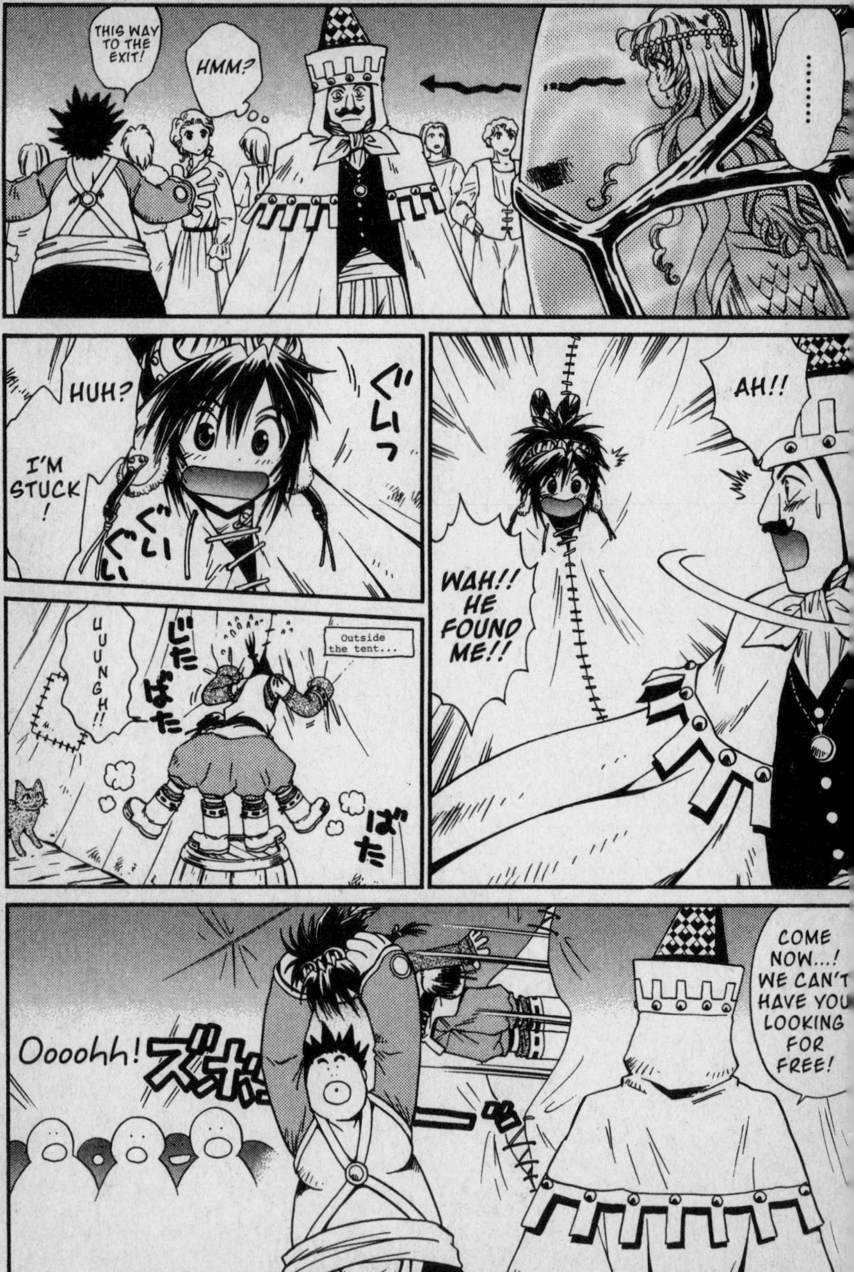

......
HMM?
THIS WAY TO THE EXIT!
AH!!
WAH!! HE FOUND ME!!
ぐいっ
HUH?
I'M STUCK!
ぐい ぐい
Outside the tent...
じた ばた
UUUNGH!!
ばた
COME NOW...! WE CAN'T HAVE YOU LOOKING FOR FREE!
ズボ
Oooohh!

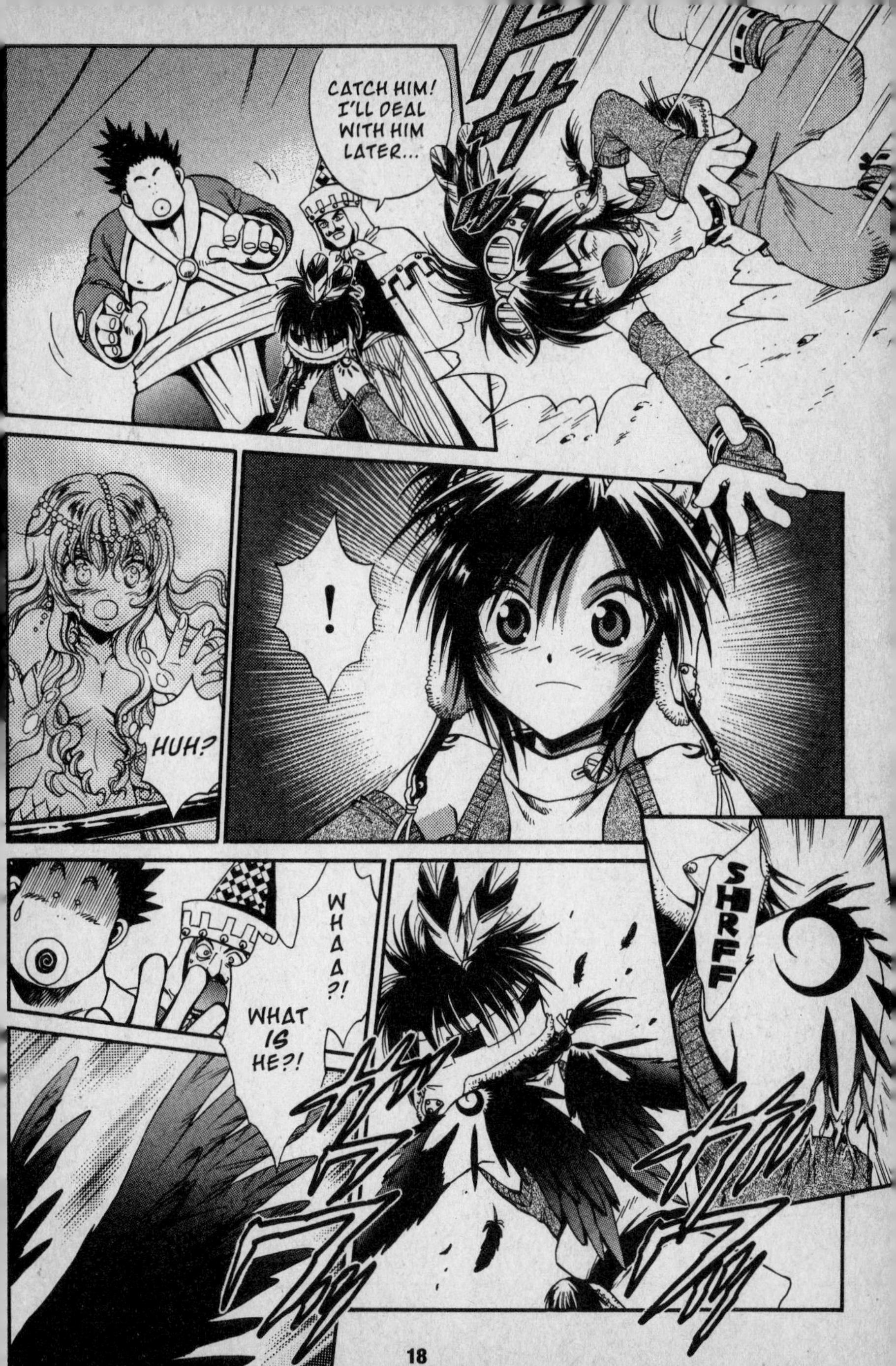
CATCH HIM! I'LL DEAL WITH HIM LATER...
!
HUH?
SHRFF
WHAAA?!
WHAT IS HE?!

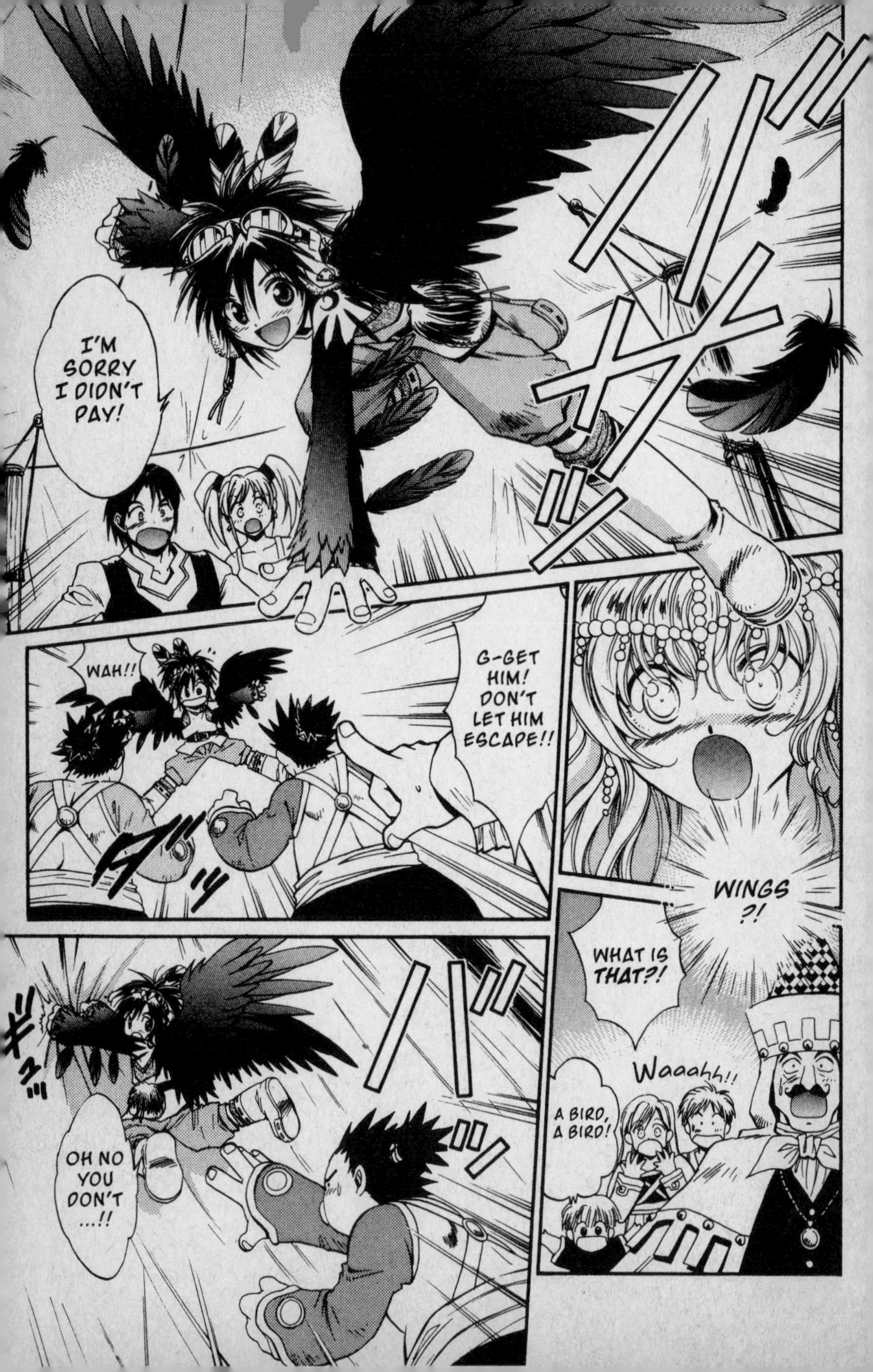

I'M SORRY I DIDN'T PAY!
WINGS?!
G-GET HIM! DON'T LET HIM ESCAPE!!
WAH!!
WHAT IS THAT?!
Waaahh!!
A BIRD, A BIRD!
OH NO YOU DON'T ...!!

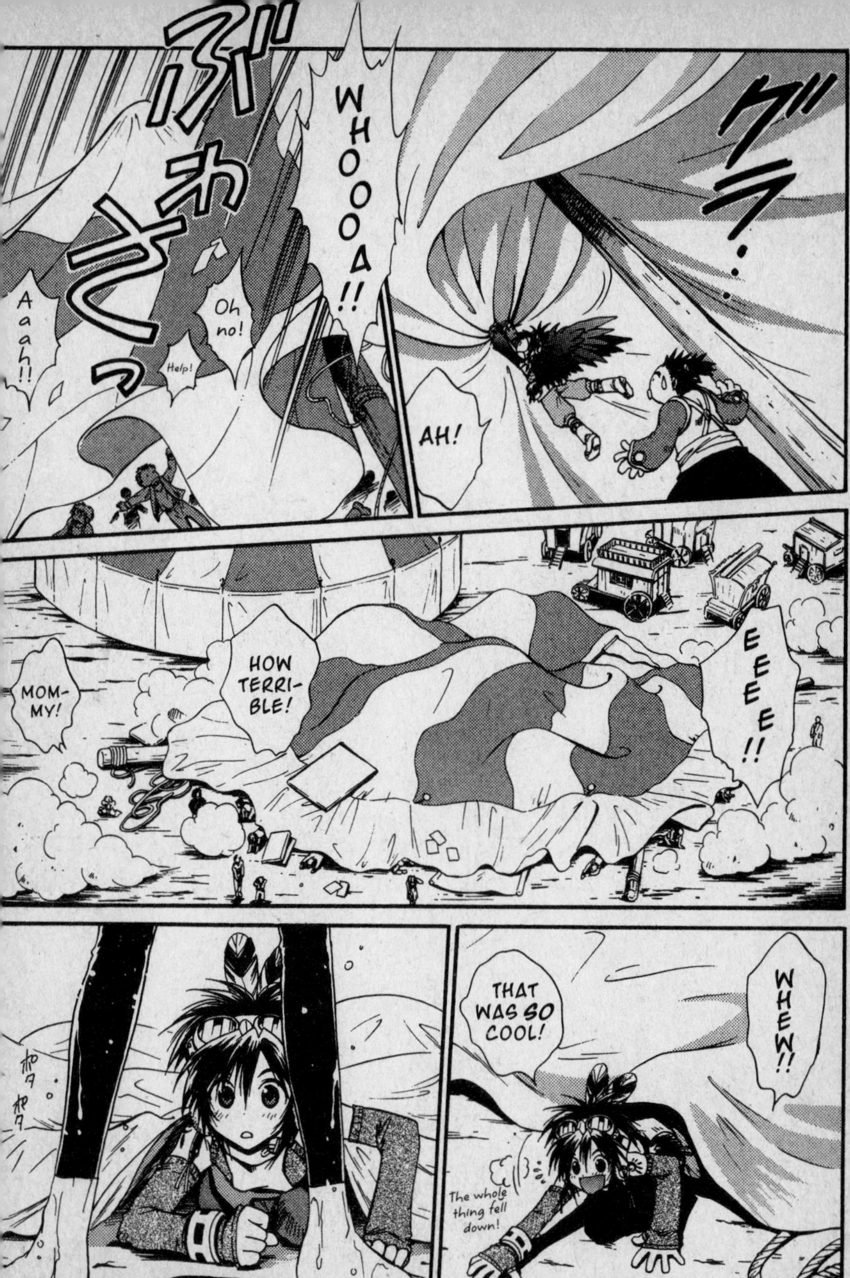
グラ…
AH!
WHOOOA!!
Oh no!
Help!
Aaaah!!
ぶわさっ
EEEE!!
HOW TERRIBLE!
MOMMY!
WHEW!!
THAT WAS SO COOL!
The whole thing fell down!
ポタ
ポタ

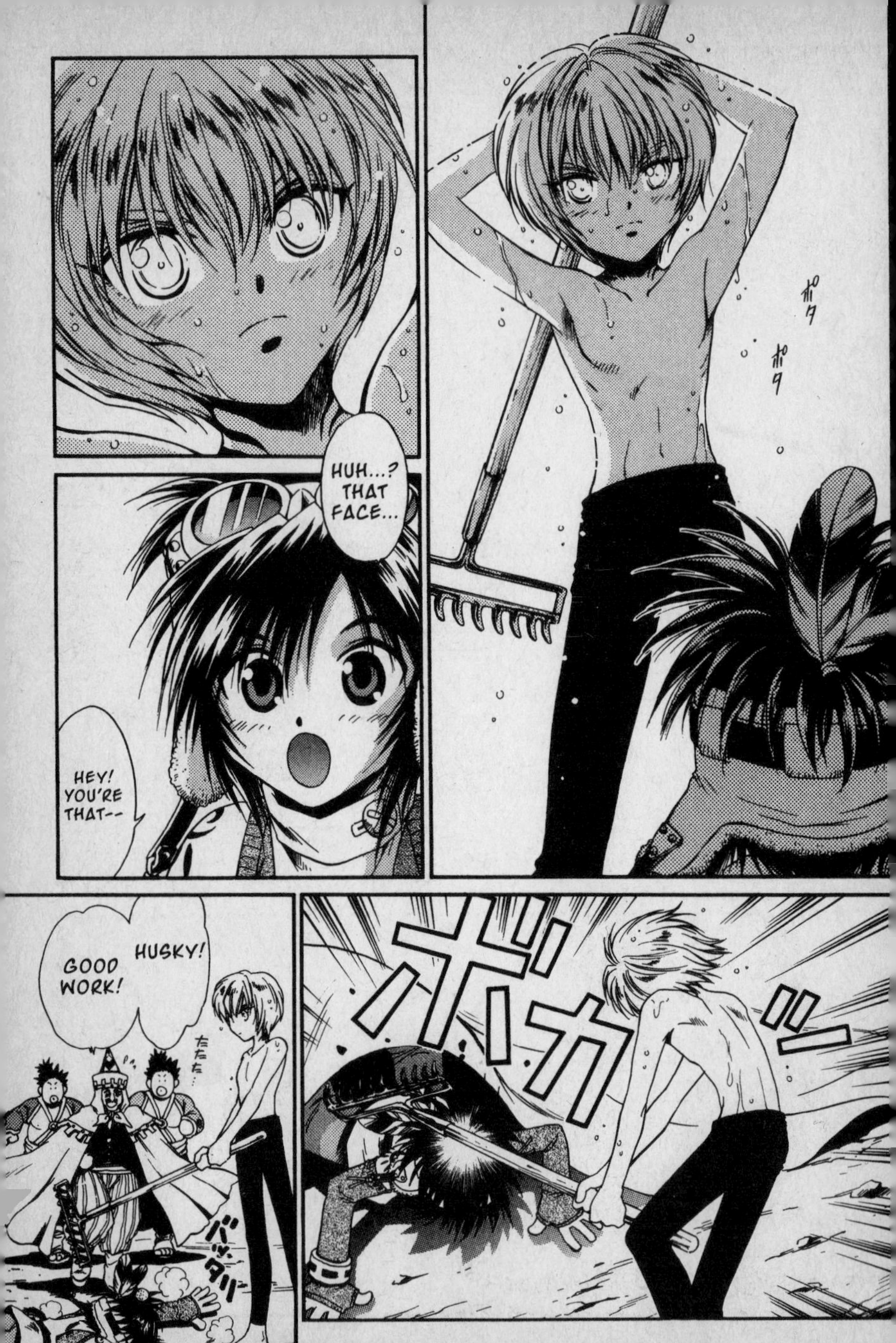
ポタ
ポタ
HUH...? THAT FACE...
HEY! YOU'RE THAT--
ボカッ
HUSKY!
GOOD WORK!
たたた
バッタ

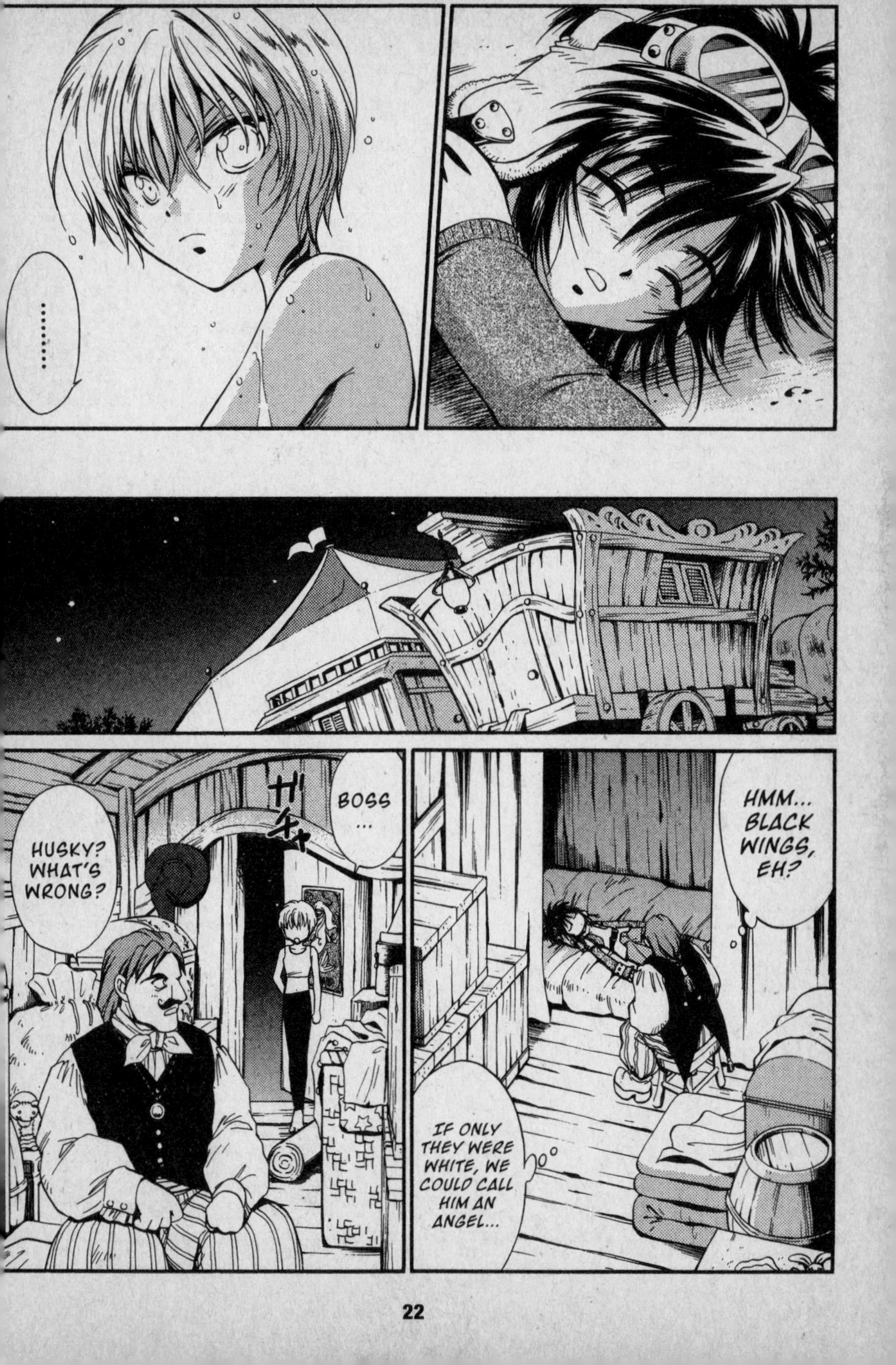
......
HMM... BLACK WINGS, EH?
IF ONLY THEY WERE WHITE, WE COULD CALL HIM AN ANGEL...
BOSS ...
ガチャ
HUSKY? WHAT'S WRONG?

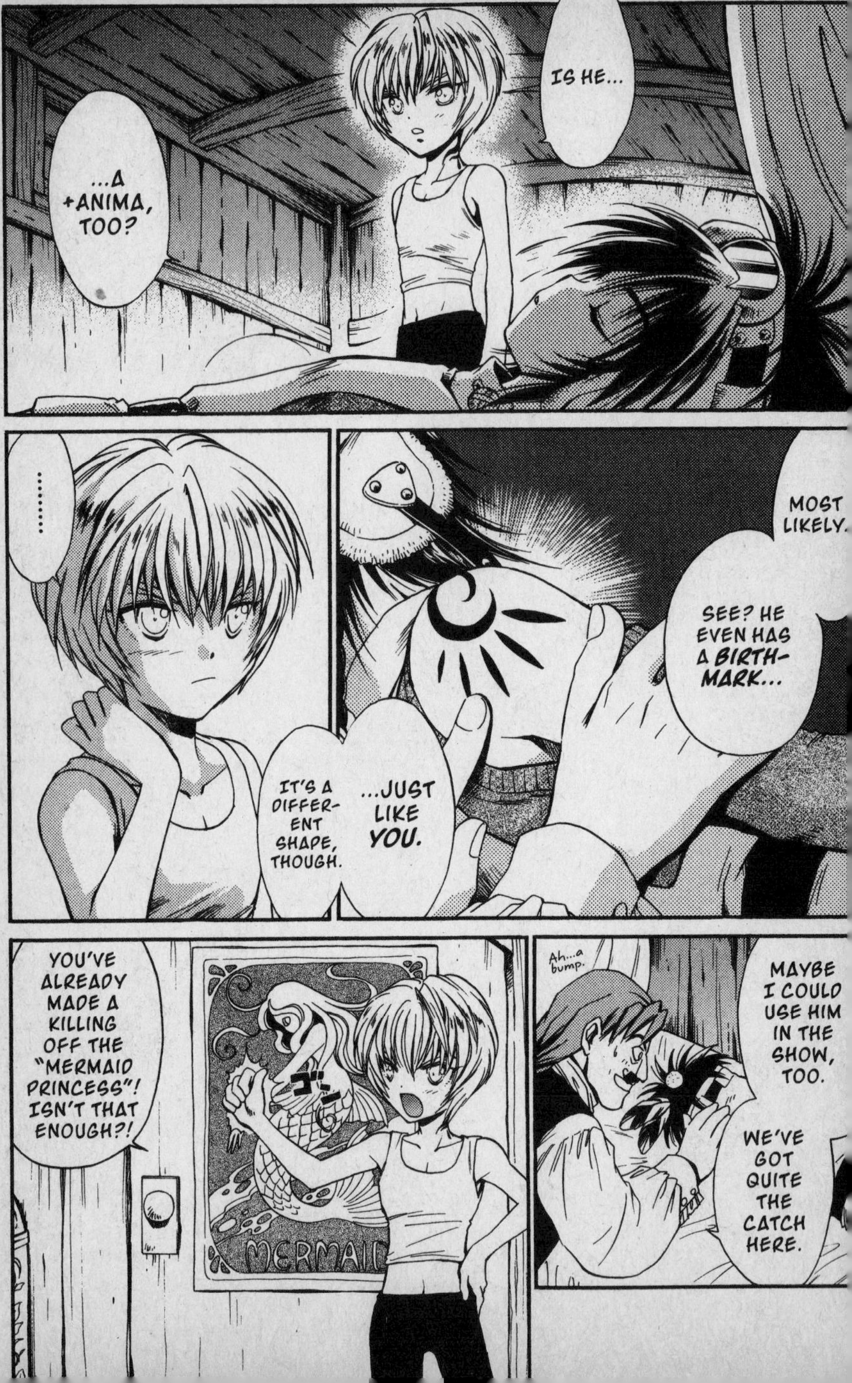
IS HE...
...A +ANIMA, TOO?
MOST LIKELY.
SEE? HE EVEN HAS A BIRTH-MARK...
...JUST LIKE YOU.
IT'S A DIFFER-ENT SHAPE, THOUGH.
......
MAYBE I COULD USE HIM IN THE SHOW, TOO.
WE'VE GOT QUITE THE CATCH HERE.
Ah...a bump.
YOU'VE ALREADY MADE A KILLING OFF THE "MERMAID PRINCESS"! ISN'T THAT ENOUGH?!
MERMAID

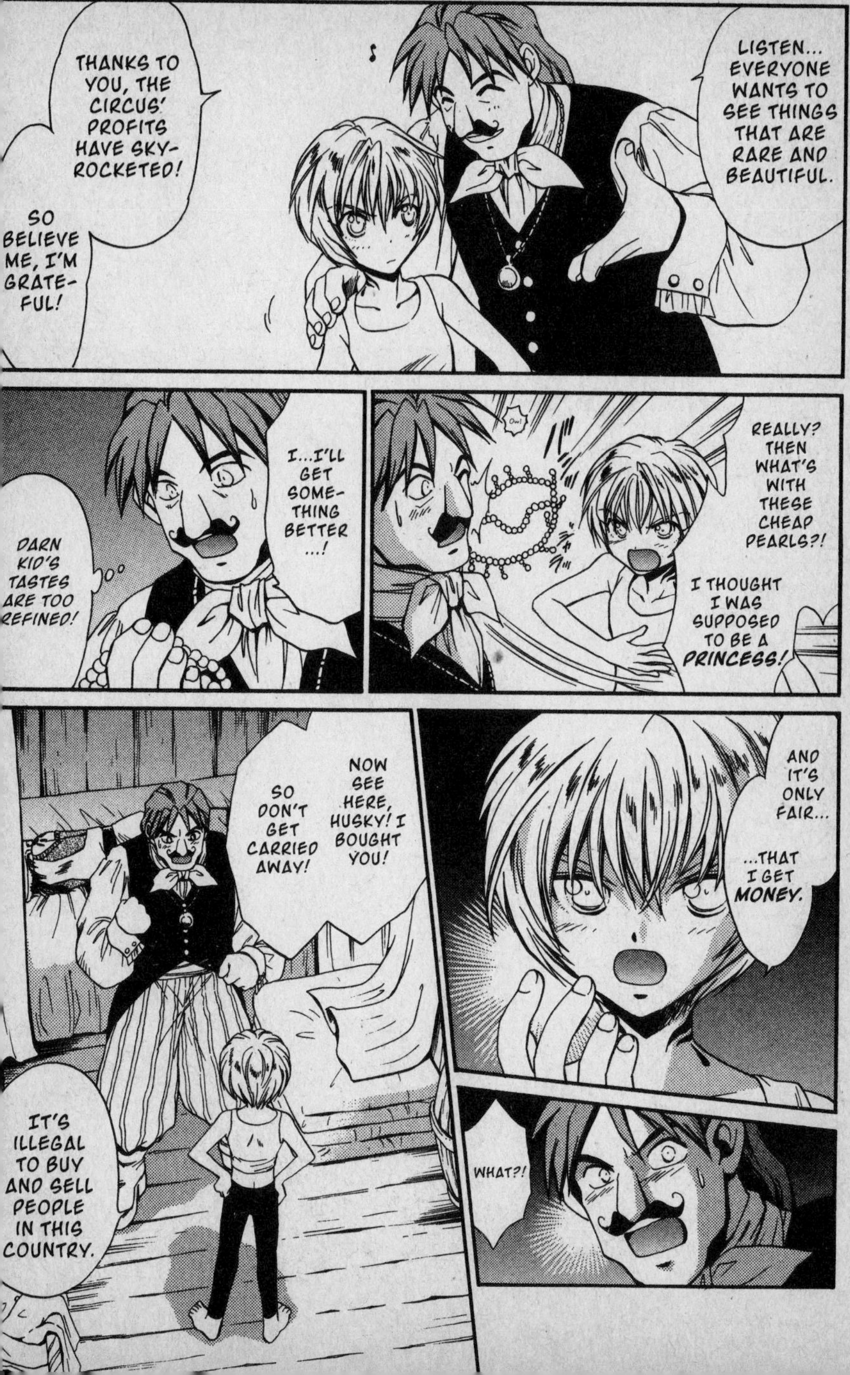
LISTEN... EVERYONE WANTS TO SEE THINGS THAT ARE RARE AND BEAUTIFUL.
THANKS TO YOU, THE CIRCUS' PROFITS HAVE SKY-ROCKETED!
SO BELIEVE ME, I'M GRATE-FUL!
Ow!
REALLY? THEN WHAT'S WITH THESE CHEAP PEARLS?!
I THOUGHT I WAS SUPPOSED TO BE A PRINCESS!
I...I'LL GET SOME-THING BETTER...!
DARN KID'S TASTES ARE TOO REFINED!
AND IT'S ONLY FAIR...
...THAT I GET MONEY.
WHAT?!
NOW SEE HERE, HUSKY! I BOUGHT YOU!
SO DON'T GET CARRIED AWAY!
IT'S ILLEGAL TO BUY AND SELL PEOPLE IN THIS COUNTRY.

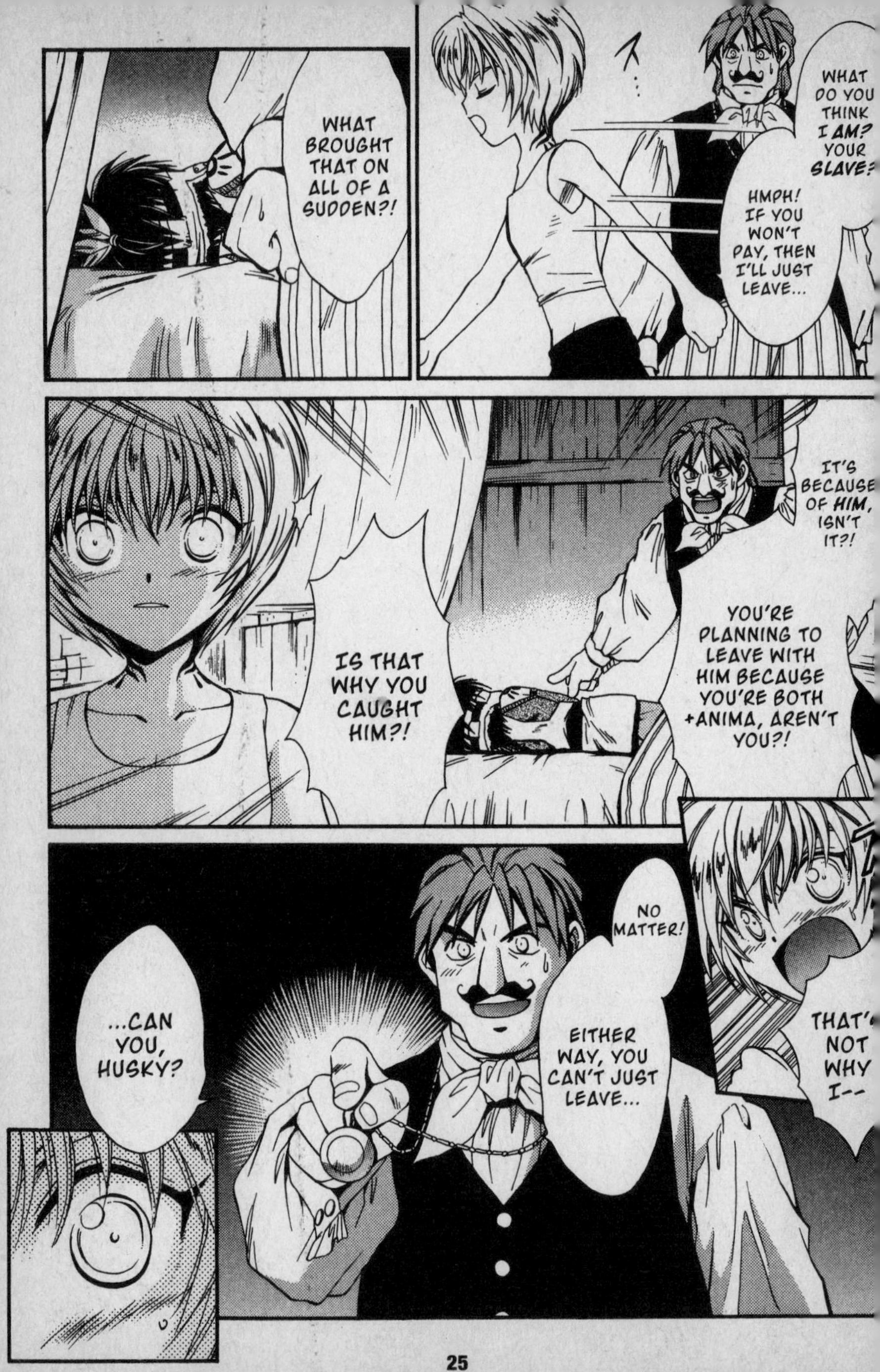
WHAT DO YOU THINK I AM? YOUR SLAVE?
HMPH! IF YOU WON'T PAY, THEN I'LL JUST LEAVE...
WHAT BROUGHT THAT ON ALL OF A SUDDEN?!
IT'S BECAUSE OF HIM, ISN'T IT?!
YOU'RE PLANNING TO LEAVE WITH HIM BECAUSE YOU'RE BOTH +ANIMA, AREN'T YOU?!
IS THAT WHY YOU CAUGHT HIM?!
THAT' NOT WHY I--
NO MATTER!
EITHER WAY, YOU CAN'T JUST LEAVE...
...CAN YOU, HUSKY?

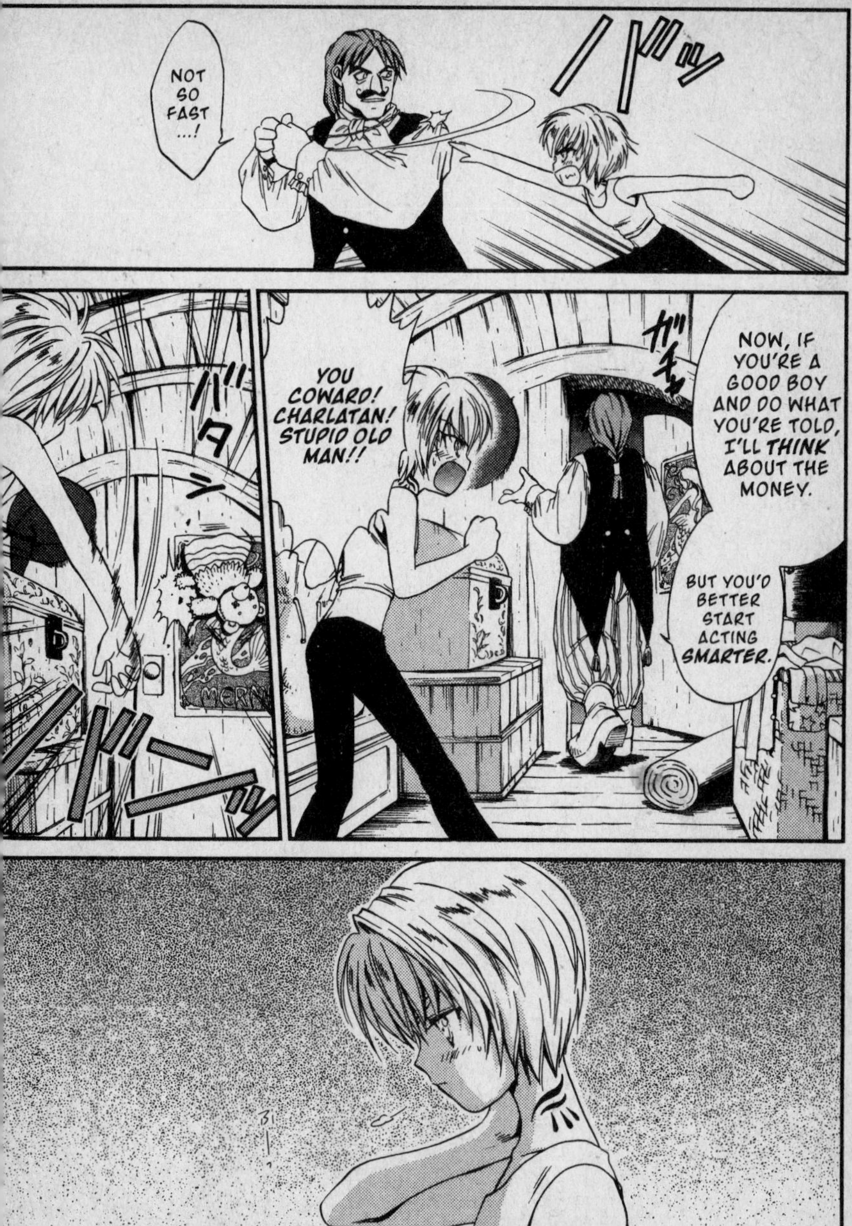
NOT SO FAST ...!
NOW, IF YOU'RE A GOOD BOY AND DO WHAT YOU'RE TOLD, I'LL THINK ABOUT THE MONEY.
BUT YOU'D BETTER START ACTING SMARTER.
YOU COWARD! CHARLATAN! STUPID OLD MAN!!

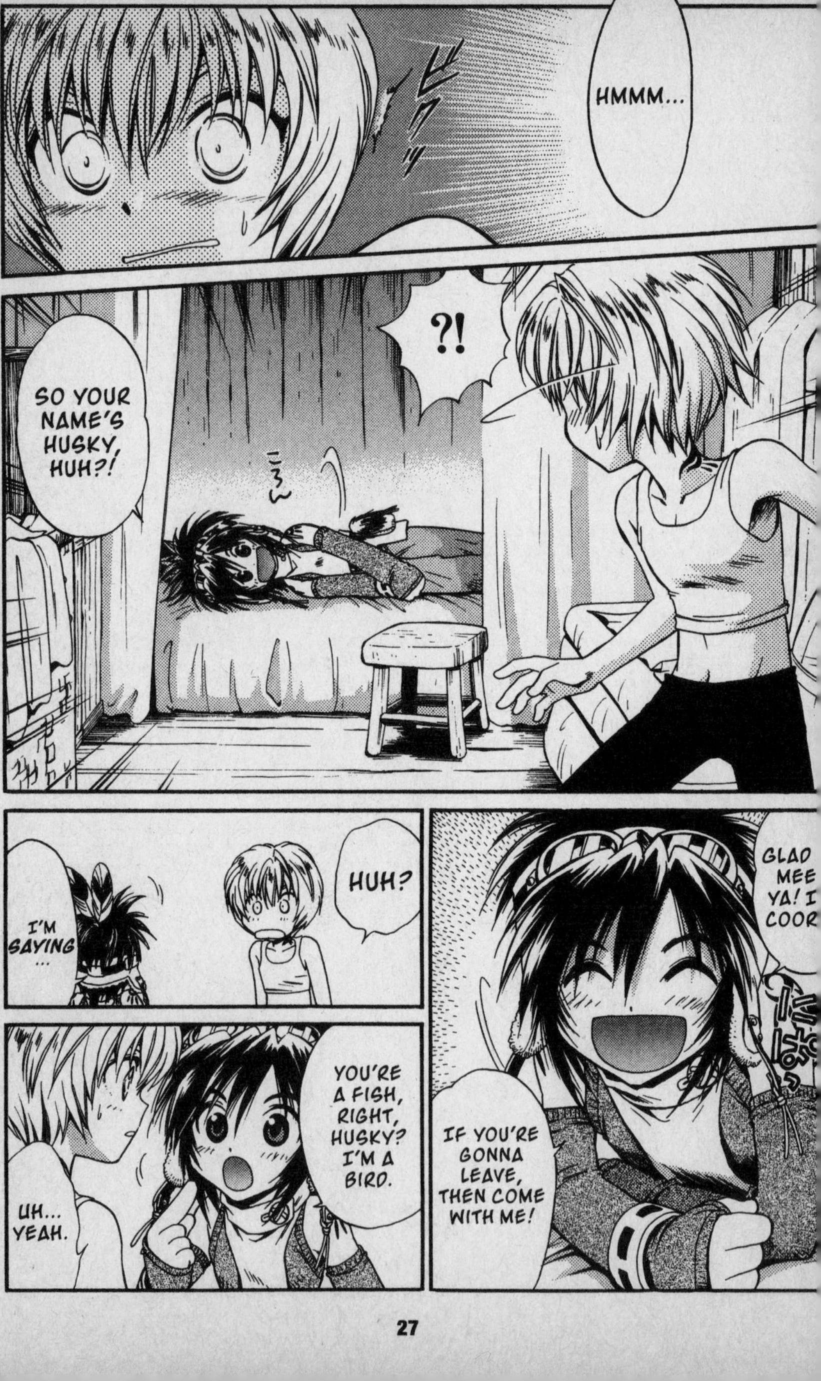
HMMM...
?!
SO YOUR NAME'S HUSKY, HUH?!
GLAD MEE YA! I COOR
IF YOU'RE GONNA LEAVE, THEN COME WITH ME!
HUH?
I'M SAYING...
YOU'RE A FISH, RIGHT, HUSKY? I'M A BIRD.
UH... YEAH.

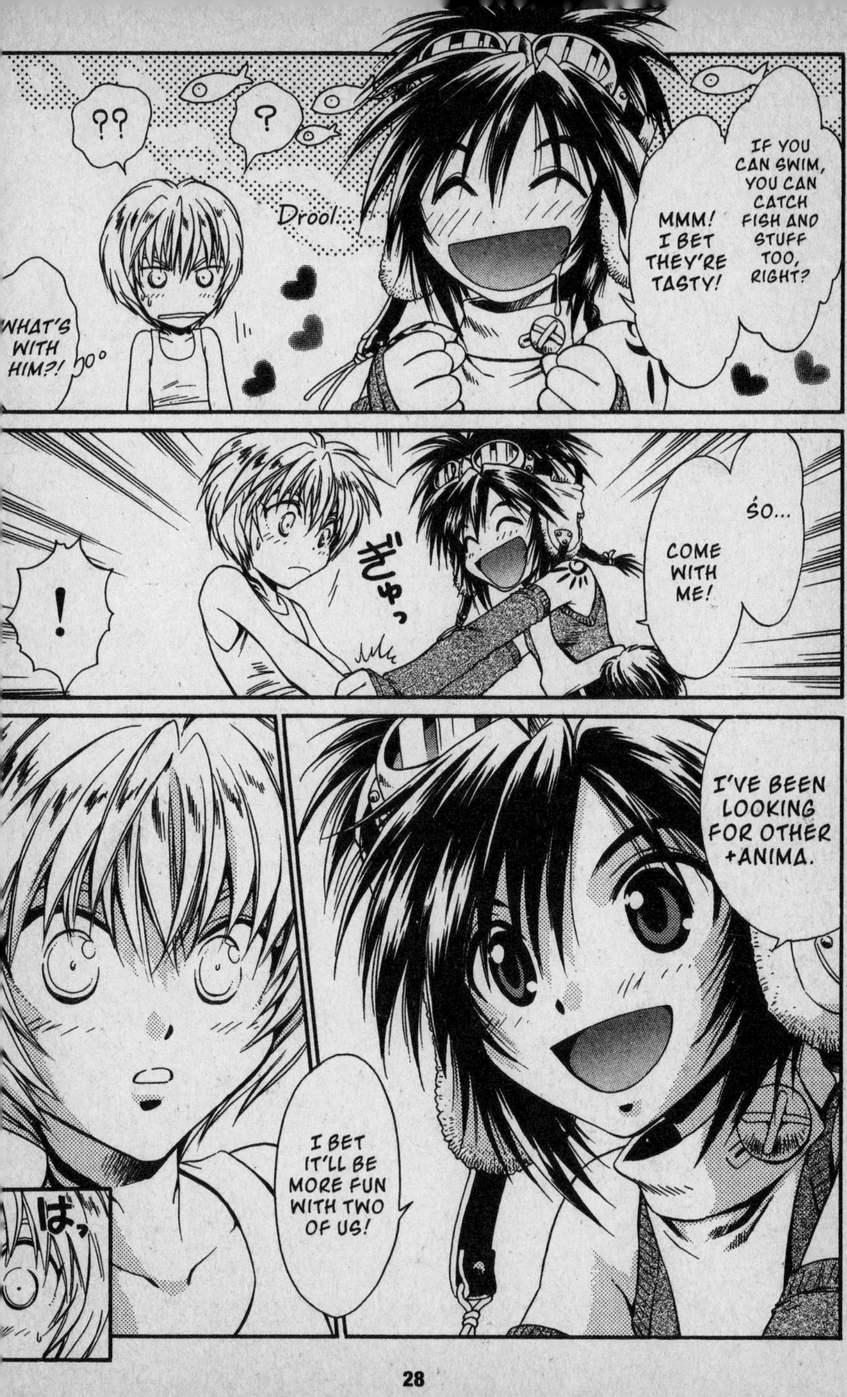
IF YOU CAN SWIM, YOU CAN CATCH FISH AND STUFF TOO, RIGHT?
MMM! I BET THEY'RE TASTY!
?
??
Drool...
WHAT'S WITH HIM?!
SO... COME WITH ME!
ぎゅっ
!
I'VE BEEN LOOKING FOR OTHER +ANIMA.
I BET IT'LL BE MORE FUN WITH TWO OF US!
ばっ

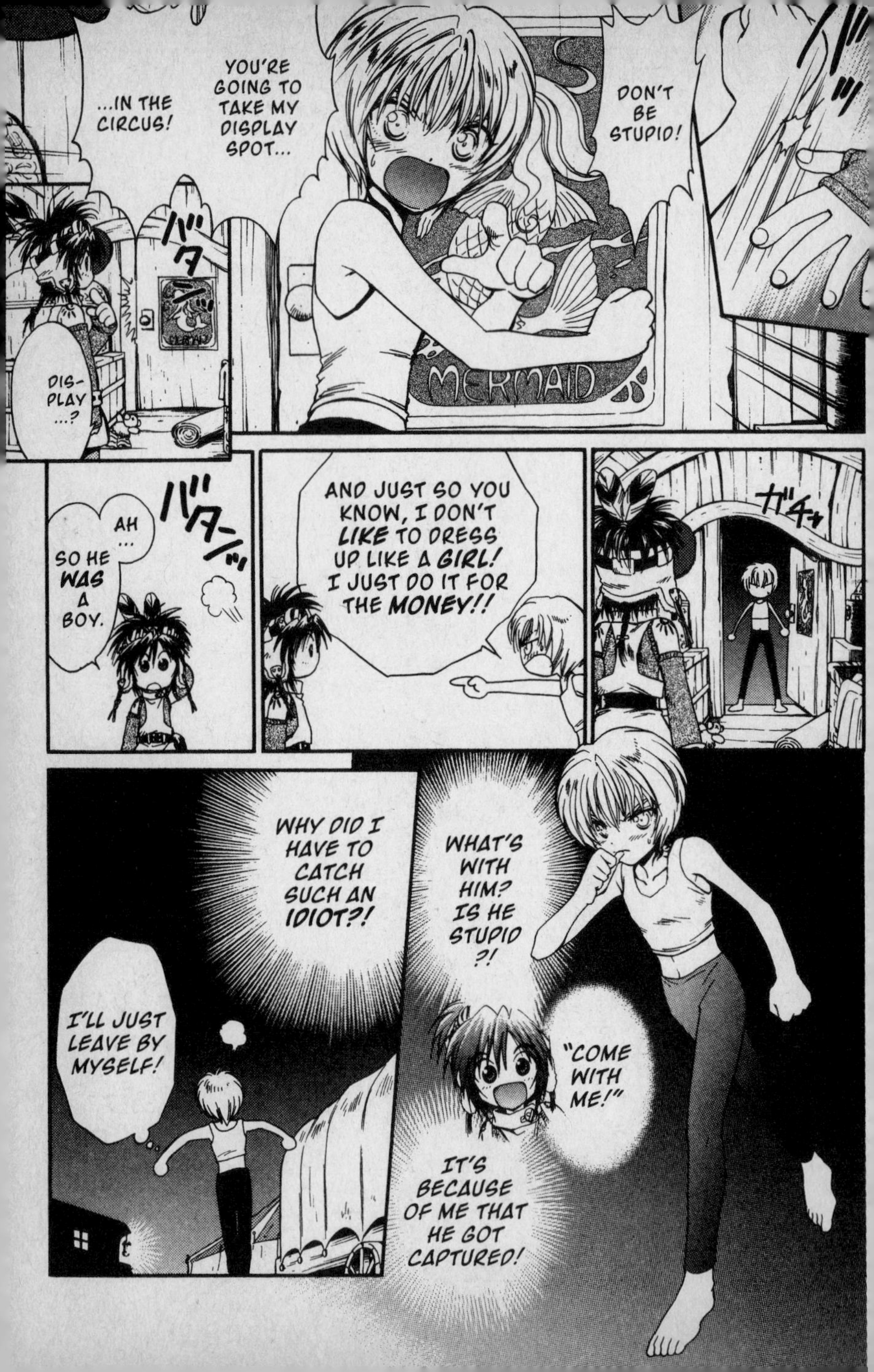
DON'T BE STUPID!
YOU'RE GOING TO TAKE MY DISPLAY SPOT...
...IN THE CIRCUS!
バタン
DIS-PLAY ...?
ガチャ
AND JUST SO YOU KNOW, I DON'T LIKE TO DRESS UP LIKE A GIRL! I JUST DO IT FOR THE MONEY!!
バターンッ
AH ...
SO HE WAS A BOY.
WHAT'S WITH HIM? IS HE STUPID ?!
WHY DID I HAVE TO CATCH SUCH AN IDIOT?!
"COME WITH ME!"
IT'S BECAUSE OF ME THAT HE GOT CAPTURED!
I'LL JUST LEAVE BY MYSELF!

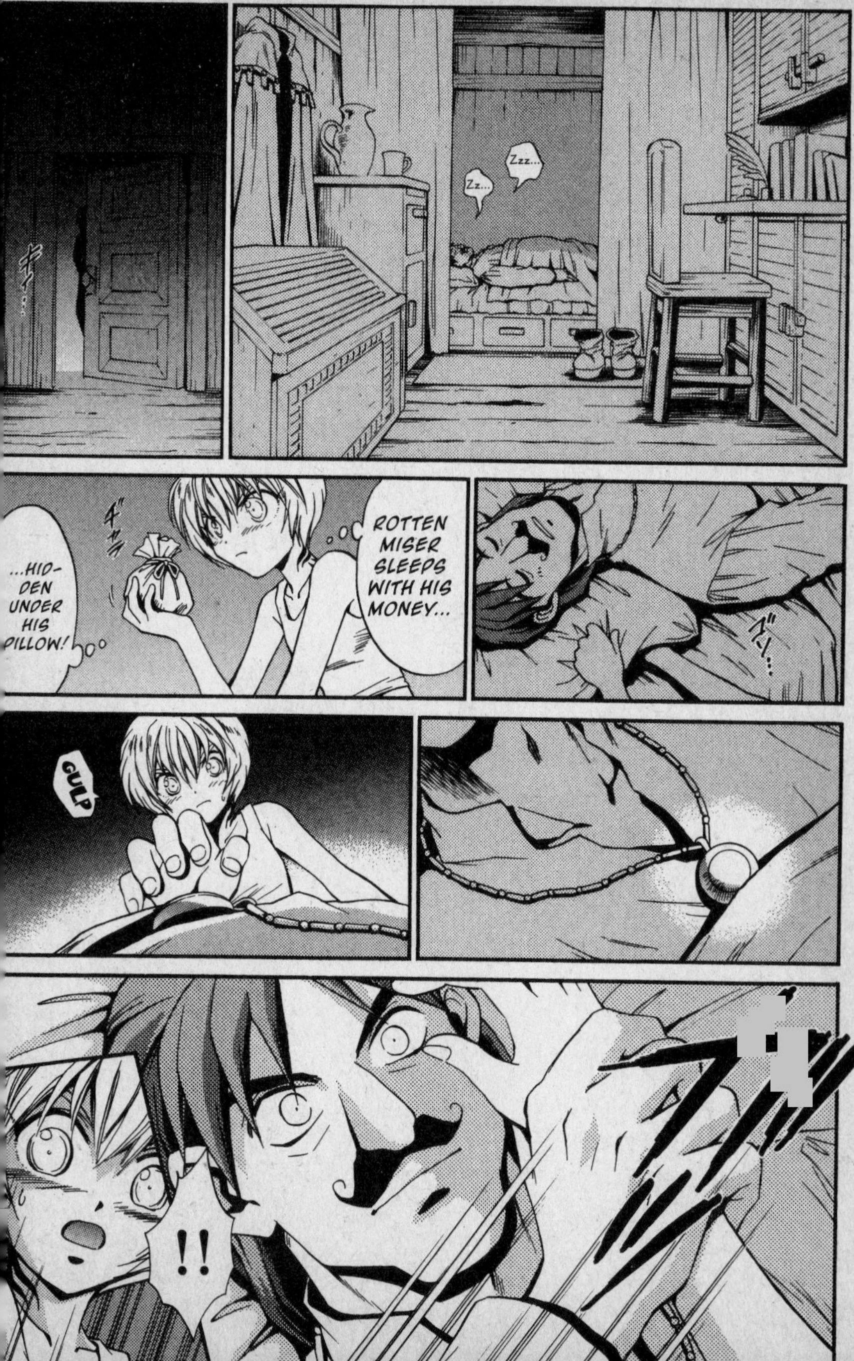
Zzz...
Zz...
ROTTEN MISER SLEEPS WITH HIS MONEY...
...HID-DEN UNDER HIS PILLOW!
GULP
!!

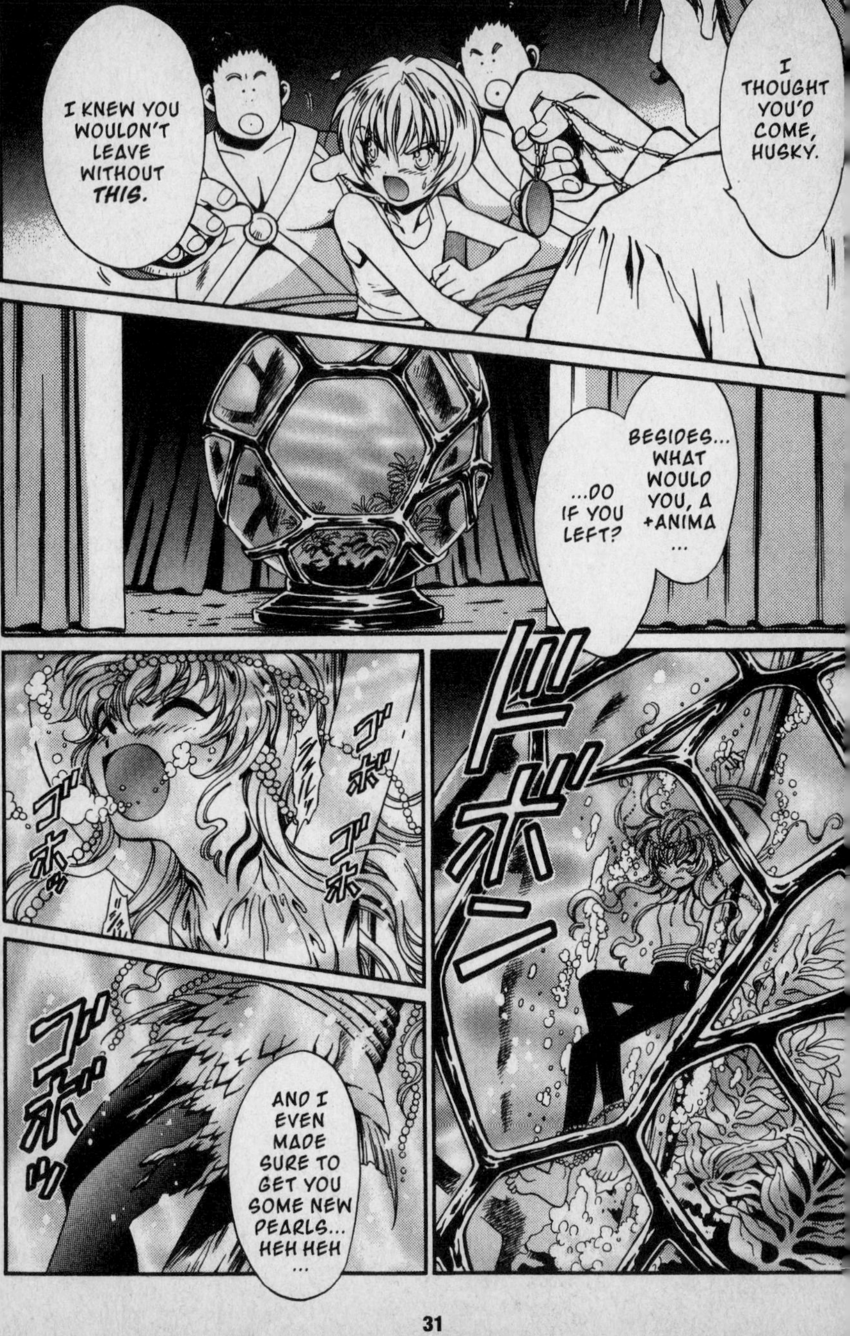
I THOUGHT YOU'D COME, HUSKY.
I KNEW YOU WOULDN'T LEAVE WITHOUT THIS.
BESIDES... WHAT WOULD YOU, A +ANIMA ...
...DO IF YOU LEFT?
AND I EVEN MADE SURE TO GET YOU SOME NEW PEARLS... HEH HEH ...

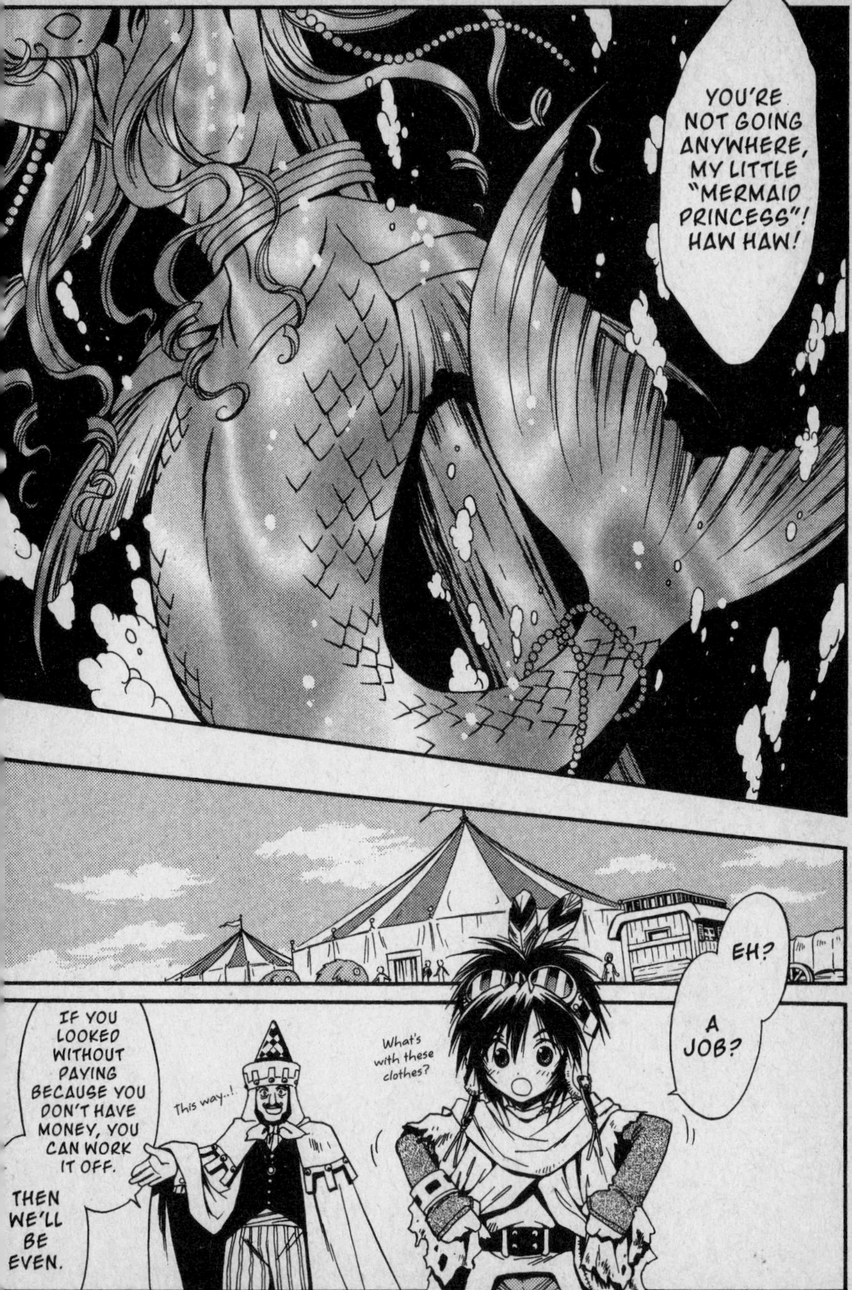
YOU'RE NOT GOING ANYWHERE, MY LITTLE "MERMAID PRINCESS"! HAW HAW!
EH?
A JOB?
What's with these clothes?
This way..!
IF YOU LOOKED WITHOUT PAYING BECAUSE YOU DON'T HAVE MONEY, YOU CAN WORK IT OFF.
THEN WE'LL BE EVEN.

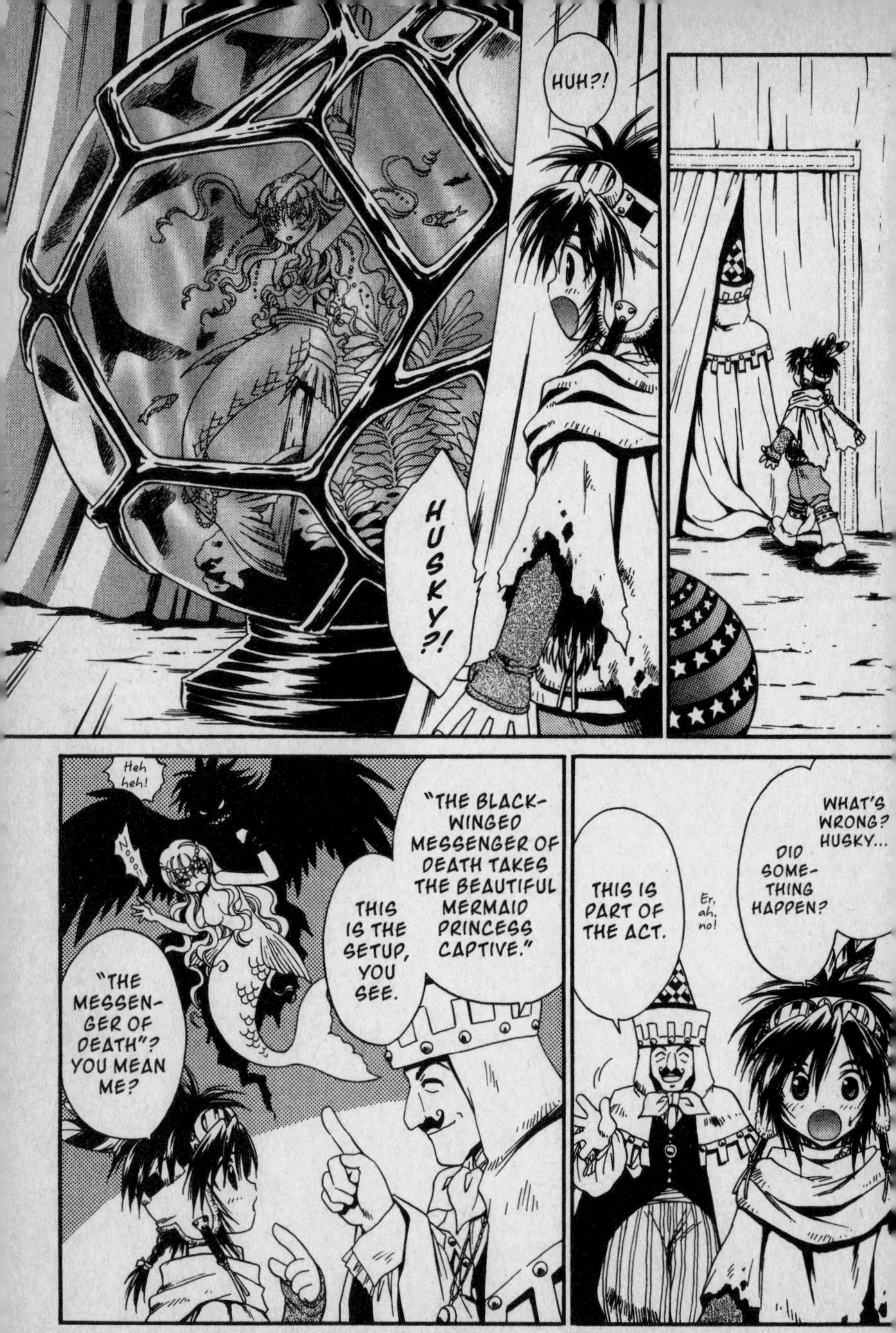
HUH?!
HUSKY?!
WHAT'S WRONG? HUSKY...
DID SOMETHING HAPPEN?
Er, ah, no!
THIS IS PART OF THE ACT.
"THE BLACK-WINGED MESSENGER OF DEATH TAKES THE BEAUTIFUL MERMAID PRINCESS CAPTIVE."
THIS IS THE SETUP, YOU SEE.
Heh heh!
Nooo!
"THE MESSENGER OF DEATH"? YOU MEAN ME?

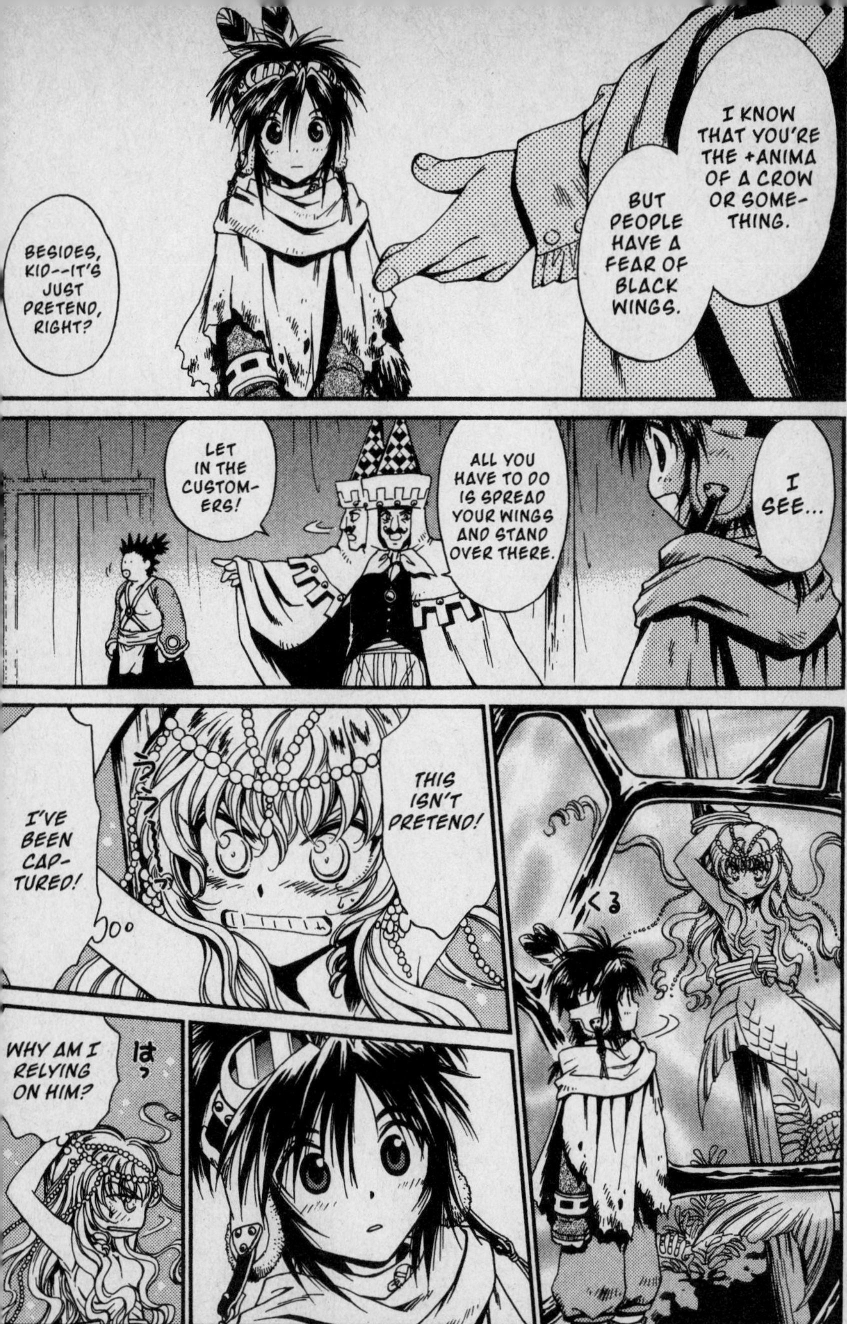
I KNOW THAT YOU'RE THE +ANIMA OF A CROW OR SOMETHING.
BUT PEOPLE HAVE A FEAR OF BLACK WINGS.
BESIDES, KID--IT'S JUST PRETEND, RIGHT?
I SEE...
ALL YOU HAVE TO DO IS SPREAD YOUR WINGS AND STAND OVER THERE.
LET IN THE CUSTOM-ERS!
くる
THIS ISN'T PRETEND!
I'VE BEEN CAP-TURED!
はっ
WHY AM I RELYING ON HIM?

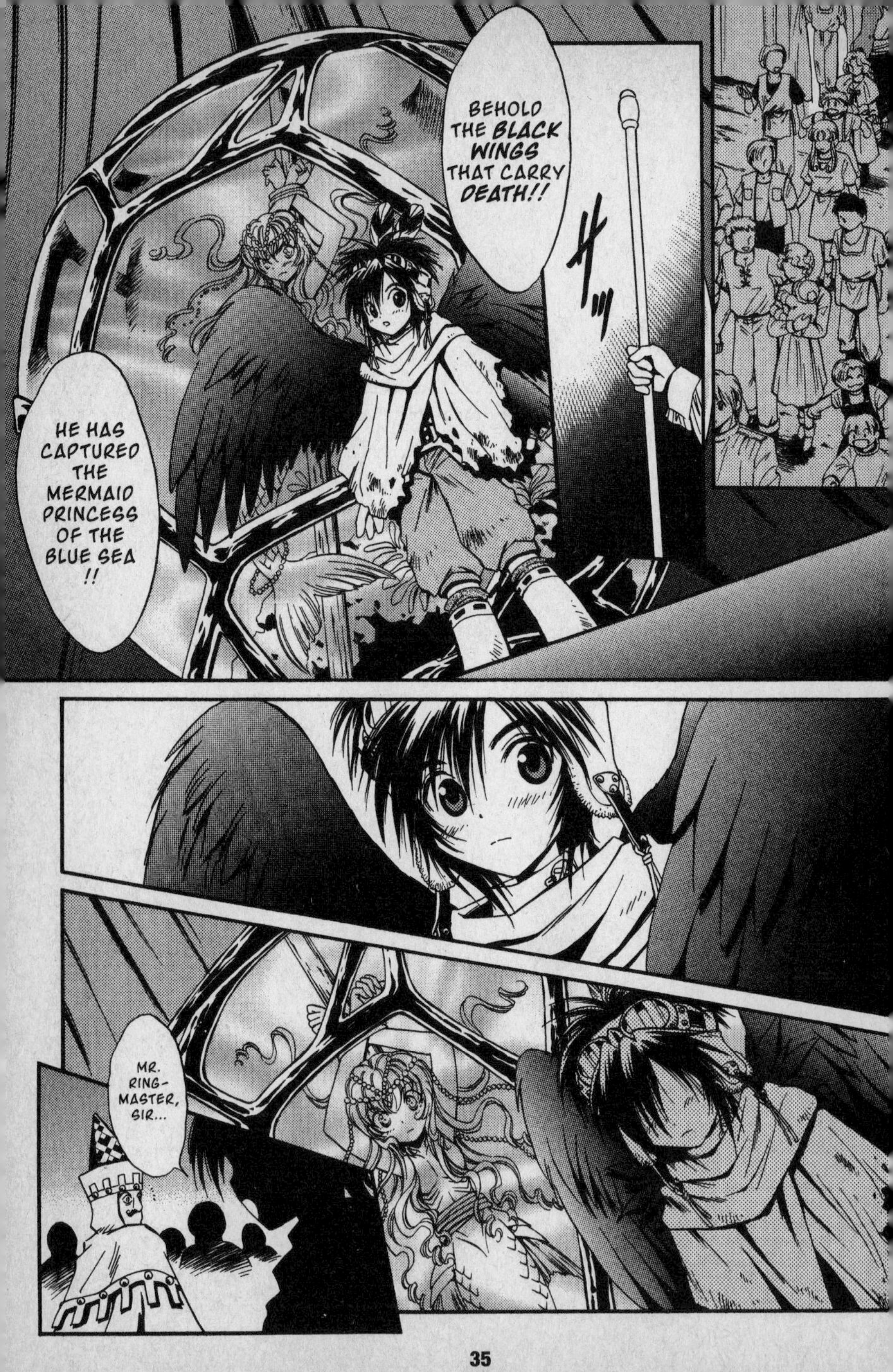
BEHOLD THE BLACK WINGS THAT CARRY DEATH!!
HE HAS CAPTURED THE MERMAID PRINCESS OF THE BLUE SEA!!
MR. RING-MASTER, SIR...

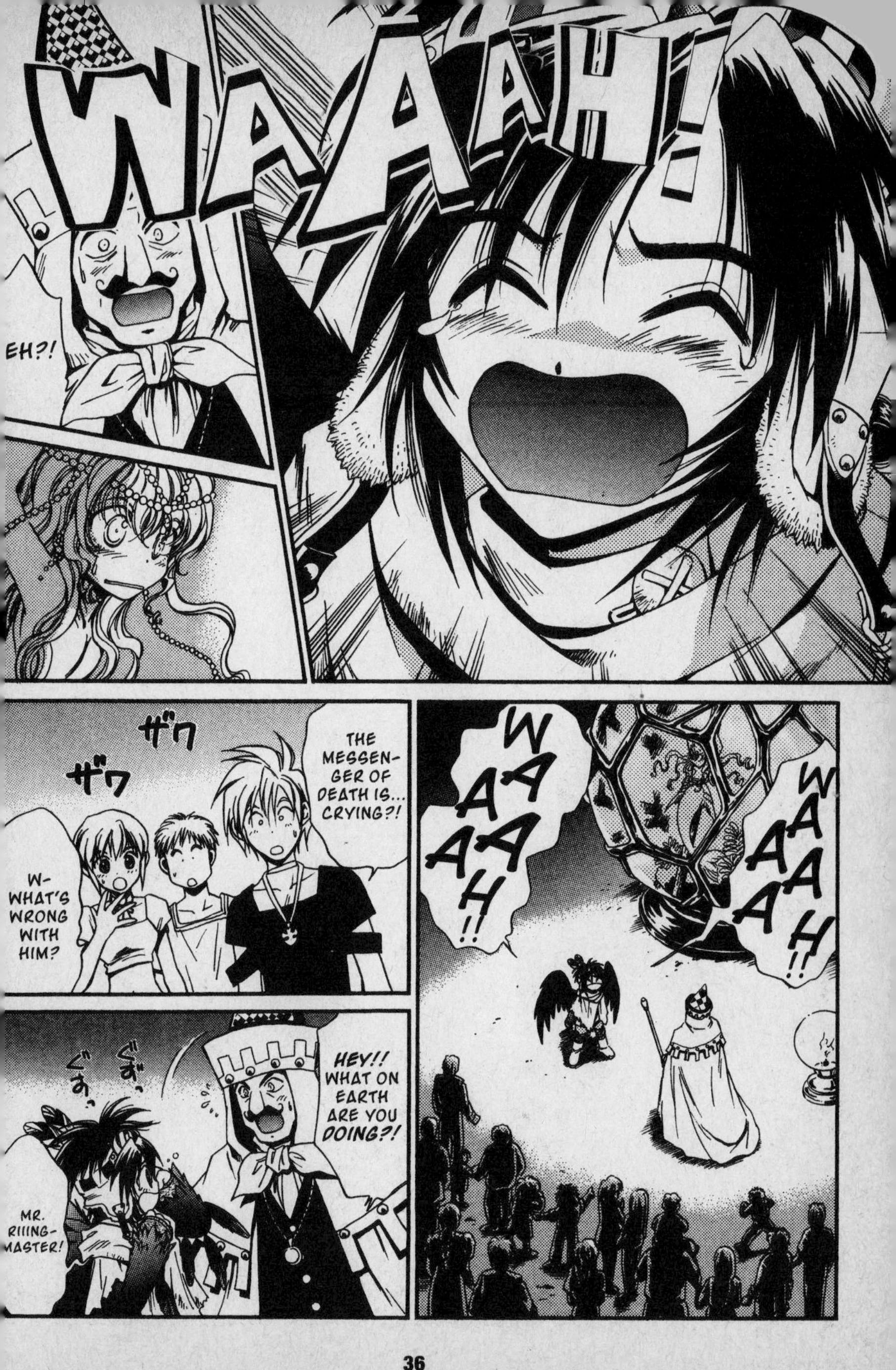
WAAAH!
EH?!
WAAAAAAH!!
WAAAAAH!!
THE MESSENGER OF DEATH IS... CRYING?!
ザワ
ザワ
W-WHAT'S WRONG WITH HIM?
HEY!! WHAT ON EARTH ARE YOU DOING?!
MR. RIIING-MASTER!

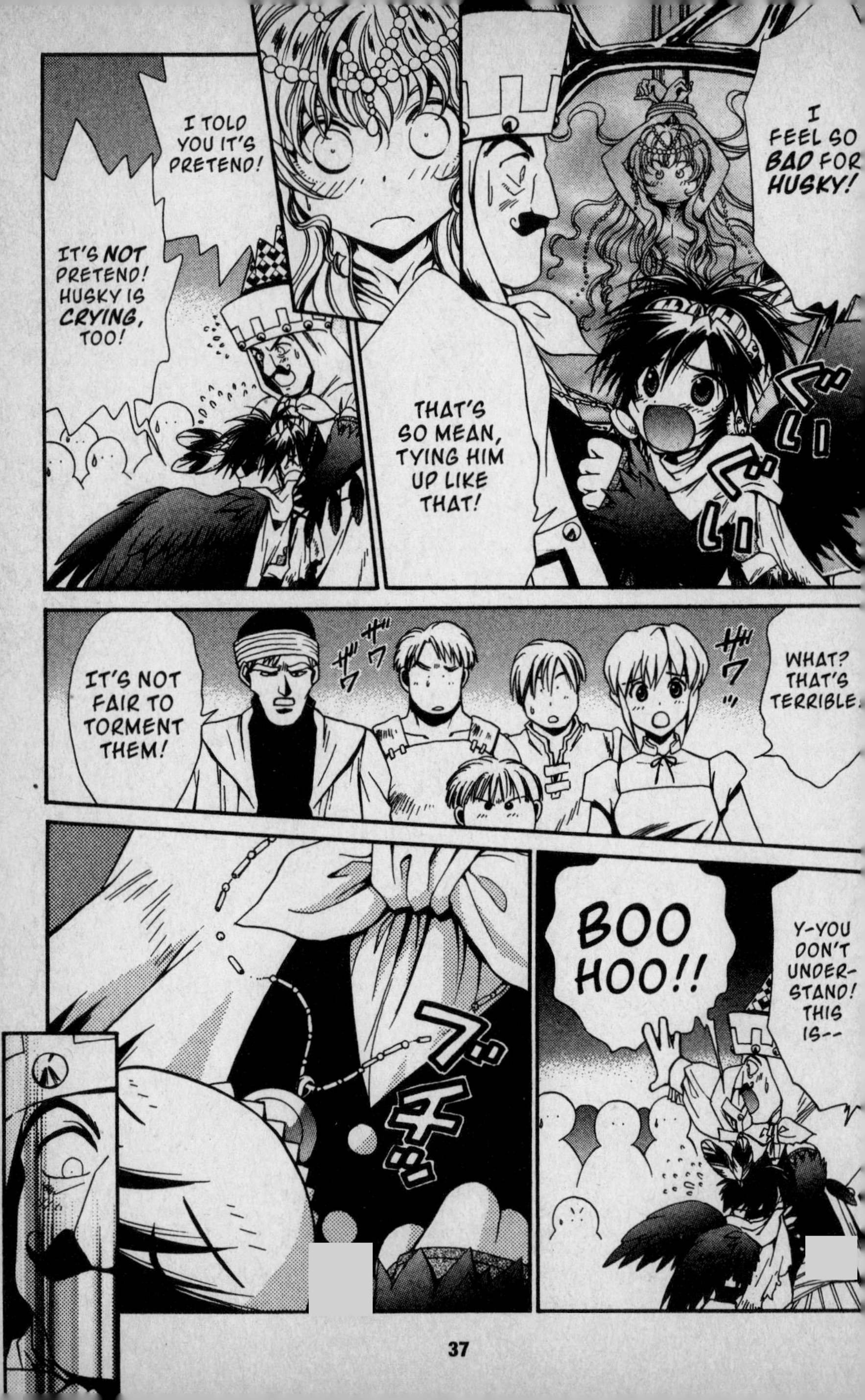
I FEEL SO BAD FOR HUSKY!
THAT'S SO MEAN, TYING HIM UP LIKE THAT!
I TOLD YOU IT'S PRETEND!
IT'S NOT PRETEND! HUSKY IS CRYING, TOO!
WHAT? THAT'S TERRIBLE.
IT'S NOT FAIR TO TORMENT THEM!
Y-YOU DON'T UNDER-STAND! THIS IS--
BOO HOO!!

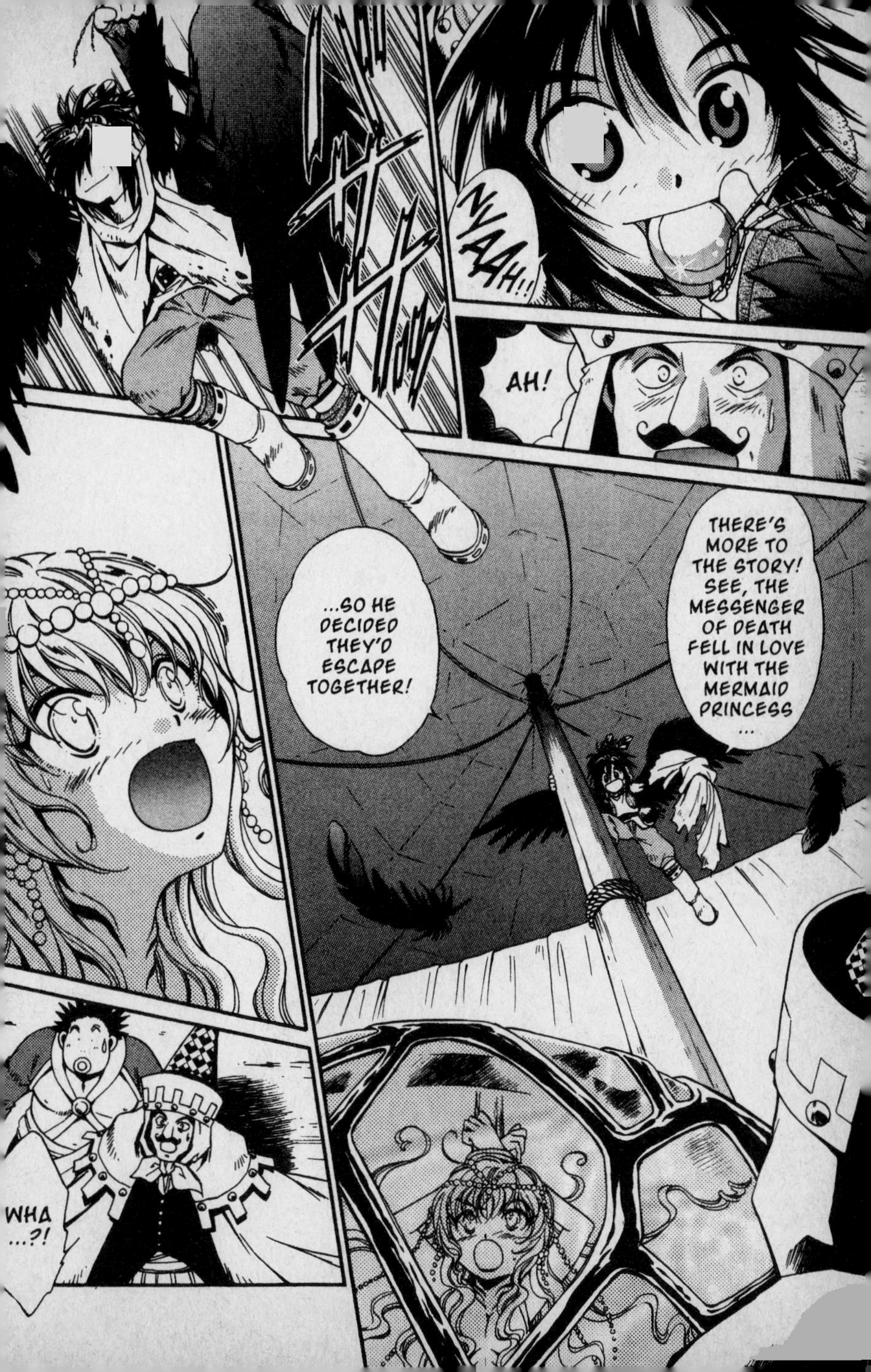
NYAAH!!
AH!
THERE'S MORE TO THE STORY! SEE, THE MESSENGER OF DEATH FELL IN LOVE WITH THE MERMAID PRINCESS ...
...SO HE DECIDED THEY'D ESCAPE TOGETHER!
WHA ...?!

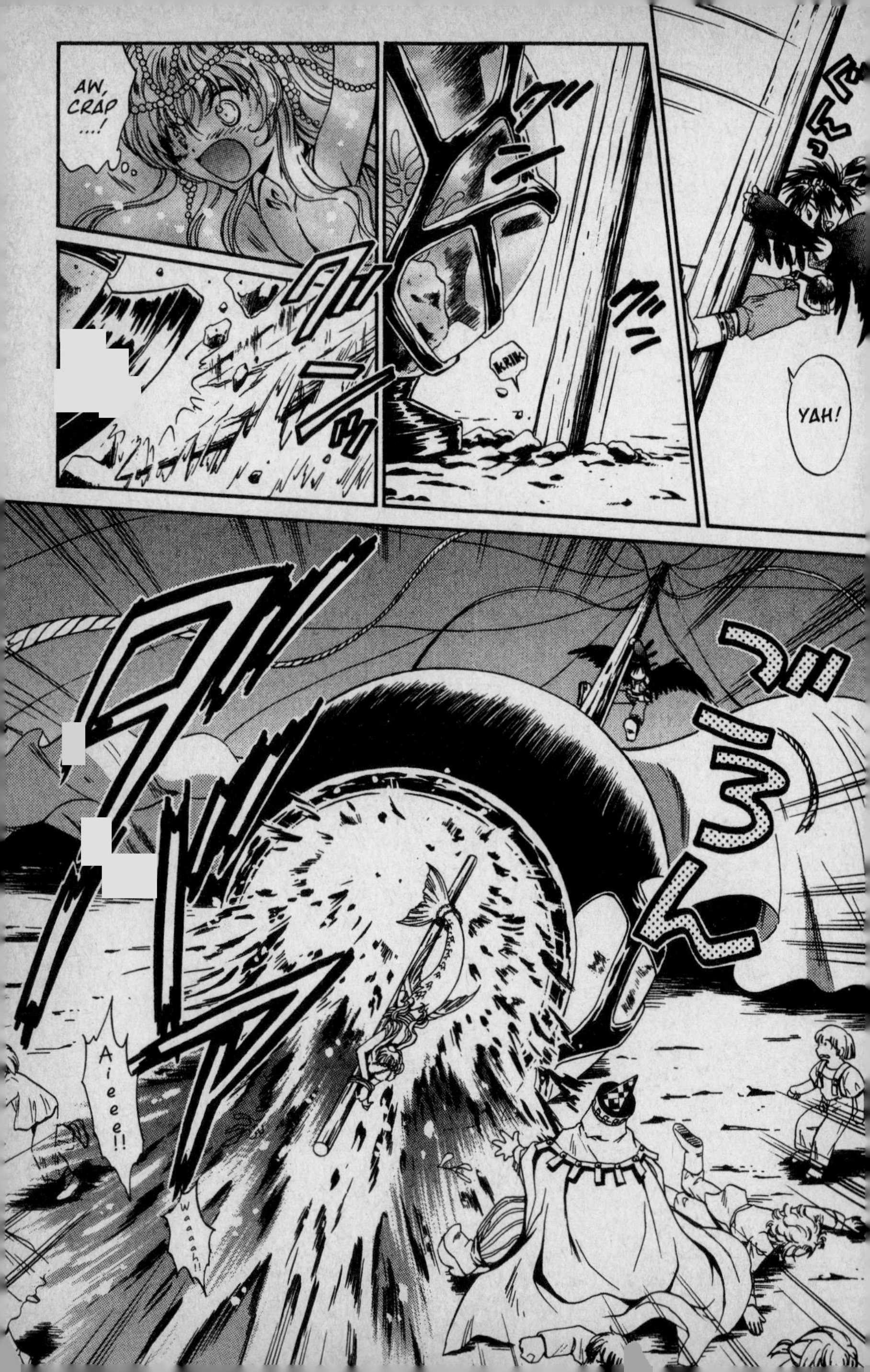
YAH!
KRIK
AW, CRAP ....!
Aieee!!
Waaaah!!

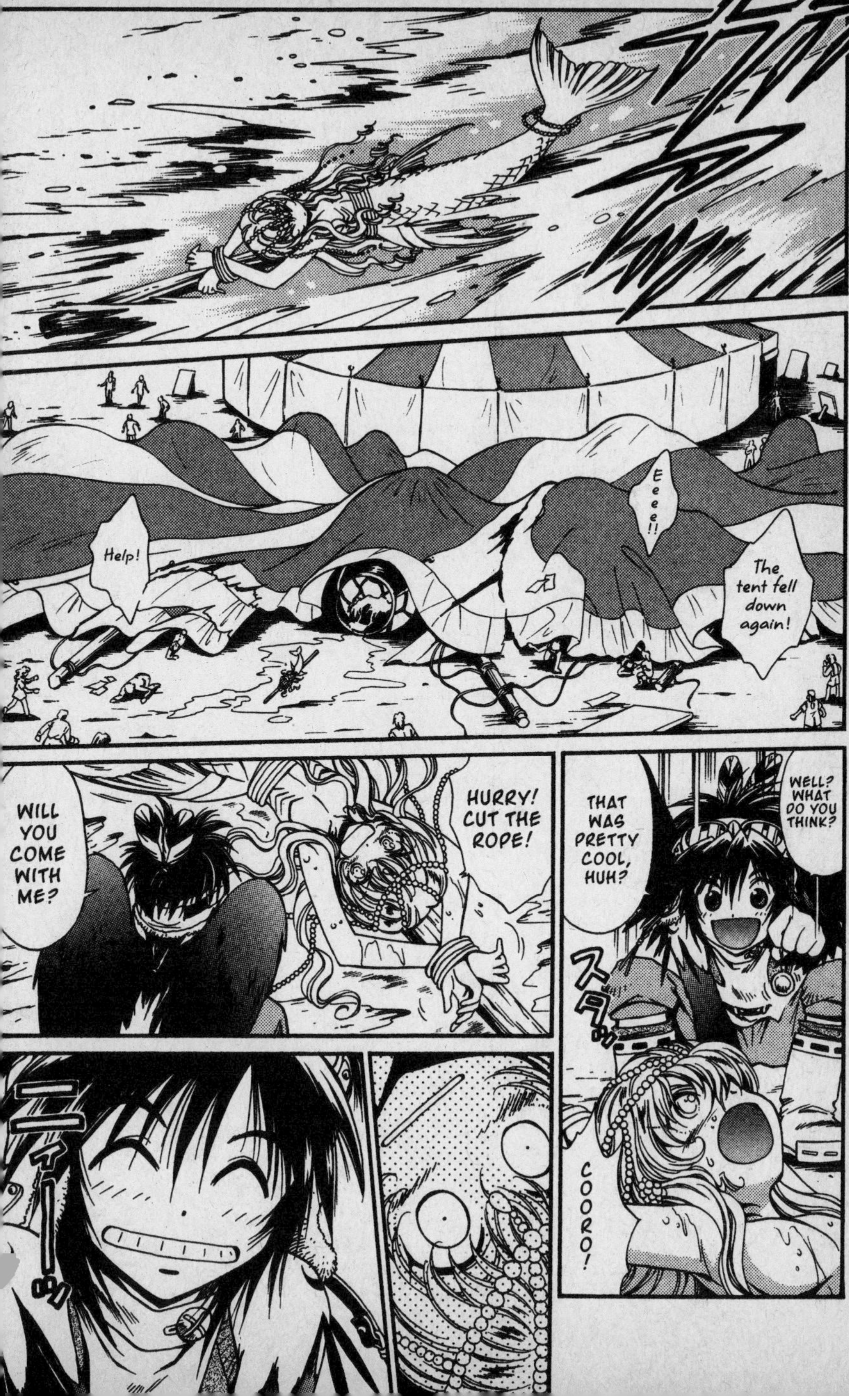
The tent fell down again!
Eeee!!
Help!
WELL? WHAT DO YOU THINK?
THAT WAS PRETTY COOL, HUH?
COORO!
HURRY! CUT THE ROPE!
WILL YOU COME WITH ME?

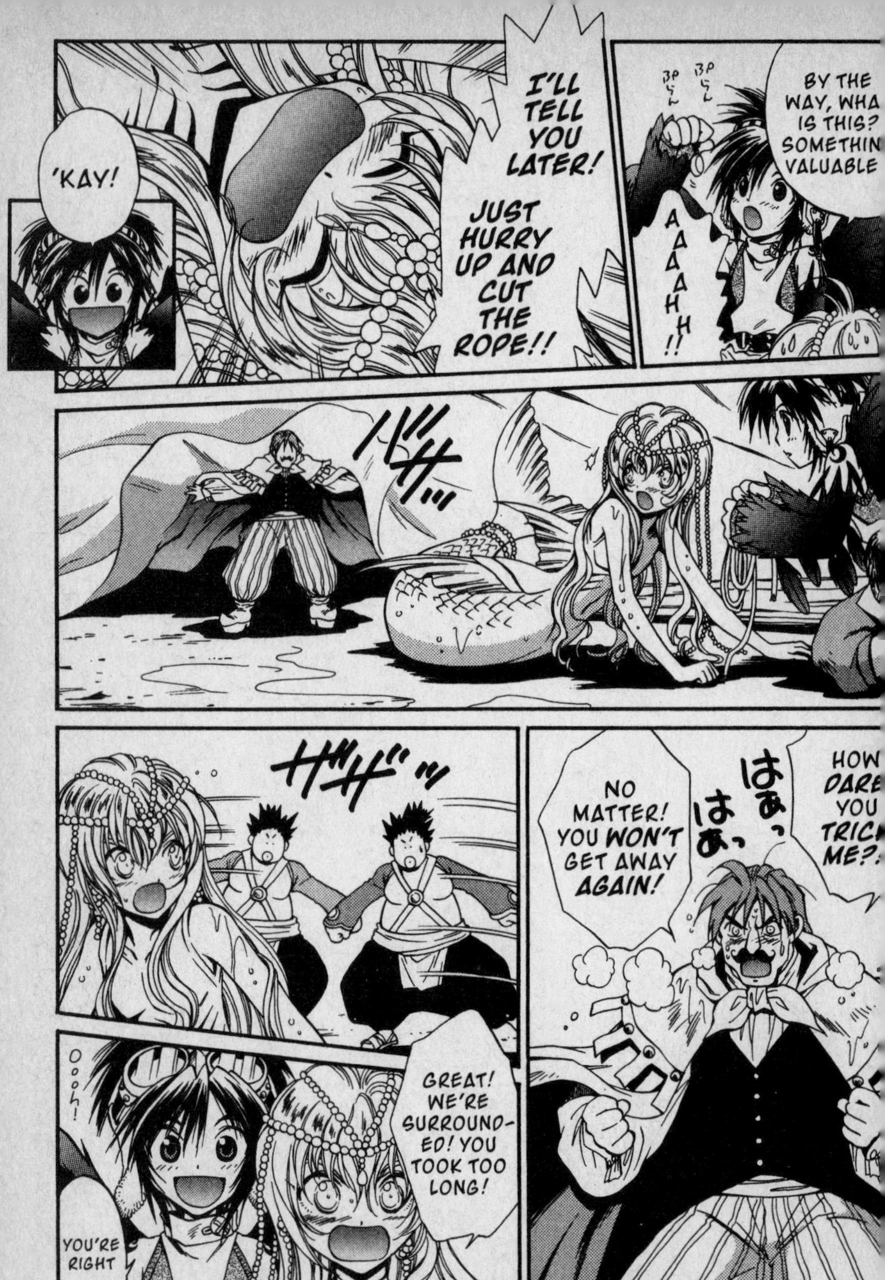

ぷらん ぷらん
BY THE WAY, WHA IS THIS? SOMETHIN VALUABLE
AAAAH!!
I'LL TELL YOU LATER!
JUST HURRY UP AND CUT THE ROPE!!
'KAY!
バサッ
HOW DARE YOU TRIC ME?!
はぁっ はぁっ
NO MATTER! YOU WON'T GET AWAY AGAIN!
ザザッ
GREAT! WE'RE SURROUND-ED! YOU TOOK TOO LONG!
Oooh!
YOU'RE RIGHT ...

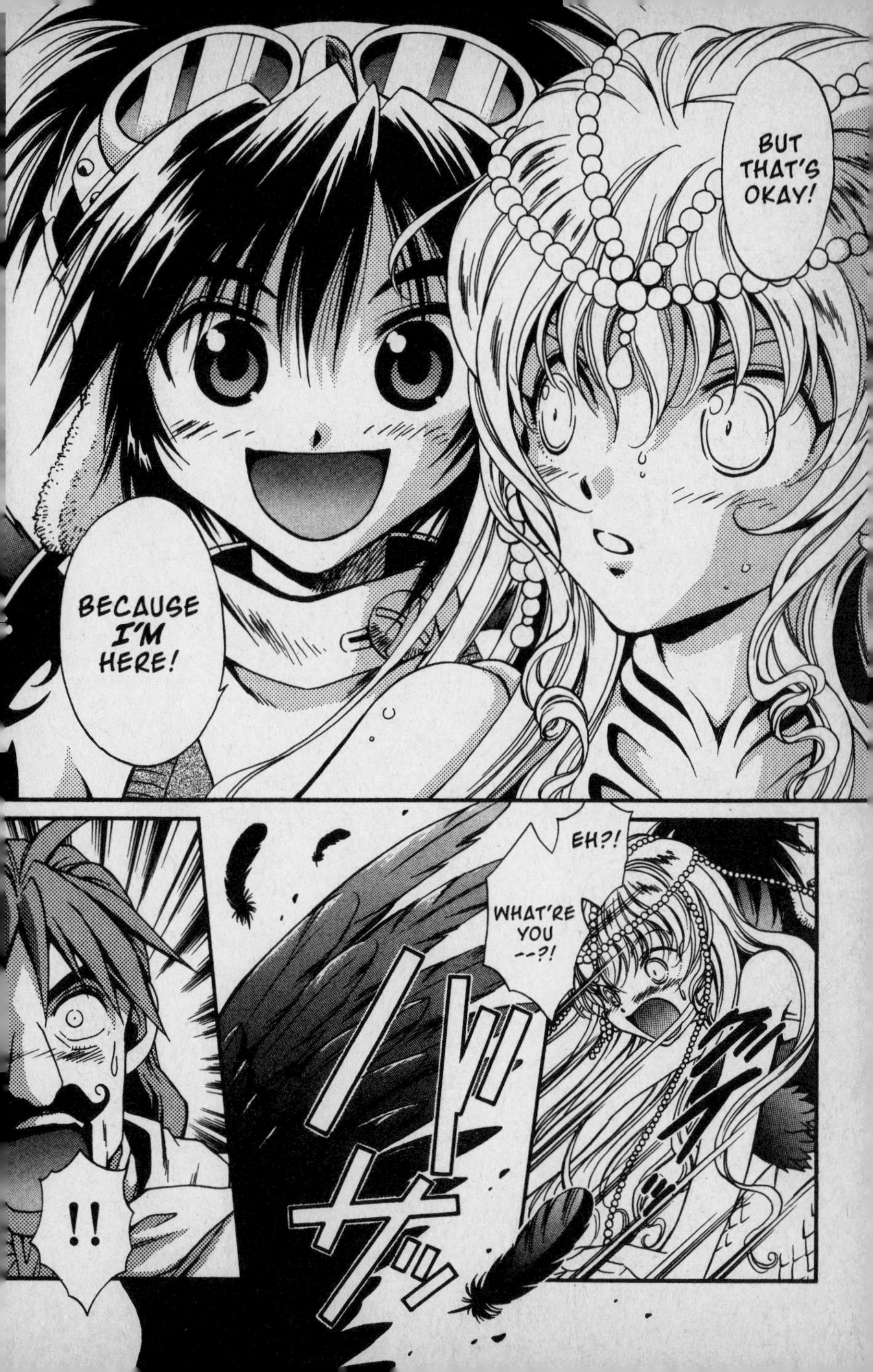
BUT THAT'S OKAY!
BECAUSE I'M HERE!
EH?!
WHAT'RE YOU --?!
!!

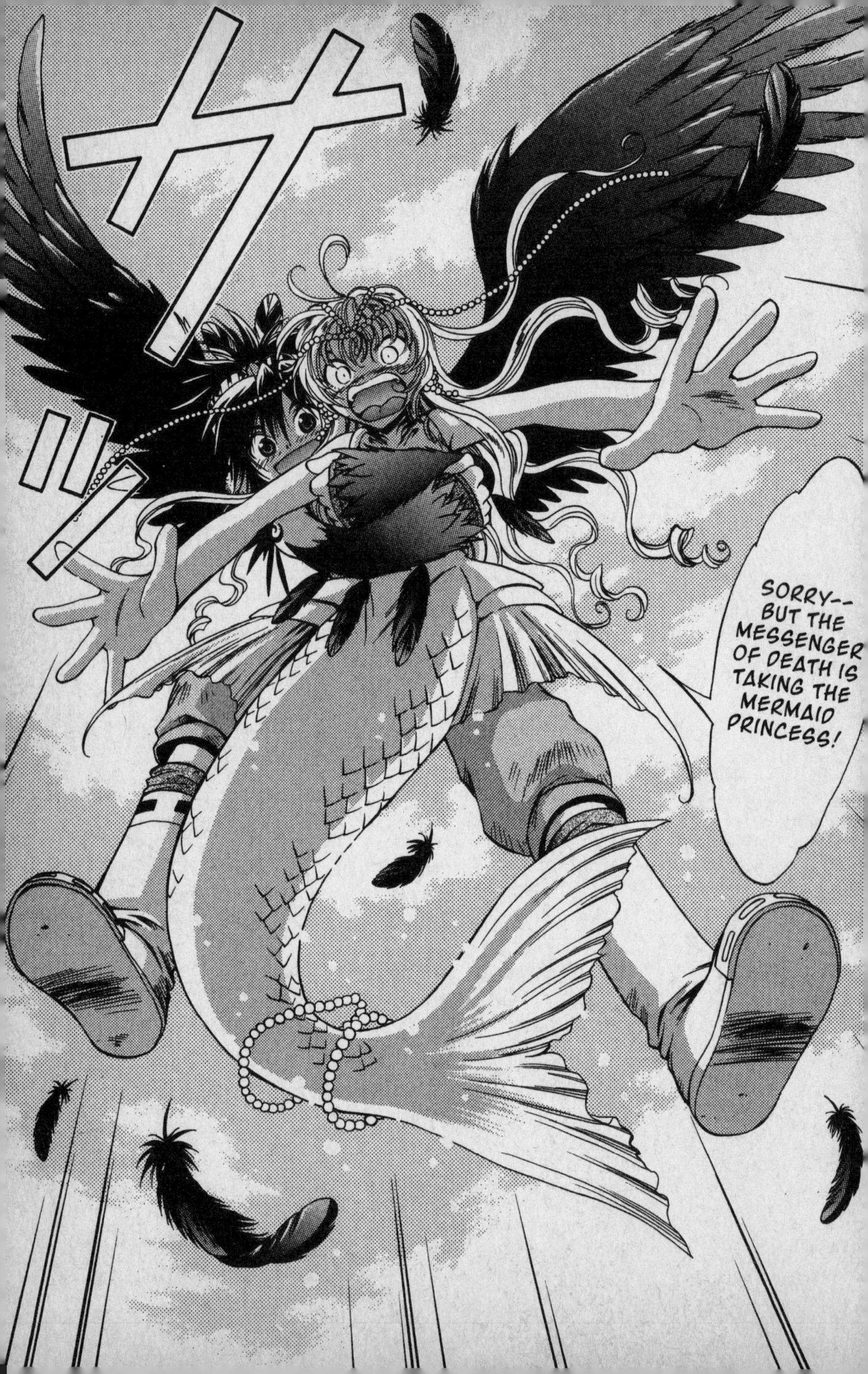
SORRY--
BUT THE MESSENGER OF DEATH IS TAKING THE MERMAID PRINCESS!

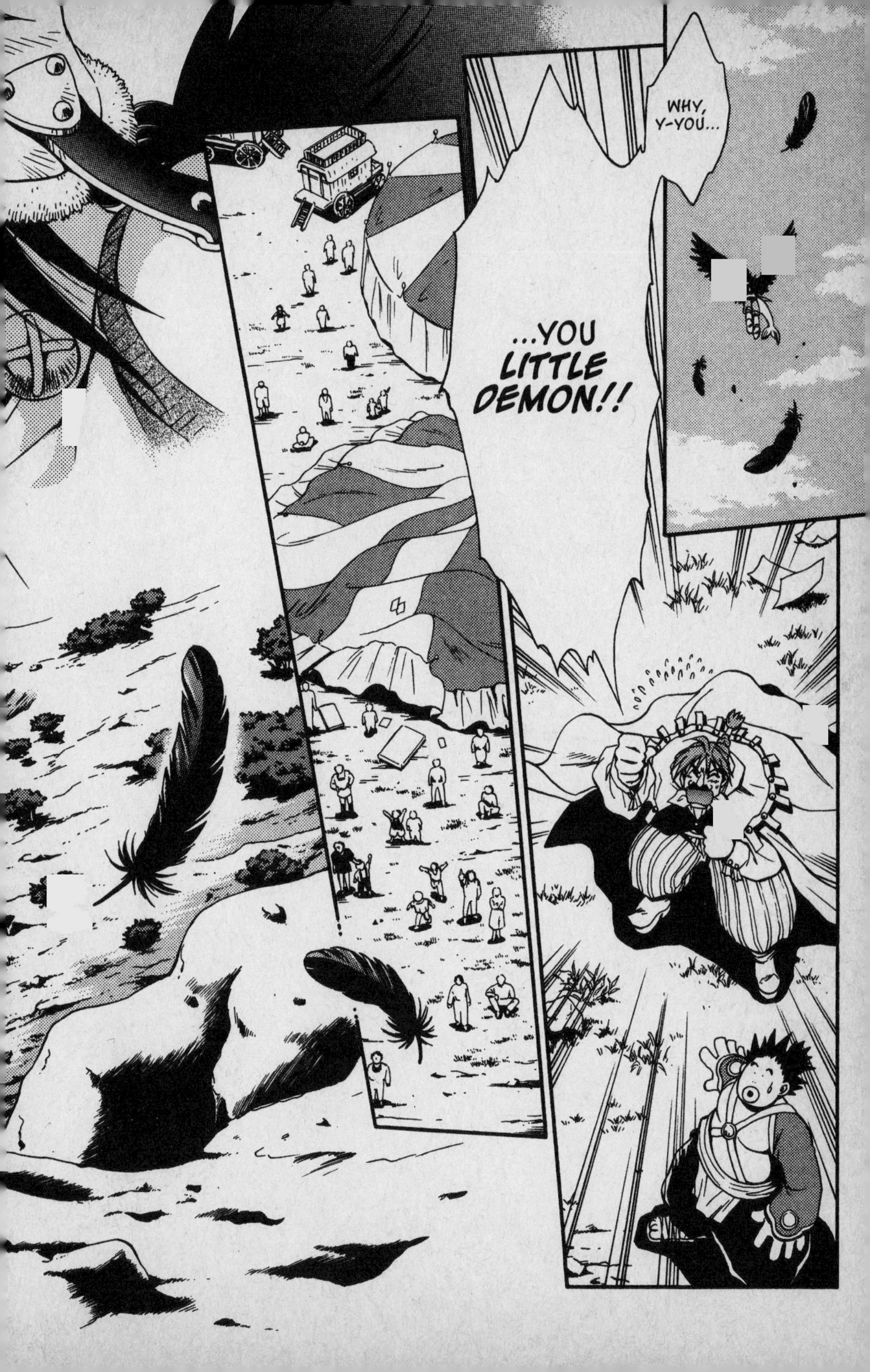
WHY, Y-YOU...
...YOU LITTLE DEMON!!

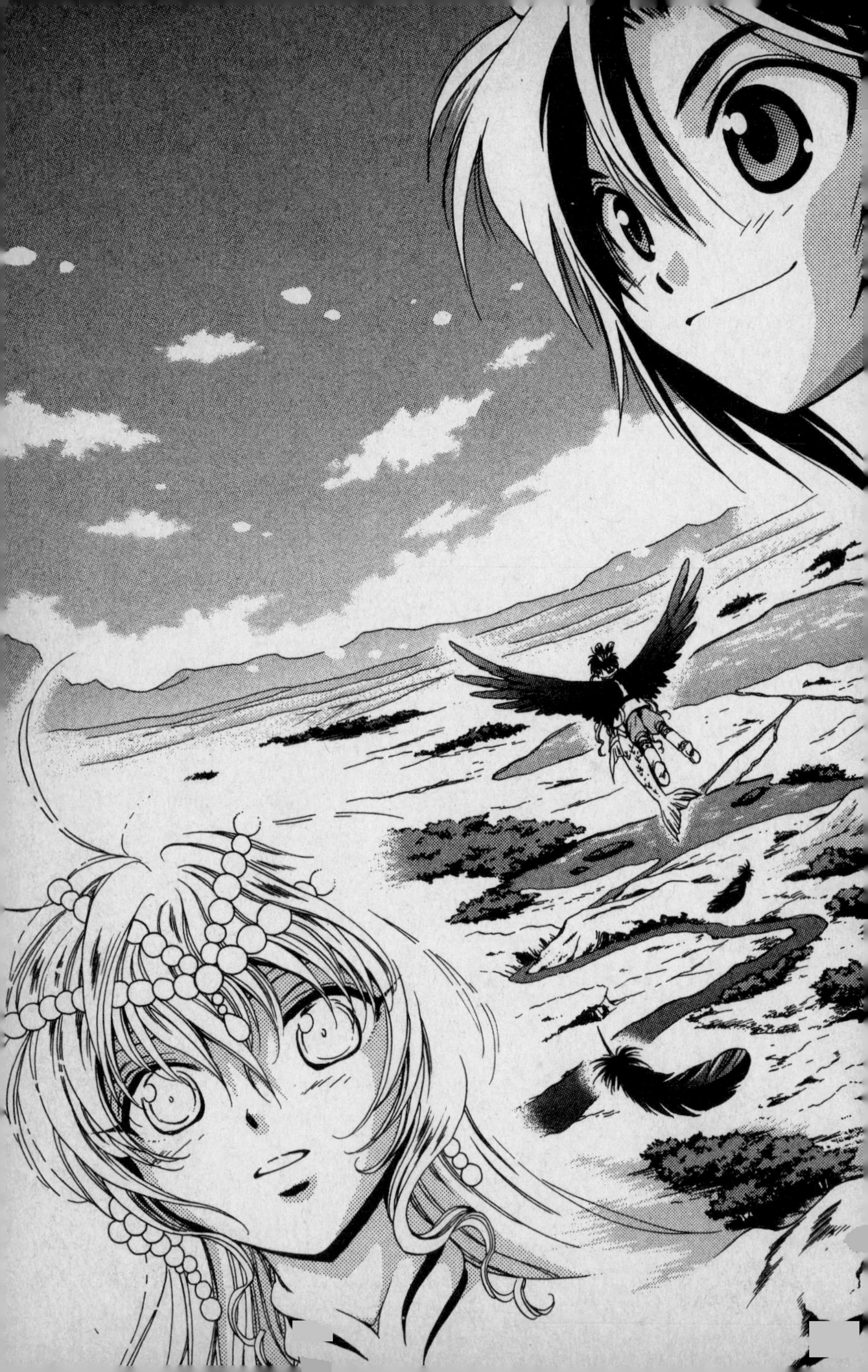

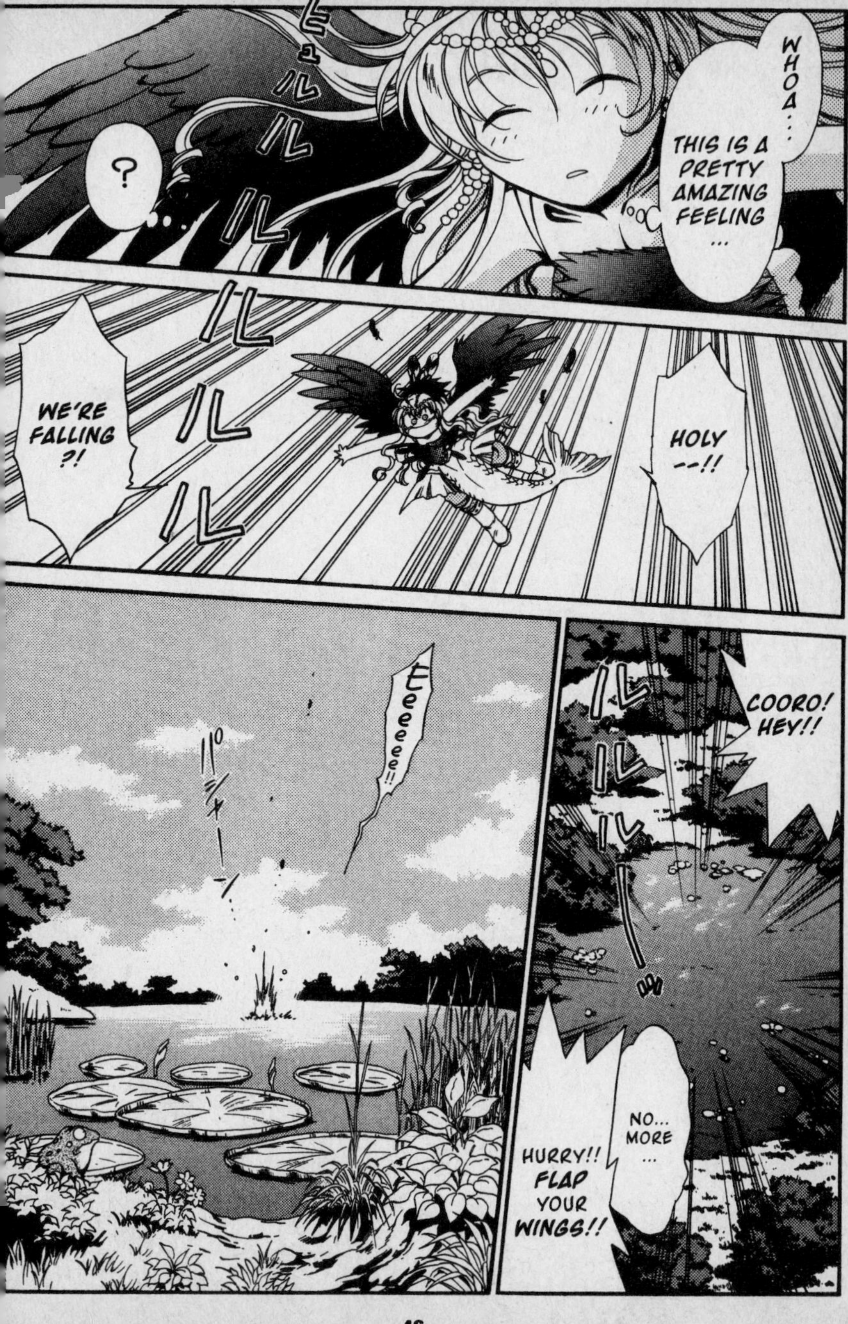
WHOA...
THIS IS A PRETTY AMAZING FEELING...
?
HOLY--!!
WE'RE FALLING?!
COORO! HEY!!
NO... MORE...
HURRY!! FLAP YOUR WINGS!!
Eeeeeee!!

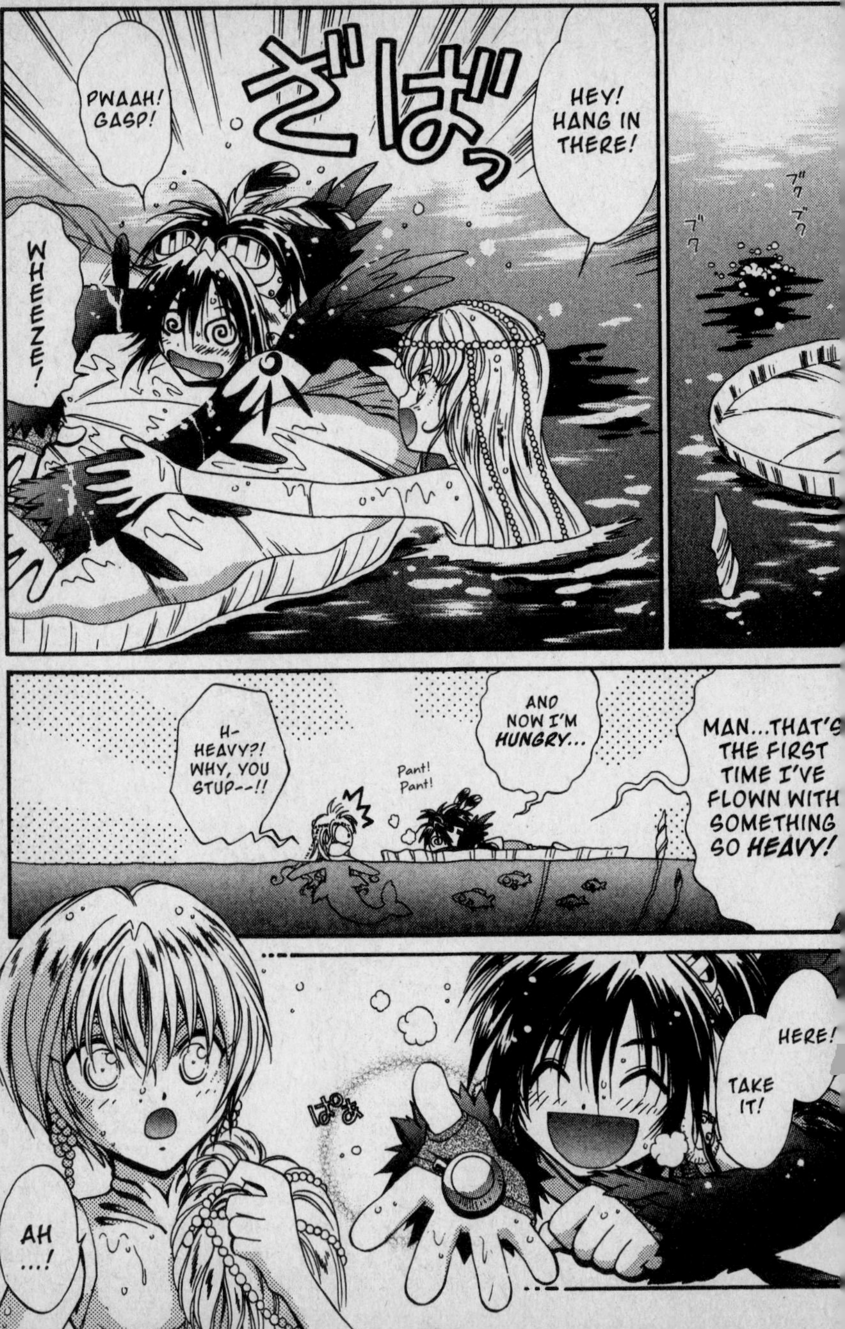
ブク ブク
ブク
ざばっ
HEY! HANG IN THERE!
PWAAH! GASP!
WHEEZE!
MAN...THAT'S THE FIRST TIME I'VE FLOWN WITH SOMETHING SO HEAVY!
AND NOW I'M HUNGRY...
Pant! Pant!
H-HEAVY?! WHY, YOU STUP--!!
HERE!
TAKE IT!
AH ...!

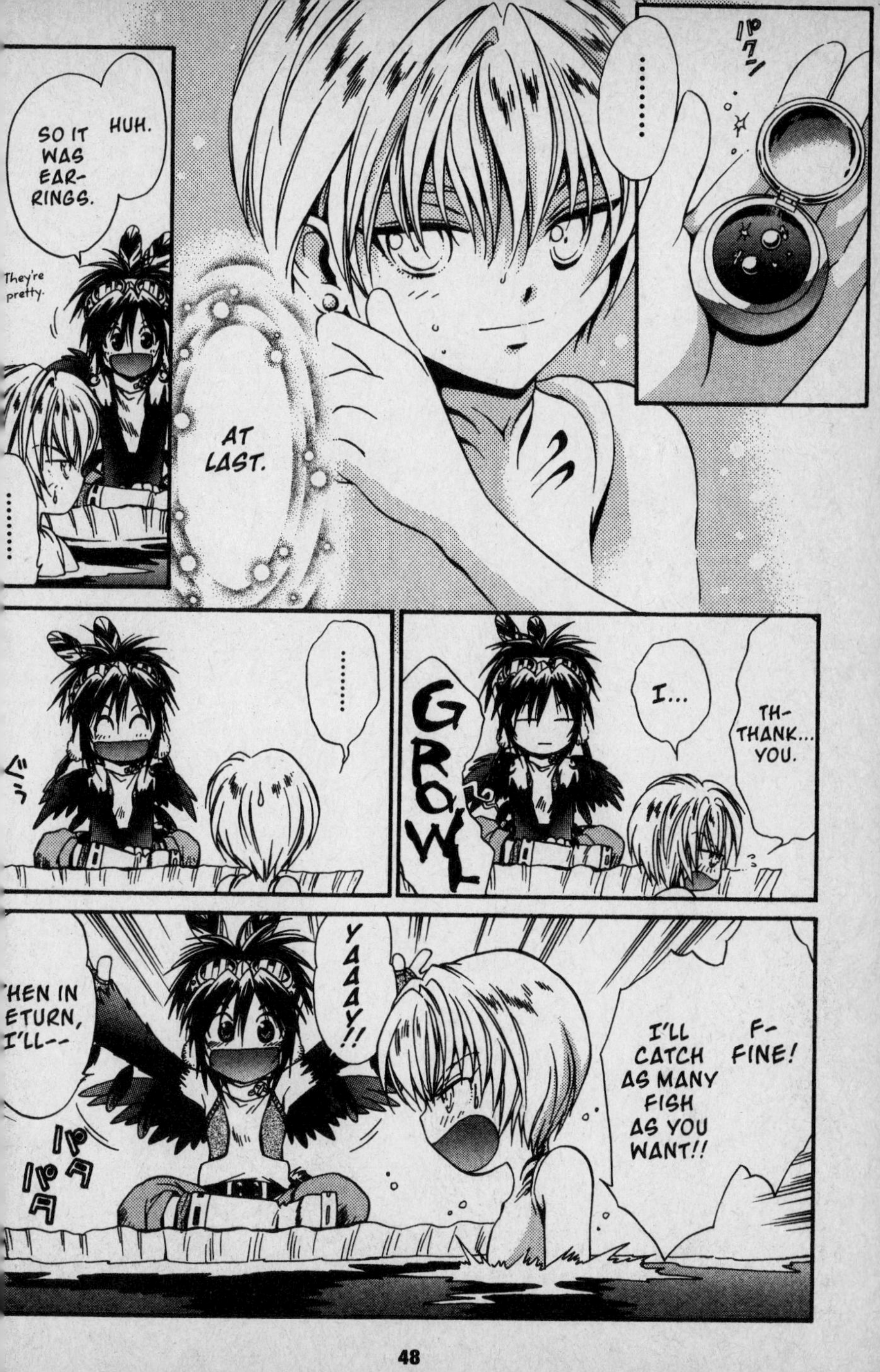

パクン
......
AT LAST.
SO IT WAS EAR-RINGS. HUH.
They're pretty.
......
TH- THANK... YOU.
I...
GROWL
......
F- FINE!
I'LL CATCH AS MANY FISH AS YOU WANT!!
YAAAAY!!
HEN IN ETURN, I'LL--
パタ パタ

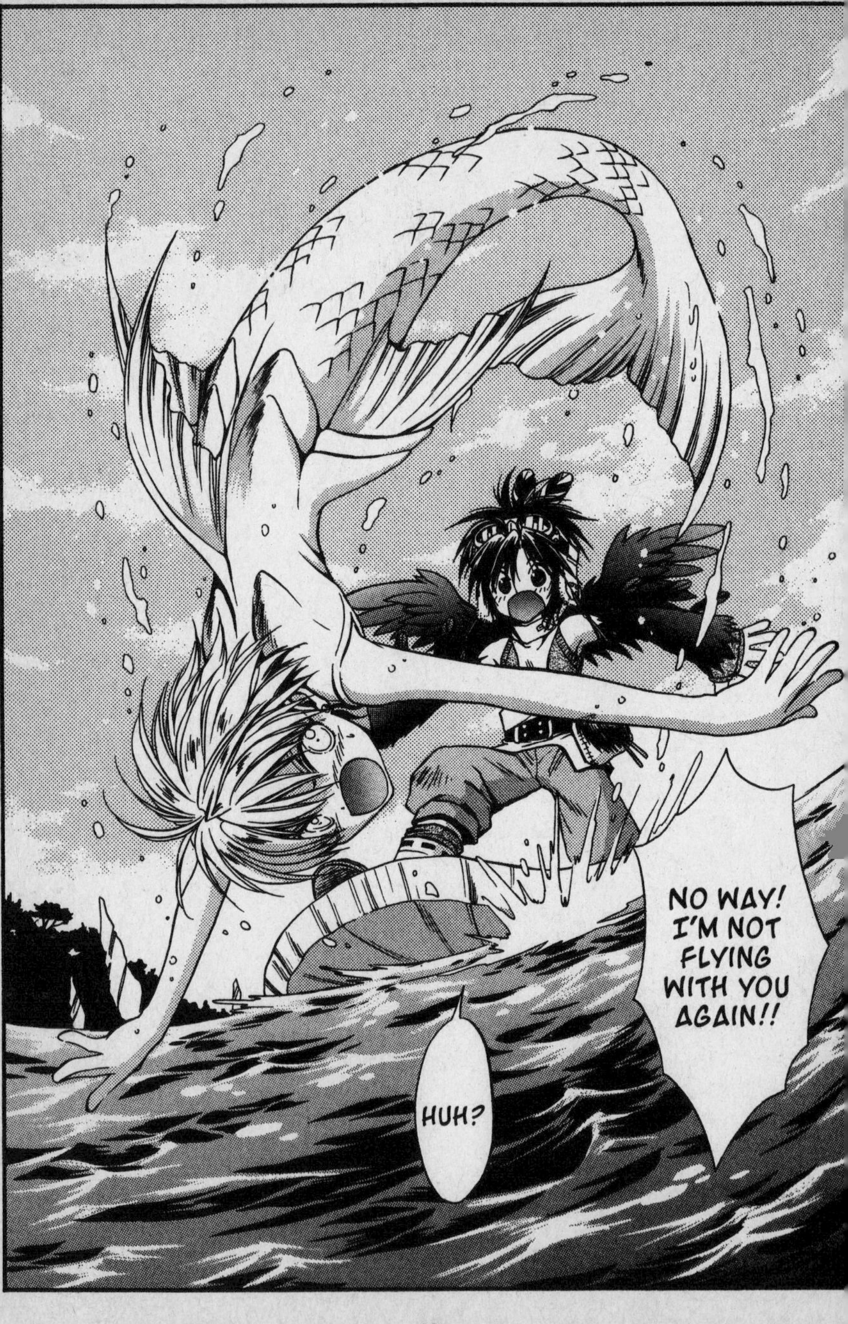
NO WAY! I'M NOT FLYING WITH YOU AGAIN!!
HUH?

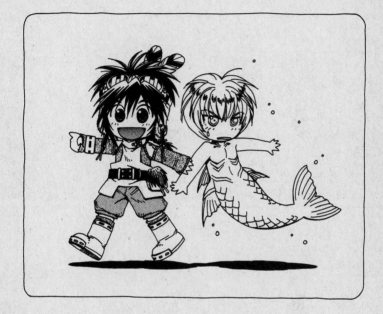

Let's go together !

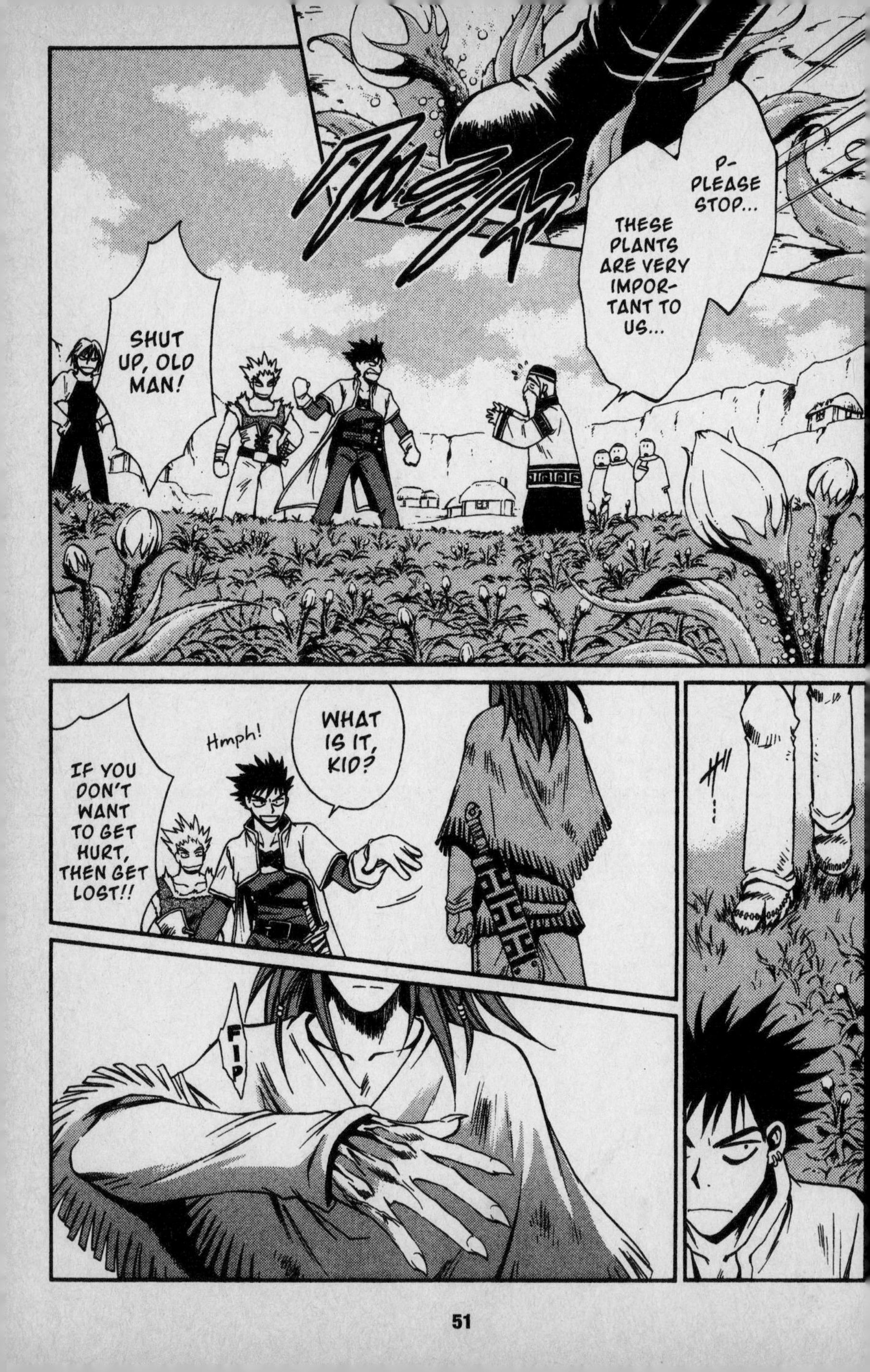
P-PLEASE STOP... THESE PLANTS ARE VERY IMPORTANT TO US...
SHUT UP, OLD MAN!
WHAT IS IT, KID?
Hmph!
IF YOU DON'T WANT TO GET HURT, THEN GET LOST!!
FIP

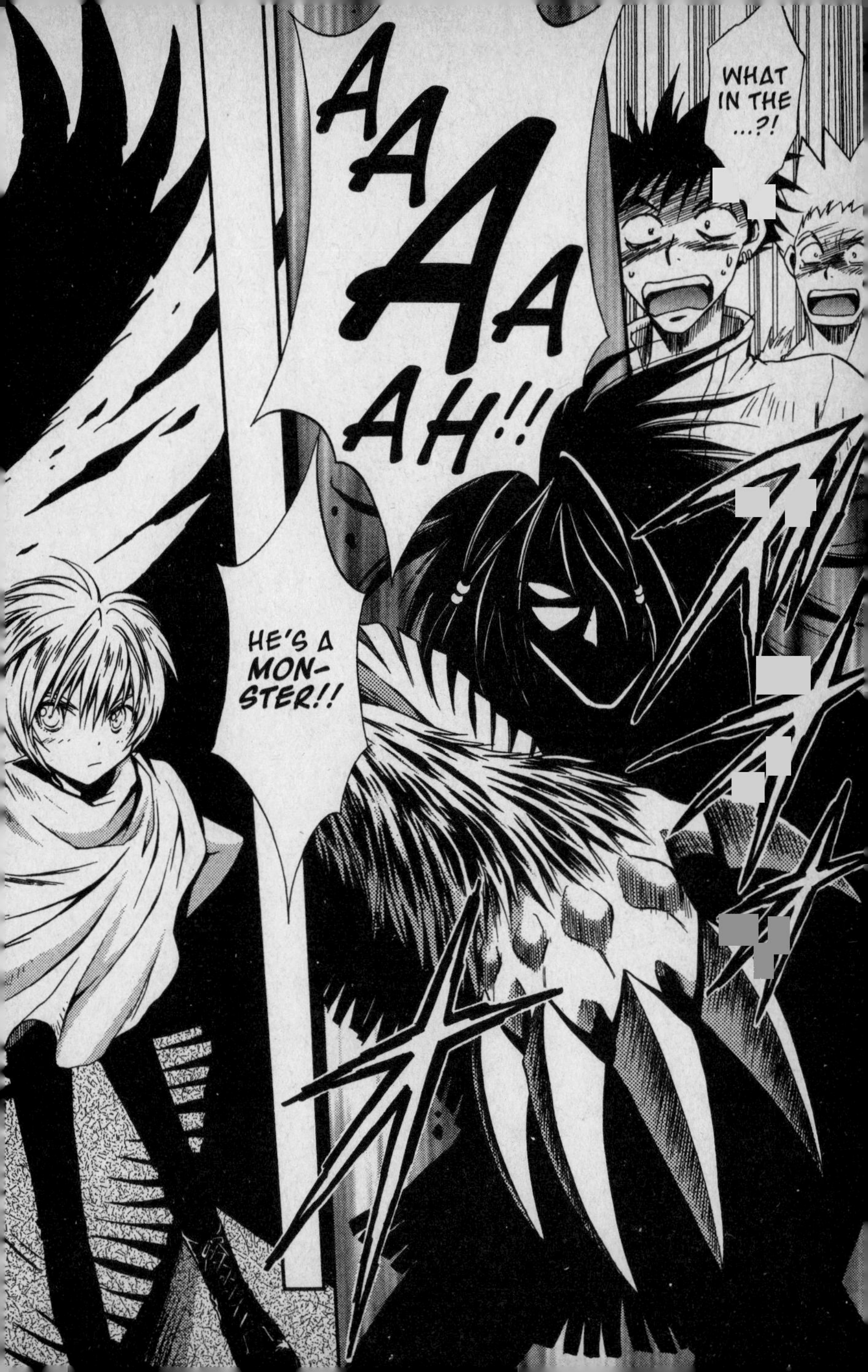
WHAT IN THE ...?!
AAAAAH!!
HE'S A MON-STER!!

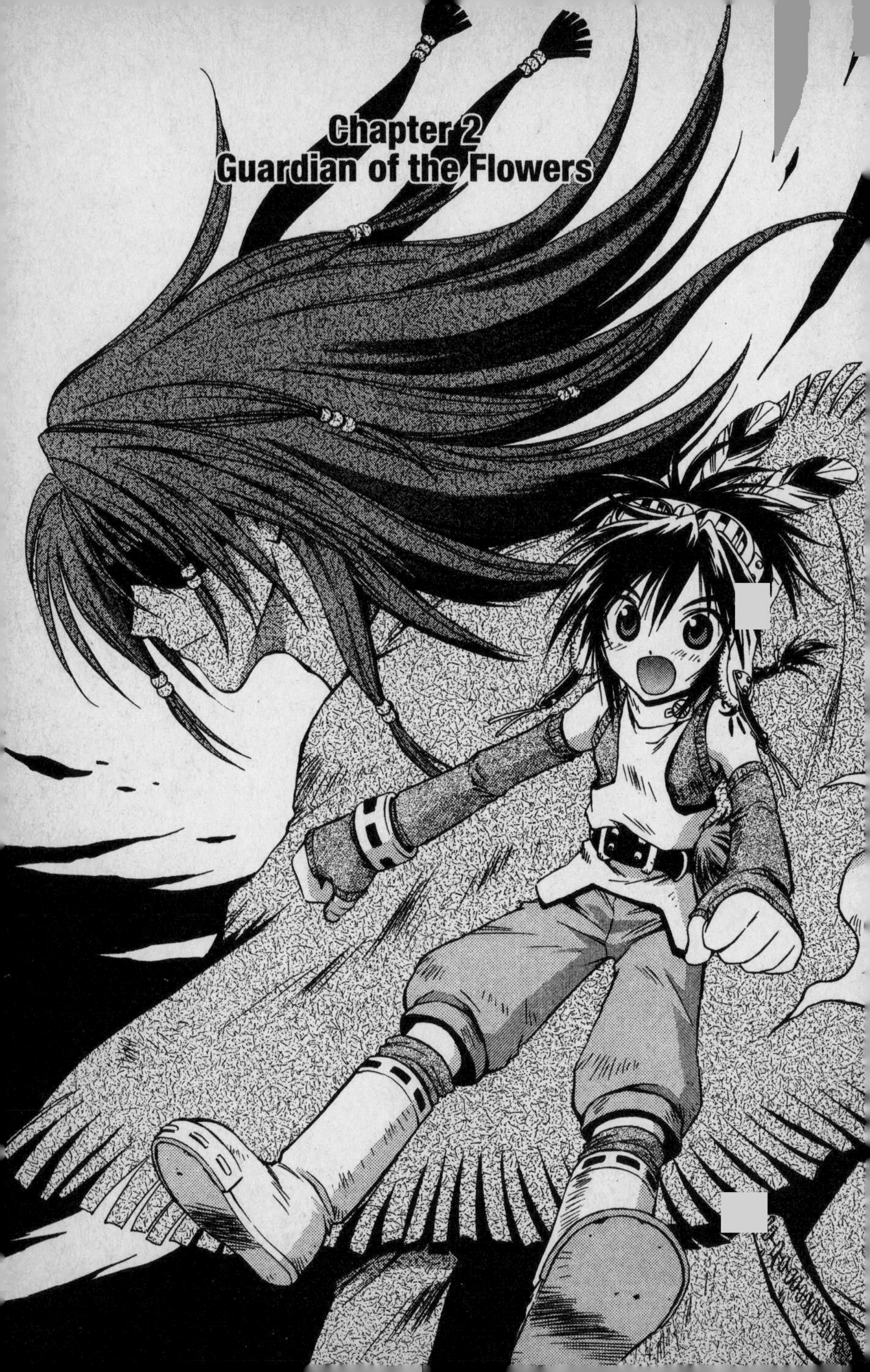
Chapter 2
Guardian of the Flowers

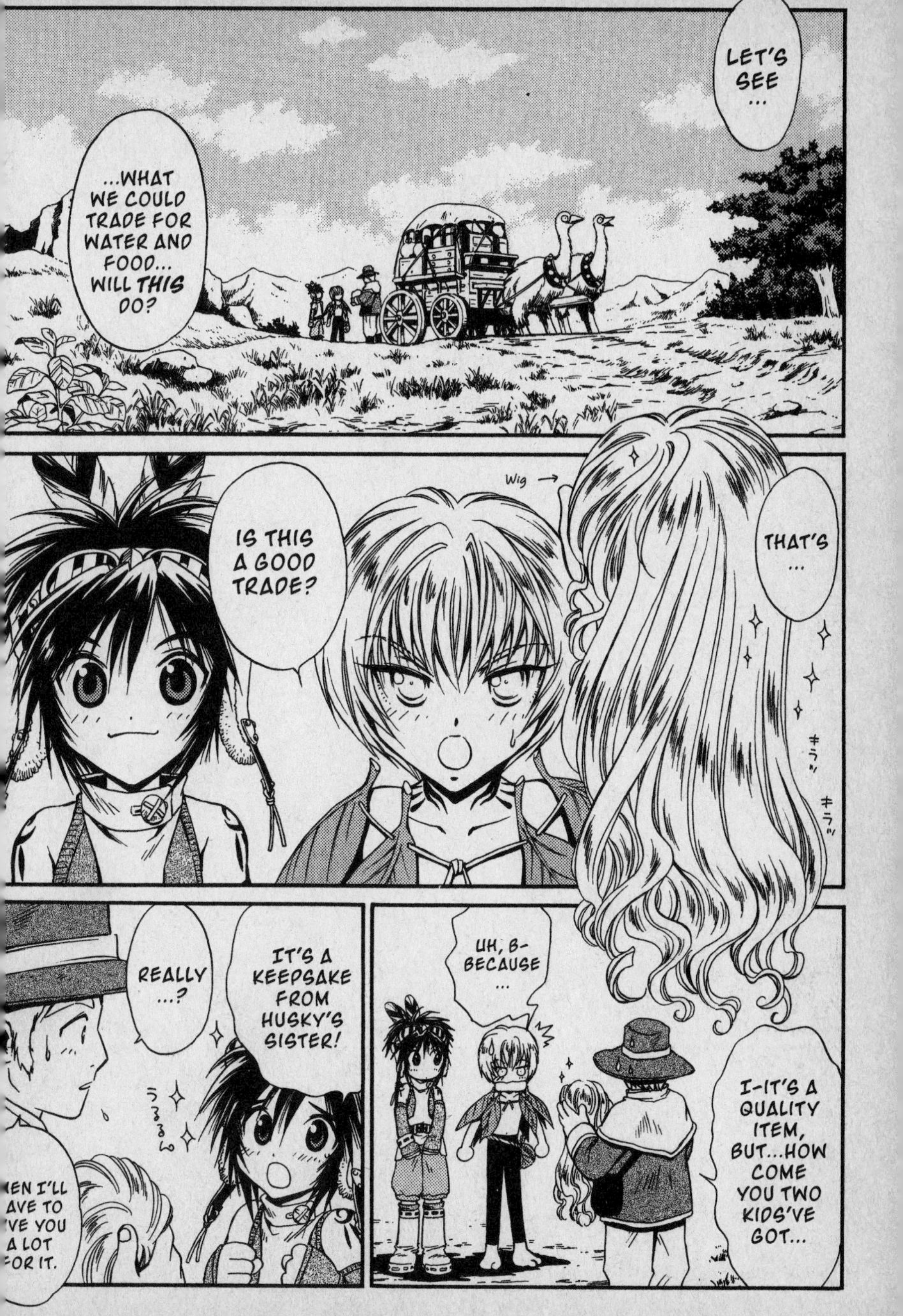
LET'S SEE ...
...WHAT WE COULD TRADE FOR WATER AND FOOD... WILL THIS DO?
THAT'S ...
Wig →
キラッ
キラッ
IS THIS A GOOD TRADE?
I-IT'S A QUALITY ITEM, BUT...HOW COME YOU TWO KIDS'VE GOT...
UH, B-BECAUSE ...
IT'S A KEEPSAKE FROM HUSKY'S SISTER!
REALLY ...?
うるるん
EN I'LL AVE TO VE YOU A LOT FOR IT.

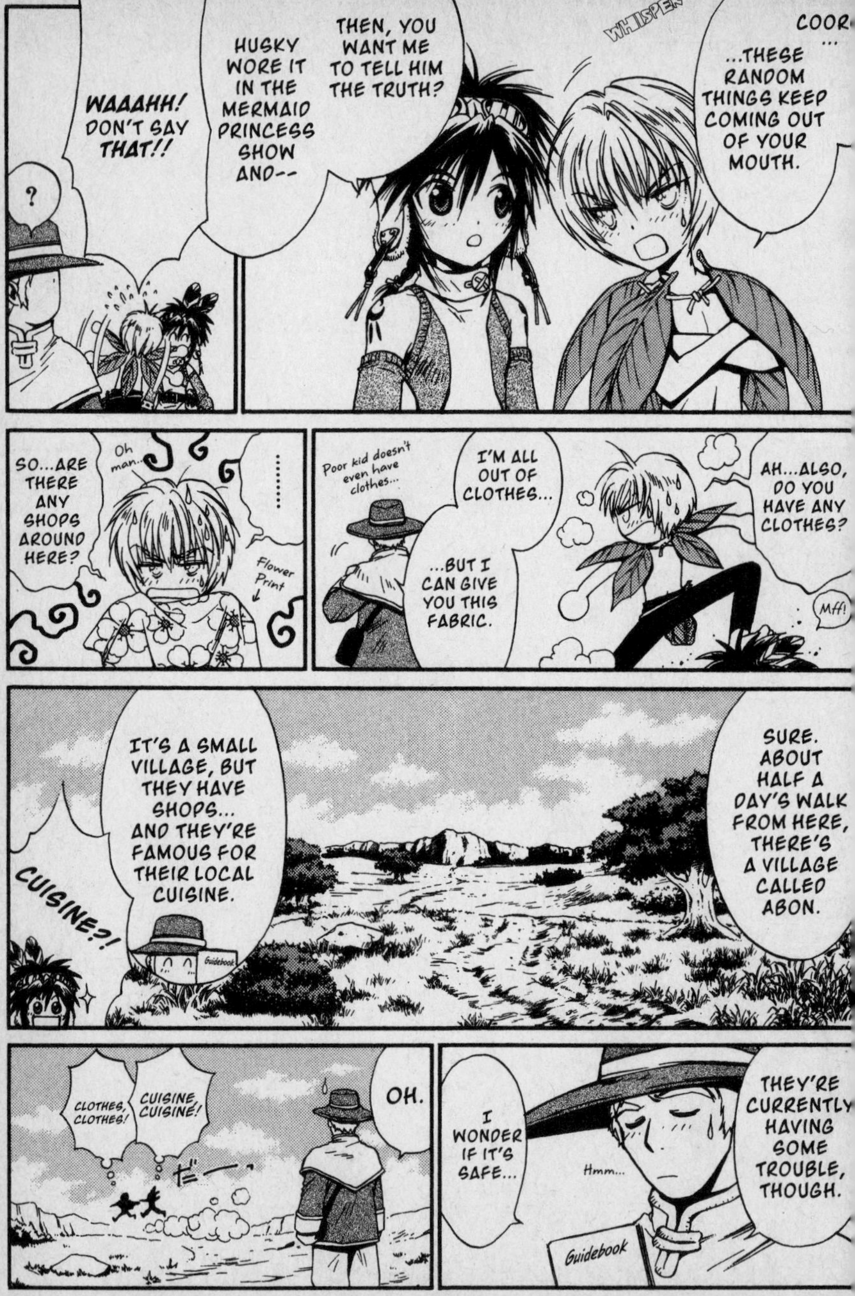

WHISPER
COOR...
...THESE RANDOM THINGS KEEP COMING OUT OF YOUR MOUTH.
THEN, YOU WANT ME TO TELL HIM THE TRUTH?
HUSKY WORE IT IN THE MERMAID PRINCESS SHOW AND--
WAAAHH! DON'T SAY THAT!!
?
AH...ALSO, DO YOU HAVE ANY CLOTHES?
Mff!
I'M ALL OUT OF CLOTHES...
...BUT I CAN GIVE YOU THIS FABRIC.
Poor kid doesn't even have clothes...
......
Oh man...
SO...ARE THERE ANY SHOPS AROUND HERE?
Flower Print
SURE. ABOUT HALF A DAY'S WALK FROM HERE, THERE'S A VILLAGE CALLED ABON.
IT'S A SMALL VILLAGE, BUT THEY HAVE SHOPS... AND THEY'RE FAMOUS FOR THEIR LOCAL CUISINE.
Guidebook
CUISINE?!
THEY'RE CURRENTLY HAVING SOME TROUBLE, THOUGH.
Hmm...
I WONDER IF IT'S SAFE...
Guidebook
OH.
CUISINE, CUISINE!
CLOTHES, CLOTHES!

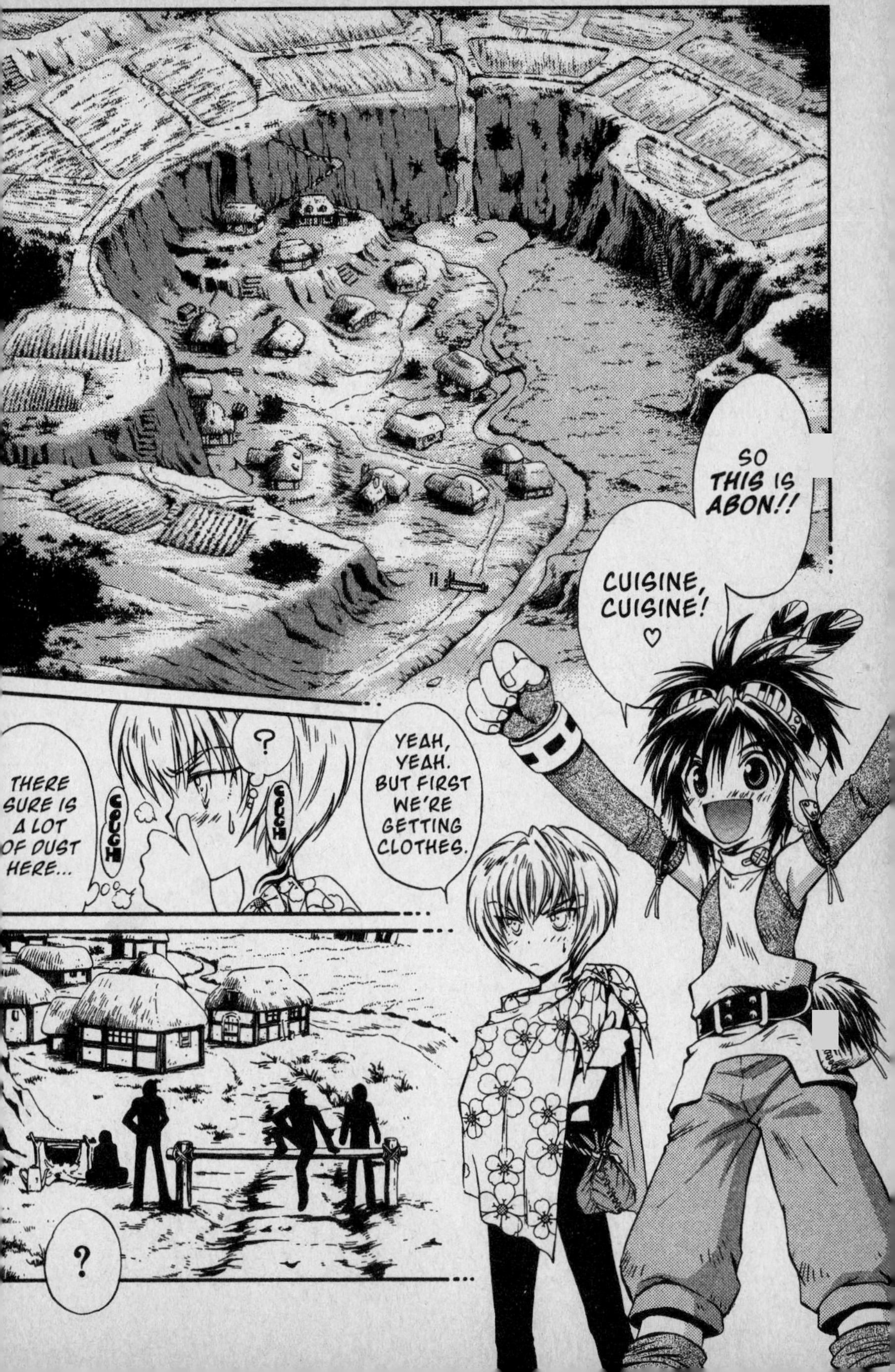
SO THIS IS ABON!!
CUISINE, CUISINE! ♡
YEAH, YEAH. BUT FIRST WE'RE GETTING CLOTHES.
?
COUGH
COUGH
THERE SURE IS A LOT OF DUST HERE...
?

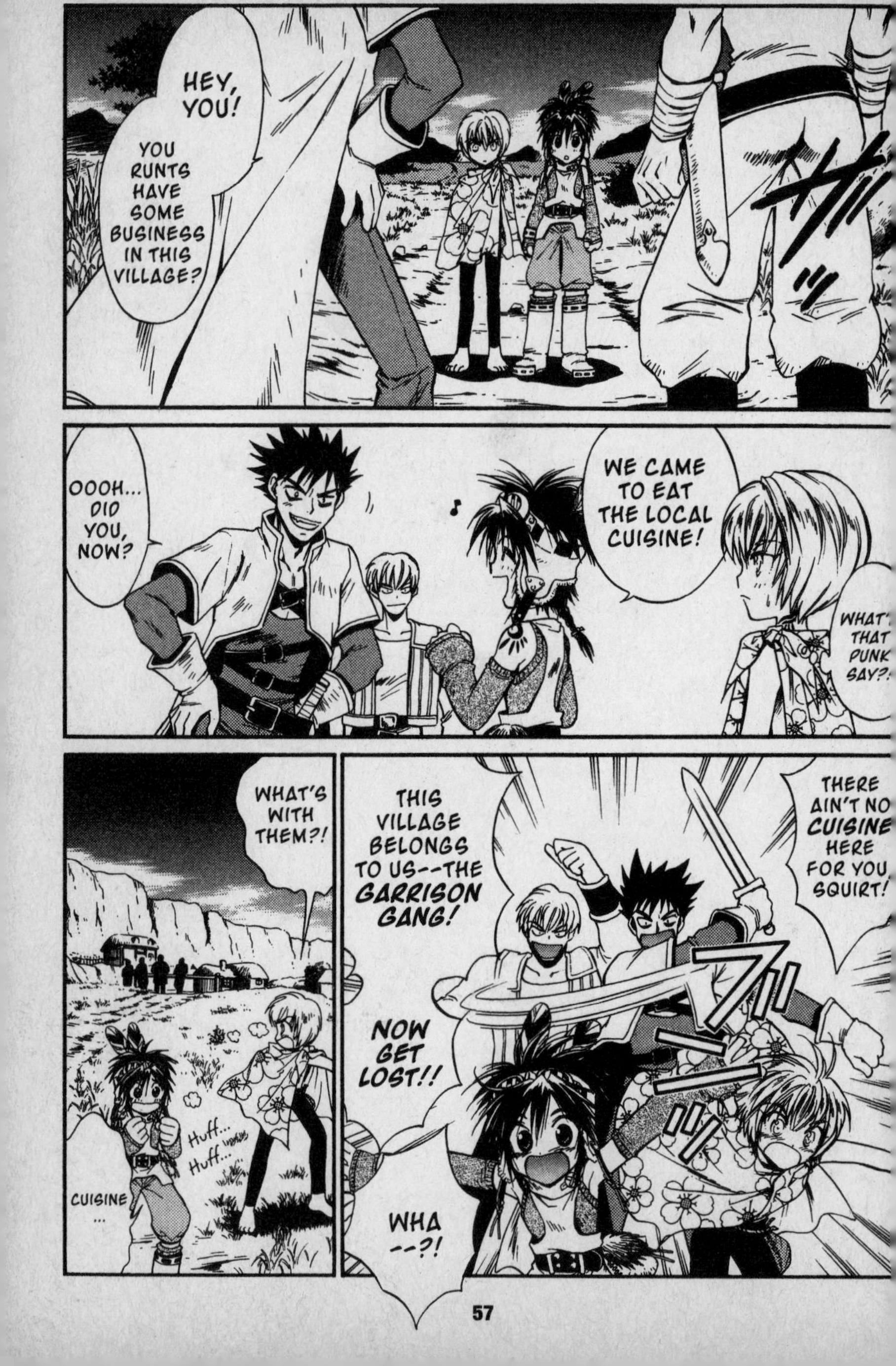
HEY, YOU!
YOU RUNTS HAVE SOME BUSINESS IN THIS VILLAGE?
WE CAME TO EAT THE LOCAL CUISINE!
OOOH... DID YOU, NOW?
WHAT' THAT PUNK SAY?!
THERE AIN'T NO CUISINE HERE FOR YOU SQUIRT!
THIS VILLAGE BELONGS TO US--THE GARRISON GANG!
NOW GET LOST!!
WHA--?!
WHAT'S WITH THEM?!
Huff... Huff...
CUISINE...

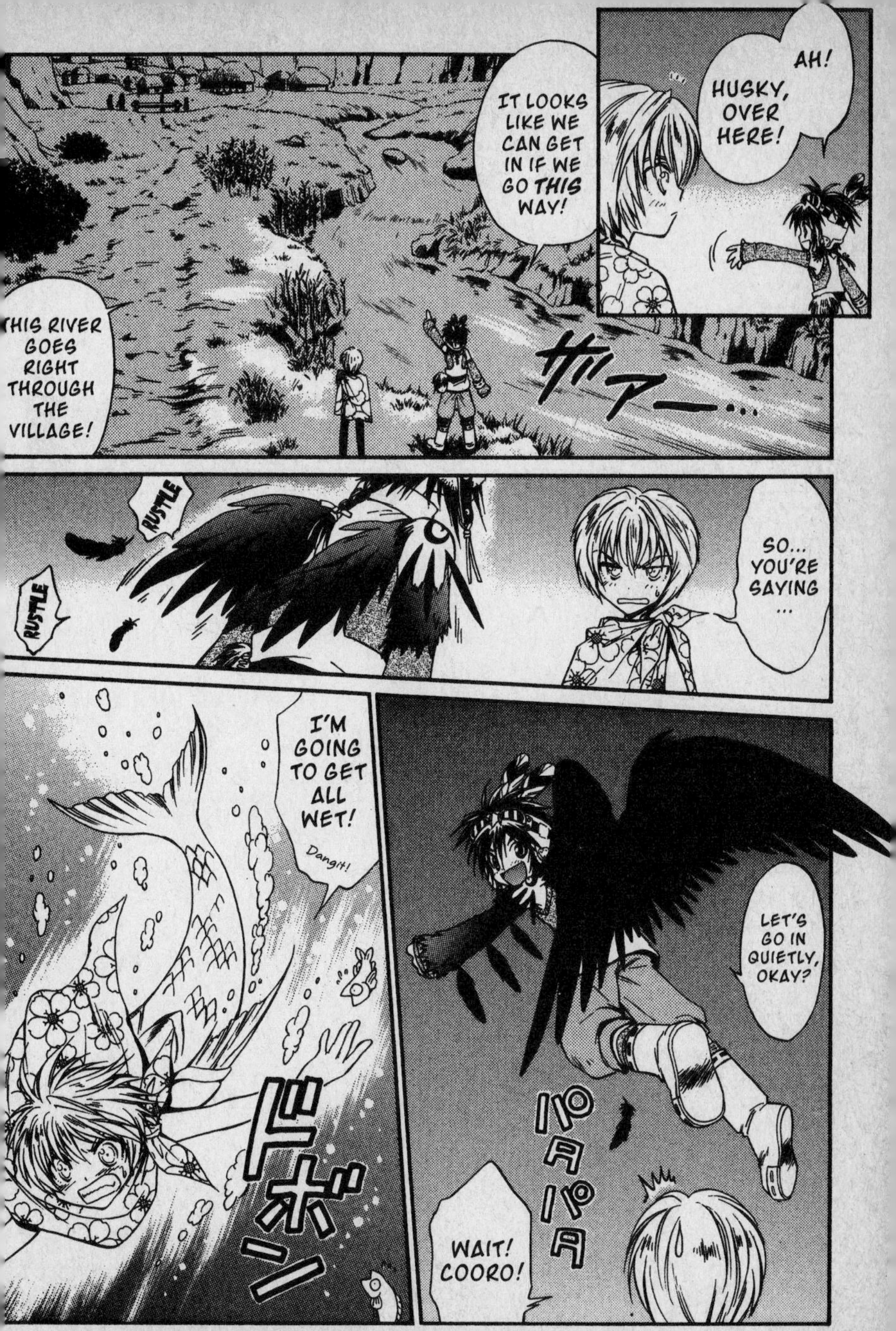
AH! HUSKY, OVER HERE!
IT LOOKS LIKE WE CAN GET IN IF WE GO THIS WAY!
ザァー…
THIS RIVER GOES RIGHT THROUGH THE VILLAGE!
SO... YOU'RE SAYING ...
RUSTLE
RUSTLE
LET'S GO IN QUIETLY, OKAY?
パタパタ
WAIT! COORO!
I'M GOING TO GET ALL WET!
Dangit!
ドボーン

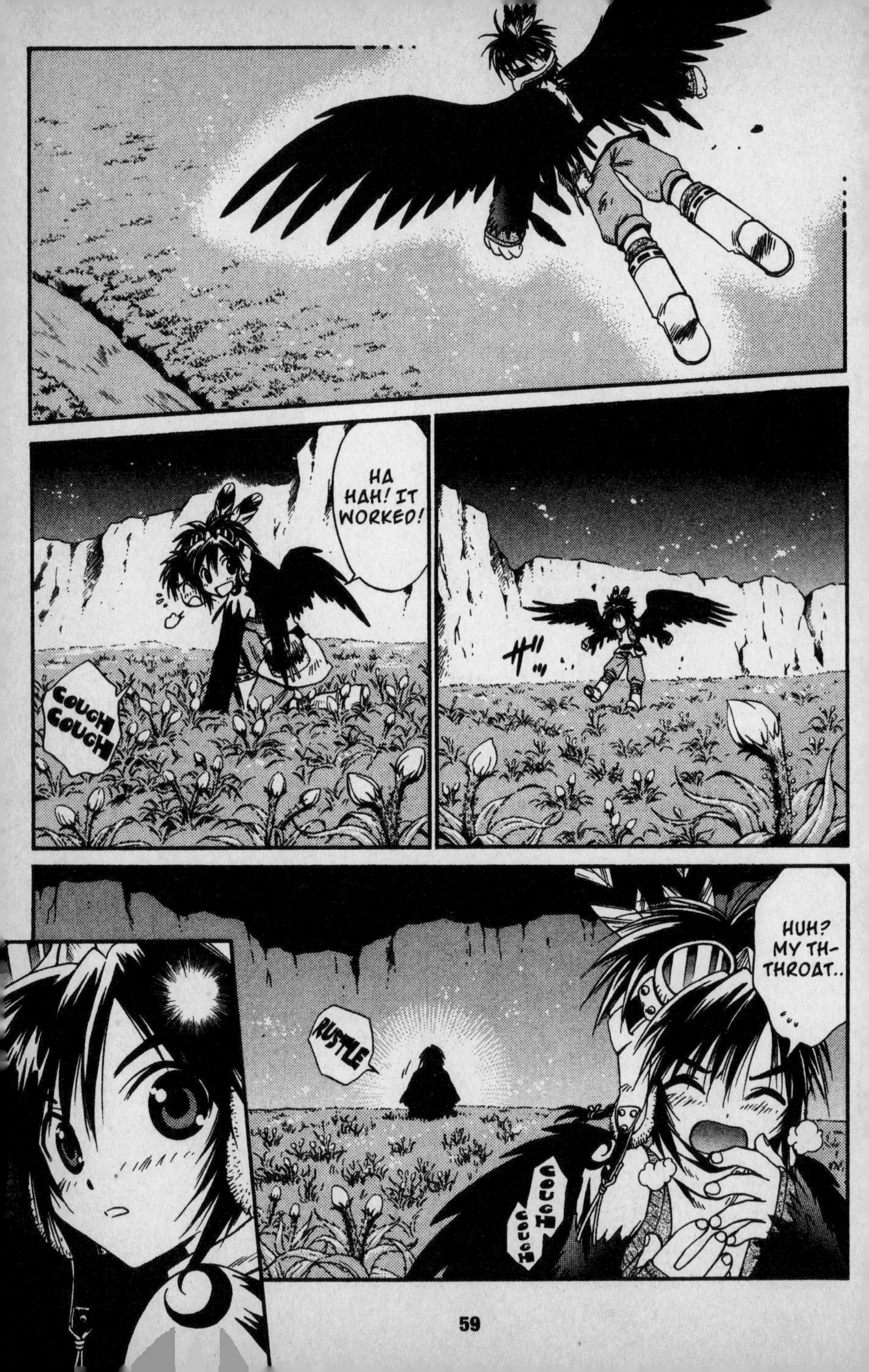
HA HAH! IT WORKED!
COUGH COUGH
HUH? MY TH-THROAT..
...
COUGH COUGH COUGH
RUSTLE

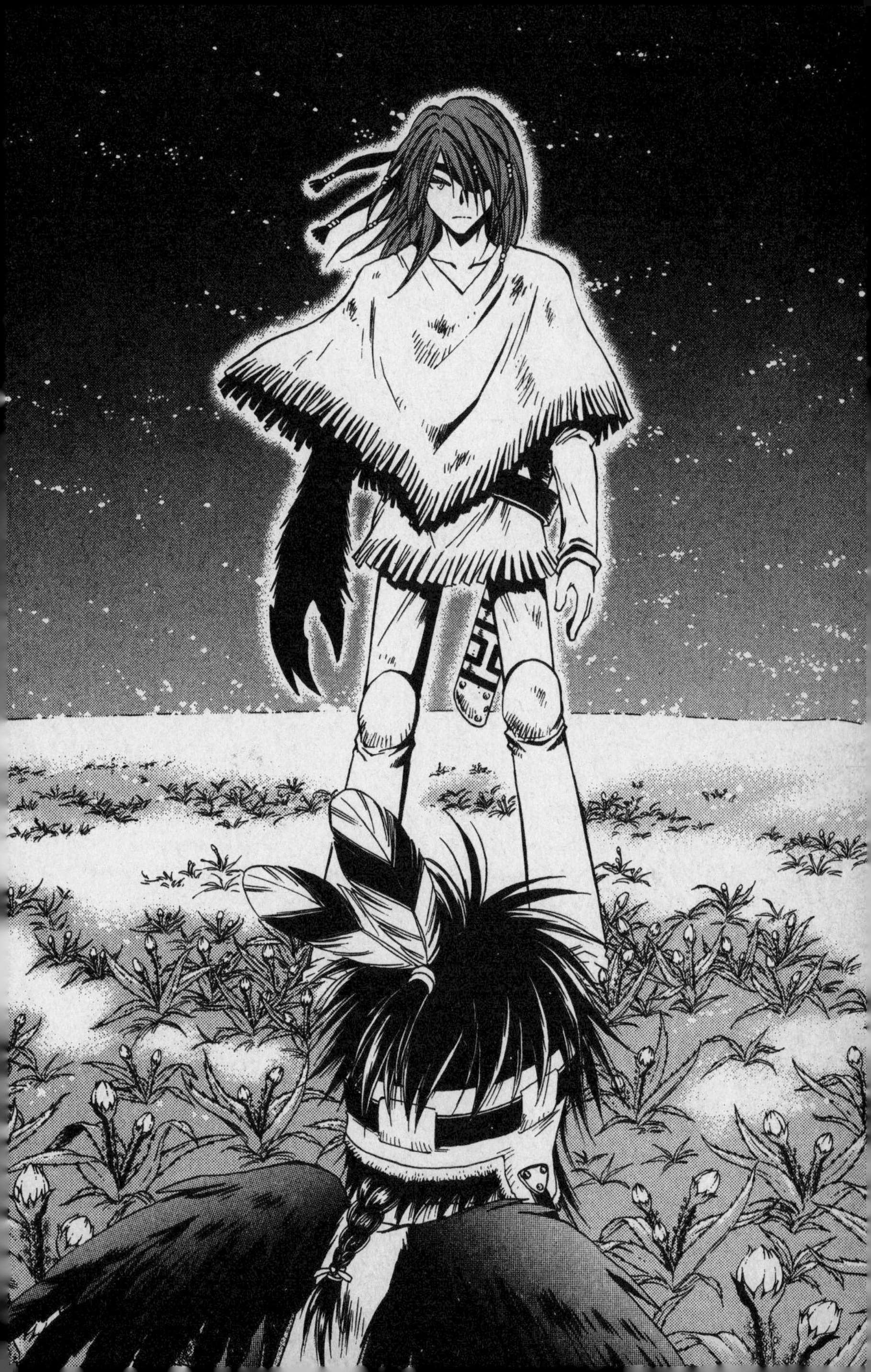

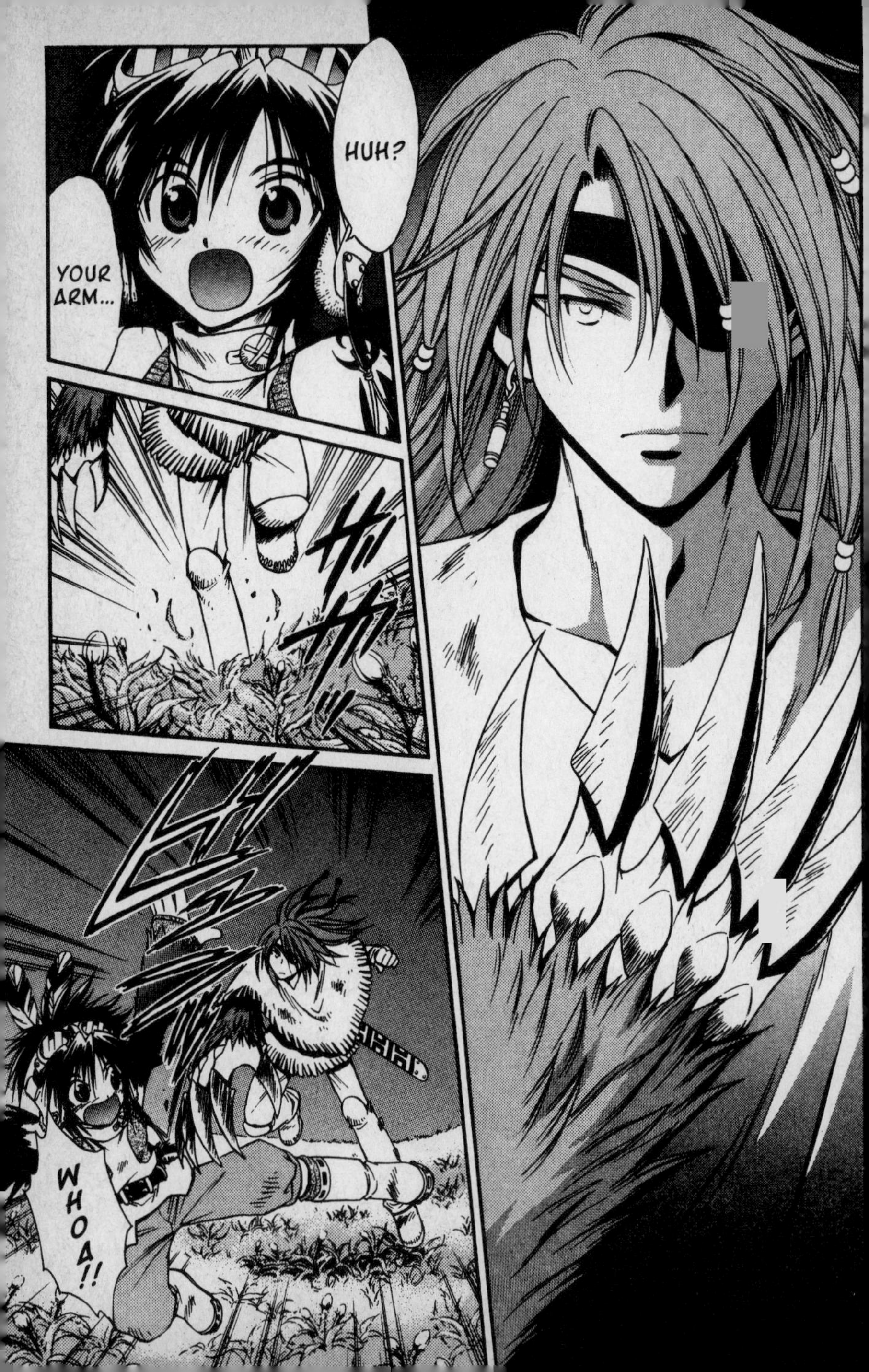
HUH?
YOUR ARM...
WHOA!!

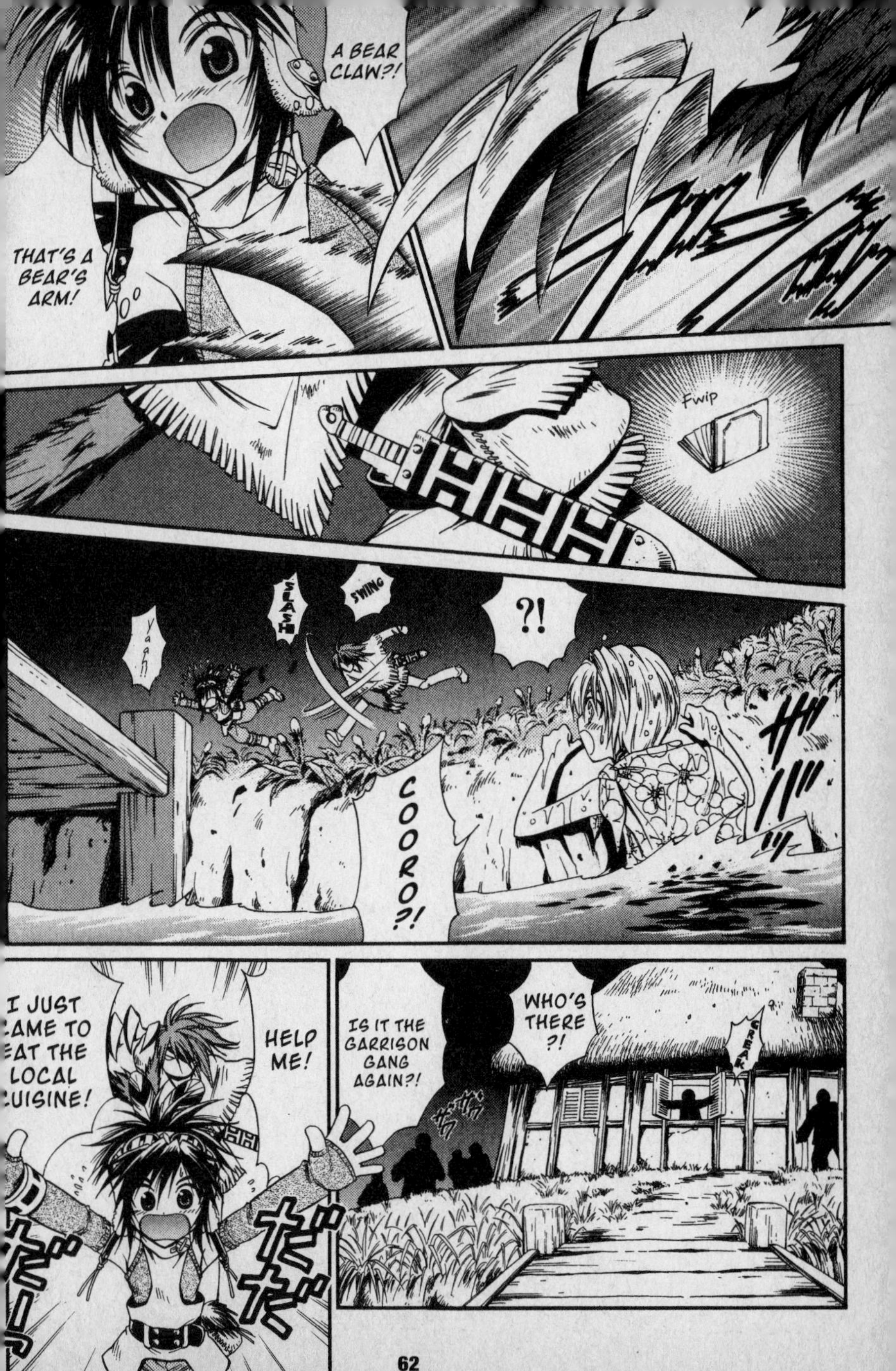

A BEAR CLAW?!
THAT'S A BEAR'S ARM!
Fwip
?!
COORO?!
SWING
SLASH
Yaah!
WHO'S THERE?!
CREAK
IS IT THE GARRISON GANG AGAIN?!
HELP ME!
I JUST AME TO AT THE LOCAL UISINE!

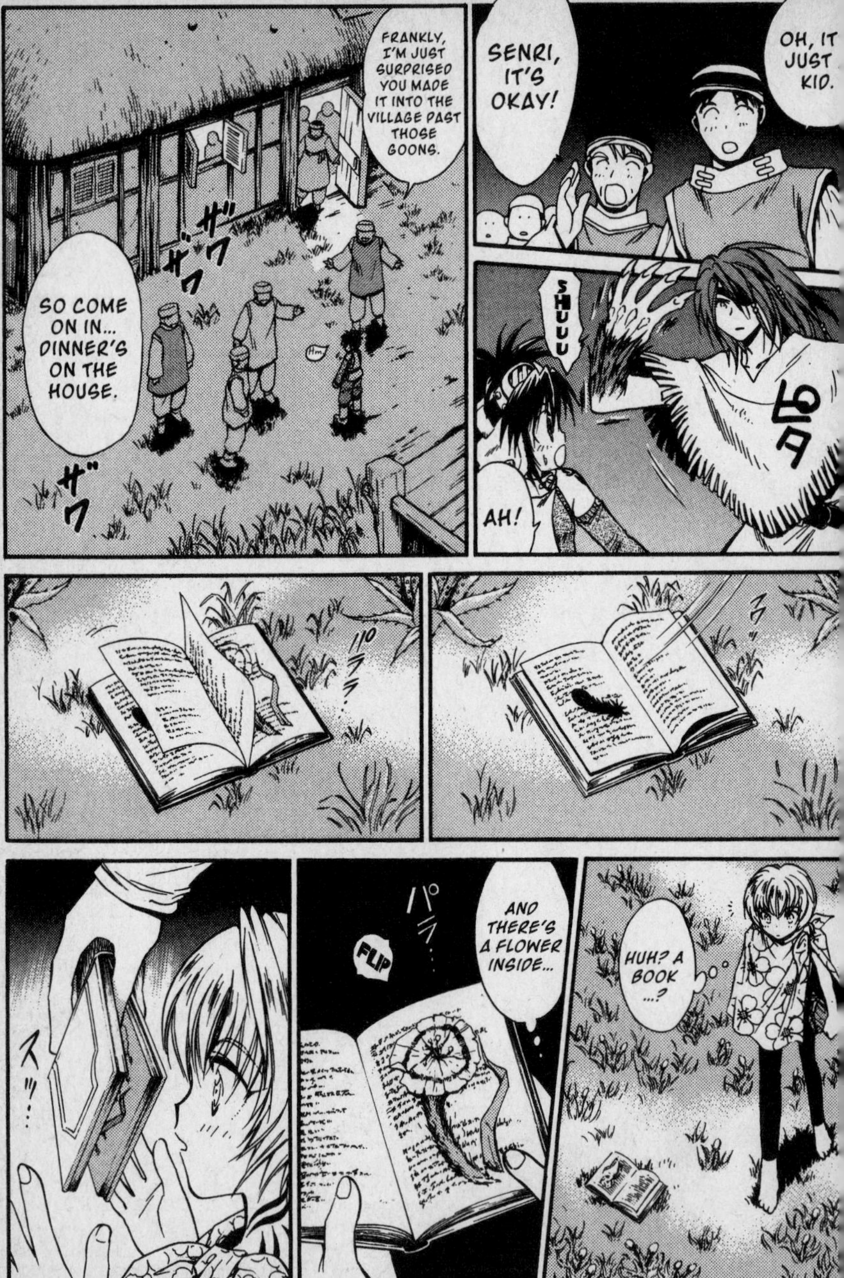
OH, IT JUST KID.
SENRI, IT'S OKAY!
SHUUU
AH!
FRANKLY, I'M JUST SURPRISED YOU MADE IT INTO THE VILLAGE PAST THOSE GOONS.
SO COME ON IN... DINNER'S ON THE HOUSE.
HUH? A BOOK ...?
AND THERE'S A FLOWER INSIDE...
FLIP

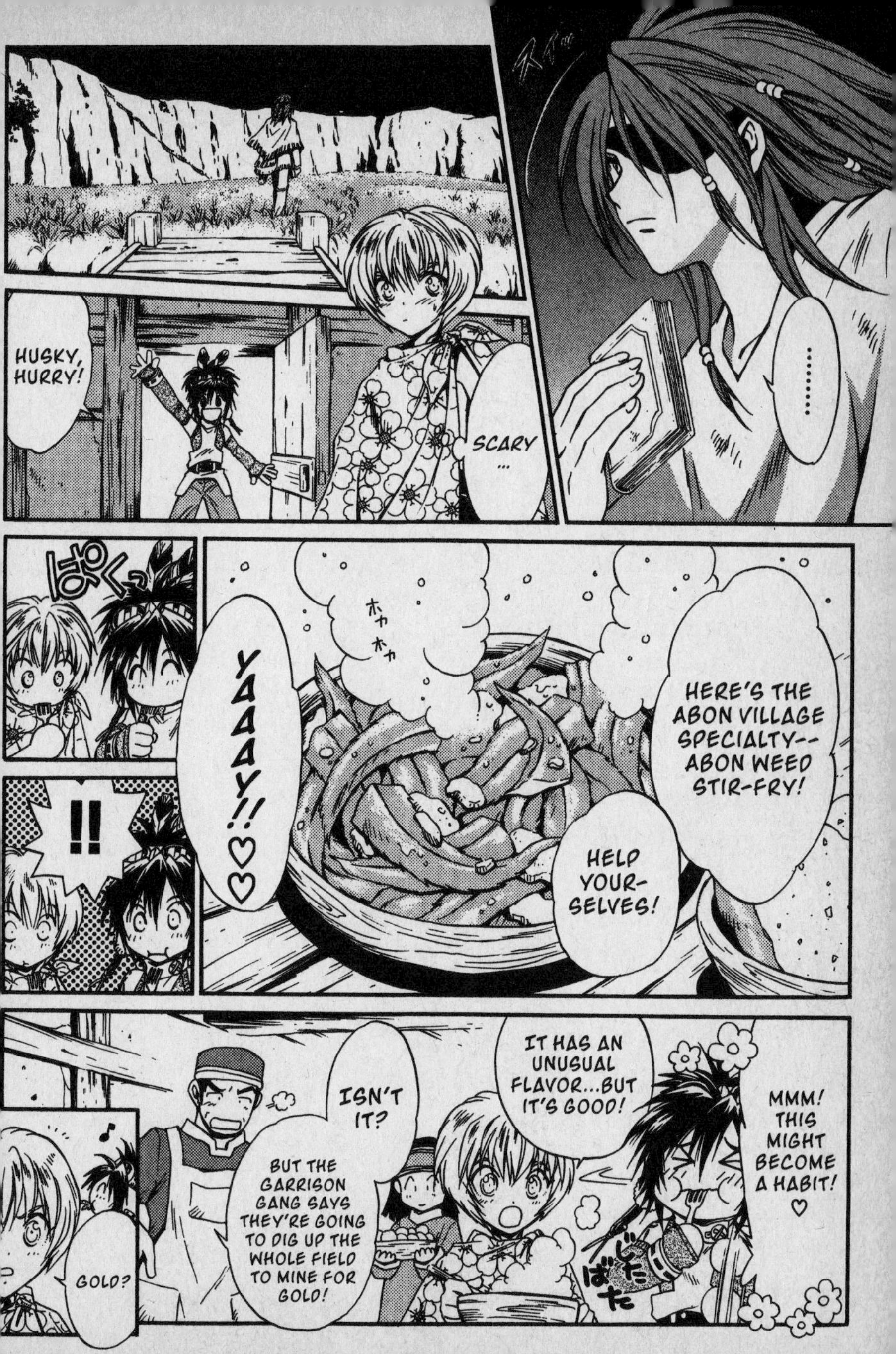
......
SCARY...
HUSKY, HURRY!
HERE'S THE ABON VILLAGE SPECIALTY--ABON WEED STIR-FRY!
ホカホカ
HELP YOURSELVES!
YAAAAY!! ♡♡
ぱくっ
!!
MMM! THIS MIGHT BECOME A HABIT! ♡
IT HAS AN UNUSUAL FLAVOR...BUT IT'S GOOD!
ISN'T IT?
じたばた
BUT THE GARRISON GANG SAYS THEY'RE GOING TO DIG UP THE WHOLE FIELD TO MINE FOR GOLD!
GOLD?

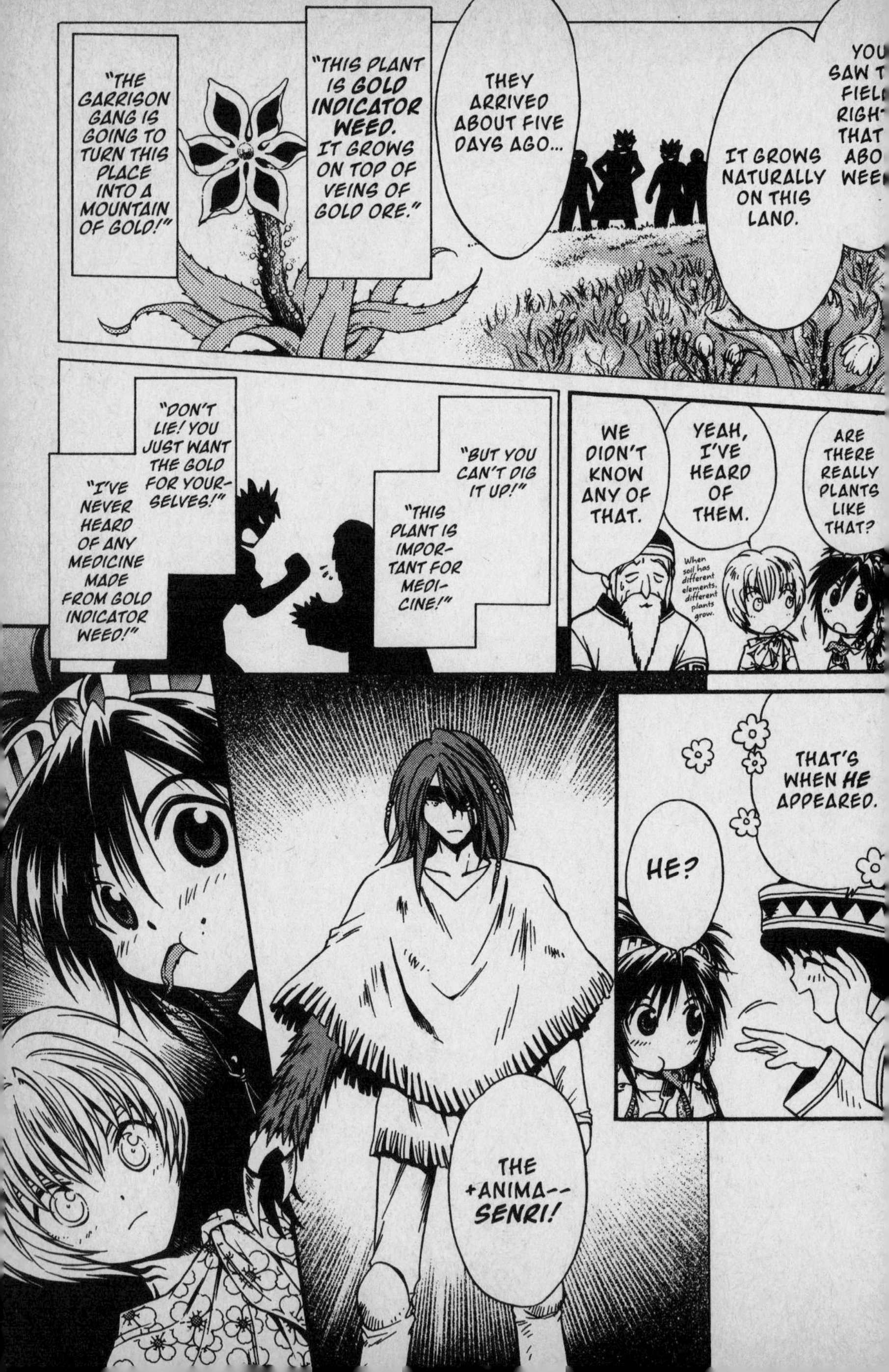
IT GROWS NATURALLY ON THIS LAND.
THEY ARRIVED ABOUT FIVE DAYS AGO...
"THIS PLANT IS GOLD INDICATOR WEED. IT GROWS ON TOP OF VEINS OF GOLD ORE."
"THE GARRISON GANG IS GOING TO TURN THIS PLACE INTO A MOUNTAIN OF GOLD!"
ARE THERE REALLY PLANTS LIKE THAT?
YEAH, I'VE HEARD OF THEM.
When soil has different elements, different plants grow.
WE DIDN'T KNOW ANY OF THAT.
"BUT YOU CAN'T DIG IT UP!"
"THIS PLANT IS IMPORTANT FOR MEDICINE!"
"DON'T LIE! YOU JUST WANT THE GOLD FOR YOURSELVES!"
"I'VE NEVER HEARD OF ANY MEDICINE MADE FROM GOLD INDICATOR WEED!"
THAT'S WHEN HE APPEARED.
HE?
THE +ANIMA--SENRI!

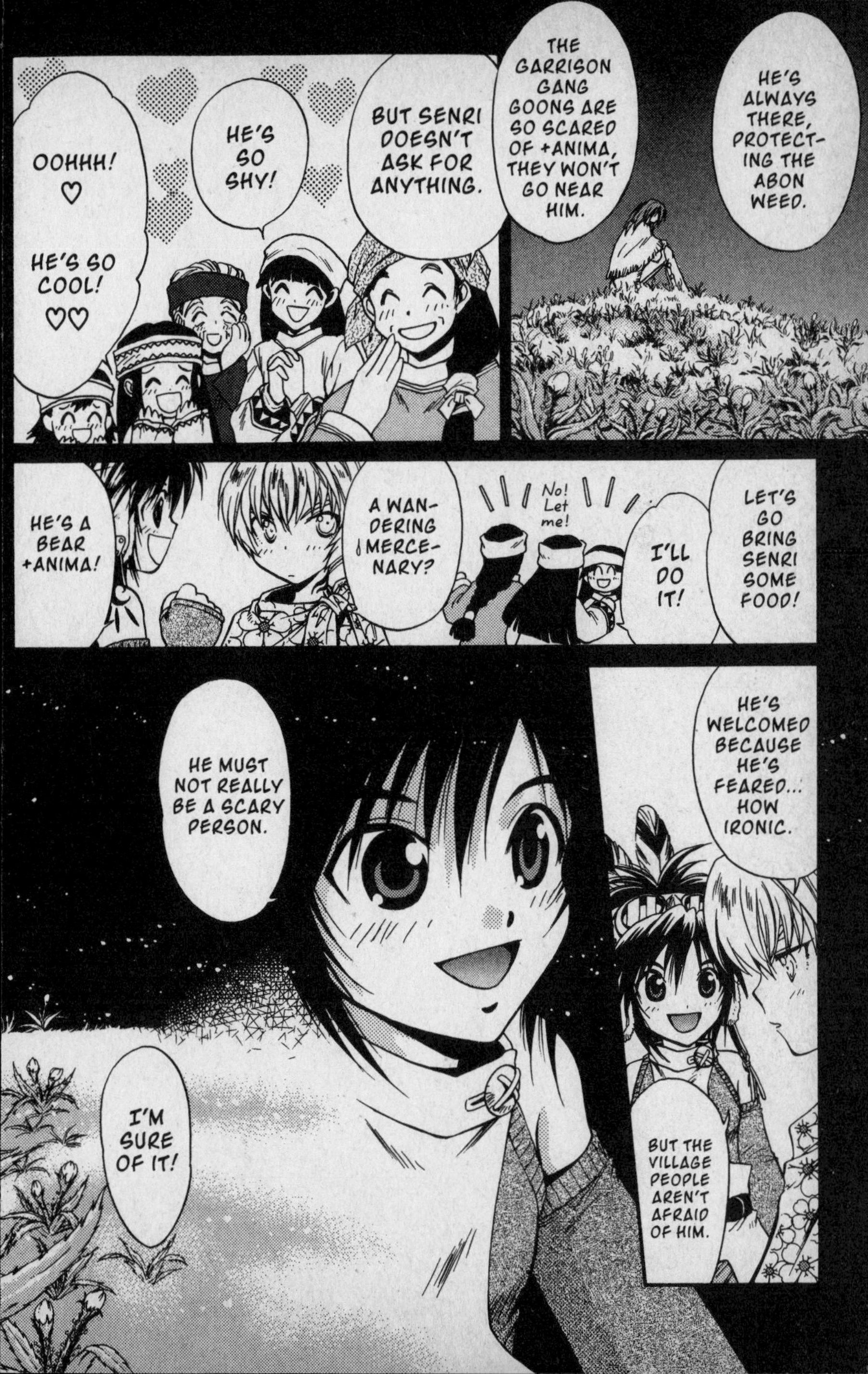
HE'S ALWAYS THERE, PROTECTING THE ABON WEED.
THE GARRISON GANG GOONS ARE SO SCARED OF +ANIMA, THEY WON'T GO NEAR HIM.
BUT SENRI DOESN'T ASK FOR ANYTHING.
HE'S SO SHY!
OOHHH! ♡
HE'S SO COOL! ♡♡
LET'S GO BRING SENRI SOME FOOD!
I'LL DO IT!
No! Let me!
A WANDERING MERCENARY?
HE'S A BEAR +ANIMA!
HE'S WELCOMED BECAUSE HE'S FEARED... HOW IRONIC.
BUT THE VILLAGE PEOPLE AREN'T AFRAID OF HIM.
HE MUST NOT REALLY BE A SCARY PERSON.
I'M SURE OF IT!

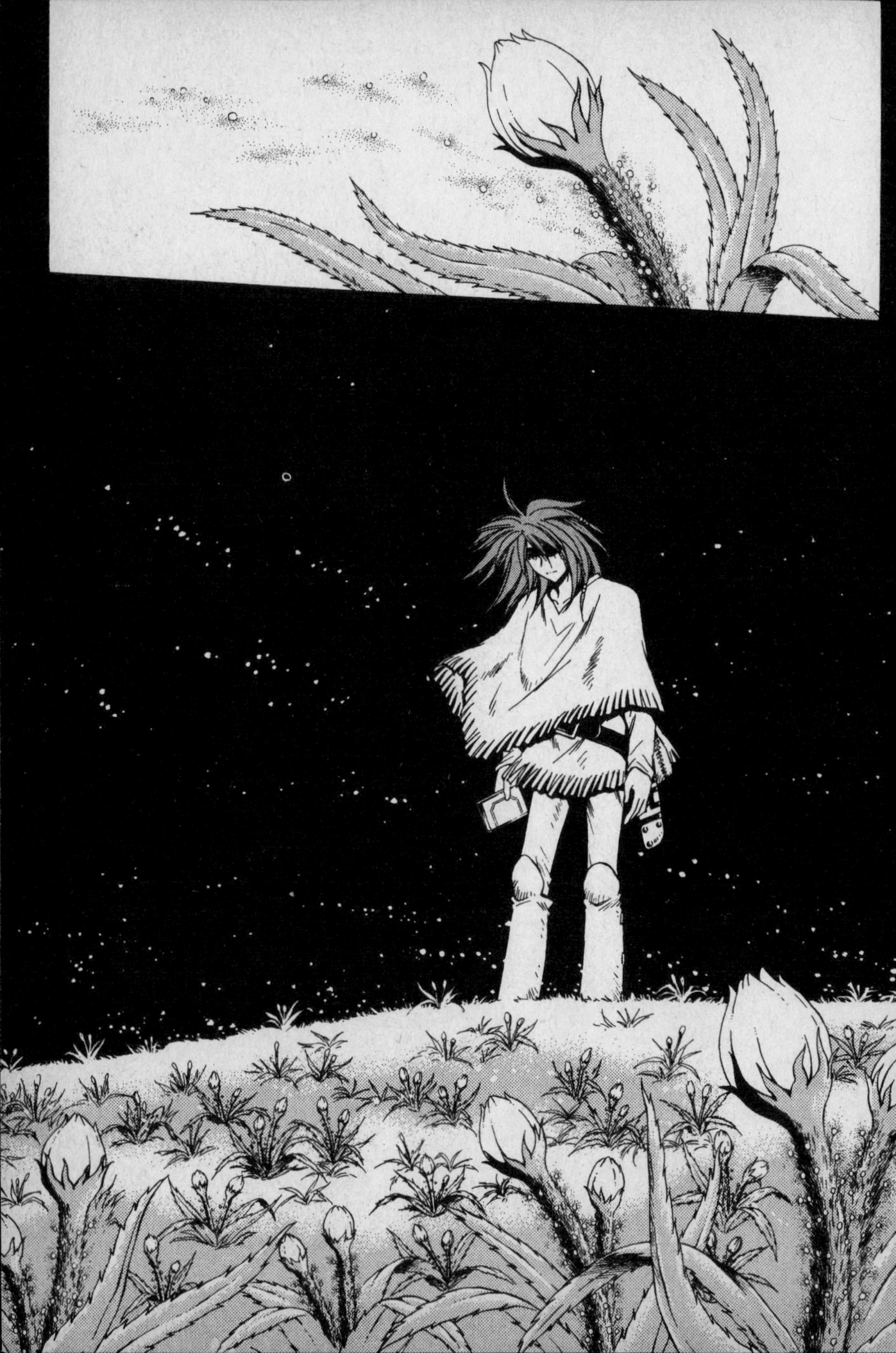

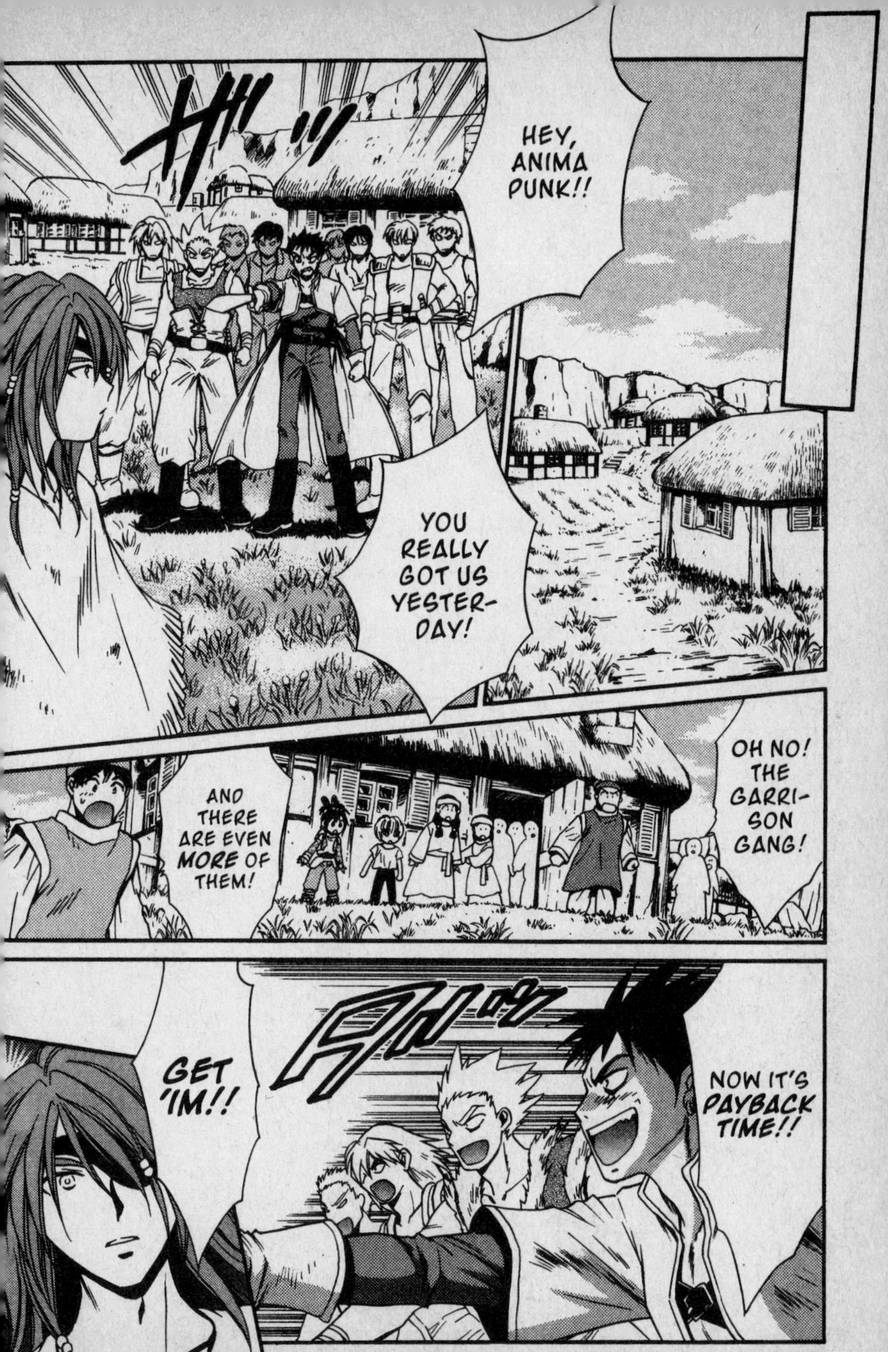
HEY, ANIMA PUNK!!
ザッ
YOU REALLY GOT US YESTER-DAY!
OH NO! THE GARRI-SON GANG!
AND THERE ARE EVEN MORE OF THEM!
NOW IT'S PAYBACK TIME!!
GET 'IM!!

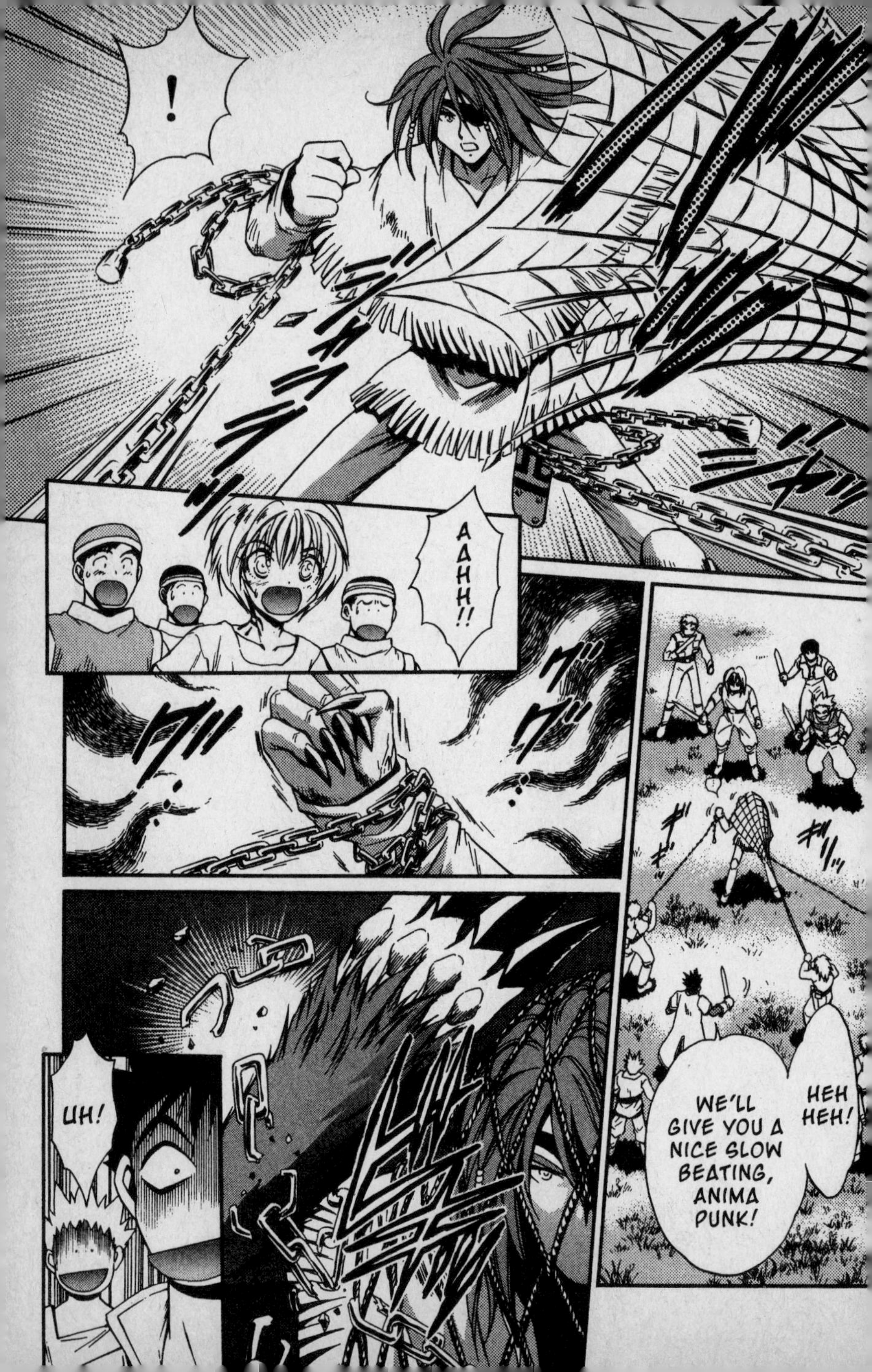
!
AAHH!!
HEH HEH!
WE'LL GIVE YOU A NICE SLOW BEATING, ANIMA PUNK!
UH!

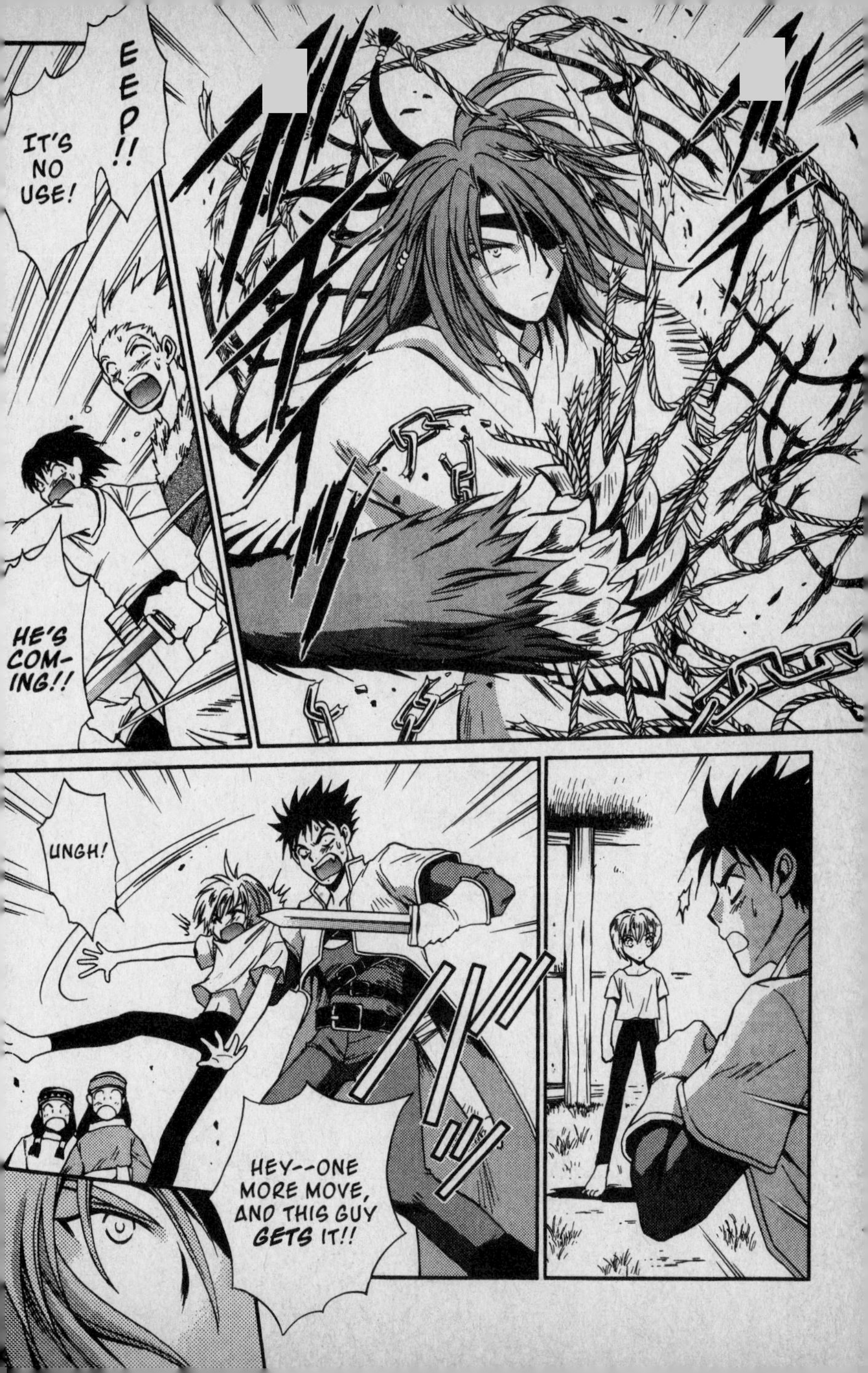
EEP!!
IT'S NO USE!
HE'S COMING!!
UNGH!
HEY--ONE MORE MOVE, AND THIS GUY GETS IT!!

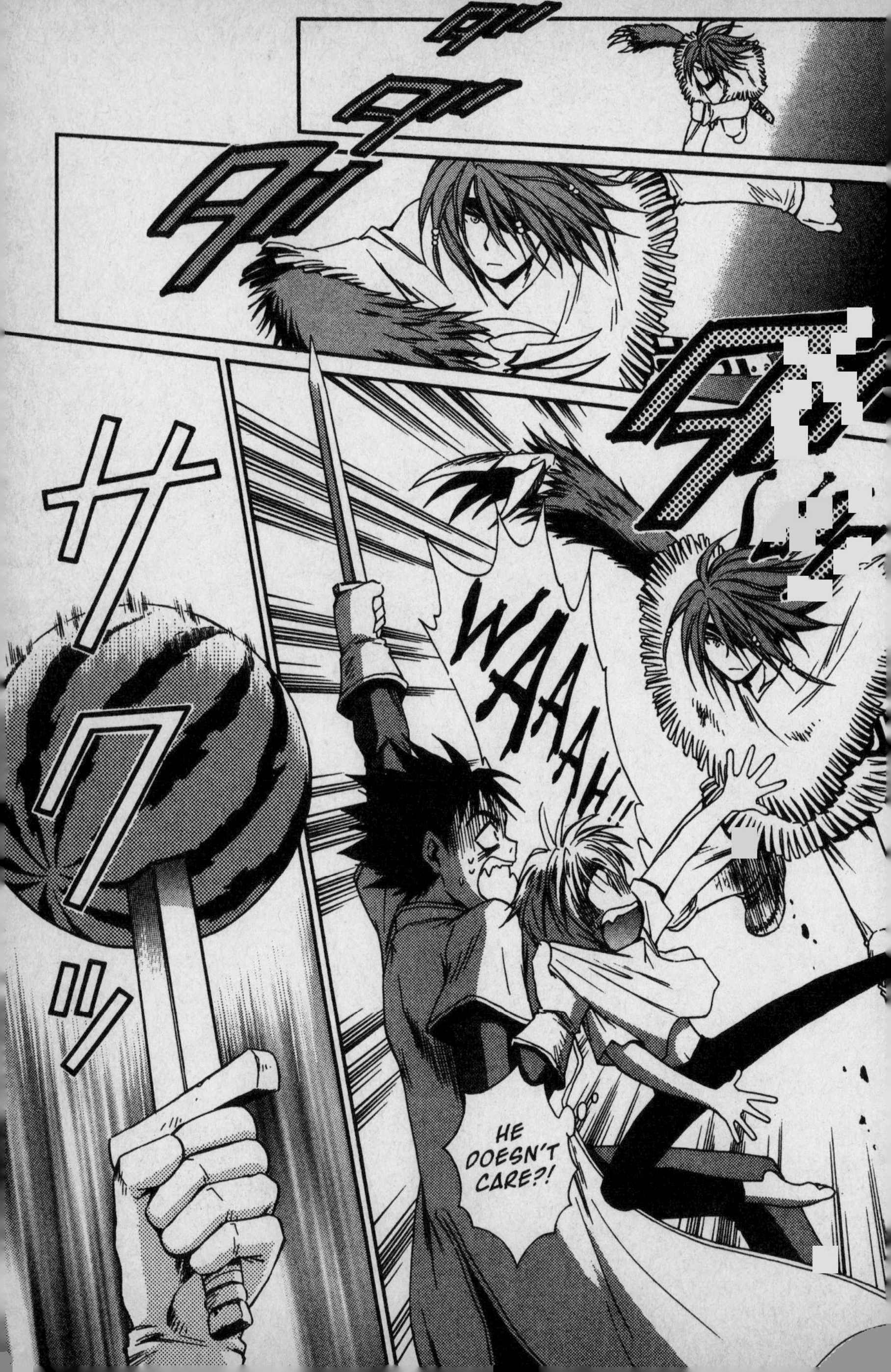
WAAAAH!!
HE DOESN'T CARE?!

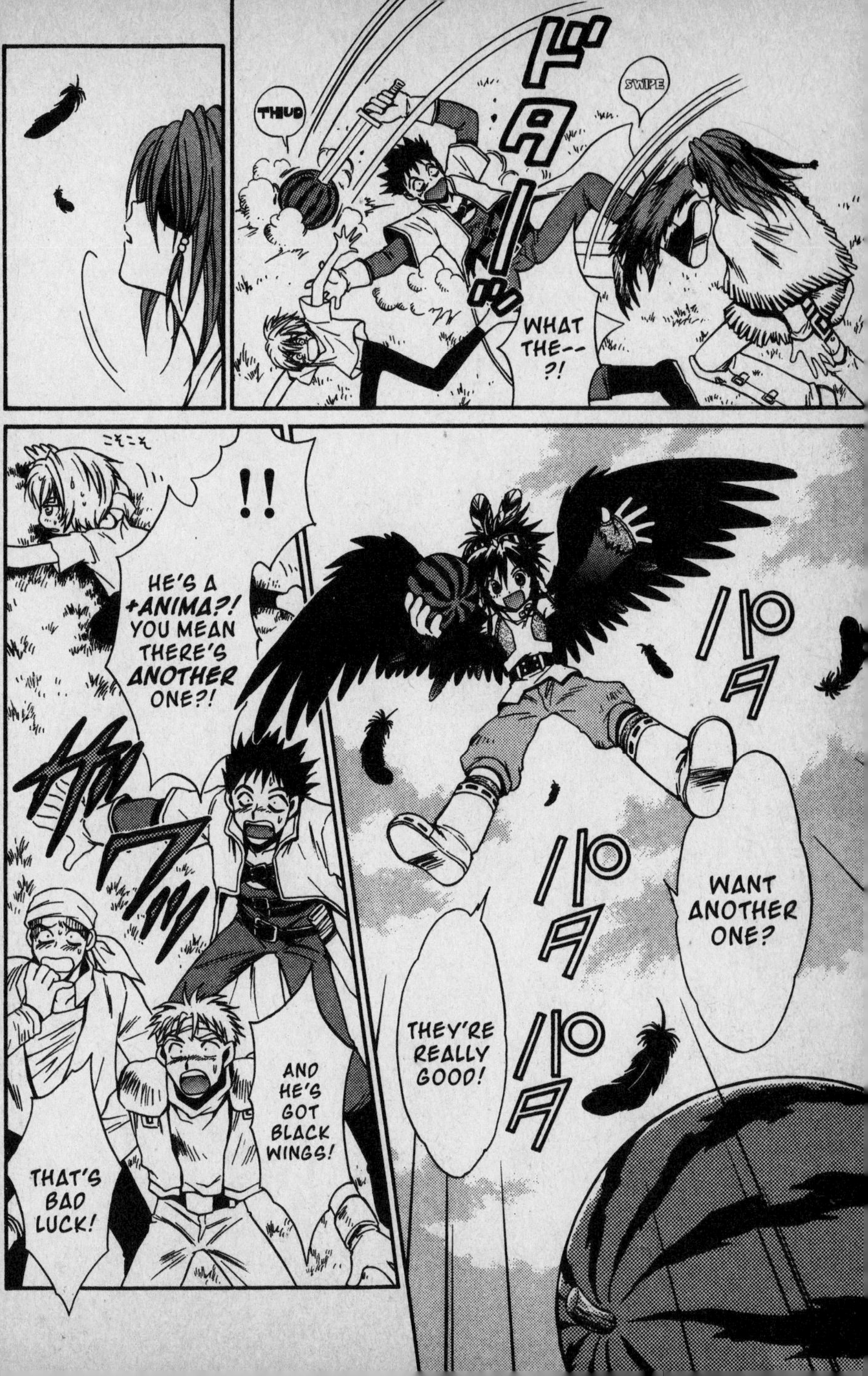
SWIPE
ドターッ
THUD
WHAT THE--?!
WANT ANOTHER ONE?
パタ
パタ
パタ
THEY'RE REALLY GOOD!
!!
こそこそ
HE'S A +ANIMA?! YOU MEAN THERE'S ANOTHER ONE?!
AND HE'S GOT BLACK WINGS!
THAT'S BAD LUCK!

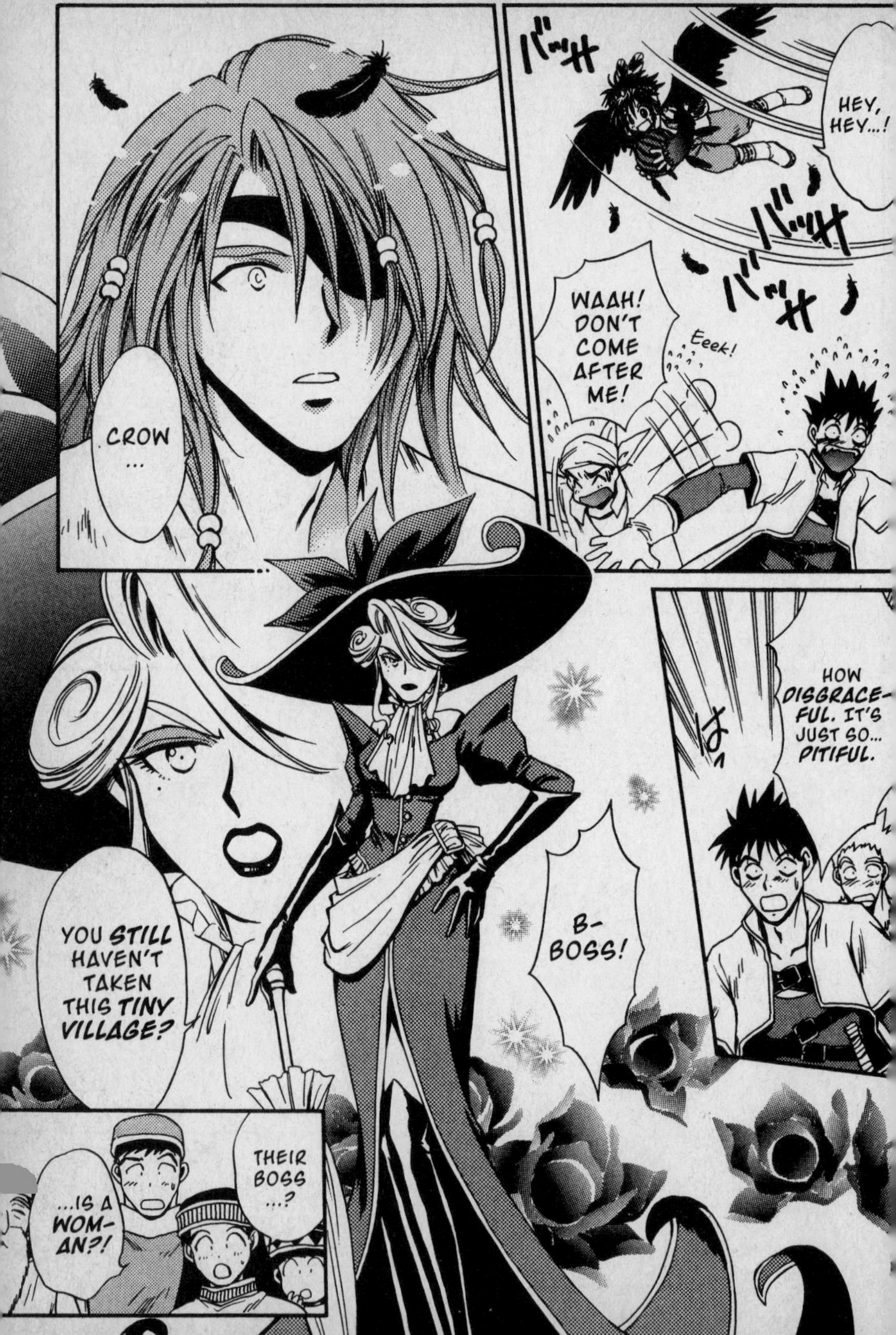

バッサ
HEY, HEY...!
バッサ
バッサ
WAAH! DON'T COME AFTER ME!
Eeek!
CROW ...
HOW DISGRACEFUL. IT'S JUST SO... PITIFUL.
は
B-BOSS!
YOU STILL HAVEN'T TAKEN THIS TINY VILLAGE?
THEIR BOSS ...?
...IS A WOMAN?!

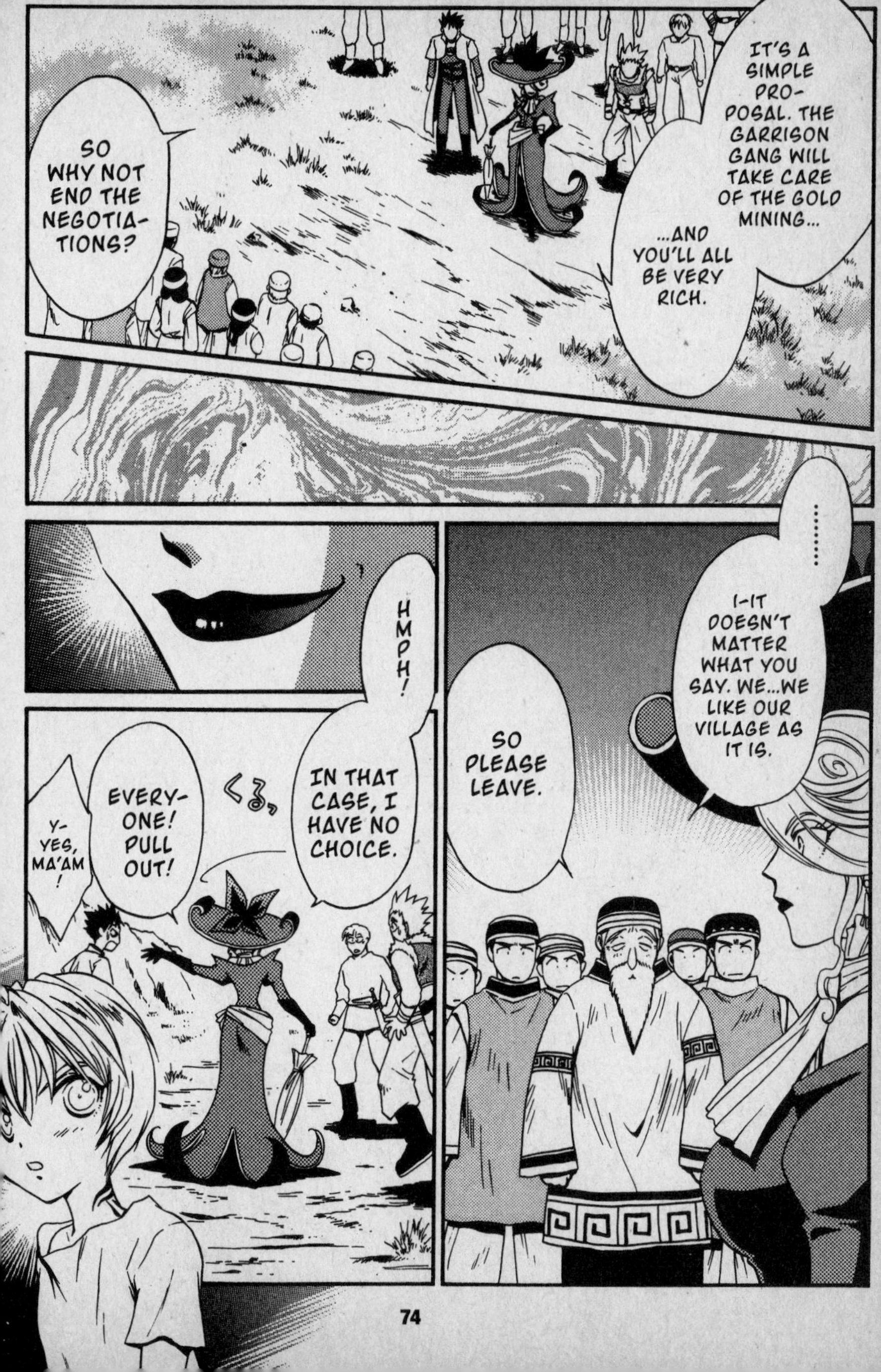
IT'S A SIMPLE PRO-POSAL. THE GARRISON GANG WILL TAKE CARE OF THE GOLD MINING...
...AND YOU'LL ALL BE VERY RICH.
SO WHY NOT END THE NEGOTIA-TIONS?
......
I-IT DOESN'T MATTER WHAT YOU SAY. WE...WE LIKE OUR VILLAGE AS IT IS.
SO PLEASE LEAVE.
HMPH!
IN THAT CASE, I HAVE NO CHOICE.
くる
EVERY-ONE! PULL OUT!
Y-YES, MA'AM!

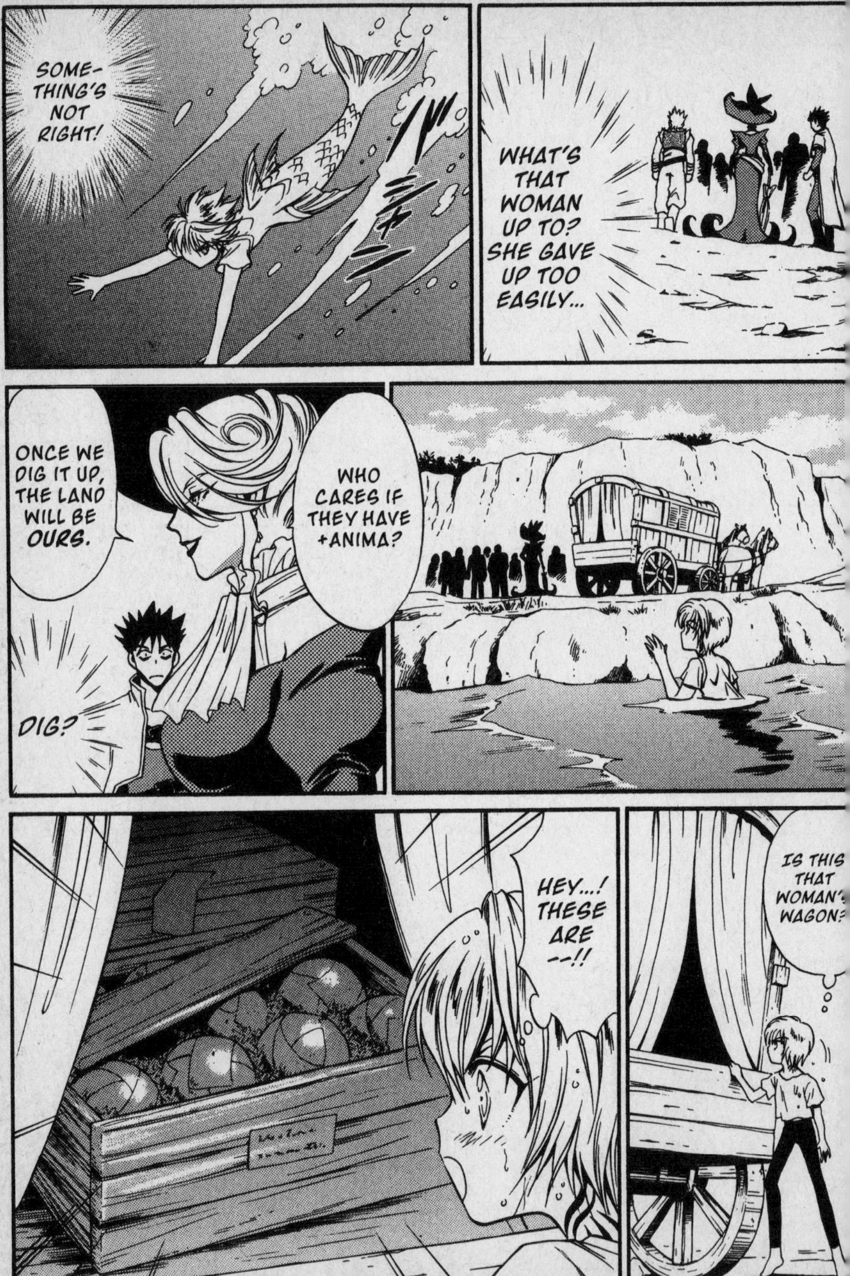
WHAT'S THAT WOMAN UP TO? SHE GAVE UP TOO EASILY...
SOME-THING'S NOT RIGHT!
WHO CARES IF THEY HAVE +ANIMA?
ONCE WE DIG IT UP, THE LAND WILL BE OURS.
DIG?
IS THIS THAT WOMAN'S WAGON?
HEY...! THESE ARE --!!

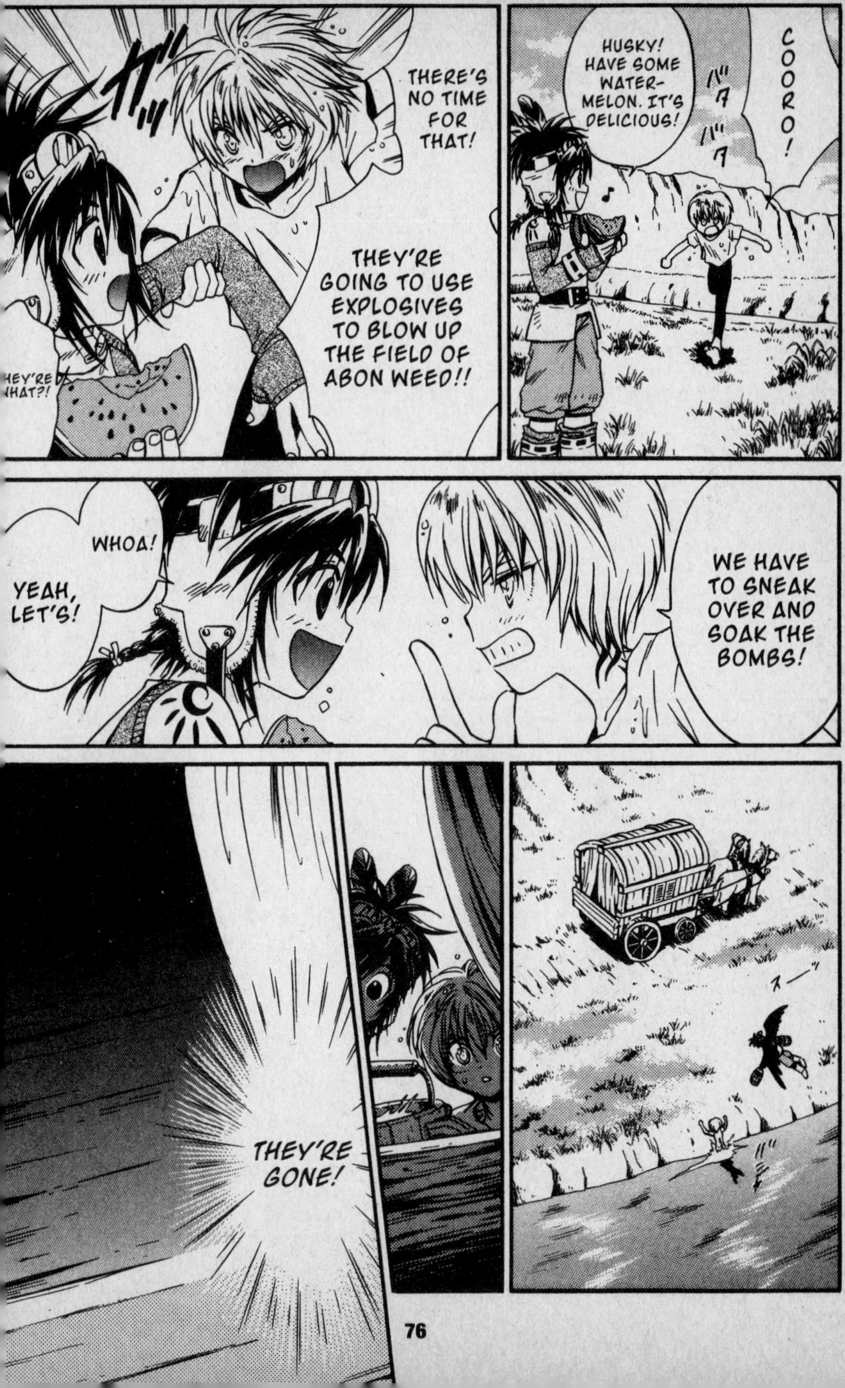
COORO!
HUSKY! HAVE SOME WATER-MELON. IT'S DELICIOUS!
THERE'S NO TIME FOR THAT!
THEY'RE GOING TO USE EXPLOSIVES TO BLOW UP THE FIELD OF ABON WEED!!
HEY'RE NHAT?!
WE HAVE TO SNEAK OVER AND SOAK THE BOMBS!
WHOA!
YEAH, LET'S!
THEY'RE GONE!

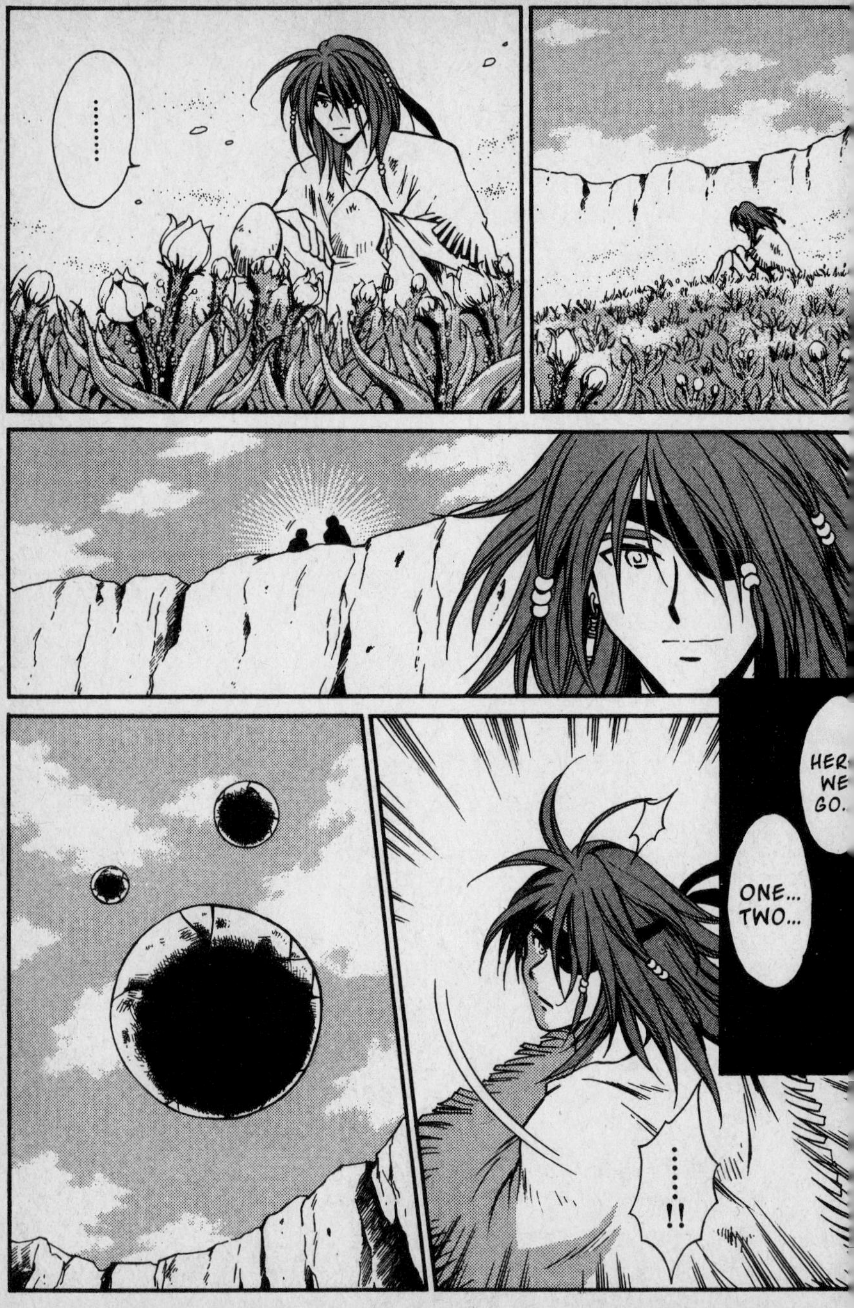
……
HER WE GO...
ONE... TWO...
……!!

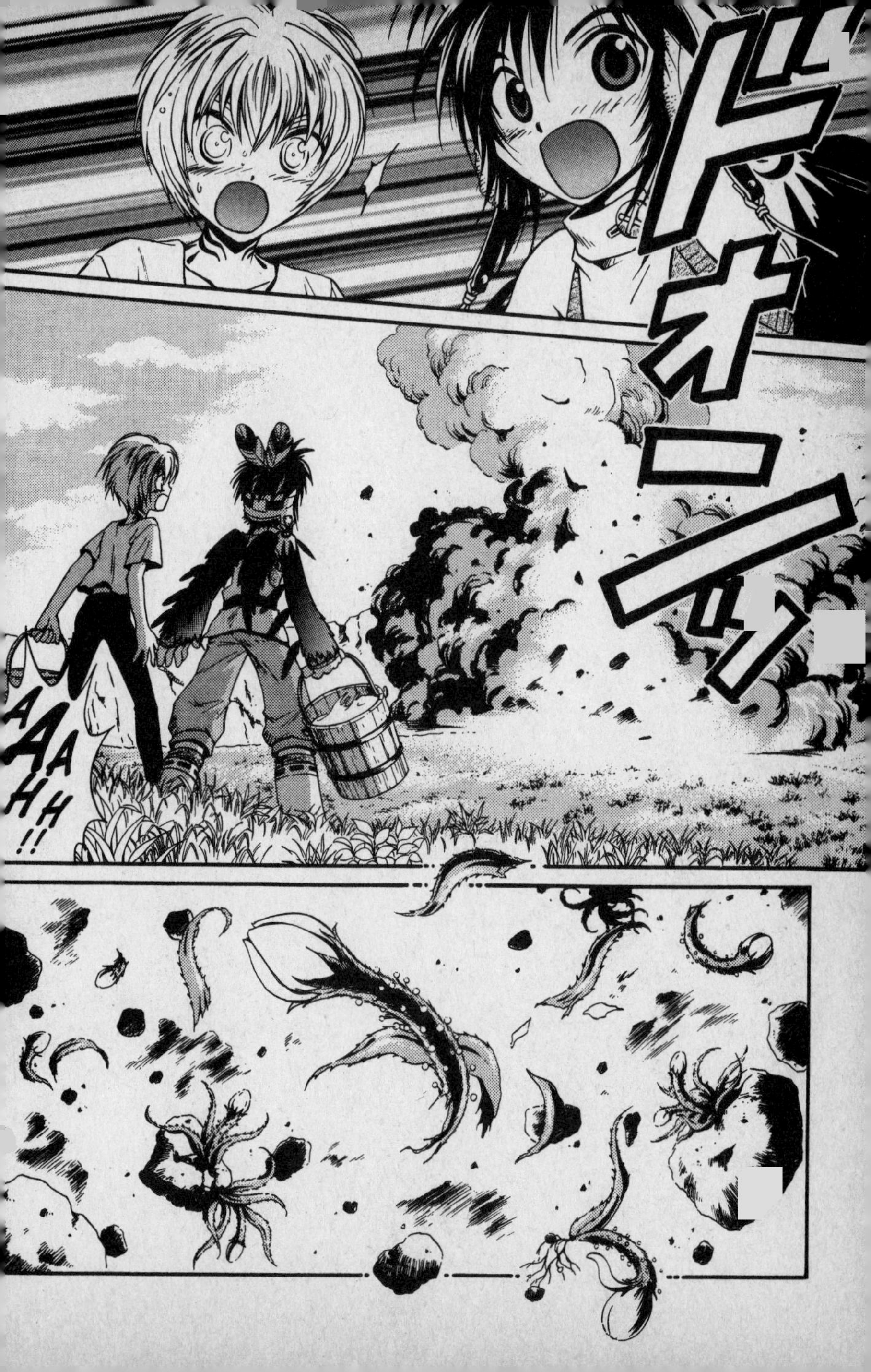
AAAHH!!

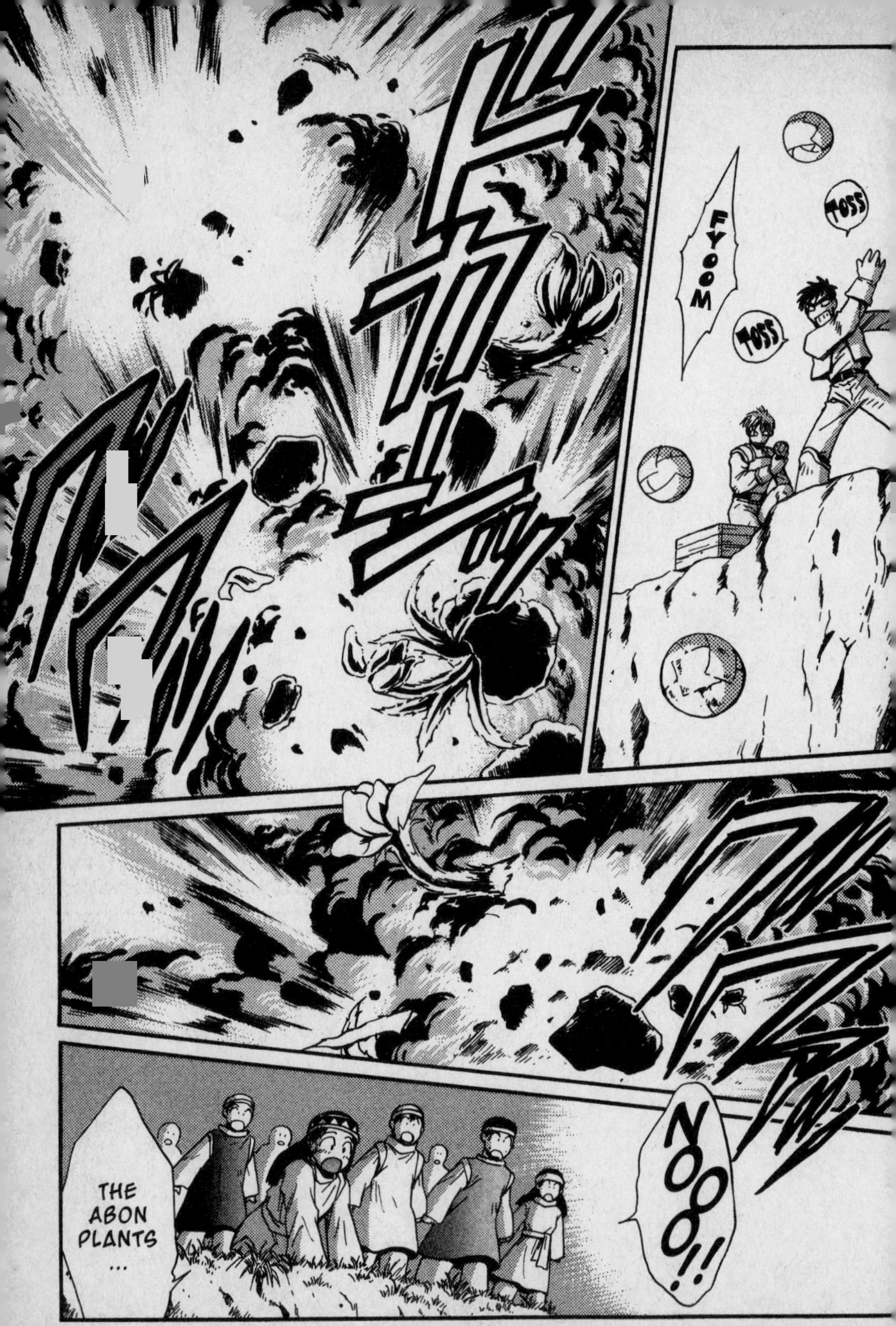
FYOOM
TOSS
TOSS
NOOOO!!
THE ABON PLANTS ...

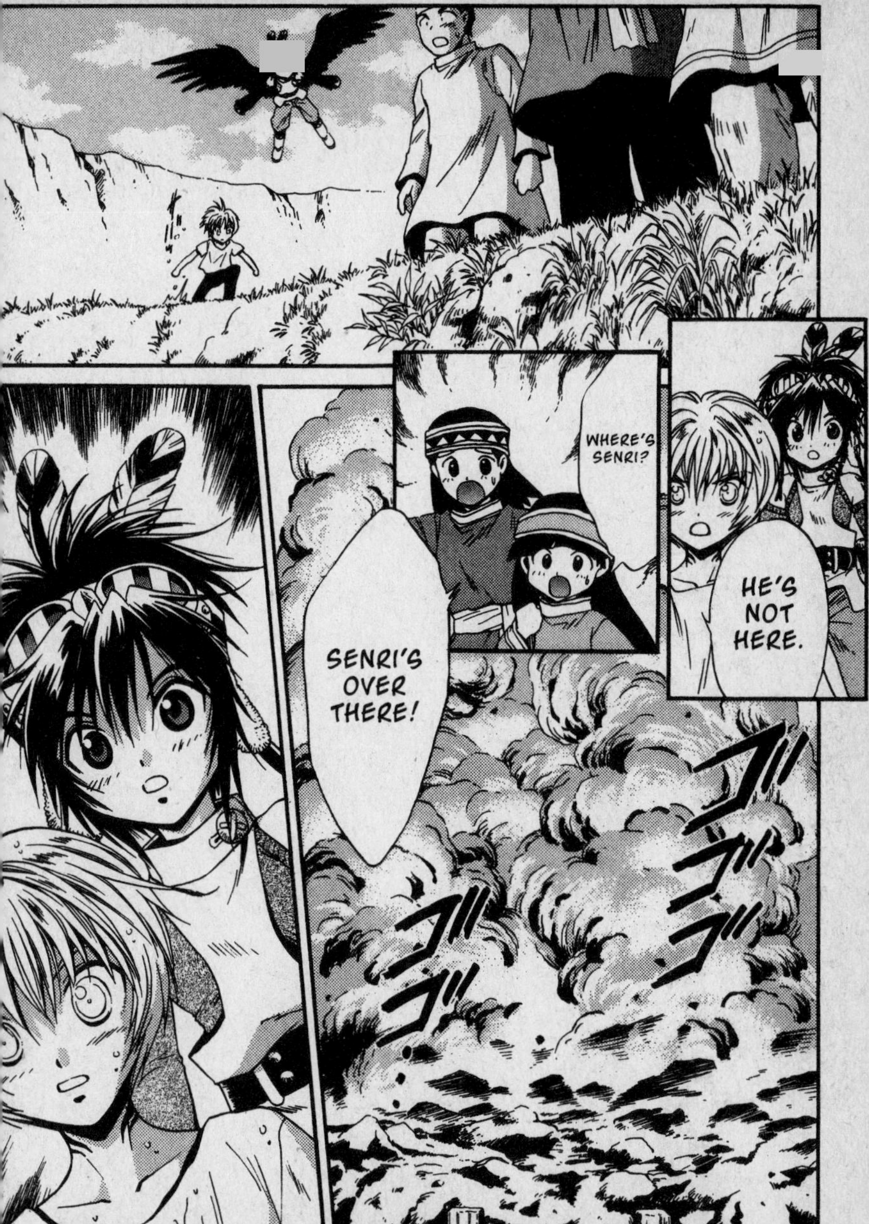
HE'S NOT HERE.
WHERE'S SENRI?
SENRI'S OVER THERE!

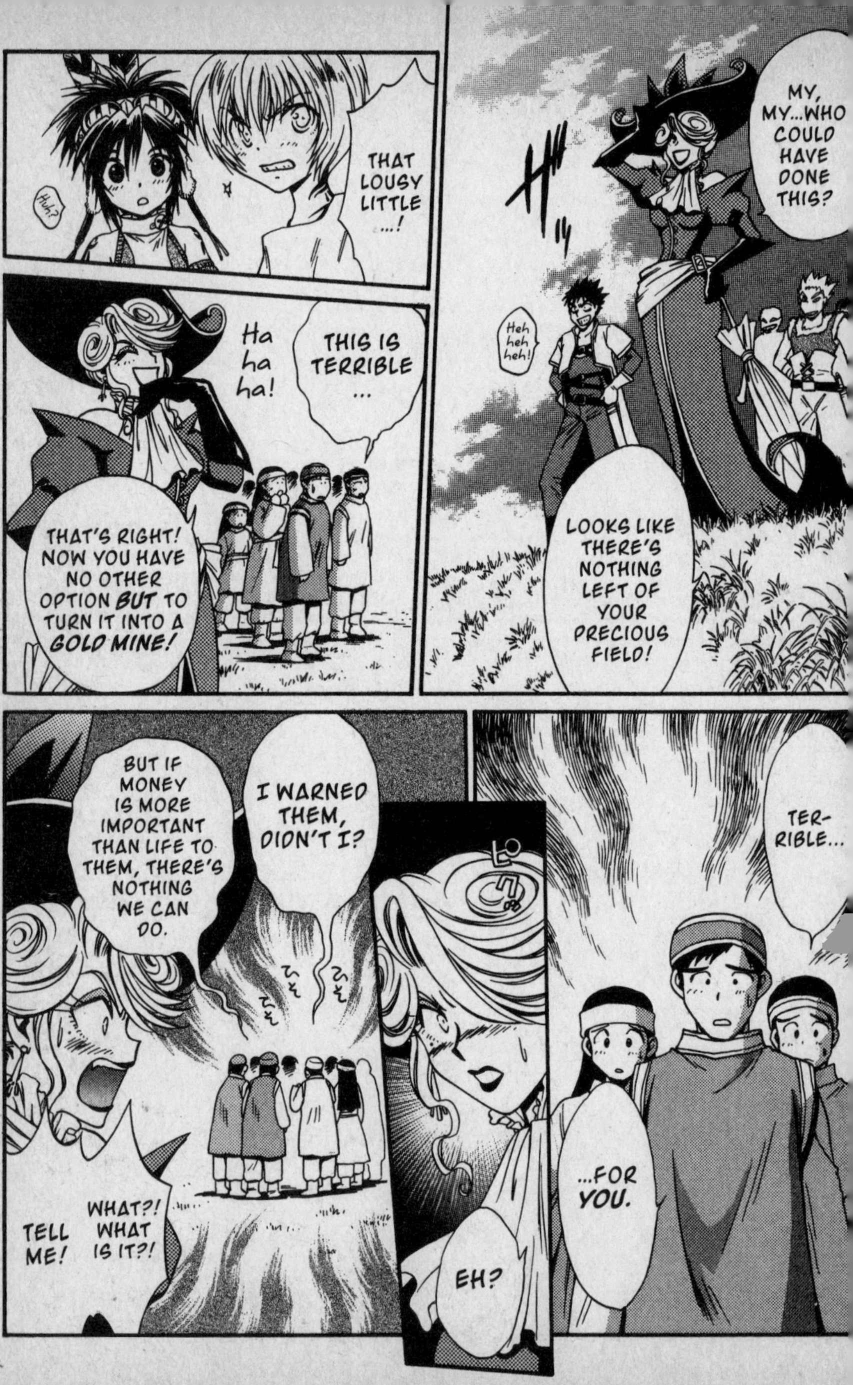
MY, MY...WHO COULD HAVE DONE THIS?
Heh heh heh!
LOOKS LIKE THERE'S NOTHING LEFT OF YOUR PRECIOUS FIELD!
THAT LOUSY LITTLE ...!
Huh?
THIS IS TERRIBLE ...
Ha ha ha!
THAT'S RIGHT! NOW YOU HAVE NO OTHER OPTION BUT TO TURN IT INTO A GOLD MINE!
TER-RIBLE...
...FOR YOU.
EH?
I WARNED THEM, DIDN'T I?
BUT IF MONEY IS MORE IMPORTANT THAN LIFE TO THEM, THERE'S NOTHING WE CAN DO.
WHAT?! WHAT IS IT?!
TELL ME!

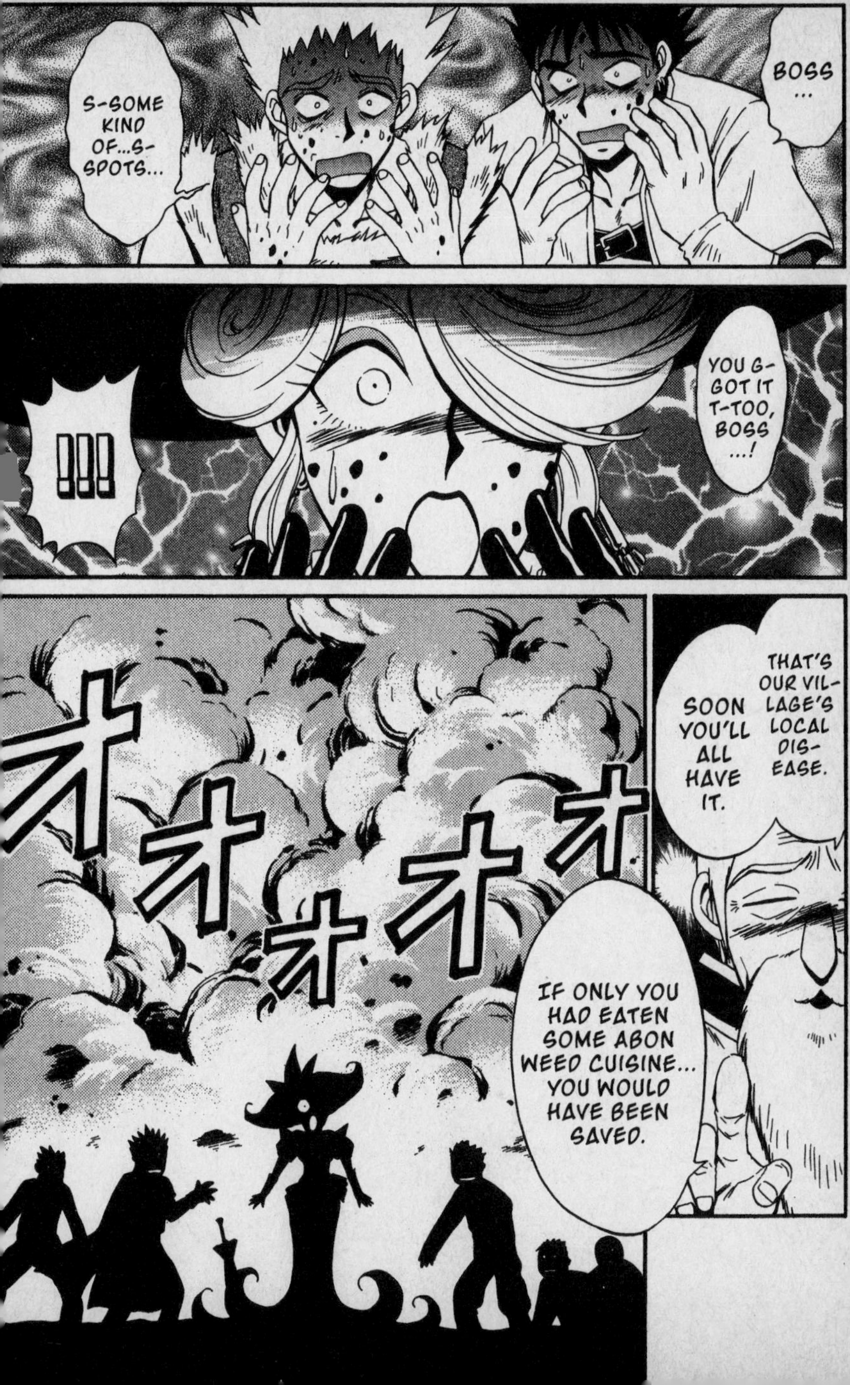
BOSS ...
S-SOME KIND OF...S-SPOTS...
YOU G-GOT IT T-TOO, BOSS ...!
!!!
THAT'S OUR VIL-LAGE'S LOCAL DIS-EASE.
SOON YOU'LL ALL HAVE IT.
IF ONLY YOU HAD EATEN SOME ABON WEED CUISINE... YOU WOULD HAVE BEEN SAVED.
オオォオオ

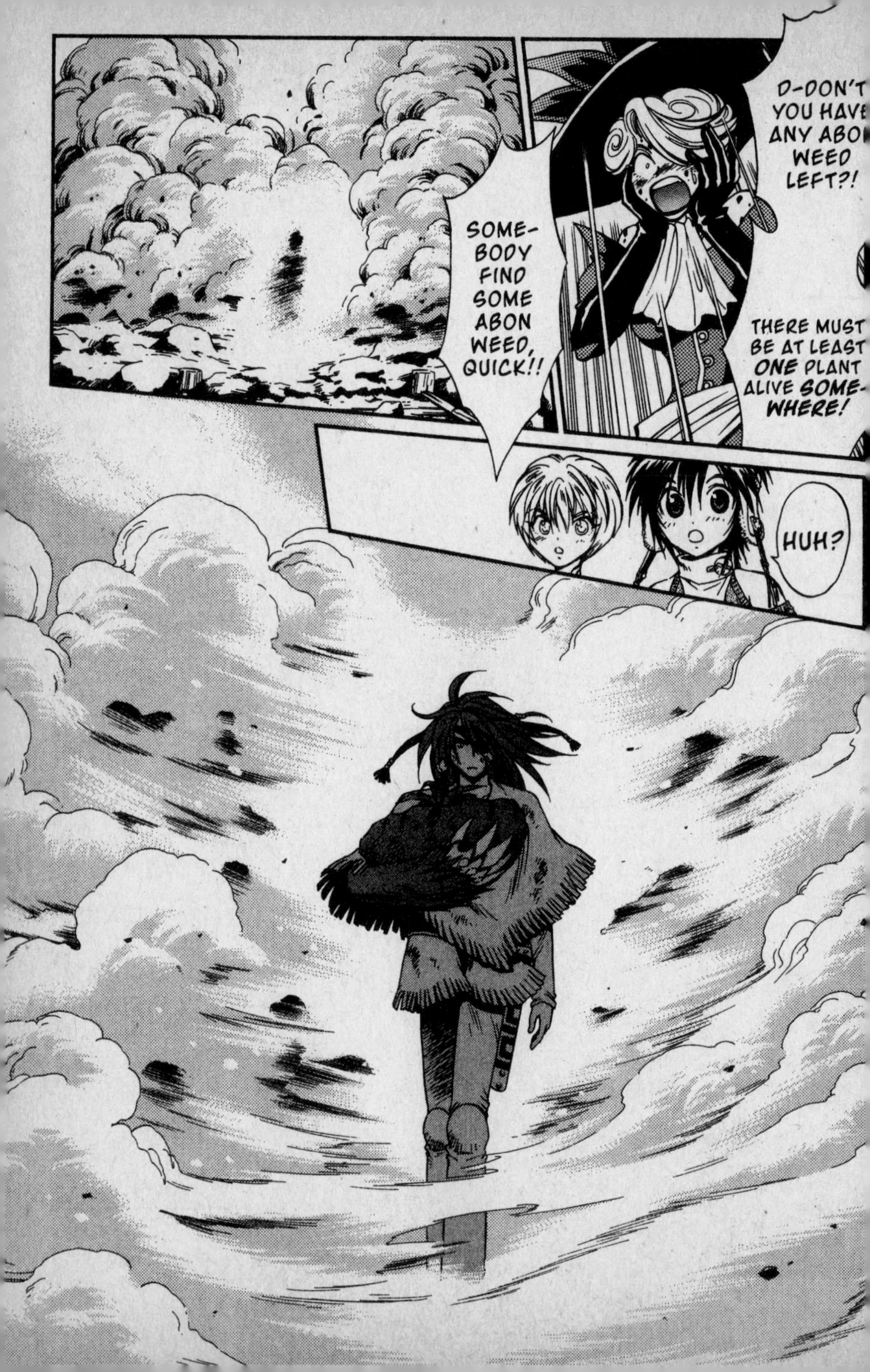
D-DON'T YOU HAVE ANY ABON WEED LEFT?!
THERE MUST BE AT LEAST ONE PLANT ALIVE SOME-WHERE!
SOME-BODY FIND SOME ABON WEED, QUICK!!
HUH?

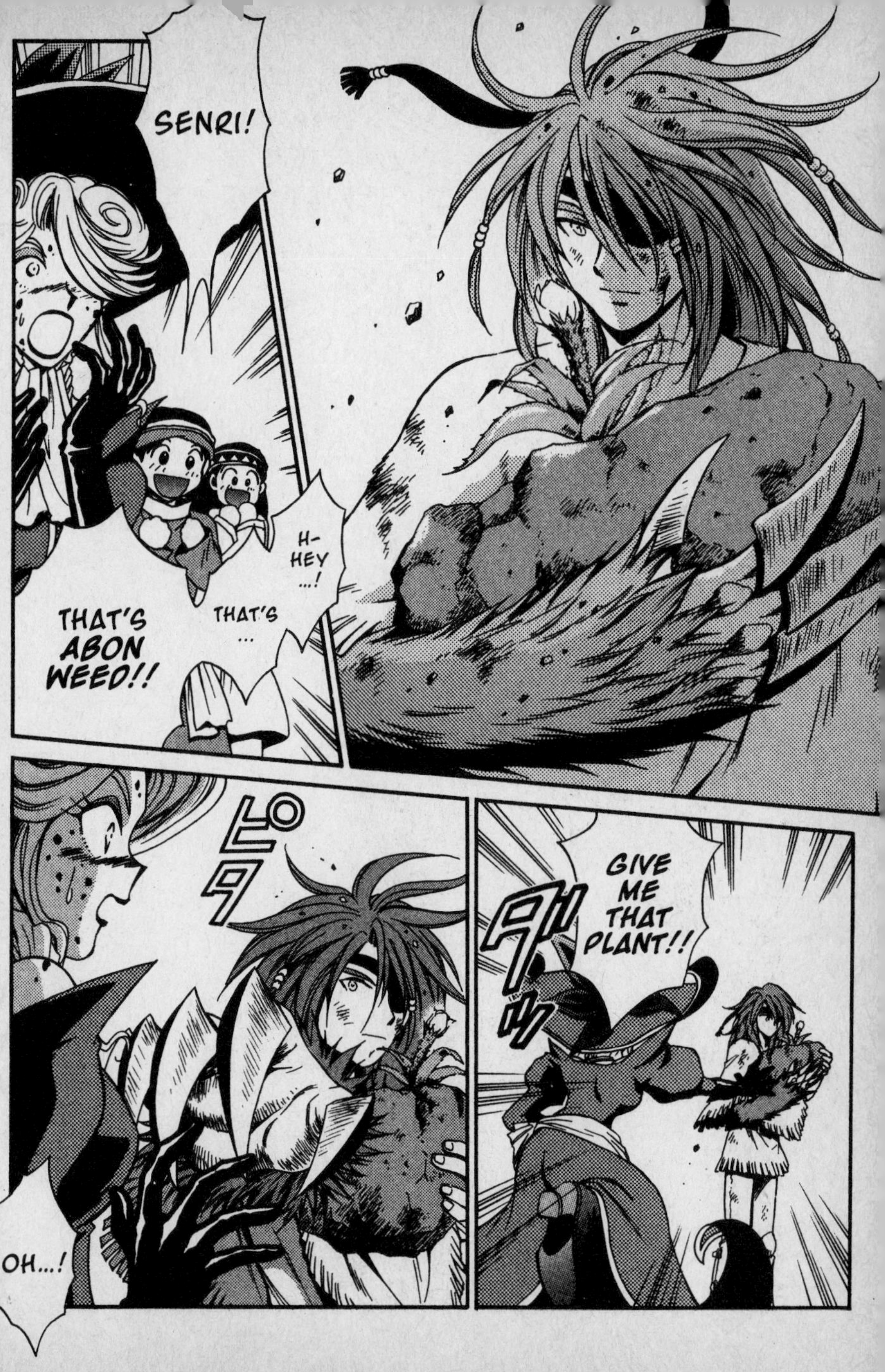
SENRI!
H-HEY ...!
THAT'S ...
THAT'S ABON WEED!!
GIVE ME THAT PLANT!!
OH...!

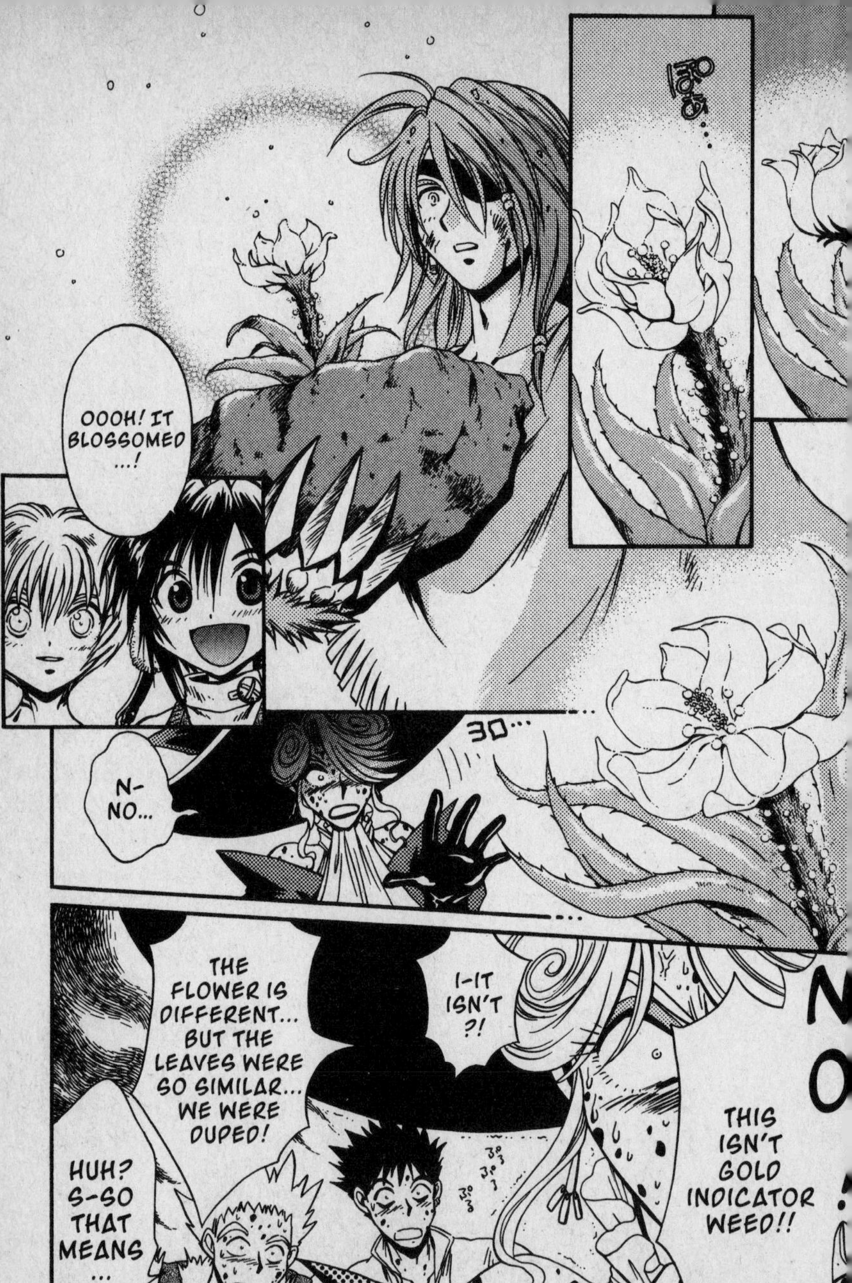

OOOH! IT BLOSSOMED ...!
SO...
N-NO...
NO
THIS ISN'T GOLD INDICATOR WEED!!
I-IT ISN'T ?!
THE FLOWER IS DIFFERENT... BUT THE LEAVES WERE SO SIMILAR... WE WERE DUPED!
HUH? S-SO THAT MEANS ...

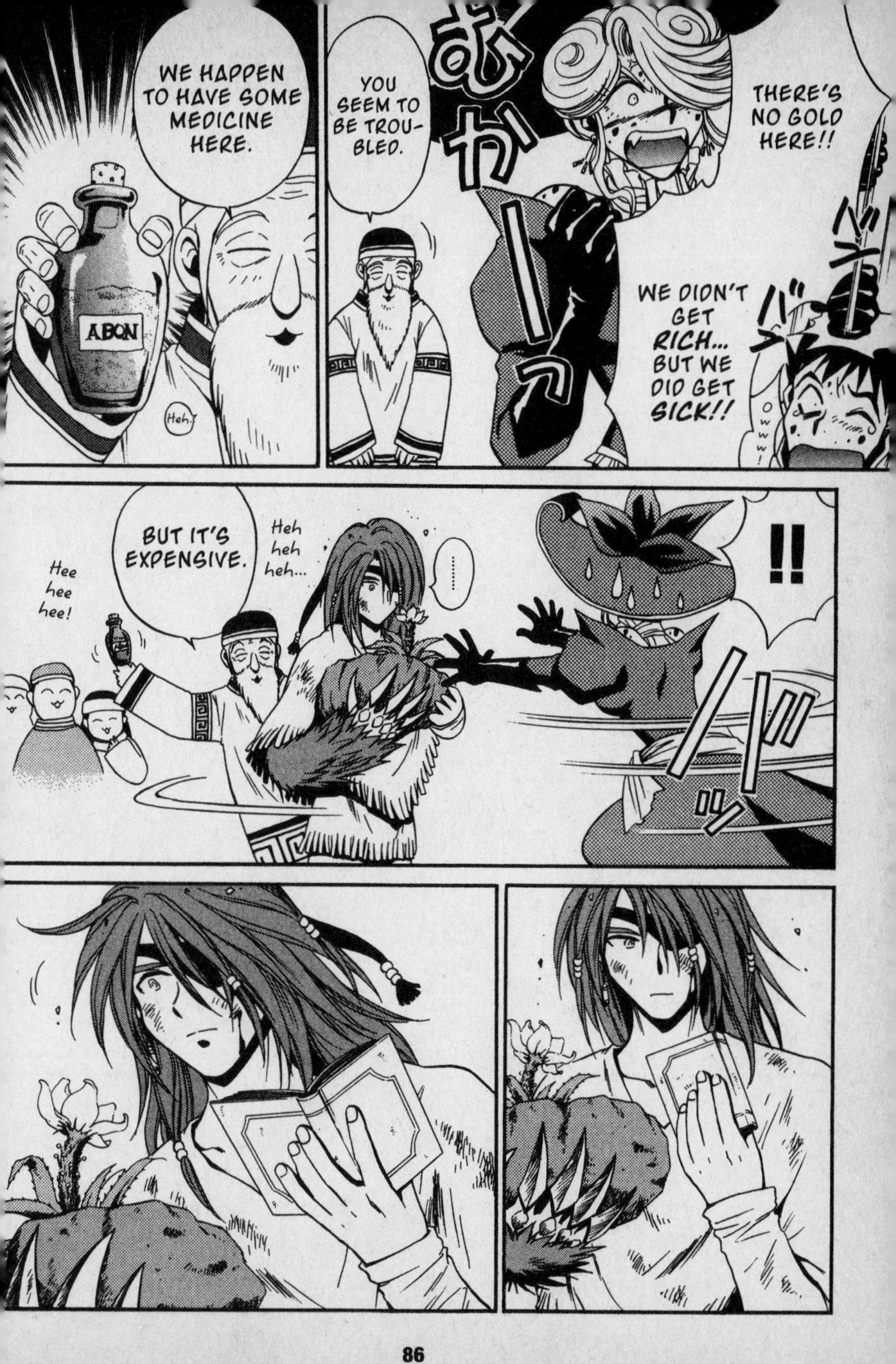

むかーっ
THERE'S NO GOLD HERE!!
WE DIDN'T GET RICH... BUT WE DID GET SICK!!
Owww!
YOU SEEM TO BE TROUBLED.
WE HAPPEN TO HAVE SOME MEDICINE HERE.
ABON
Heh.
!!
......
Heh heh heh...
BUT IT'S EXPENSIVE.
Hee hee hee!

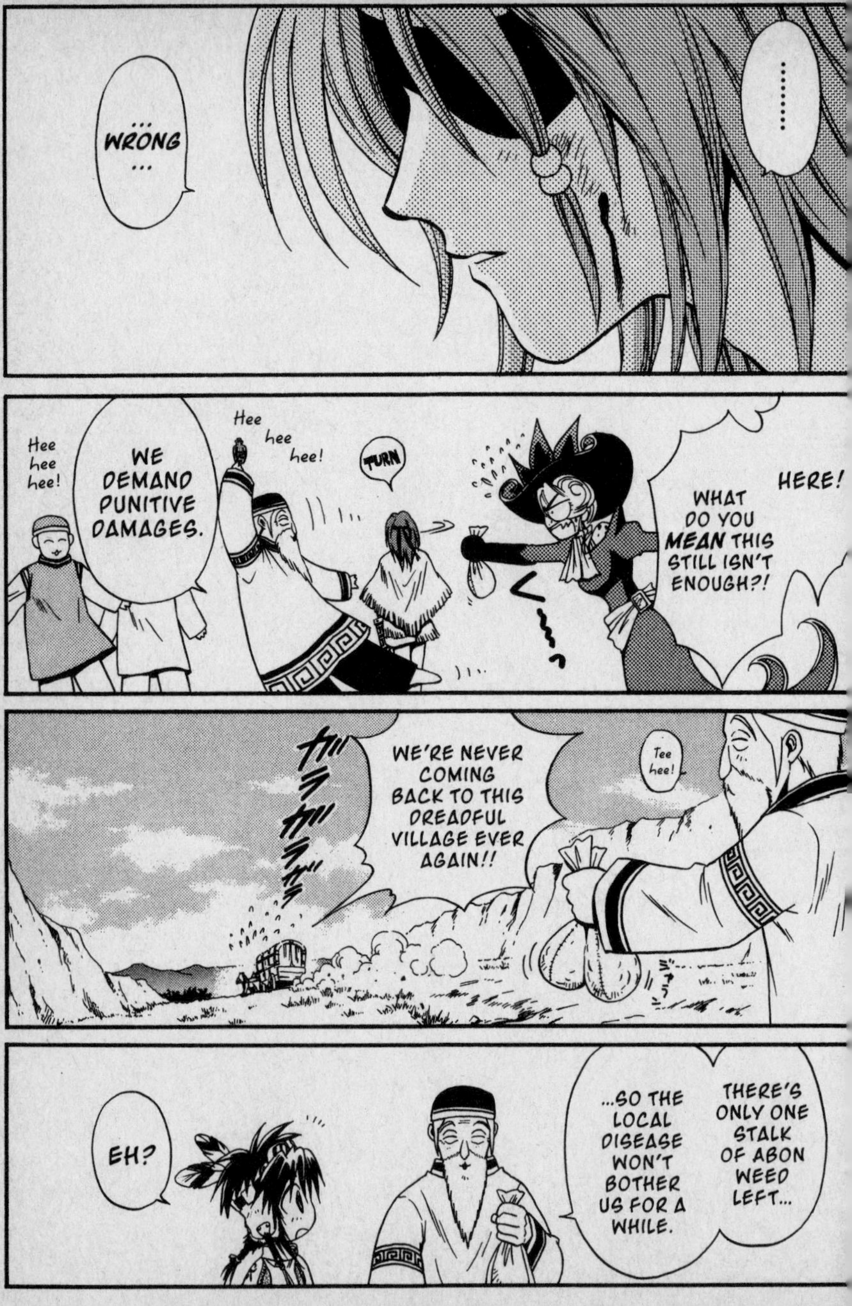
......
...WRONG...
HERE!
WHAT DO YOU MEAN THIS STILL ISN'T ENOUGH?!
TURN
Hee hee hee!
WE DEMAND PUNITIVE DAMAGES.
Hee hee hee!
Tee hee!
WE'RE NEVER COMING BACK TO THIS DREADFUL VILLAGE EVER AGAIN!!
THERE'S ONLY ONE STALK OF ABON WEED LEFT...
...SO THE LOCAL DISEASE WON'T BOTHER US FOR A WHILE.
EH?

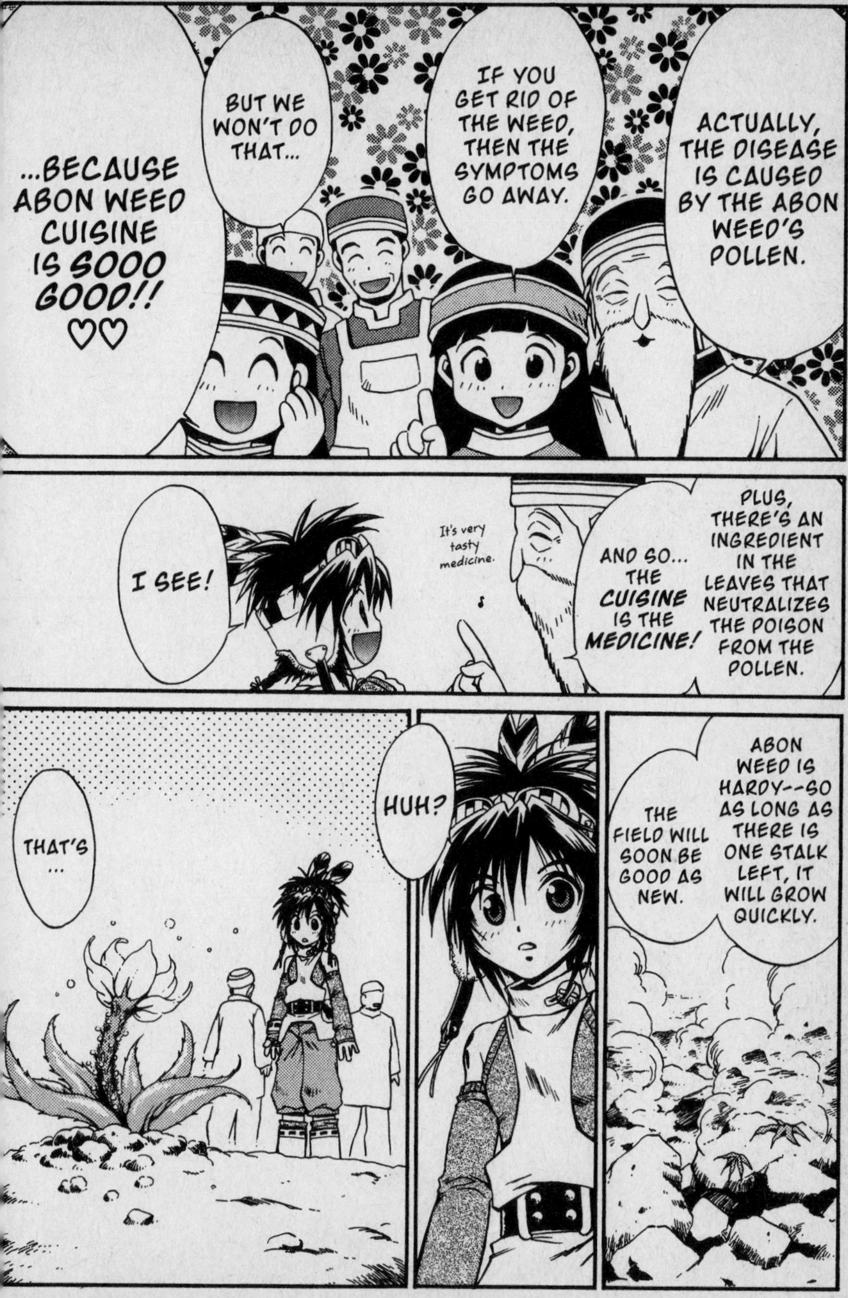
ACTUALLY, THE DISEASE IS CAUSED BY THE ABON WEED'S POLLEN.
IF YOU GET RID OF THE WEED, THEN THE SYMPTOMS GO AWAY.
BUT WE WON'T DO THAT...
...BECAUSE ABON WEED CUISINE IS SOOO GOOD!! ♡♡
PLUS, THERE'S AN INGREDIENT IN THE LEAVES THAT NEUTRALIZES THE POISON FROM THE POLLEN.
AND SO... THE CUISINE IS THE MEDICINE!
It's very tasty medicine. ♪
I SEE!
ABON WEED IS HARDY--SO AS LONG AS THERE IS ONE STALK LEFT, IT WILL GROW QUICKLY.
THE FIELD WILL SOON BE GOOD AS NEW.
HUH?
THAT'S ...

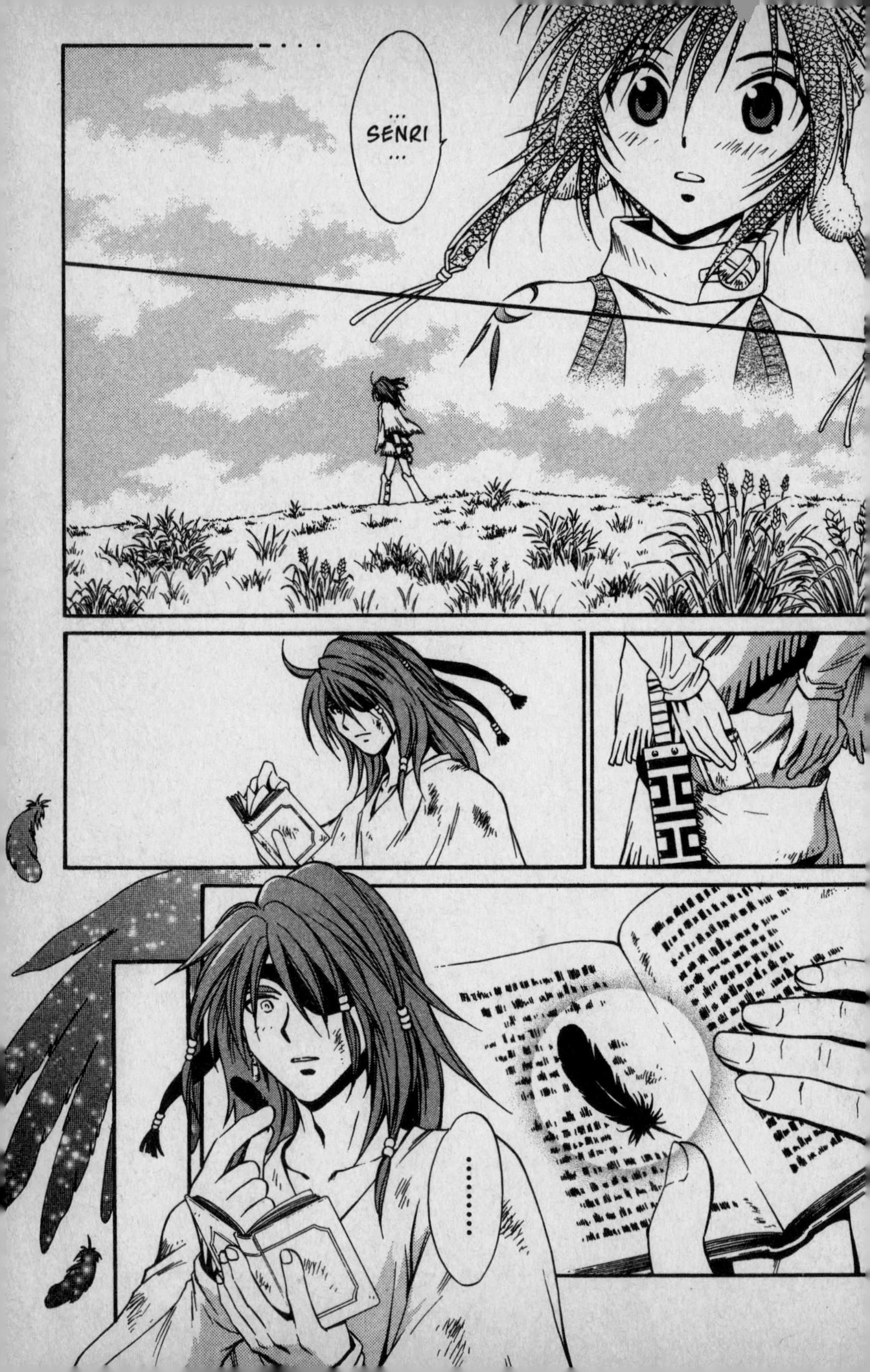

... SENRI ...
......

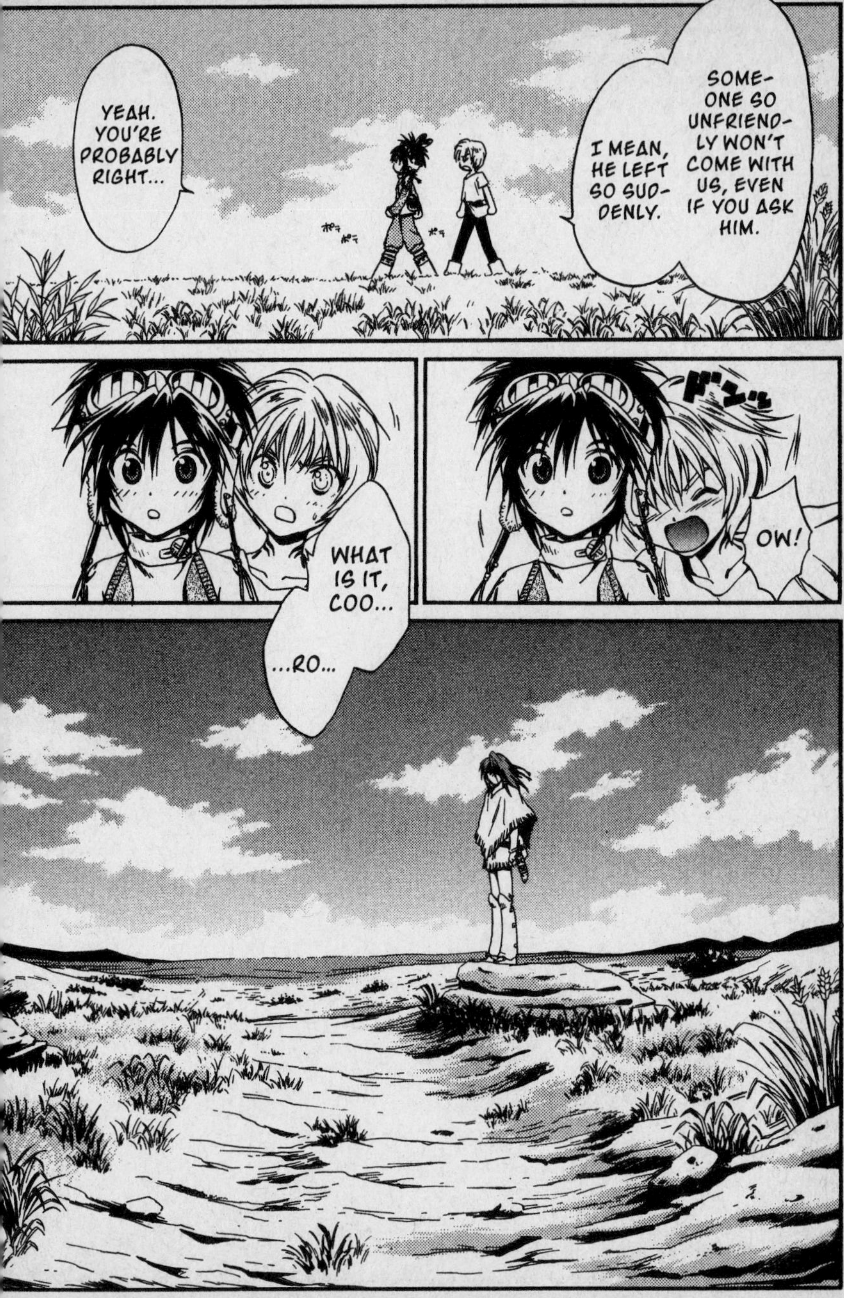
SOME-ONE SO UNFRIEND-LY WON'T COME WITH US, EVEN IF YOU ASK HIM.
I MEAN, HE LEFT SO SUD-DENLY.
YEAH. YOU'RE PROBABLY RIGHT...
OW!
WHAT IS IT, COO...
...RO...

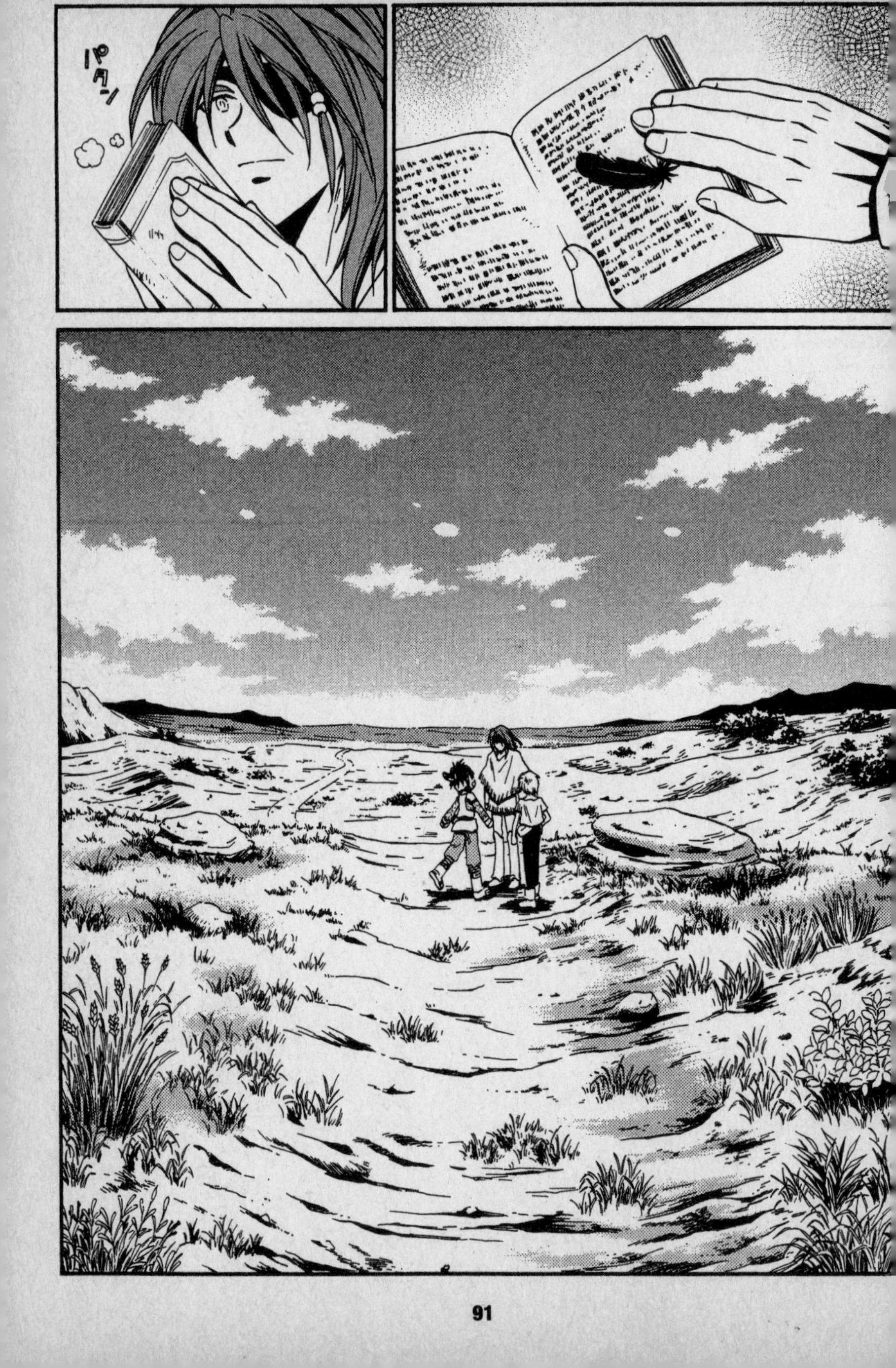
パタン

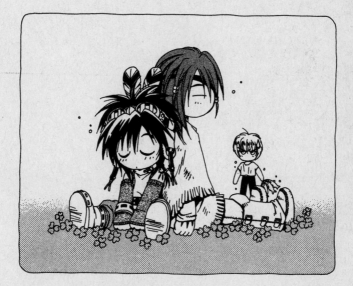

Daytime sleep

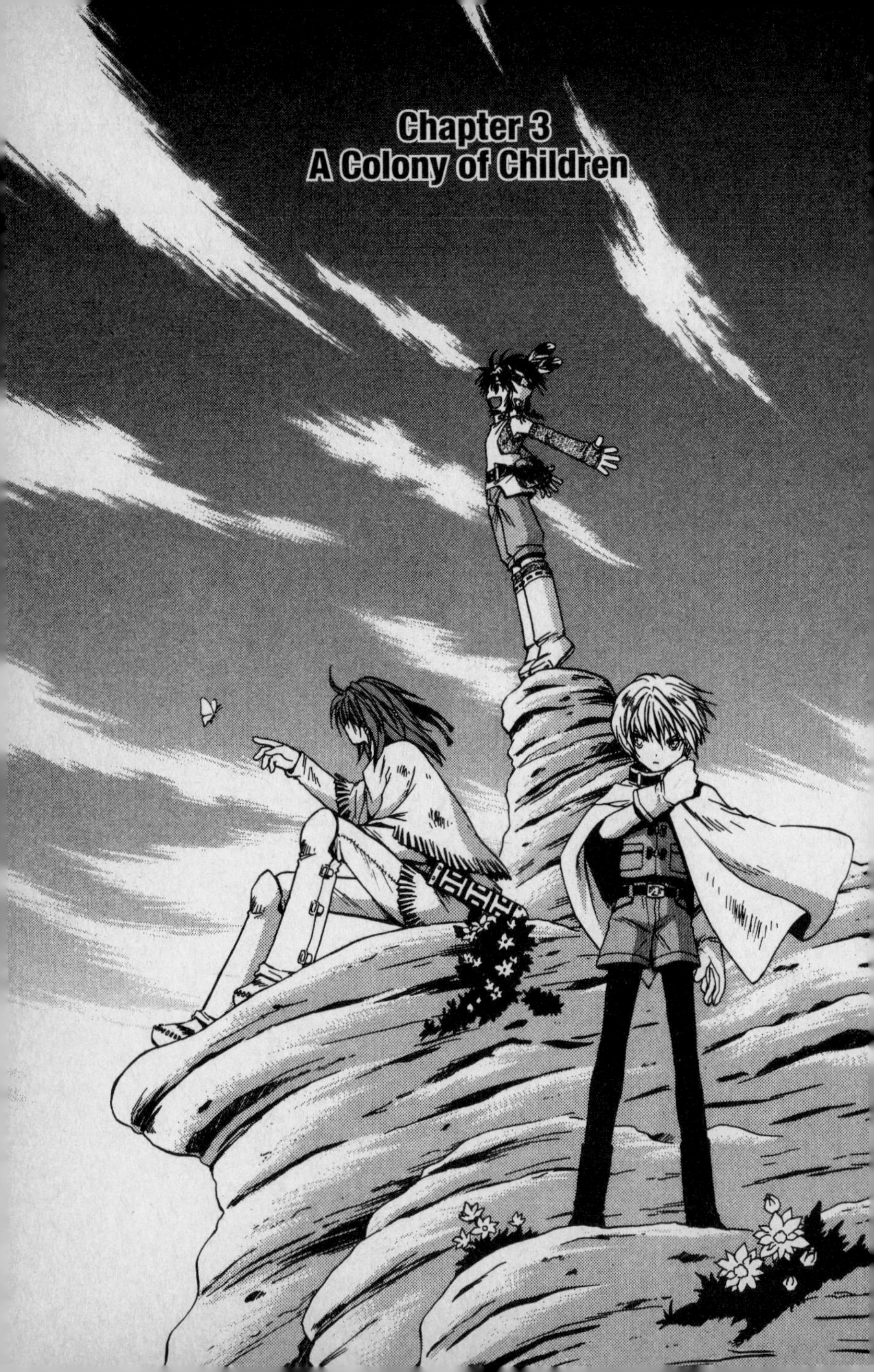
Chapter 3
A Colony of Children

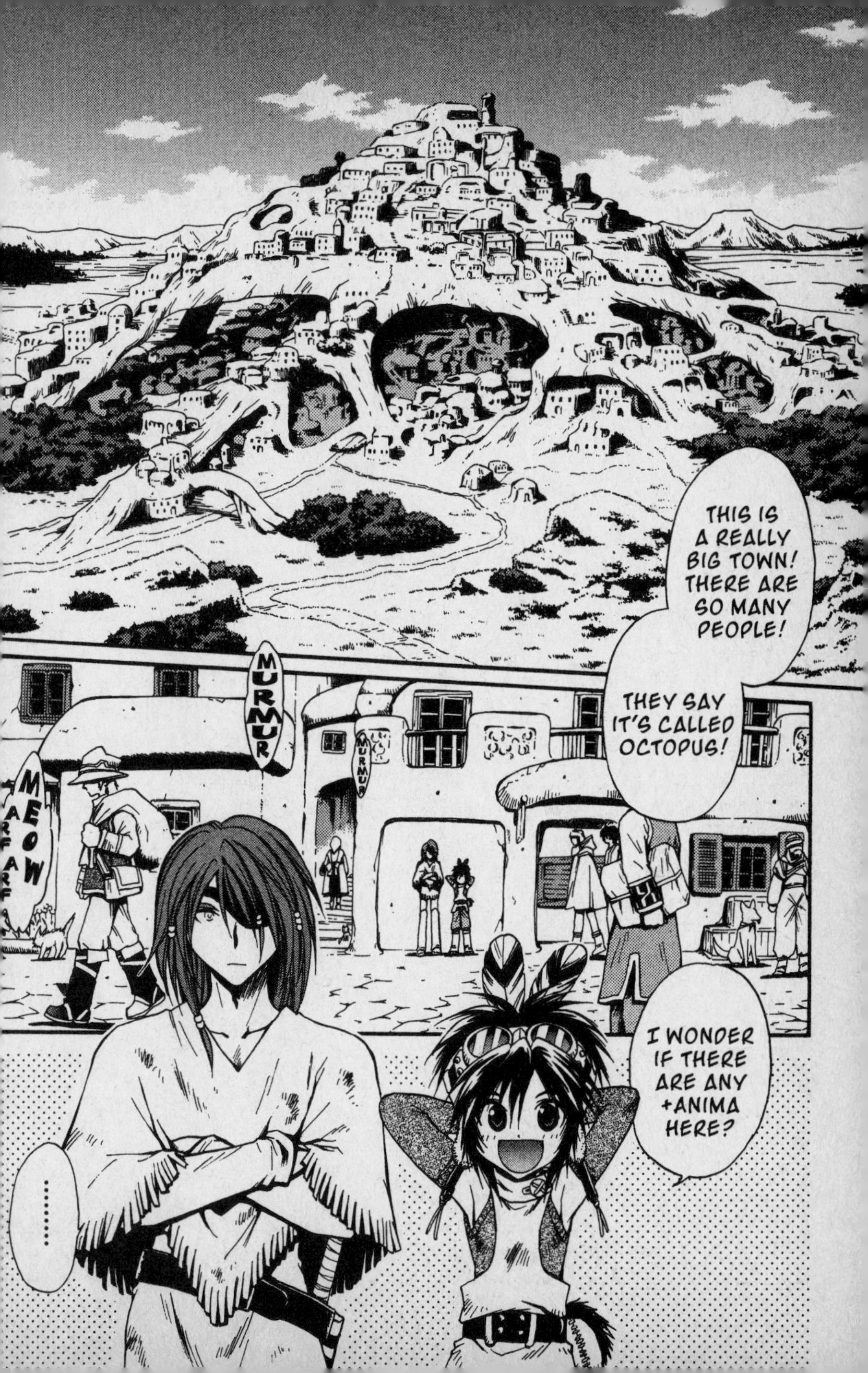
THIS IS A REALLY BIG TOWN! THERE ARE SO MANY PEOPLE!
THEY SAY IT'S CALLED OCTOPUS!
MURMUR
MURMUR
MEOW
ARF ARF
I WONDER IF THERE ARE ANY +ANIMA HERE?
......

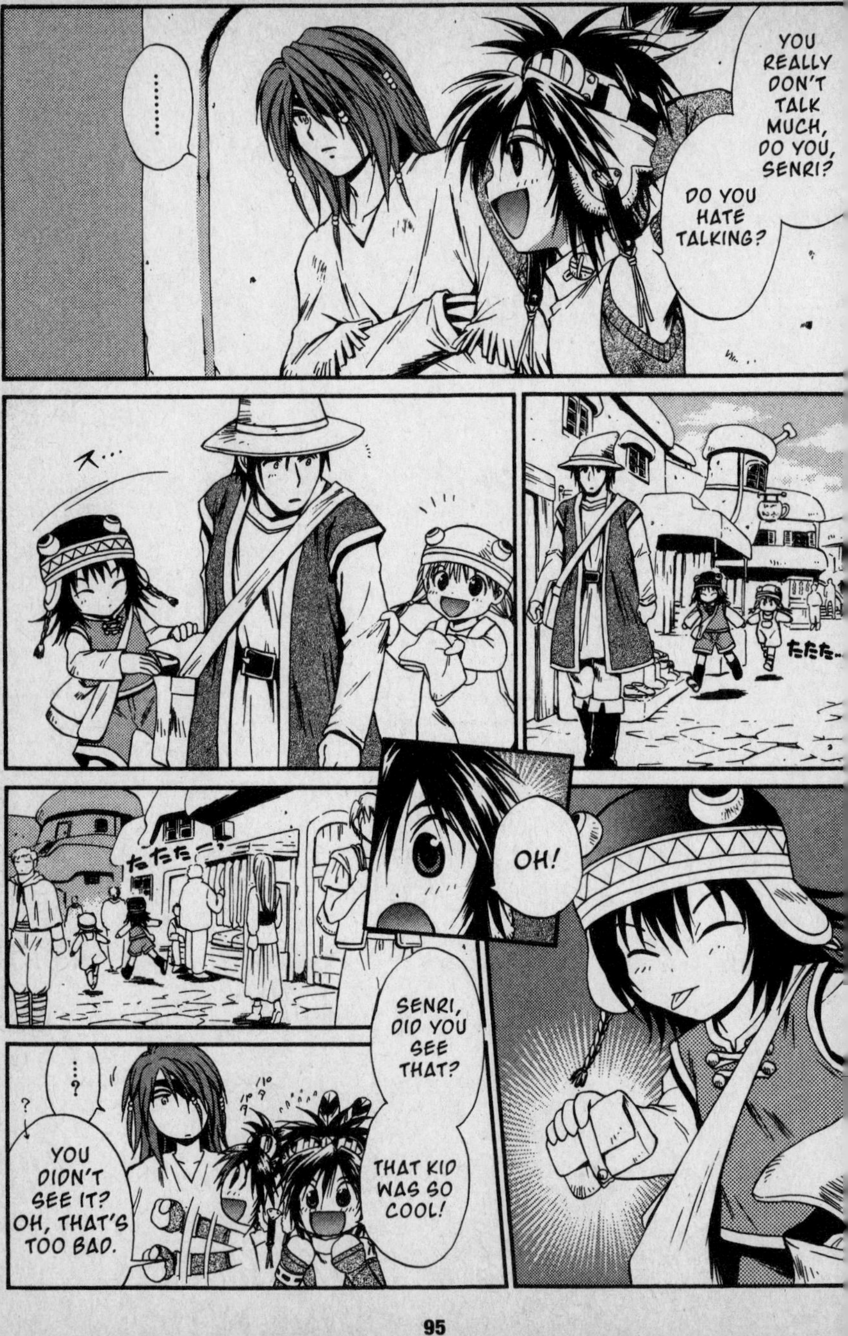
YOU REALLY DON'T TALK MUCH, DO YOU, SENRI?
DO YOU HATE TALKING?
......
たたた...
ス...
OH!
たたたー
SENRI, DID YOU SEE THAT?
THAT KID WAS SO COOL!
...?
YOU DIDN'T SEE IT? OH, THAT'S TOO BAD.

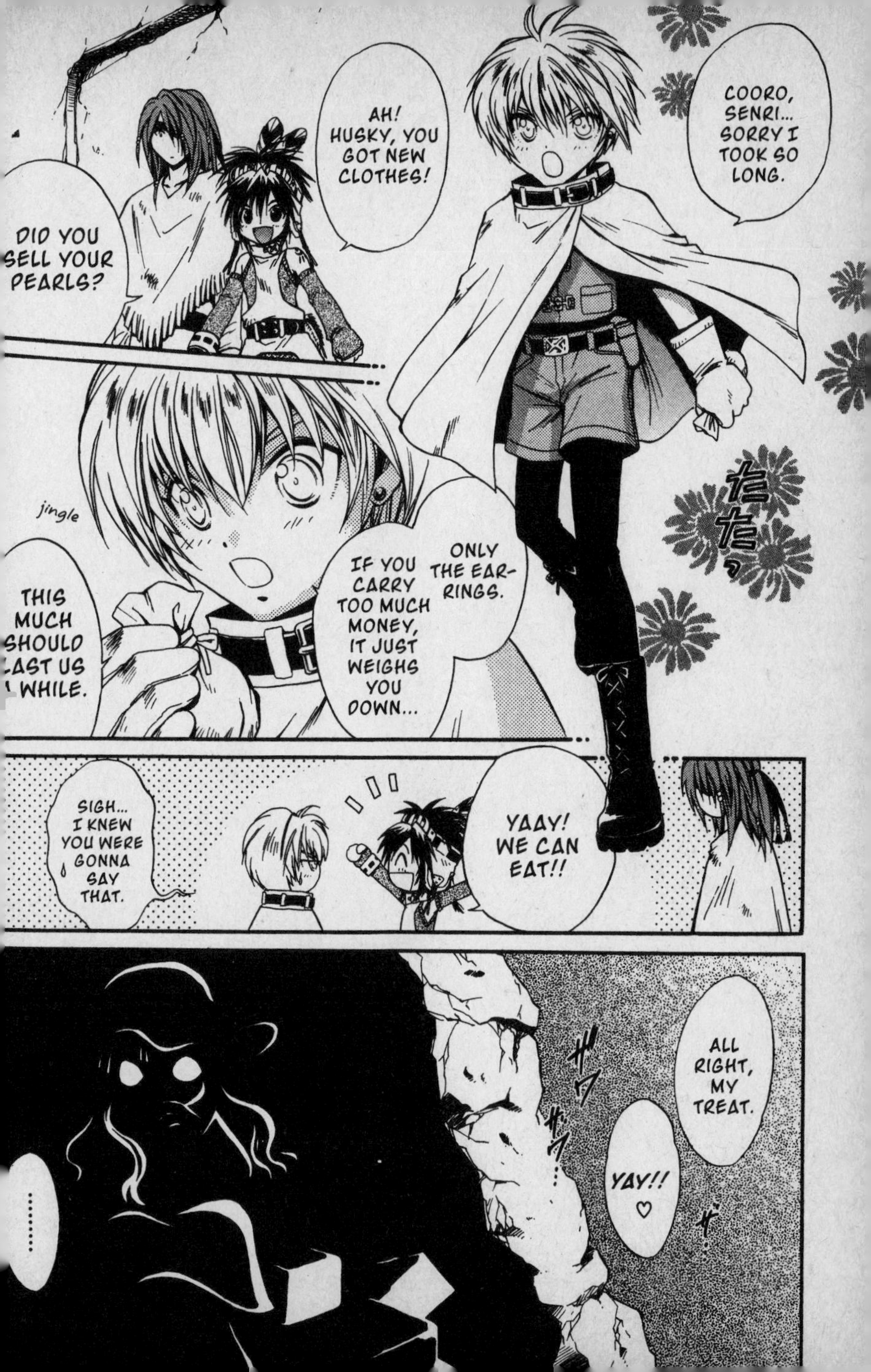
COORO, SENRI... SORRY I TOOK SO LONG.
たたっ
AH! HUSKY, YOU GOT NEW CLOTHES!
DID YOU SELL YOUR PEARLS?
ONLY THE EAR-RINGS.
IF YOU CARRY TOO MUCH MONEY, IT JUST WEIGHS YOU DOWN...
jingle
THIS MUCH SHOULD LAST US A WHILE.
YAAY! WE CAN EAT!!
SIGH... I KNEW YOU WERE GONNA SAY THAT.
ALL RIGHT, MY TREAT.
YAY!! ♡
......

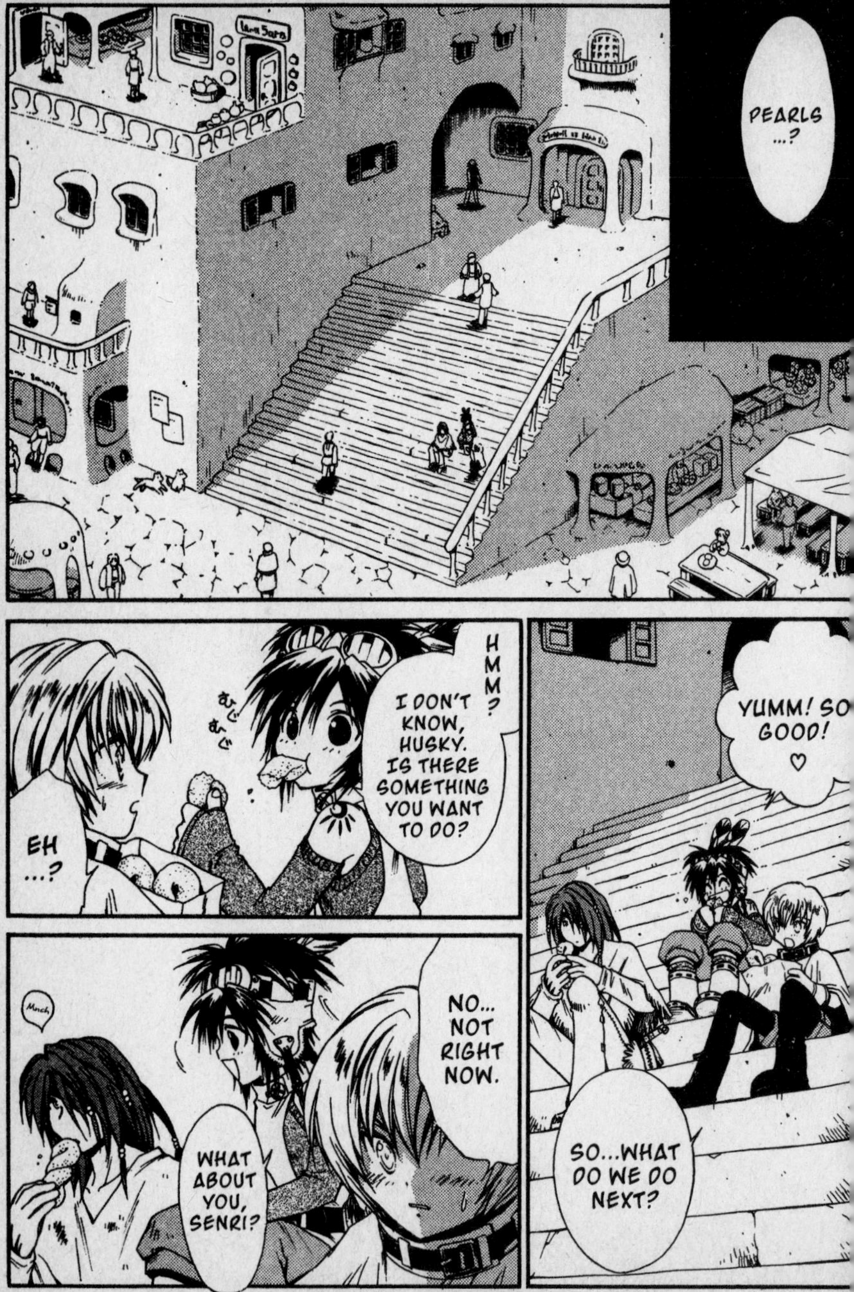
PEARLS ...?
YUMM! SO GOOD! ♡
SO...WHAT DO WE DO NEXT?
HMM? I DON'T KNOW, HUSKY. IS THERE SOMETHING YOU WANT TO DO?
むぐ むぐ
EH ...?
NO... NOT RIGHT NOW.
WHAT ABOUT YOU, SENRI?
Munch

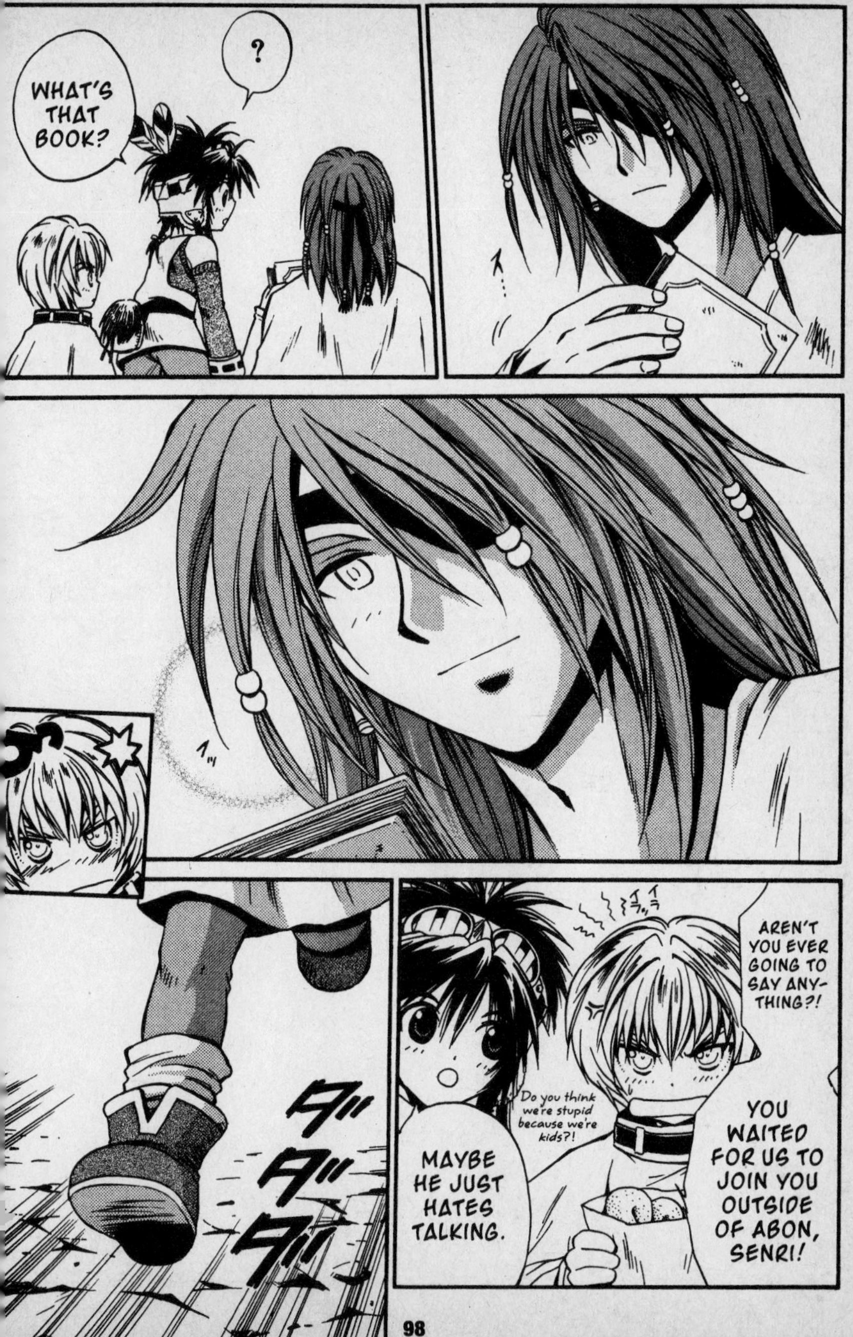
?
WHAT'S THAT BOOK?
AREN'T YOU EVER GOING TO SAY ANY-THING?!
YOU WAITED FOR US TO JOIN YOU OUTSIDE OF ABON, SENRI!
Do you think we're stupid because we're kids?!
MAYBE HE JUST HATES TALKING.

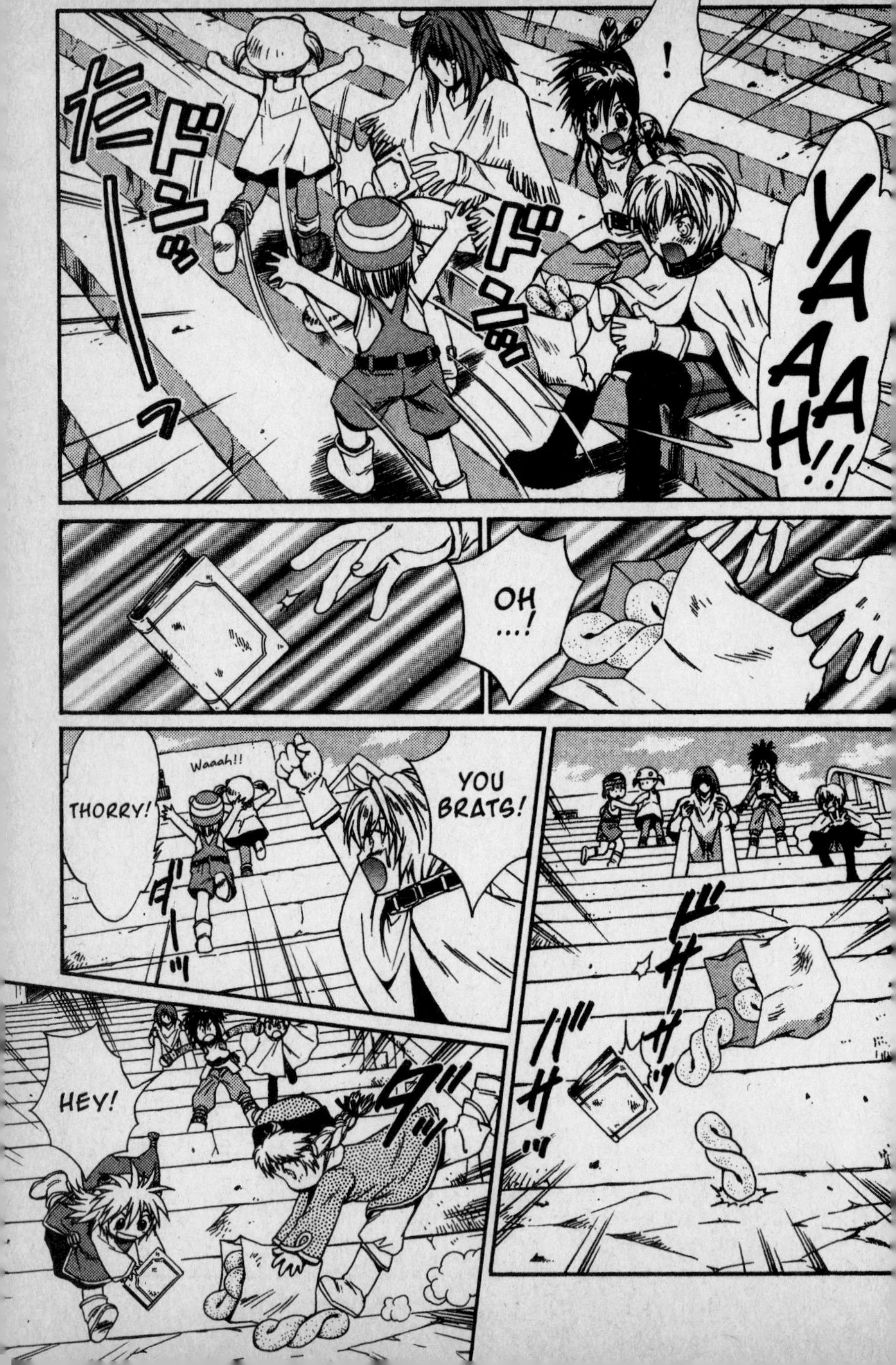
!
YAAAH!!
OH ...!
YOU BRATS!
Waaah!!
THORRY!
HEY!

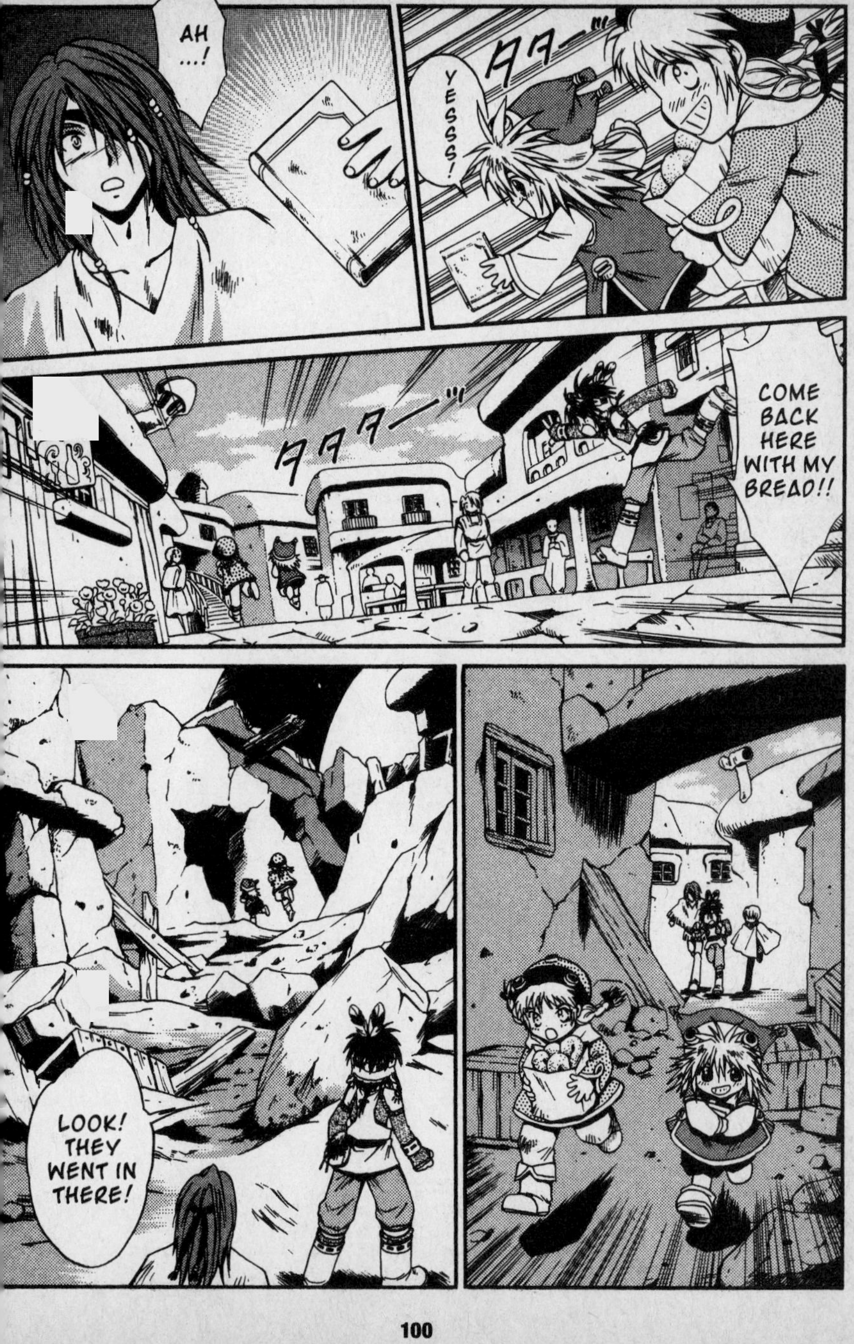
タターッ
YESSS!
AH ...!
COME BACK HERE WITH MY BREAD!!
タタターッ
LOOK! THEY WENT IN THERE!

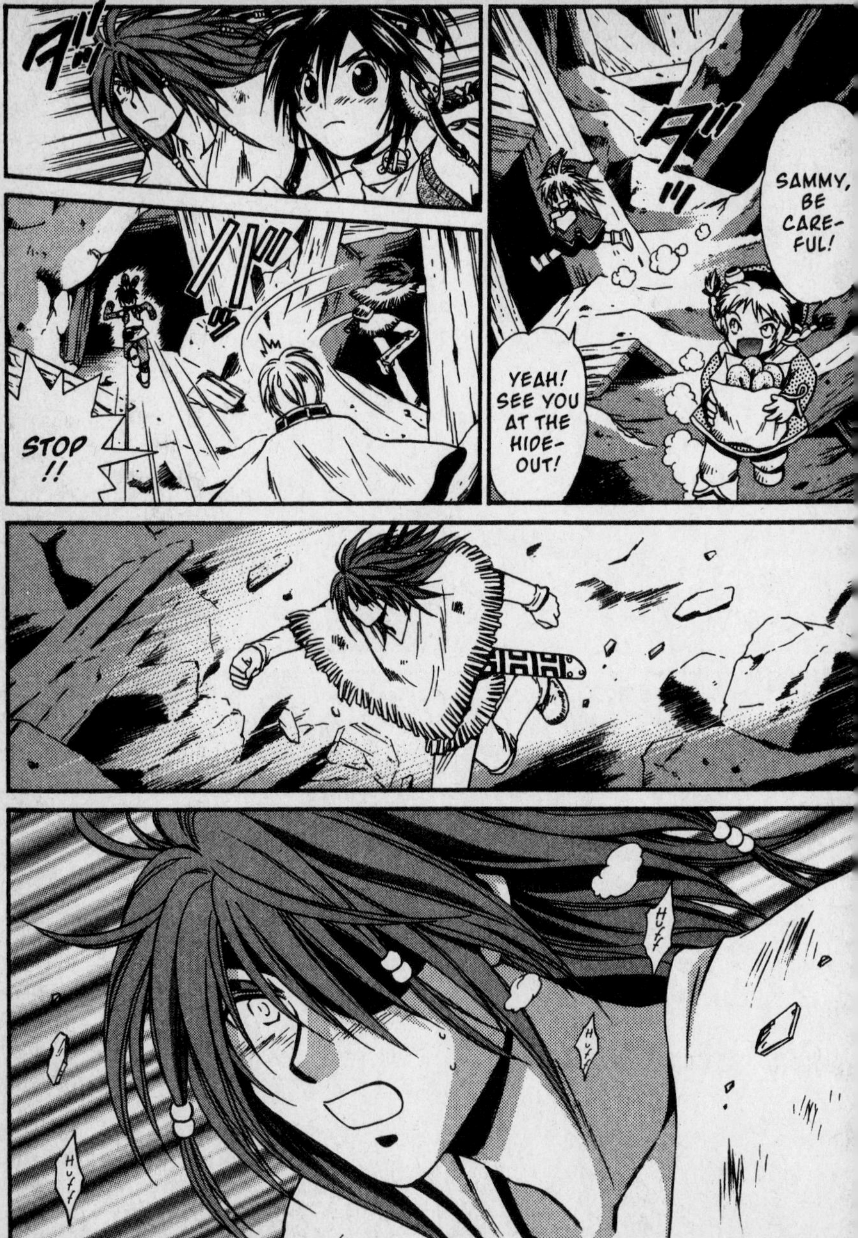
SAMMY, BE CAREFUL!
YEAH! SEE YOU AT THE HIDE-OUT!
STOP!!
HUFF
HUFF
HUFF

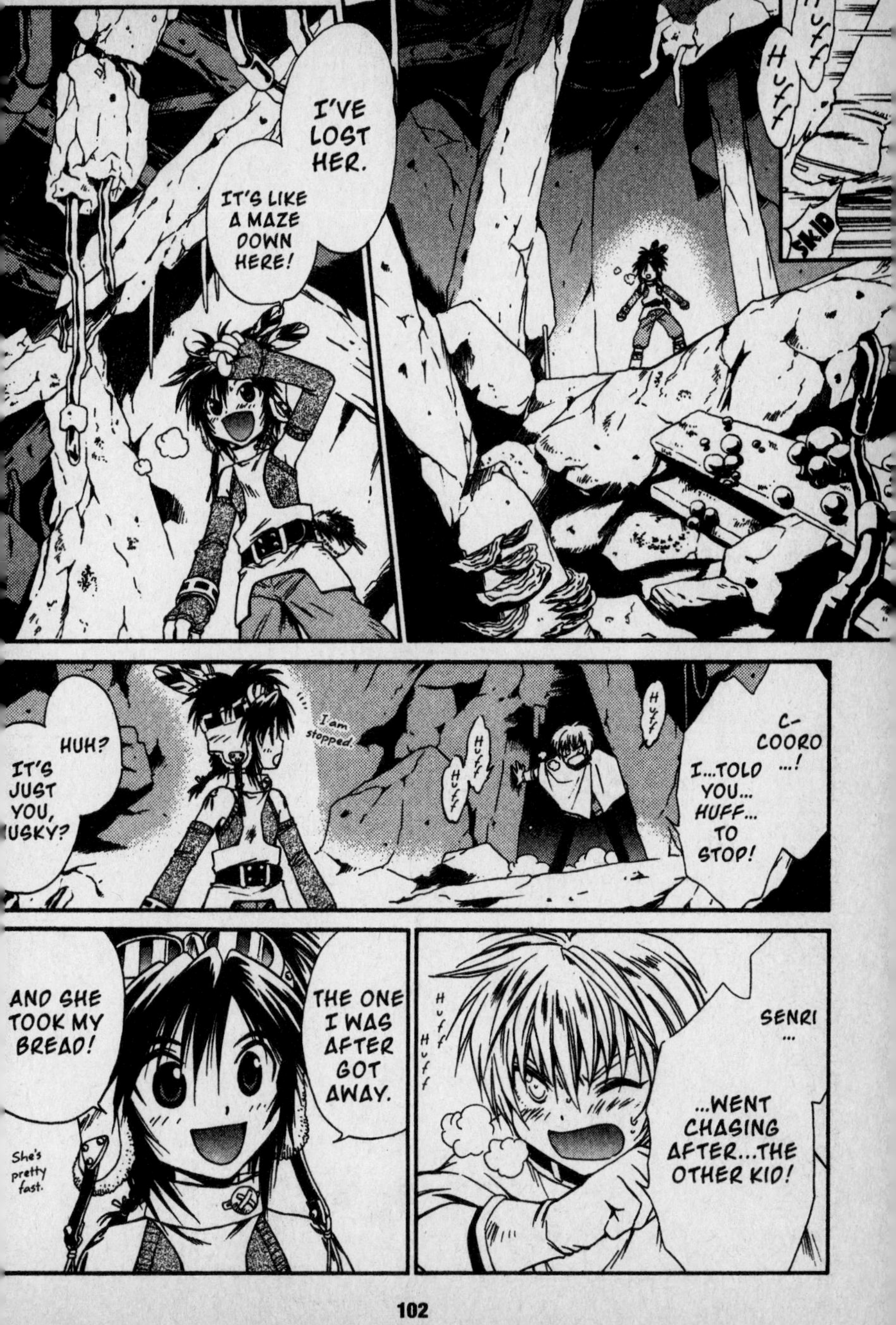
Huff
Huff
SKID
I'VE LOST HER.
IT'S LIKE A MAZE DOWN HERE!
C-COORO ...!
I...TOLD YOU... HUFF... TO STOP!
Huff
Huff
Huff
I am stopped.
HUH? IT'S JUST YOU, USKY?
SENRI ...
...WENT CHASING AFTER...THE OTHER KID!
Huff
Huff
THE ONE I WAS AFTER GOT AWAY.
AND SHE TOOK MY BREAD!
She's pretty fast.

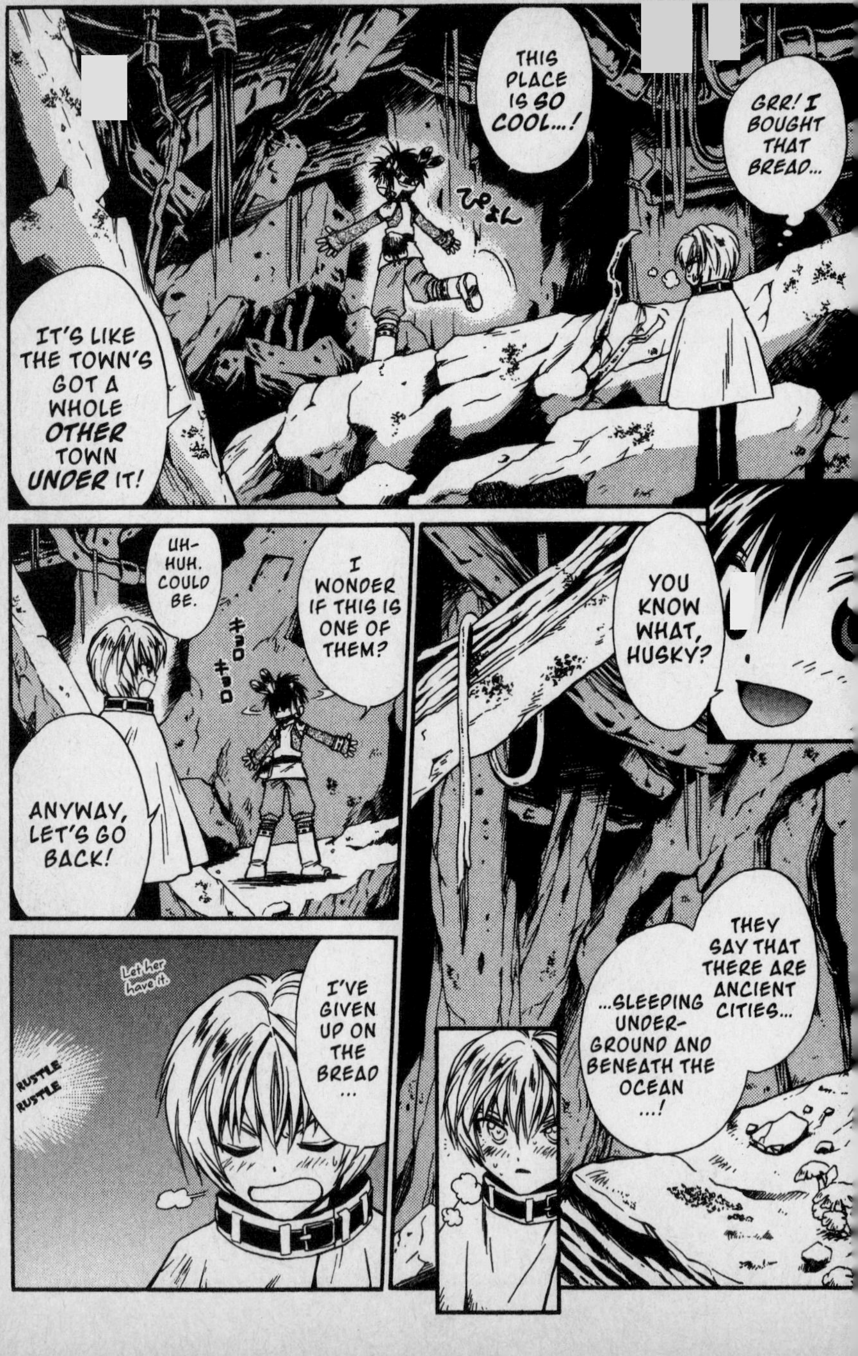
GRR! I BOUGHT THAT BREAD...
THIS PLACE IS SO COOL...!
ぴょん
IT'S LIKE THE TOWN'S GOT A WHOLE OTHER TOWN UNDER IT!
YOU KNOW WHAT, HUSKY?
THEY SAY THAT THERE ARE ANCIENT CITIES...
...SLEEPING UNDER-GROUND AND BENEATH THE OCEAN ...!
I WONDER IF THIS IS ONE OF THEM?
UH-HUH. COULD BE.
キョロ キョロ
ANYWAY, LET'S GO BACK!
I'VE GIVEN UP ON THE BREAD ...
Let her have it.
RUSTLE RUSTLE

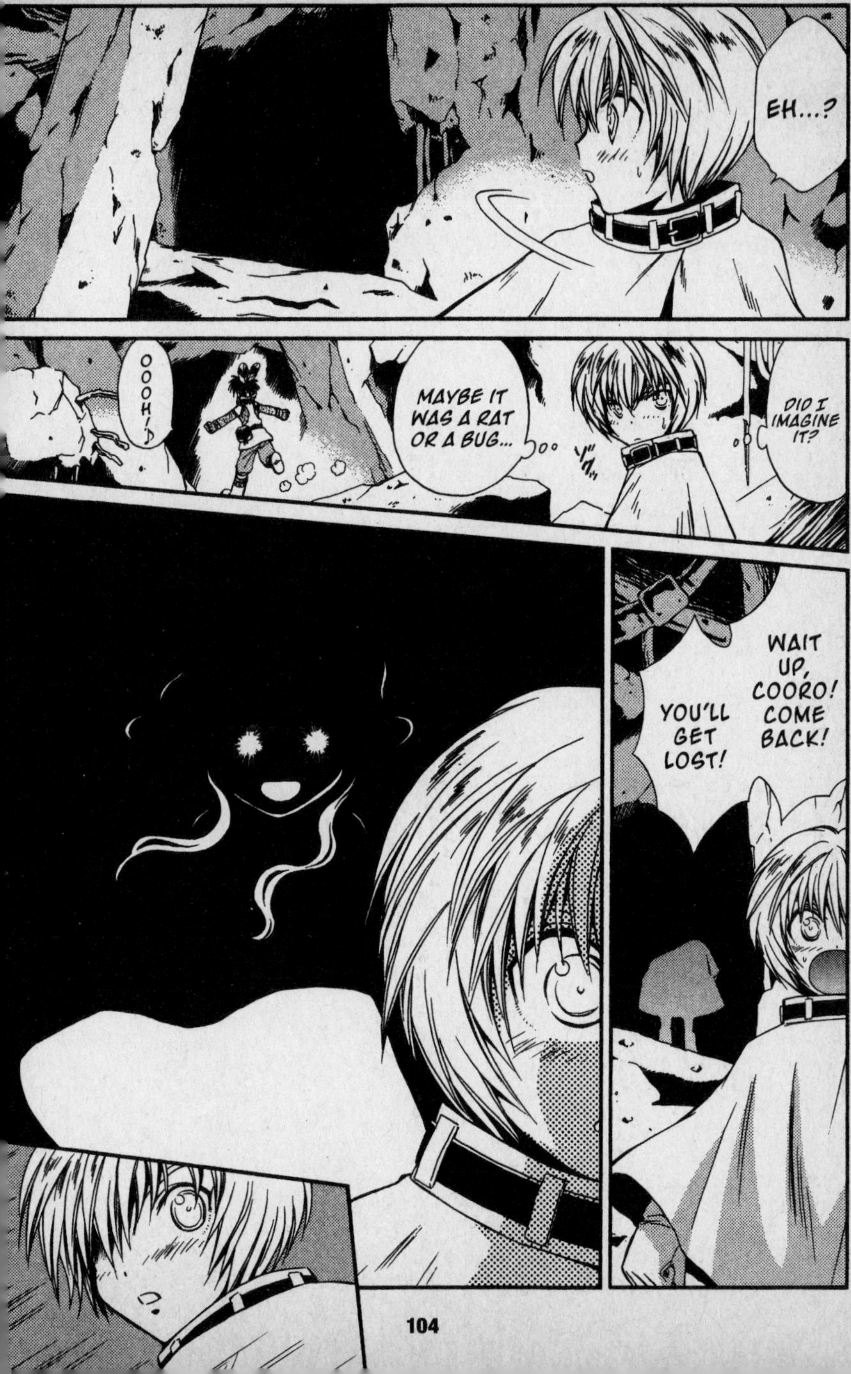
EH...?
DID I IMAGINE IT?
MAYBE IT WAS A RAT OR A BUG...
OOOH!♪
WAIT UP, COORO! COME BACK!
YOU'LL GET LOST!

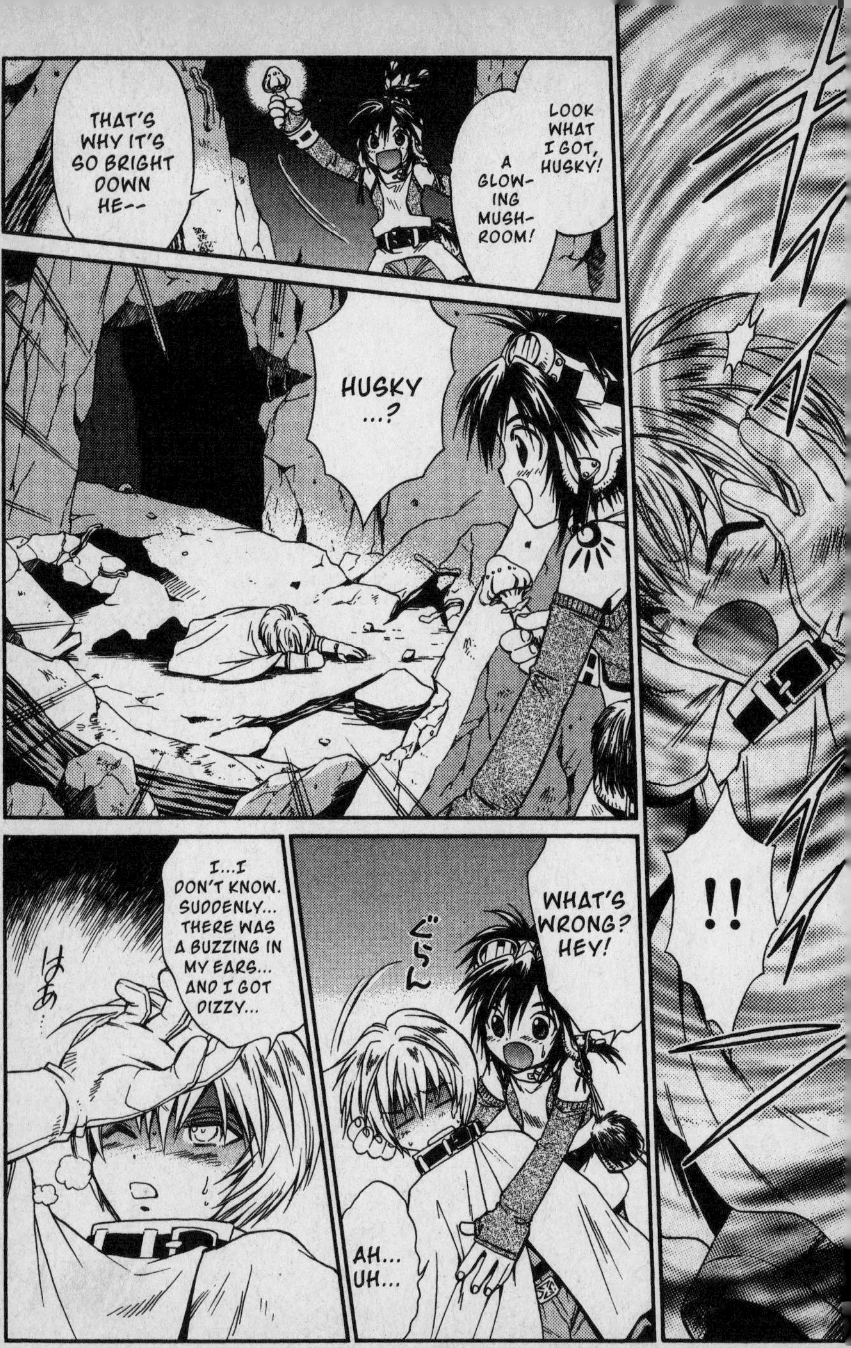
!!
LOOK WHAT I GOT, HUSKY!
A GLOWING MUSHROOM!
THAT'S WHY IT'S SO BRIGHT DOWN HE--
HUSKY ...?
WHAT'S WRONG? HEY!
ぐらん
AH... UH...
I...I DON'T KNOW. SUDDENLY... THERE WAS A BUZZING IN MY EARS... AND I GOT DIZZY...
はあ…

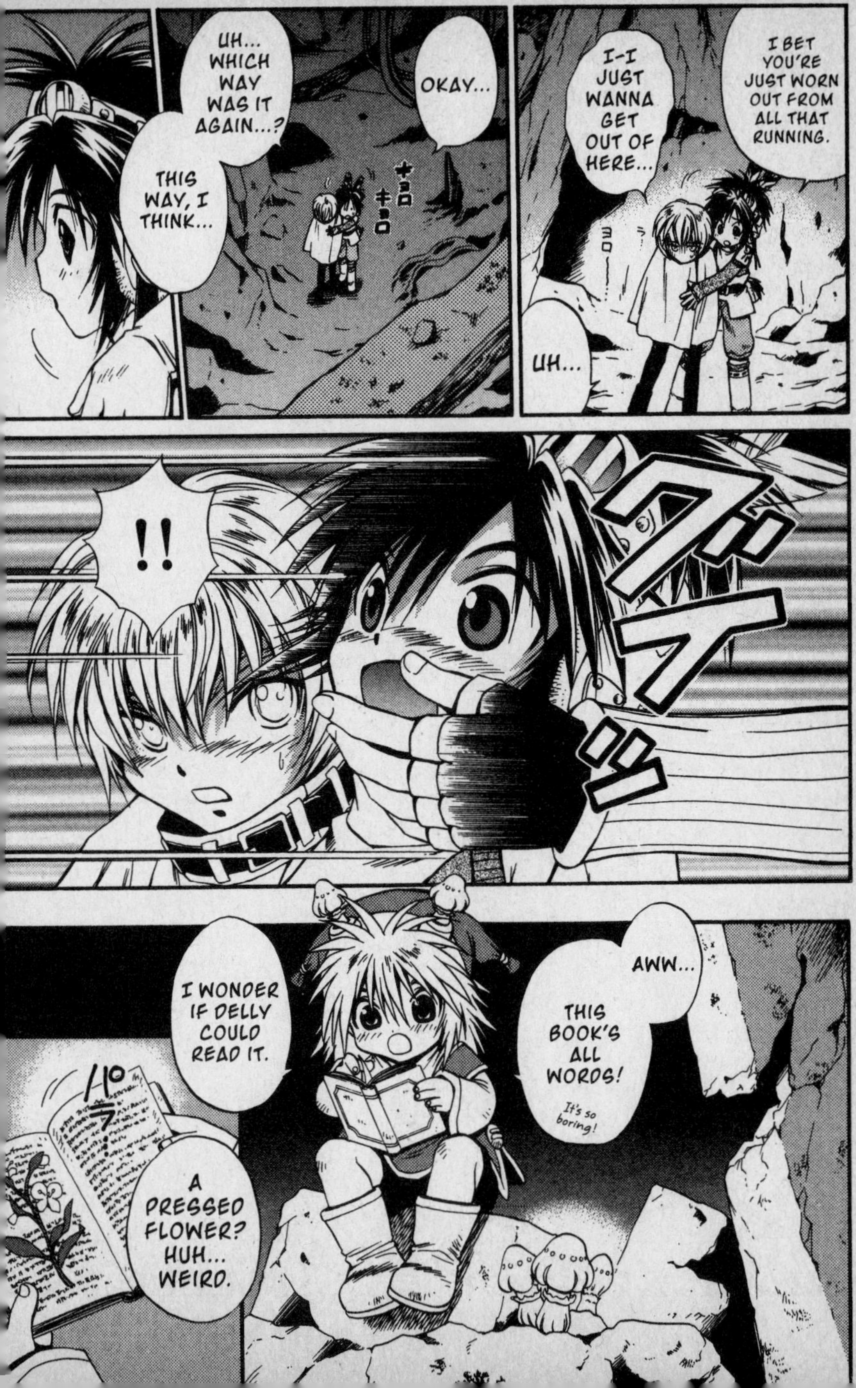
I BET YOU'RE JUST WORN OUT FROM ALL THAT RUNNING.
I-I JUST WANNA GET OUT OF HERE...
UH...
OKAY...
キョロ キョロ
UH... WHICH WAY WAS IT AGAIN...?
THIS WAY, I THINK...
!!
AWW...
THIS BOOK'S ALL WORDS!
It's so boring!
I WONDER IF DELLY COULD READ IT.
A PRESSED FLOWER? HUH... WEIRD.

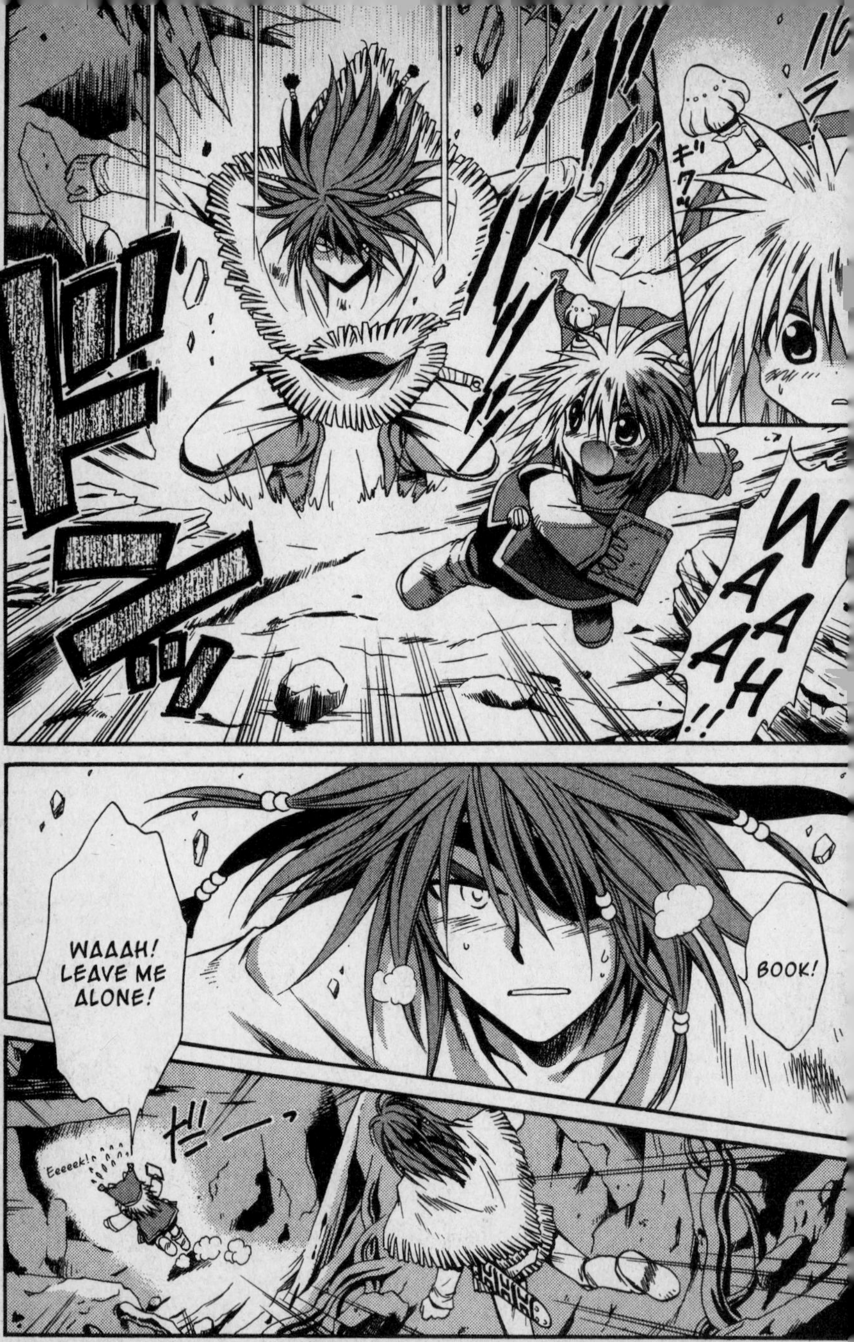
WAAAAH!!
BOOK!
WAAAH! LEAVE ME ALONE!
Eeeeek!

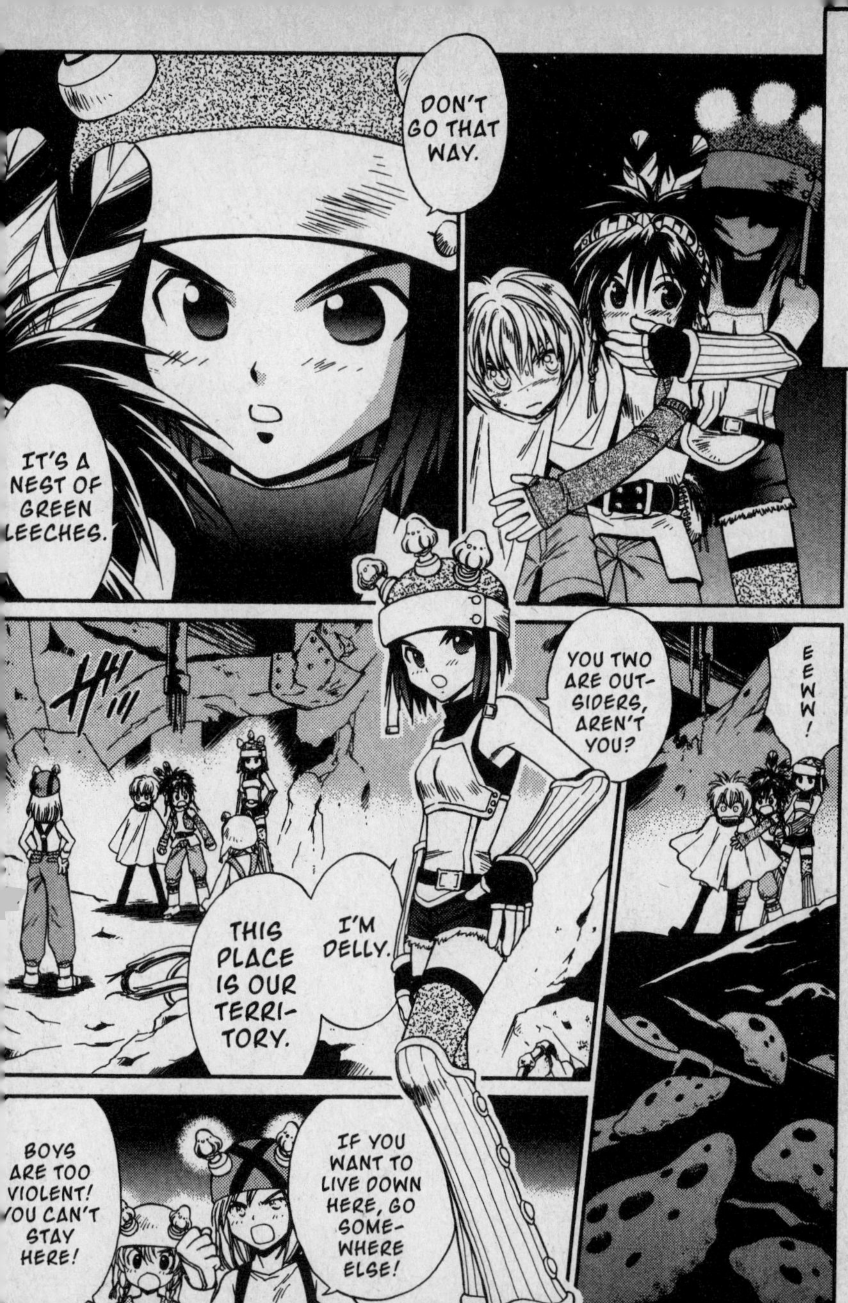

DON'T GO THAT WAY.
IT'S A NEST OF GREEN LEECHES.
EEWW!
YOU TWO ARE OUT-SIDERS, AREN'T YOU?
I'M DELLY.
THIS PLACE IS OUR TERRI-TORY.
IF YOU WANT TO LIVE DOWN HERE, GO SOME-WHERE ELSE!
BOYS ARE TOO VIOLENT! YOU CAN'T STAY HERE!

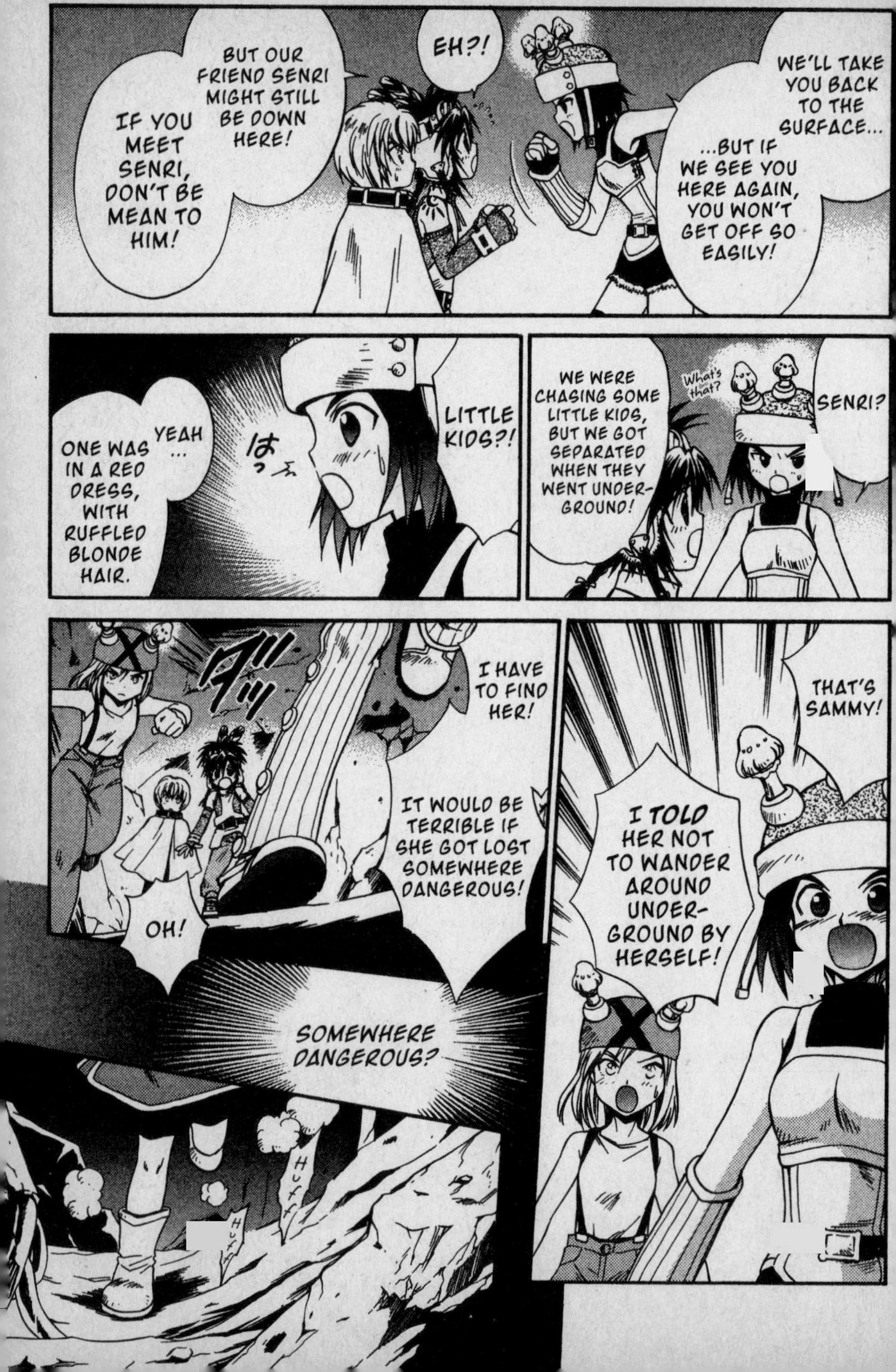
WE'LL TAKE YOU BACK TO THE SURFACE...
...BUT IF WE SEE YOU HERE AGAIN, YOU WON'T GET OFF SO EASILY!
EH?!
BUT OUR FRIEND SENRI MIGHT STILL BE DOWN HERE!
IF YOU MEET SENRI, DON'T BE MEAN TO HIM!
SENRI?
What's that?
WE WERE CHASING SOME LITTLE KIDS, BUT WE GOT SEPARATED WHEN THEY WENT UNDER-GROUND!
LITTLE KIDS?!
はっ
YEAH ...
ONE WAS IN A RED DRESS, WITH RUFFLED BLONDE HAIR.
THAT'S SAMMY!
I TOLD HER NOT TO WANDER AROUND UNDER-GROUND BY HERSELF!
I HAVE TO FIND HER!
IT WOULD BE TERRIBLE IF SHE GOT LOST SOMEWHERE DANGEROUS!
ダッ
OH!
SOMEWHERE DANGEROUS?
Huff
Huff

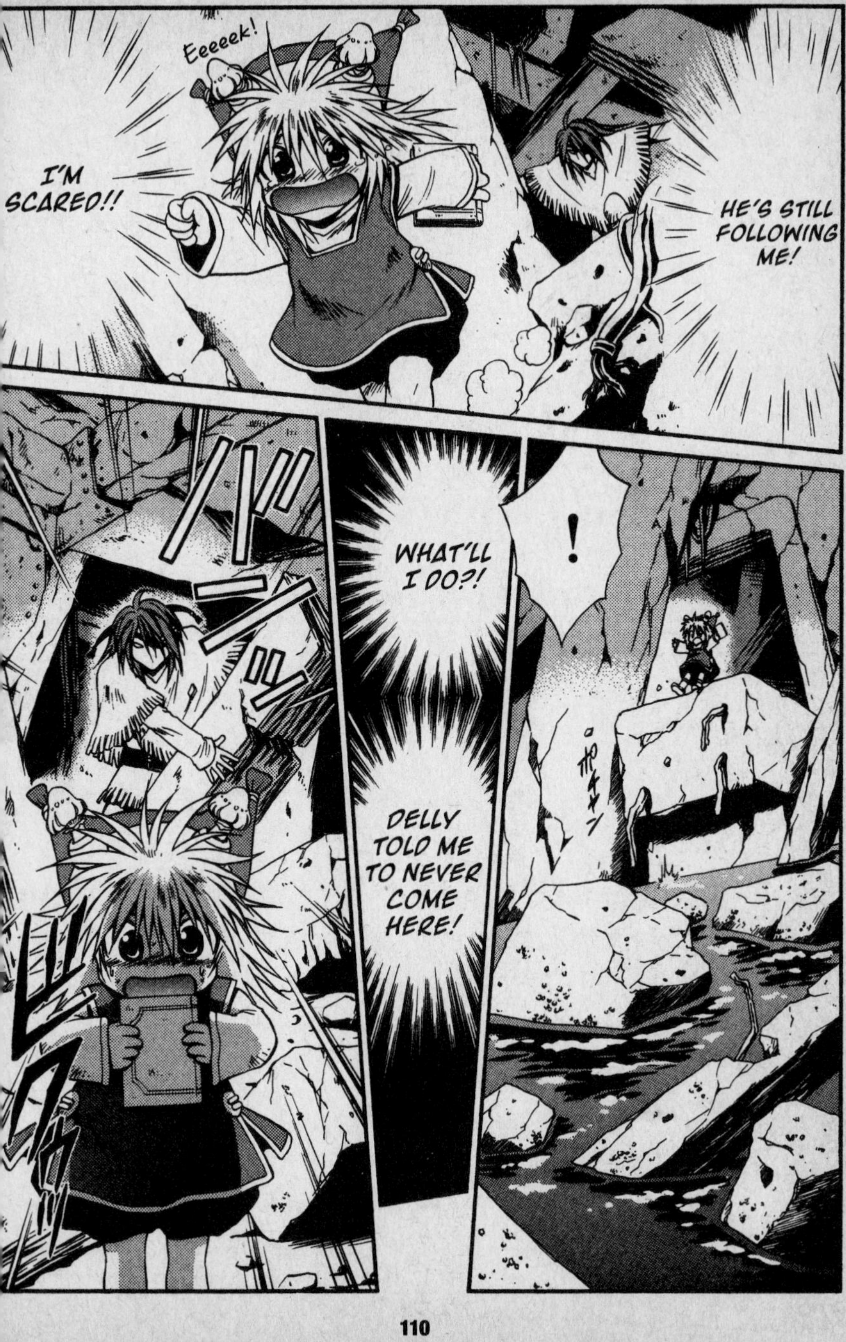
Eeeeek!
HE'S STILL FOLLOWING ME!
I'M SCARED!!
!
WHAT'LL I DO?!
DELLY TOLD ME TO NEVER COME HERE!

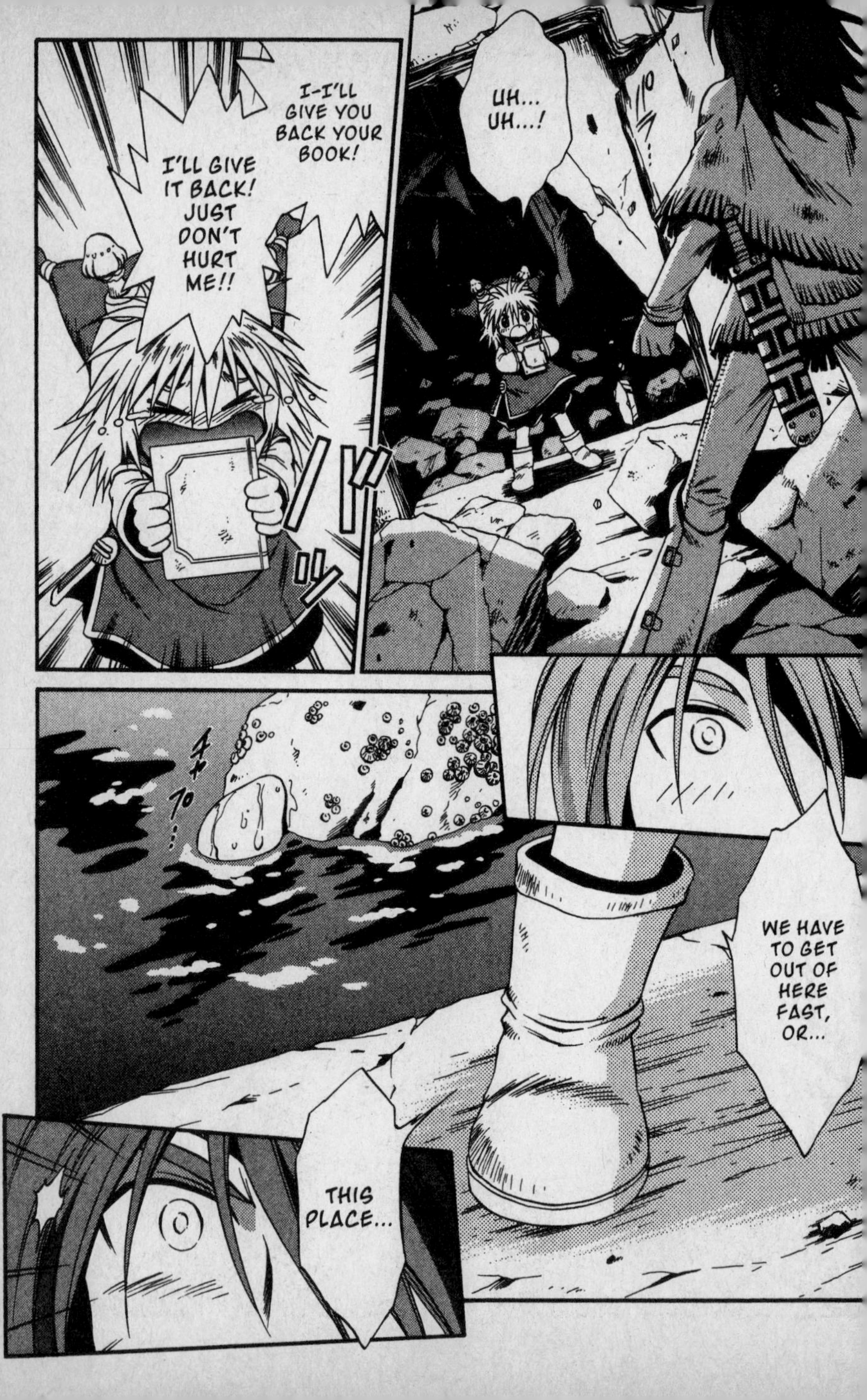
UH... UH...!
I-I'LL GIVE YOU BACK YOUR BOOK!
I'LL GIVE IT BACK! JUST DON'T HURT ME!!
WE HAVE TO GET OUT OF HERE FAST, OR...
THIS PLACE...

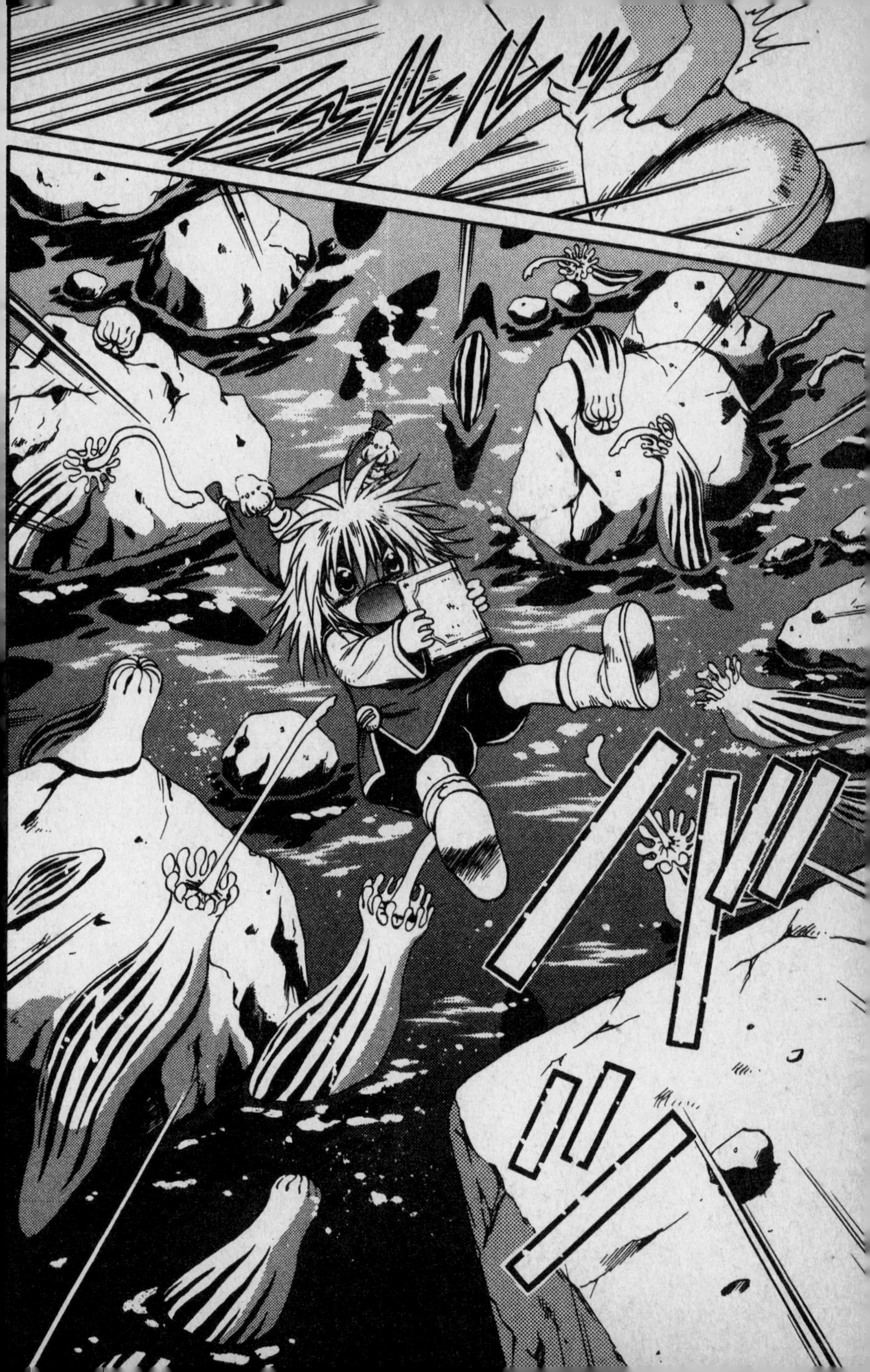

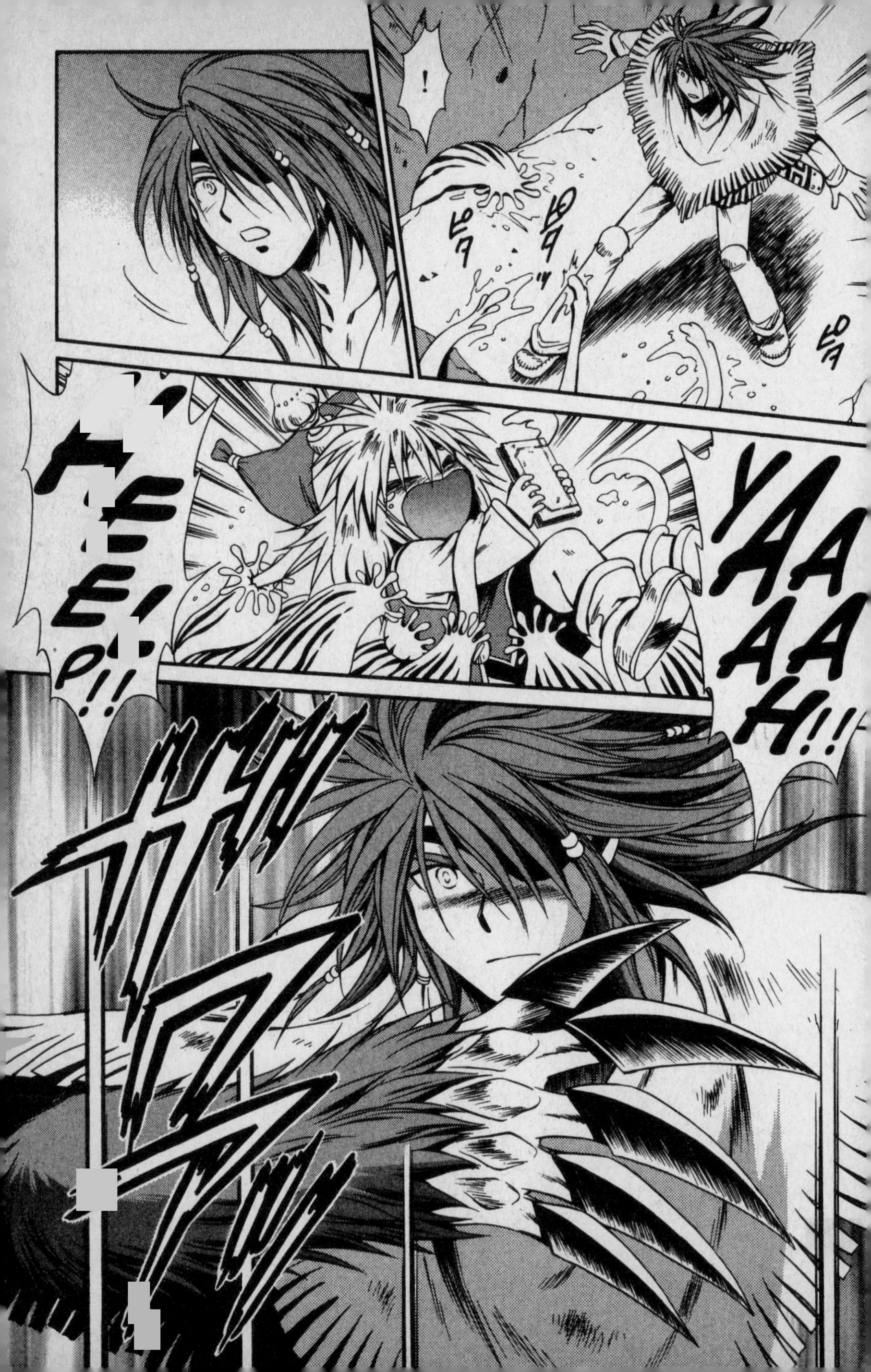
!
ピタ
ピタッ
ピタ
YAAAAAH!!
HEEEEP!!

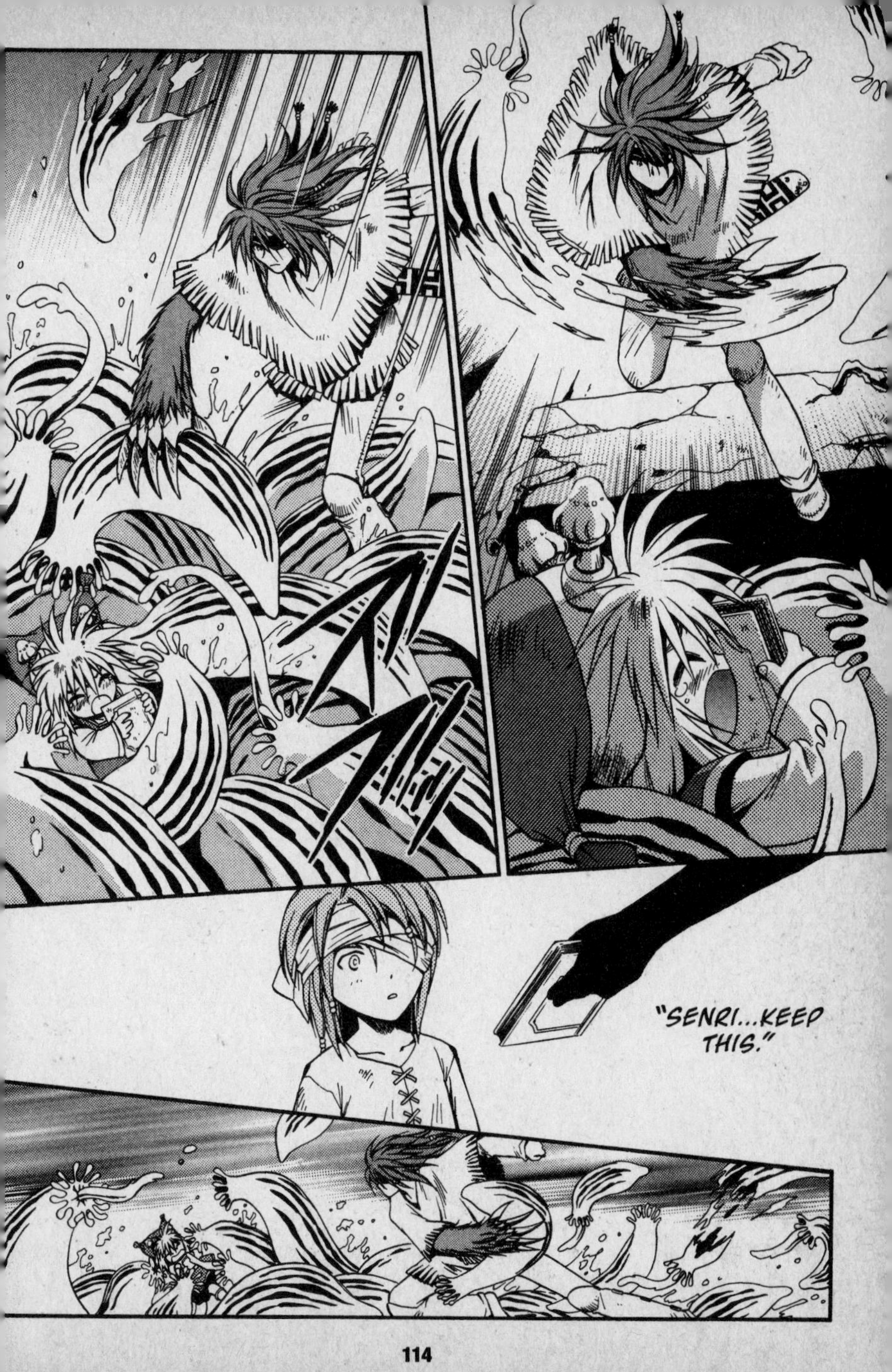
"SENRI...KEEP THIS."

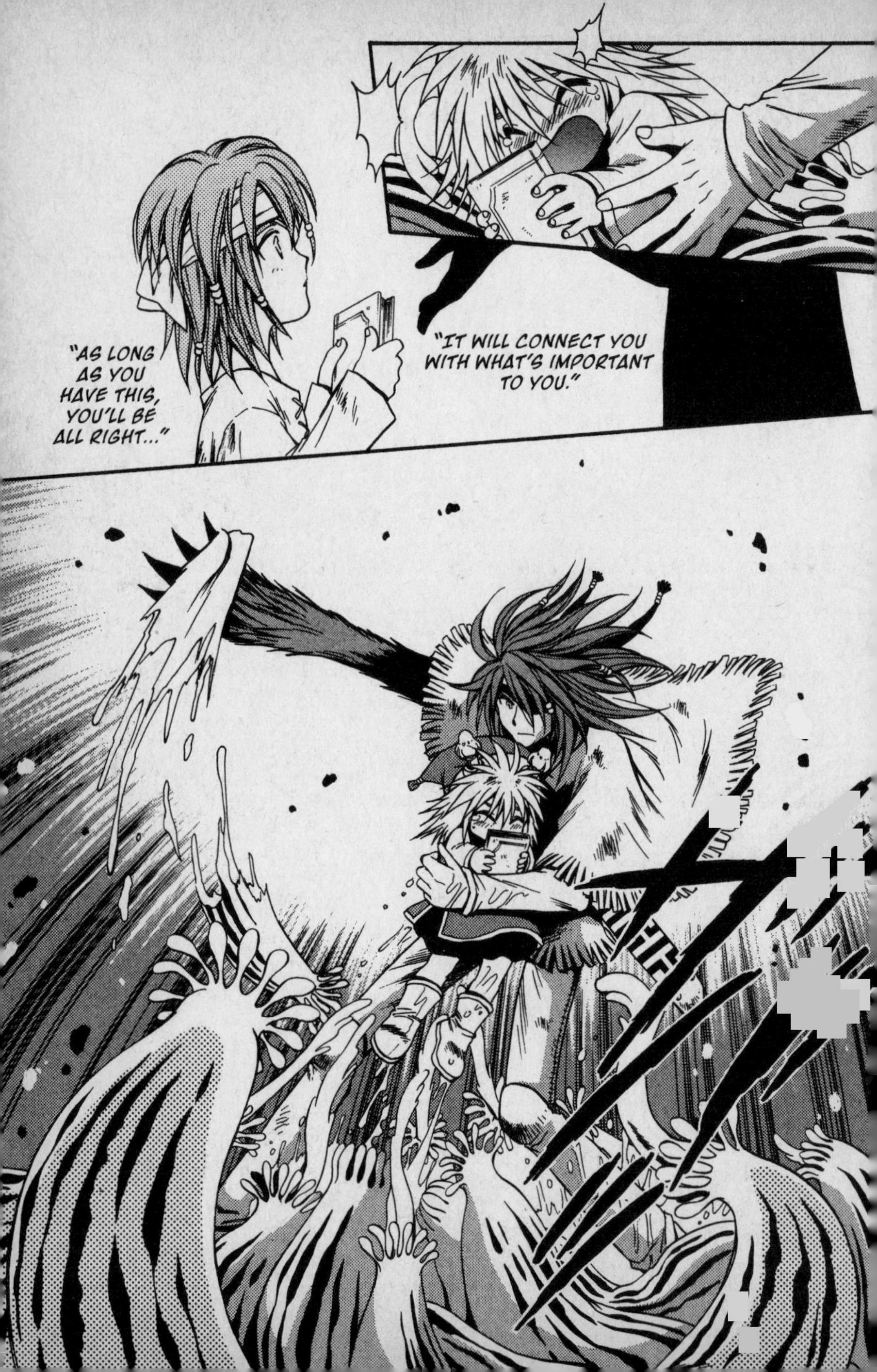
"IT WILL CONNECT YOU WITH WHAT'S IMPORTANT TO YOU."
"AS LONG AS YOU HAVE THIS, YOU'LL BE ALL RIGHT..."

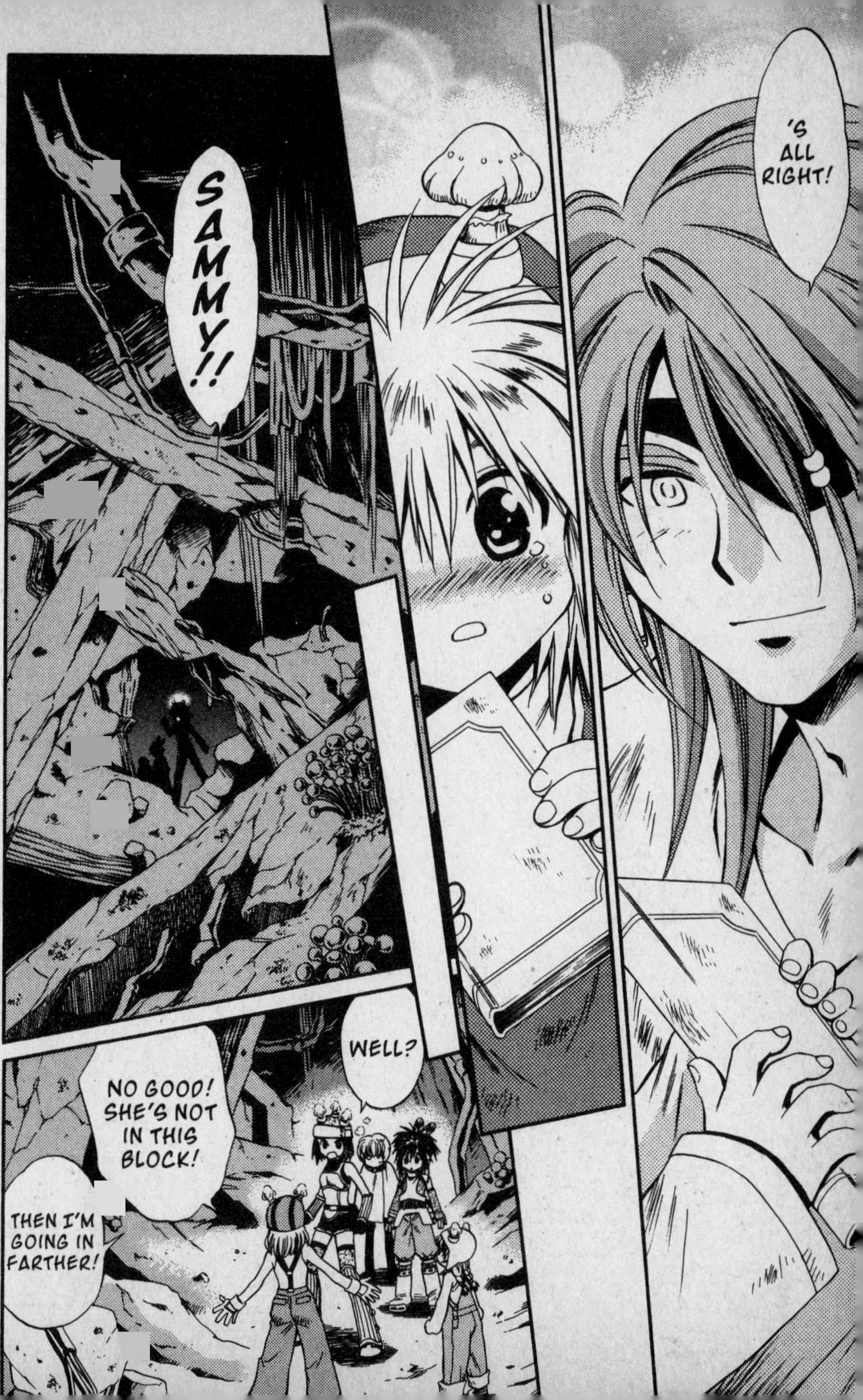
'S ALL RIGHT!
SAMMY!!
WELL?
NO GOOD! SHE'S NOT IN THIS BLOCK!
THEN I'M GOING IN FARTHER!

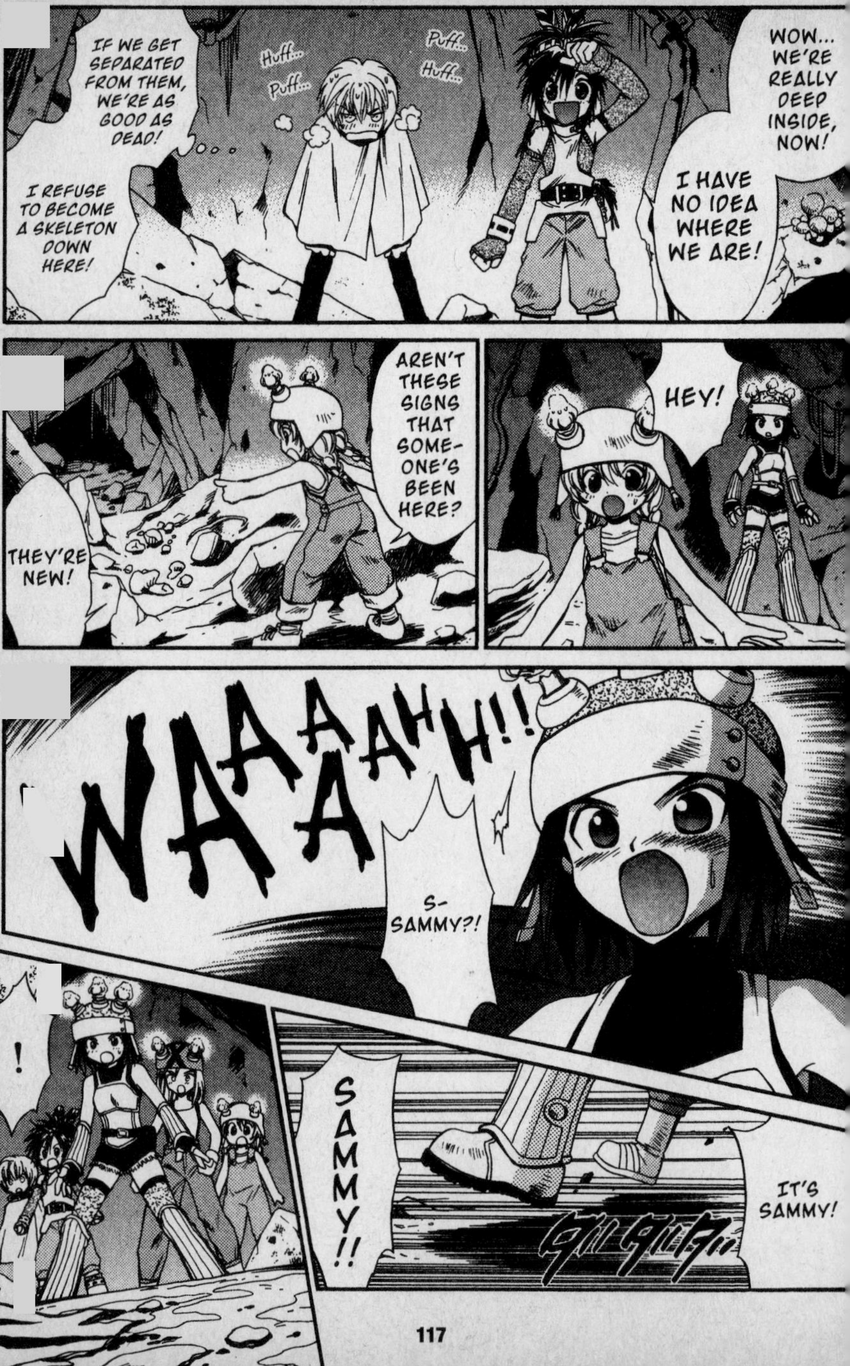
WOW... WE'RE REALLY DEEP INSIDE, NOW!
I HAVE NO IDEA WHERE WE ARE!
Puff... Huff...
Huff... Puff...
IF WE GET SEPARATED FROM THEM, WE'RE AS GOOD AS DEAD!
I REFUSE TO BECOME A SKELETON DOWN HERE!
HEY!
AREN'T THESE SIGNS THAT SOME-ONE'S BEEN HERE?
THEY'RE NEW!
WAAAAAHH!!
S-SAMMY?!
IT'S SAMMY!
SAMMY!!
!

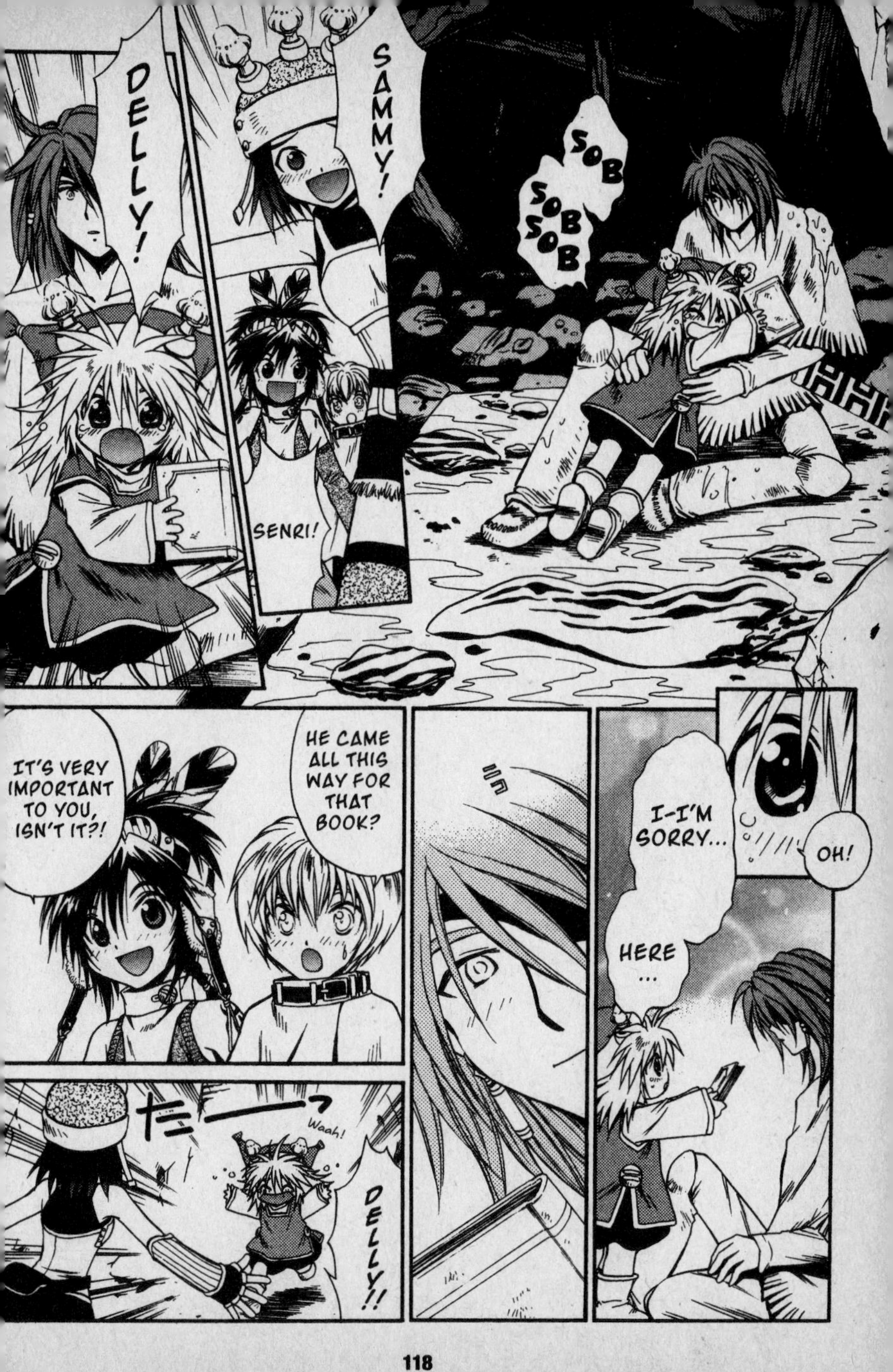
SOB
SOB
SOB
SAMMY!
SENRI!
DELLY!
OH!
I-I'M SORRY...
HERE ...
HE CAME ALL THIS WAY FOR THAT BOOK?
IT'S VERY IMPORTANT TO YOU, ISN'T IT?!
Waah!
DELLY!!

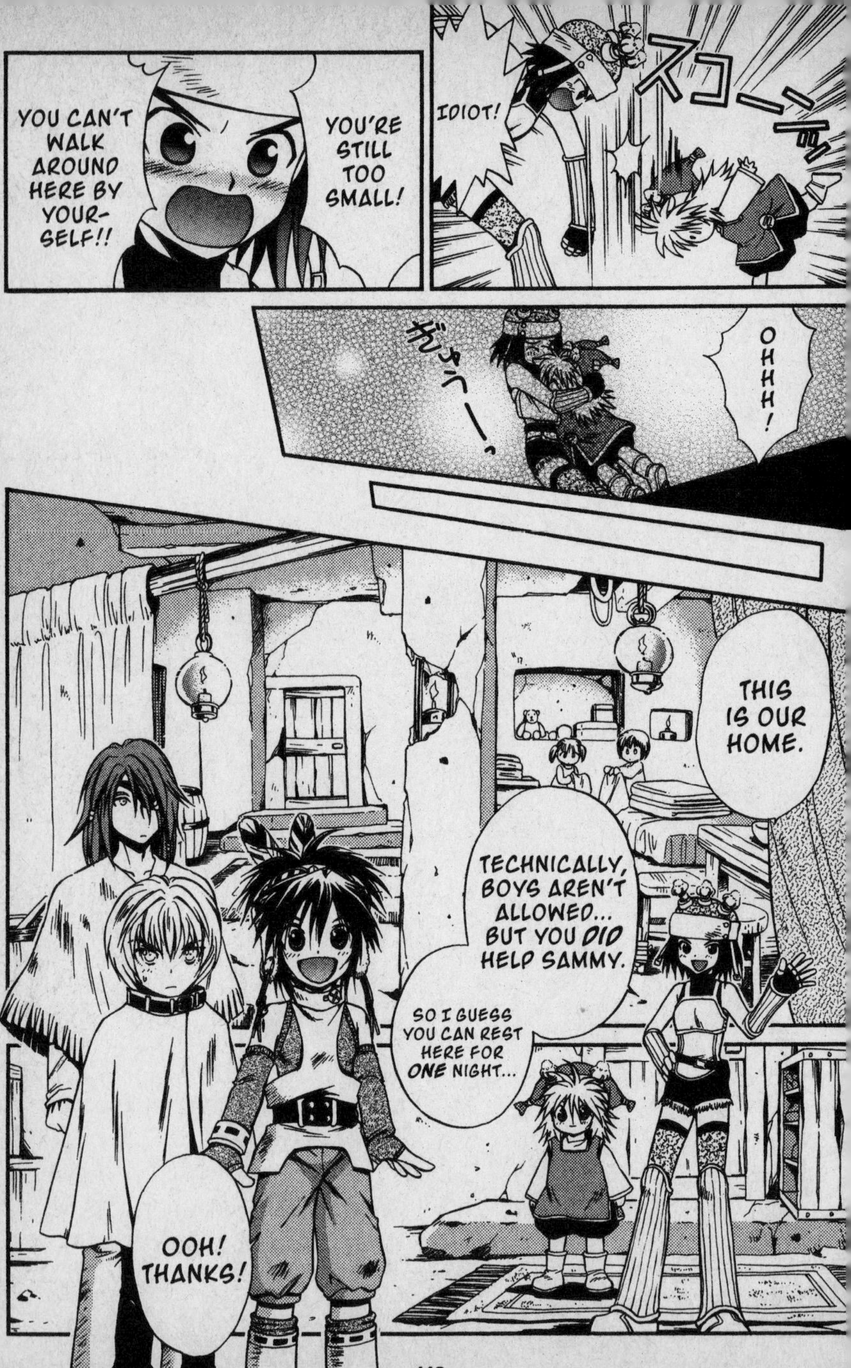
IDIOT!
YOU'RE STILL TOO SMALL!
YOU CAN'T WALK AROUND HERE BY YOUR-SELF!!
OHHHH!
THIS IS OUR HOME.
TECHNICALLY, BOYS AREN'T ALLOWED... BUT YOU *DID* HELP SAMMY.
SO I GUESS YOU CAN REST HERE FOR *ONE* NIGHT...
OOH! THANKS!

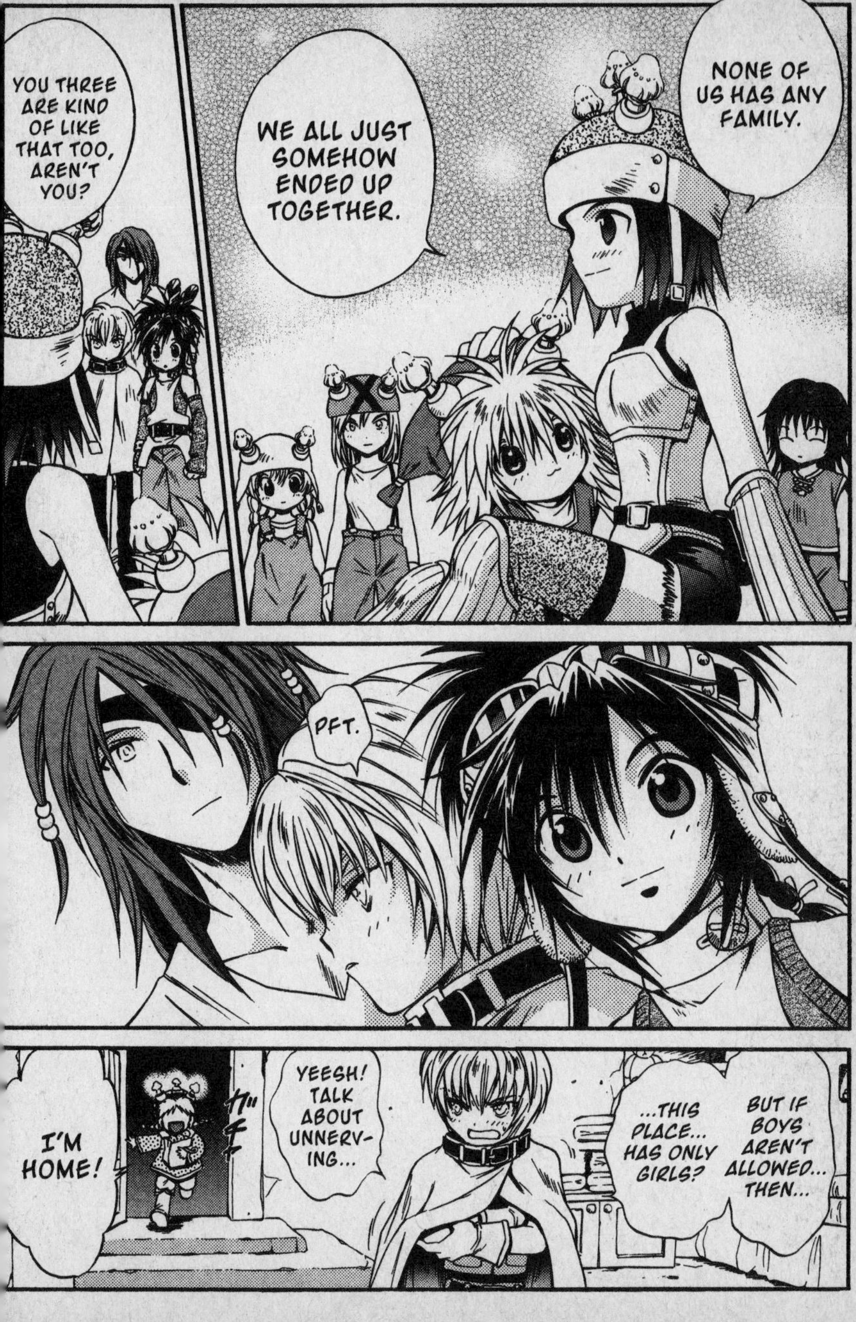
NONE OF US HAS ANY FAMILY.
WE ALL JUST SOMEHOW ENDED UP TOGETHER.
YOU THREE ARE KIND OF LIKE THAT TOO, AREN'T YOU?
PFT.
BUT IF BOYS AREN'T ALLOWED... THEN...
...THIS PLACE... HAS ONLY GIRLS?
YEESH! TALK ABOUT UNNERV-ING...
I'M HOME!

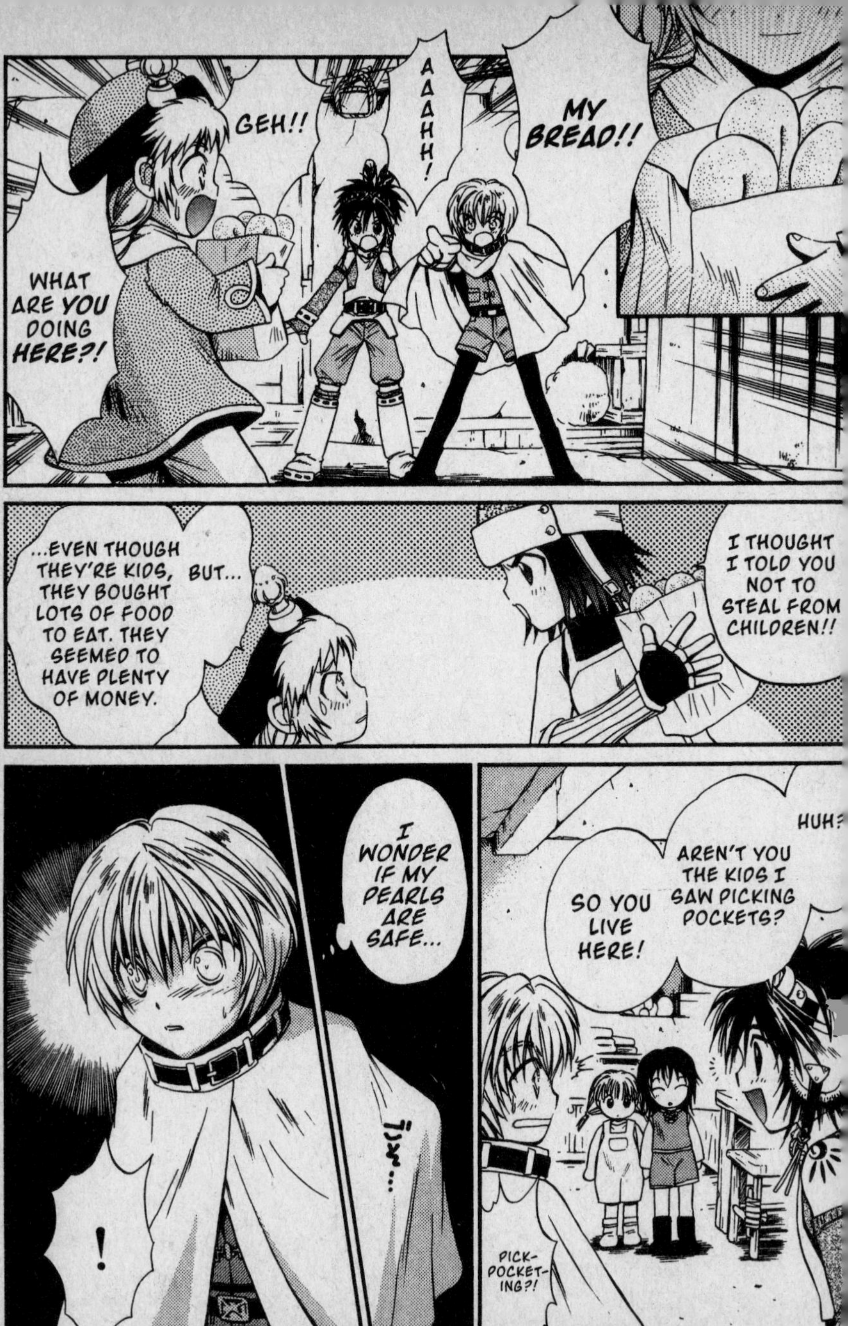
MY BREAD!!
AAAHH!
GEH!!
WHAT ARE YOU DOING HERE?!
I THOUGHT I TOLD YOU NOT TO STEAL FROM CHILDREN!!
BUT...
...EVEN THOUGH THEY'RE KIDS, THEY BOUGHT LOTS OF FOOD TO EAT. THEY SEEMED TO HAVE PLENTY OF MONEY.
HUH?
AREN'T YOU THE KIDS I SAW PICKING POCKETS?
SO YOU LIVE HERE!
PICK-POCKETING?!
I WONDER IF MY PEARLS ARE SAFE...
!

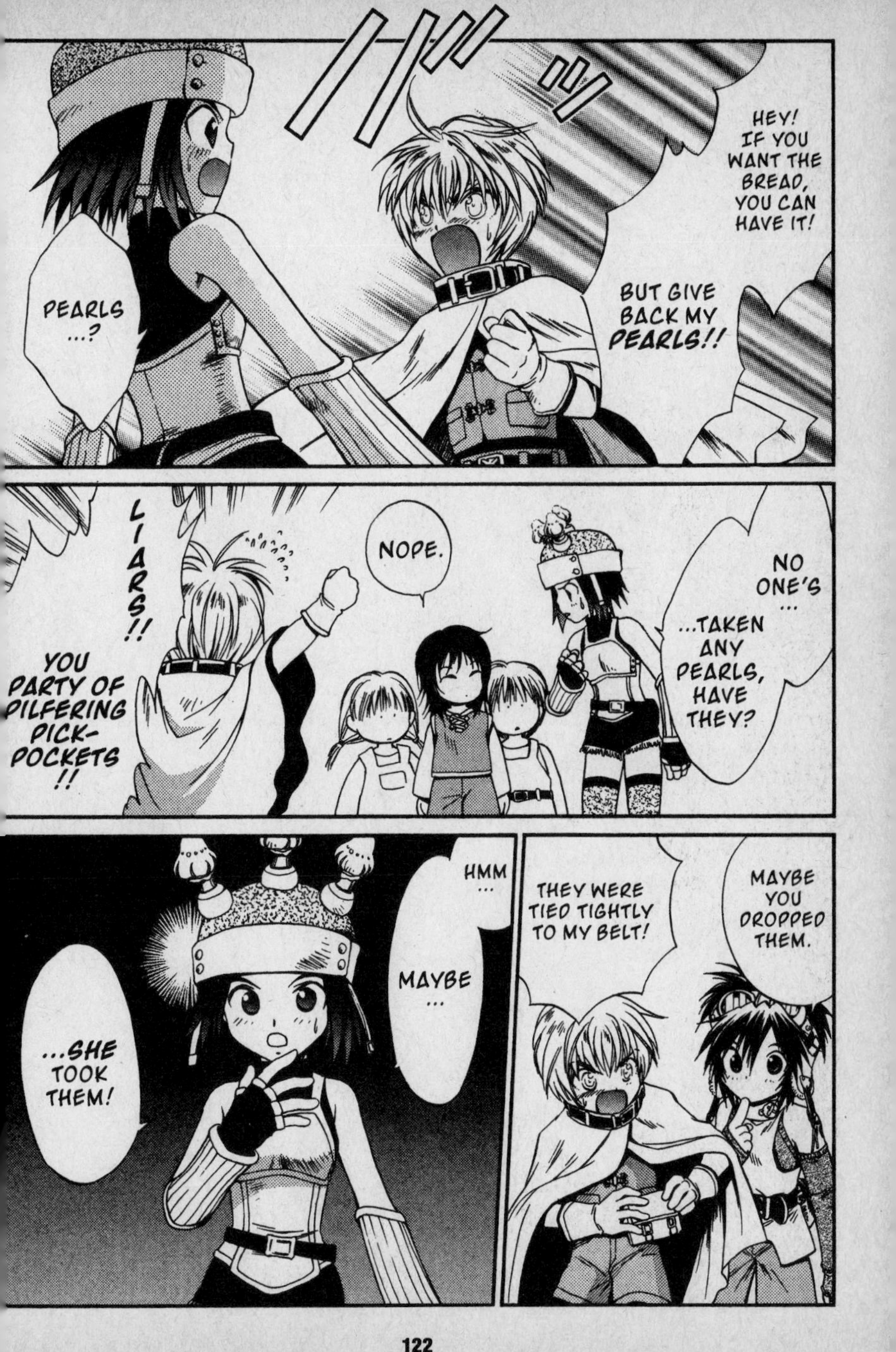
HEY! IF YOU WANT THE BREAD, YOU CAN HAVE IT!
BUT GIVE BACK MY PEARLS!!
PEARLS ...?
NO ONE'S ...
...TAKEN ANY PEARLS, HAVE THEY?
NOPE.
LIARS!!
YOU PARTY OF PILFERING PICK-POCKETS!!
MAYBE YOU DROPPED THEM.
THEY WERE TIED TIGHTLY TO MY BELT!
HMM ...
MAYBE ...
...SHE TOOK THEM!

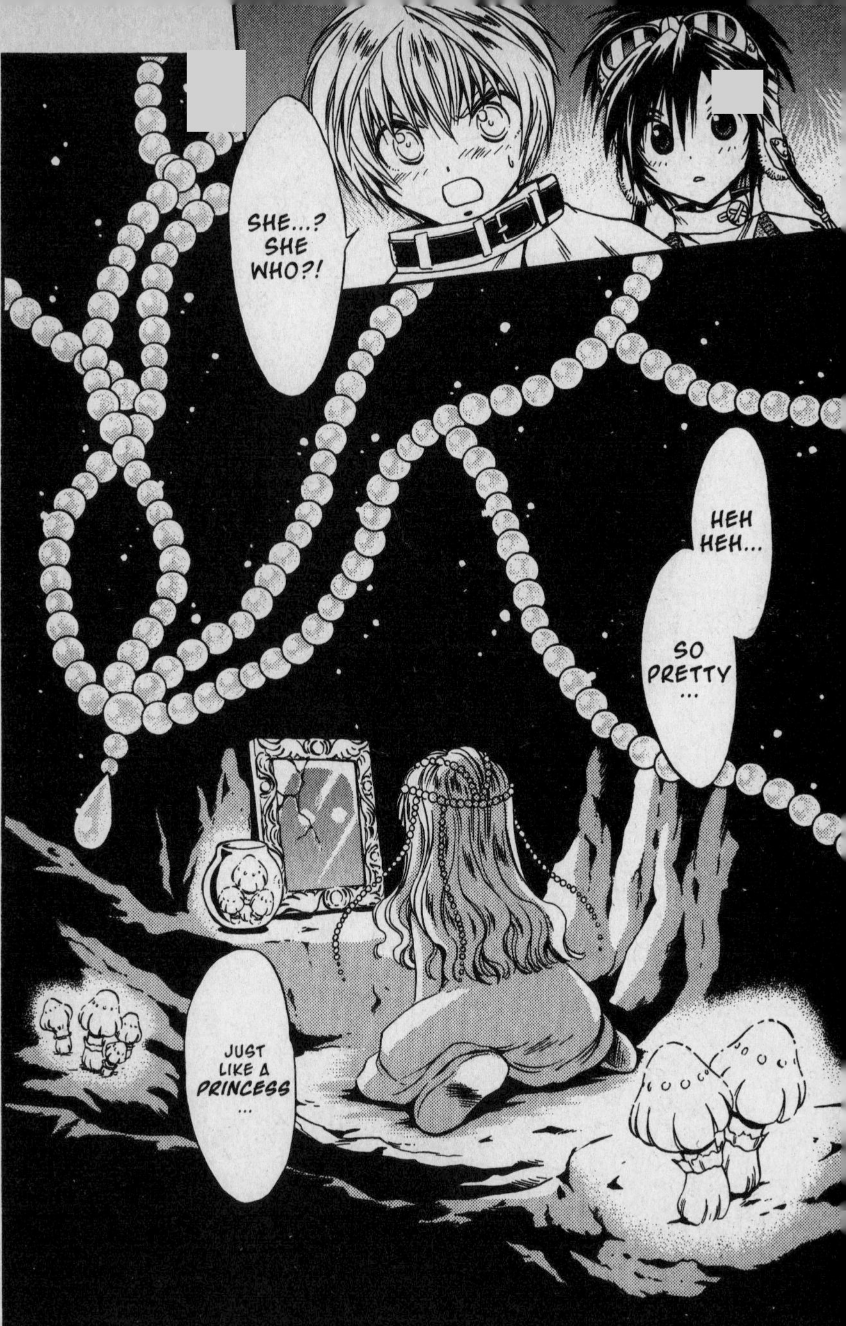
SHE...? SHE WHO?!
HEH HEH...
SO PRETTY ...
JUST LIKE A PRINCESS ...

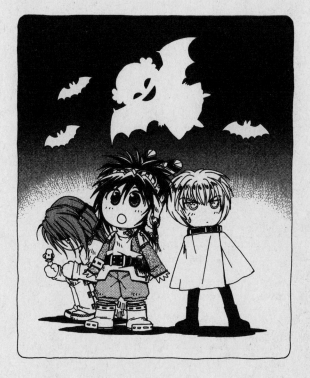

Mysterious bat ?

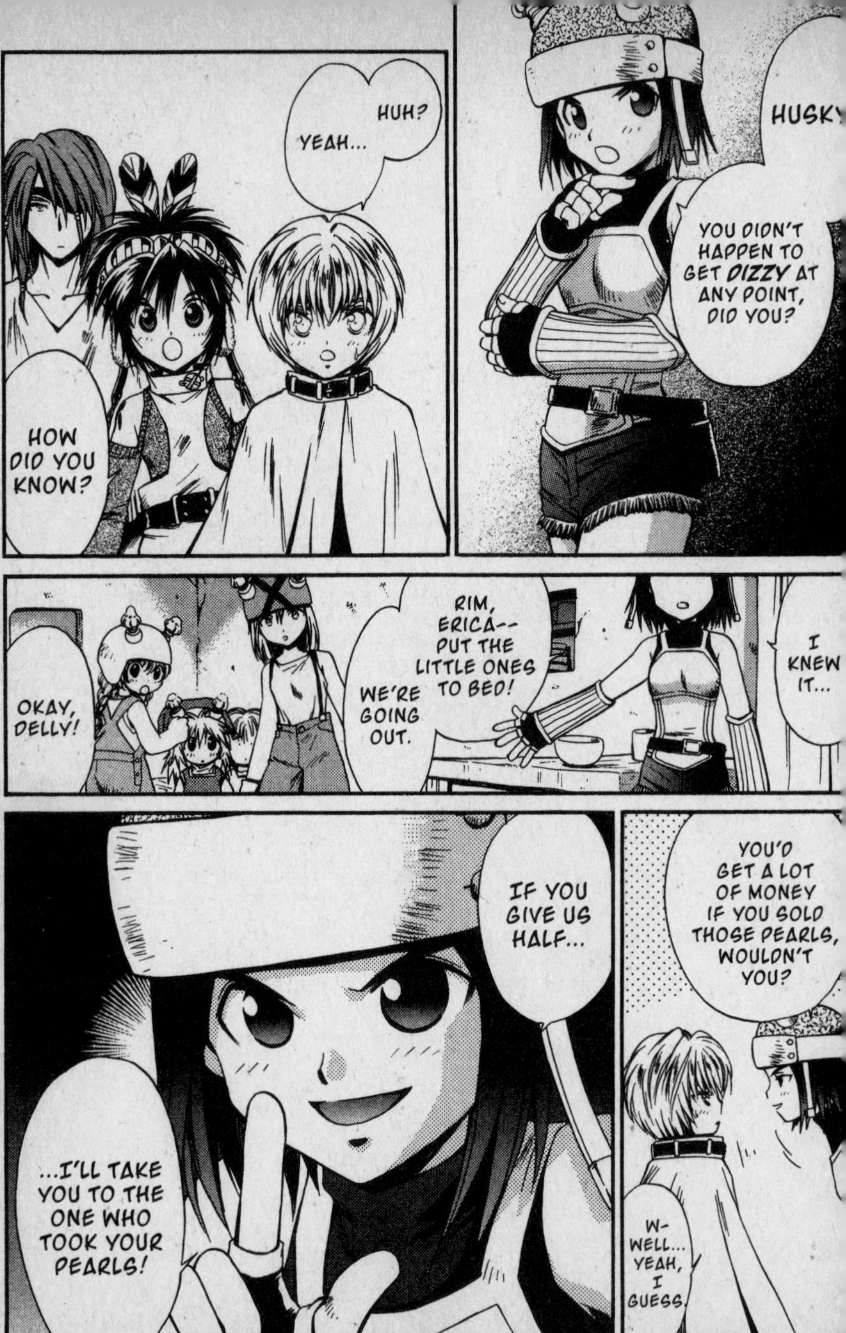
HUSKY
YOU DIDN'T HAPPEN TO GET *DIZZY* AT ANY POINT, DID YOU?
HUH? YEAH...
HOW DID YOU KNOW?
I KNEW IT...
RIM, ERICA-- PUT THE LITTLE ONES TO BED!
WE'RE GOING OUT.
OKAY, DELLY!
YOU'D GET A LOT OF MONEY IF YOU SOLD THOSE PEARLS, WOULDN'T YOU?
W- WELL... YEAH, I GUESS.
IF YOU GIVE US HALF...
...I'LL TAKE YOU TO THE ONE WHO TOOK YOUR PEARLS!

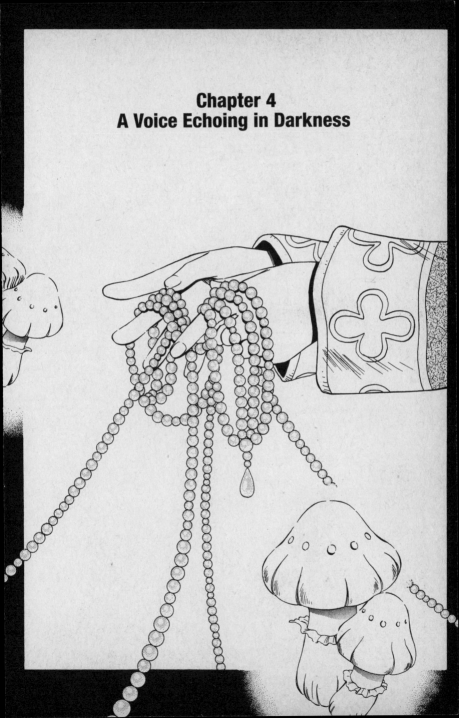

Chapter 4
A Voice Echoing in Darkness

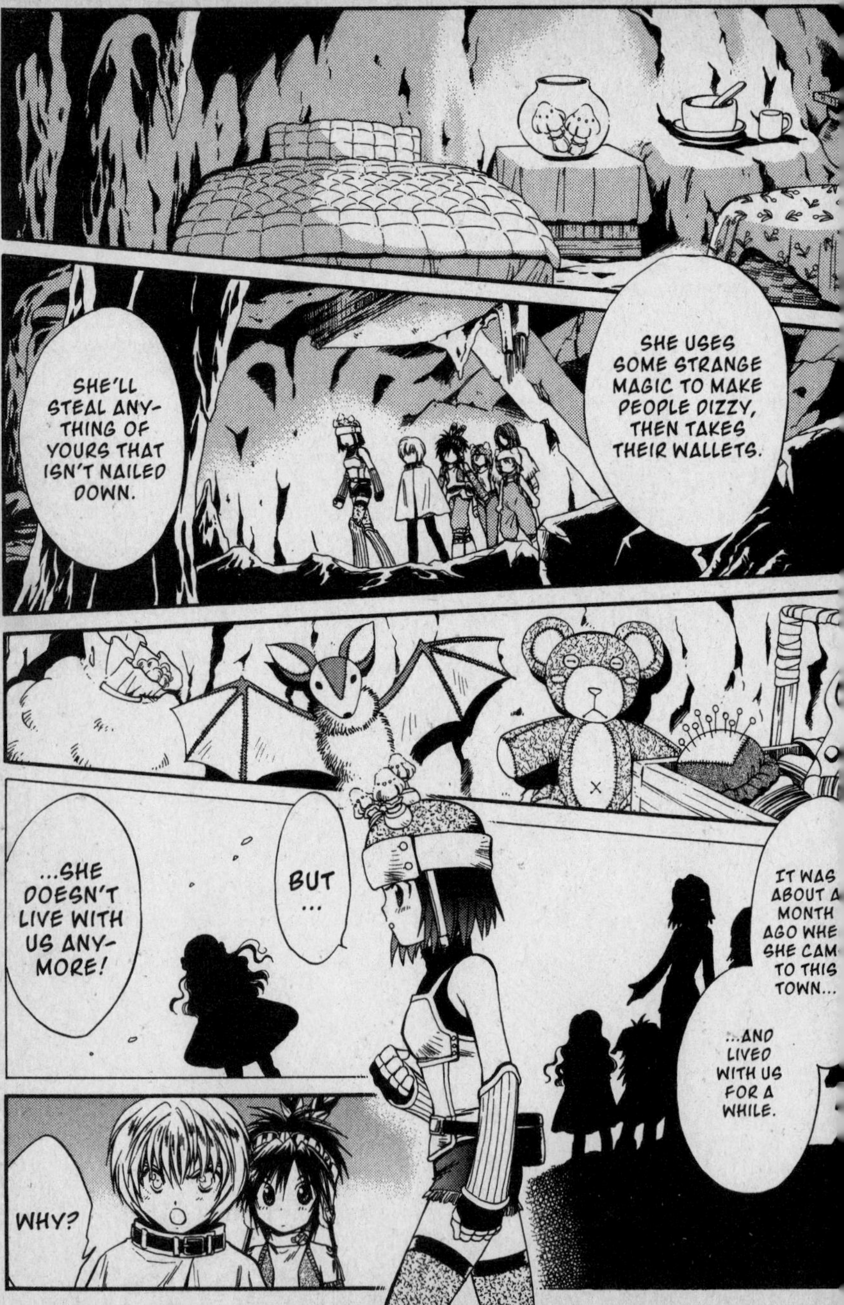

SHE USES SOME STRANGE MAGIC TO MAKE PEOPLE DIZZY, THEN TAKES THEIR WALLETS.
SHE'LL STEAL ANY-THING OF YOURS THAT ISN'T NAILED DOWN.
IT WAS ABOUT A MONTH AGO WHE SHE CAM TO THIS TOWN...
...AND LIVED WITH US FOR A WHILE.
BUT ...
...SHE DOESN'T LIVE WITH US ANY-MORE!
WHY?

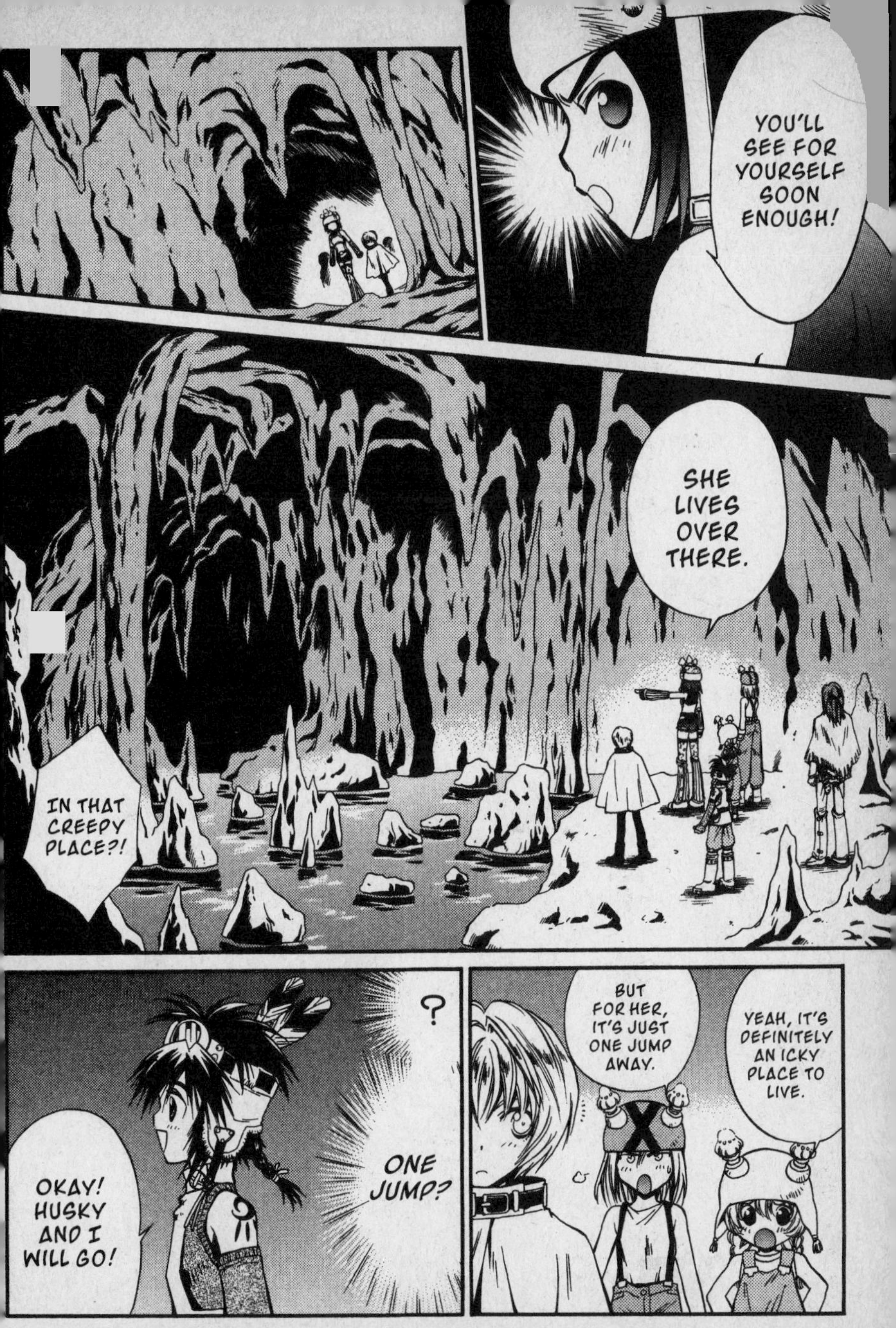
YOU'LL SEE FOR YOURSELF SOON ENOUGH!
SHE LIVES OVER THERE.
IN THAT CREEPY PLACE?!
YEAH, IT'S DEFINITELY AN ICKY PLACE TO LIVE.
BUT FOR HER, IT'S JUST ONE JUMP AWAY.
?
ONE JUMP?
OKAY! HUSKY AND I WILL GO!

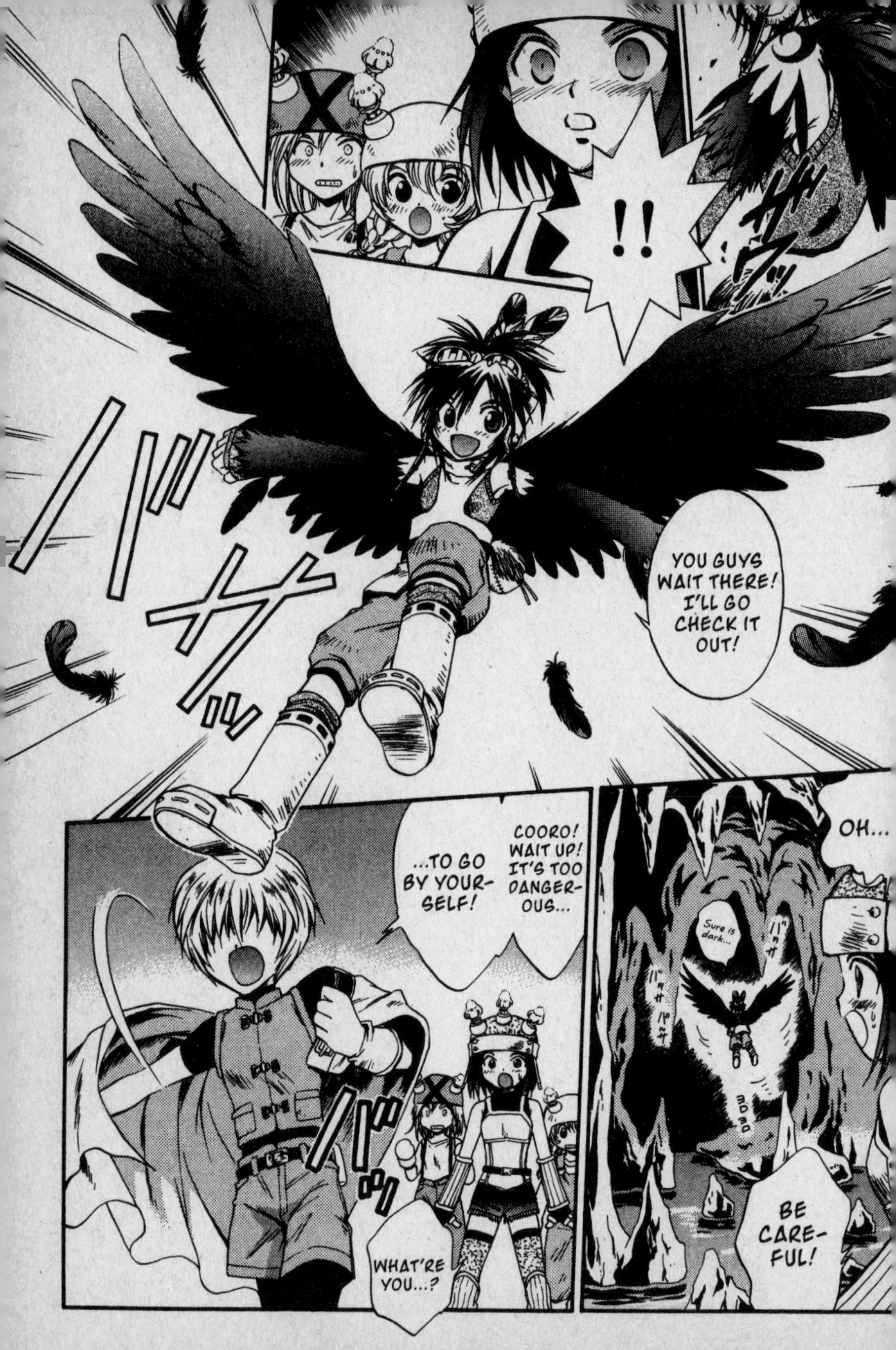
!!
YOU GUYS WAIT THERE! I'LL GO CHECK IT OUT!
OH...
Sure is dark...
BE CARE-FUL!
COORO! WAIT UP! IT'S TOO DANGER-OUS...
...TO GO BY YOUR-SELF!
WHAT'RE YOU...?

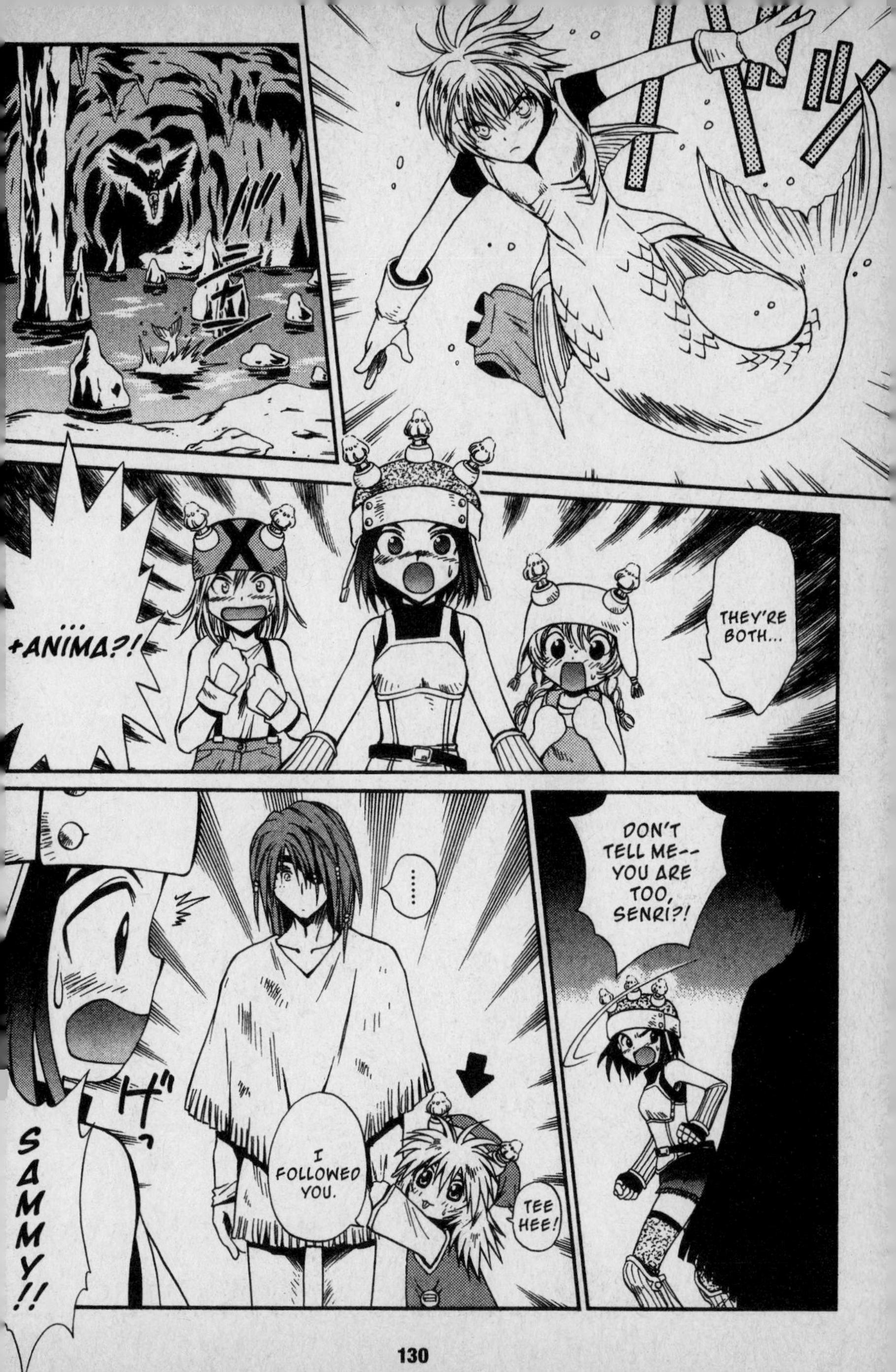
THEY'RE BOTH...
...+ANIMA?!
DON'T TELL ME-- YOU ARE TOO, SENRI?!
......
I FOLLOWED YOU.
TEE HEE!
SAMMY!!

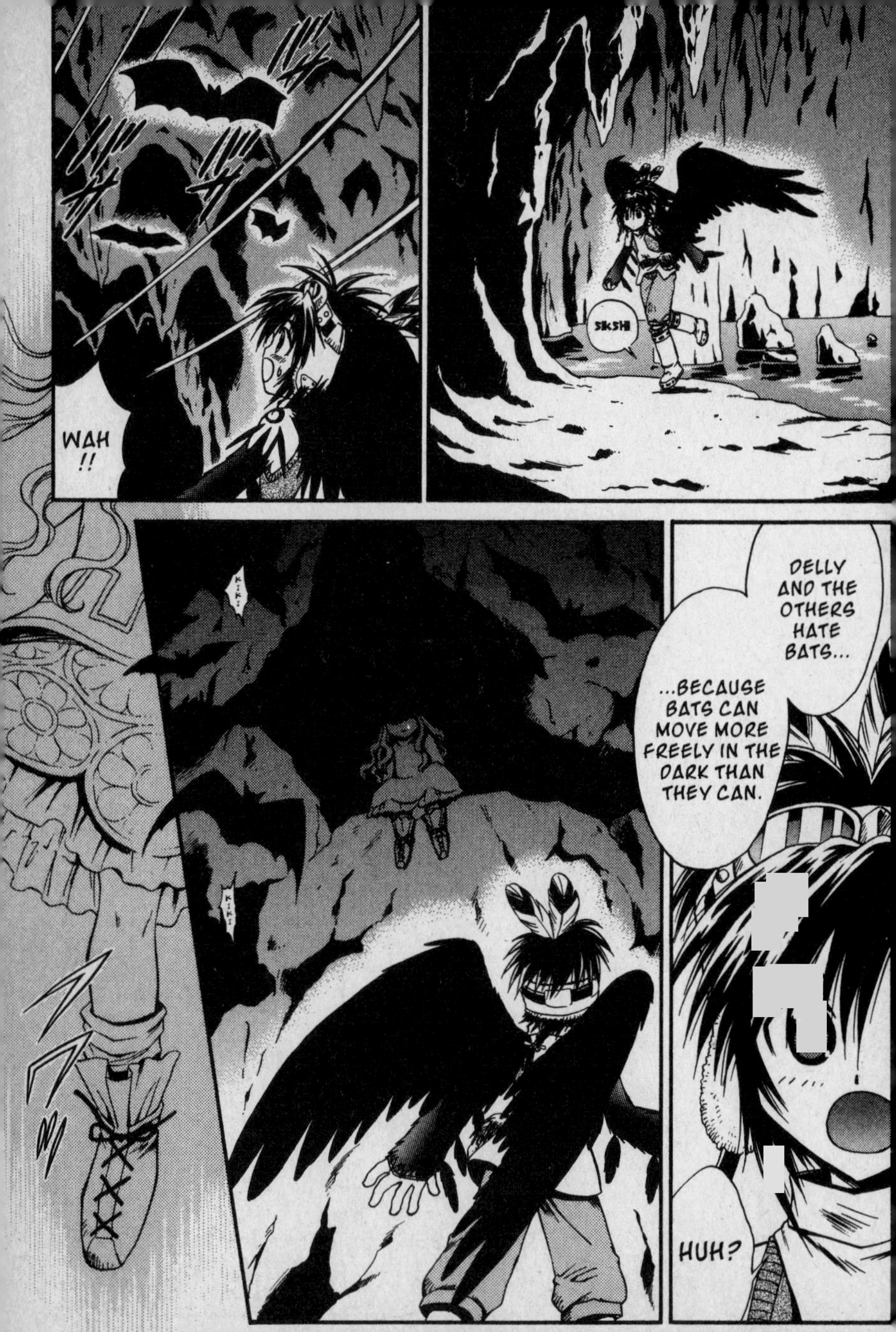
SKSH
WAH!!
DELLY AND THE OTHERS HATE BATS...
...BECAUSE BATS CAN MOVE MORE FREELY IN THE DARK THAN THEY CAN.
HUH?
KIKI
KIKI

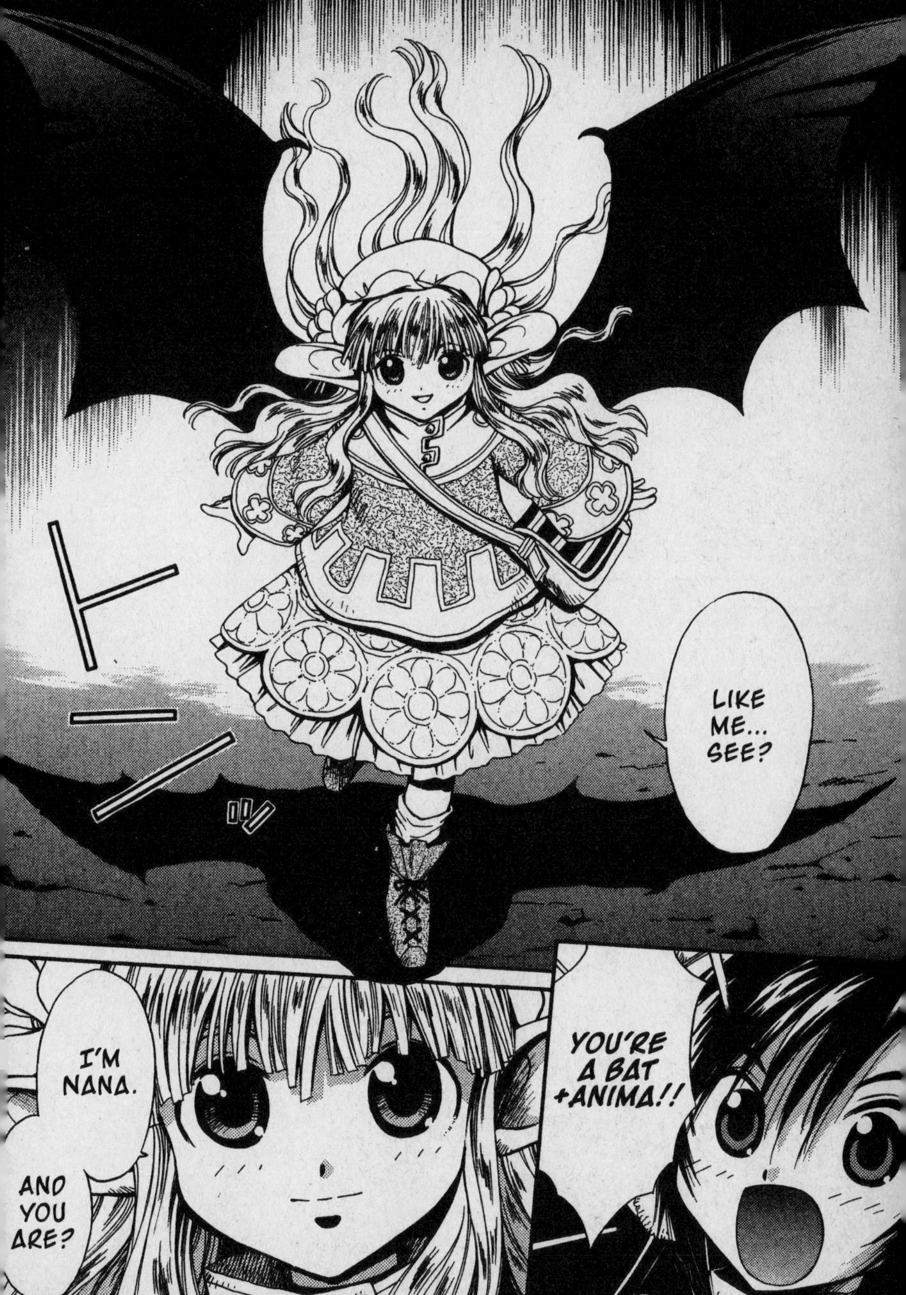
LIKE ME... SEE?
YOU'RE A BAT +ANIMA!!
I'M NANA.
AND YOU ARE?

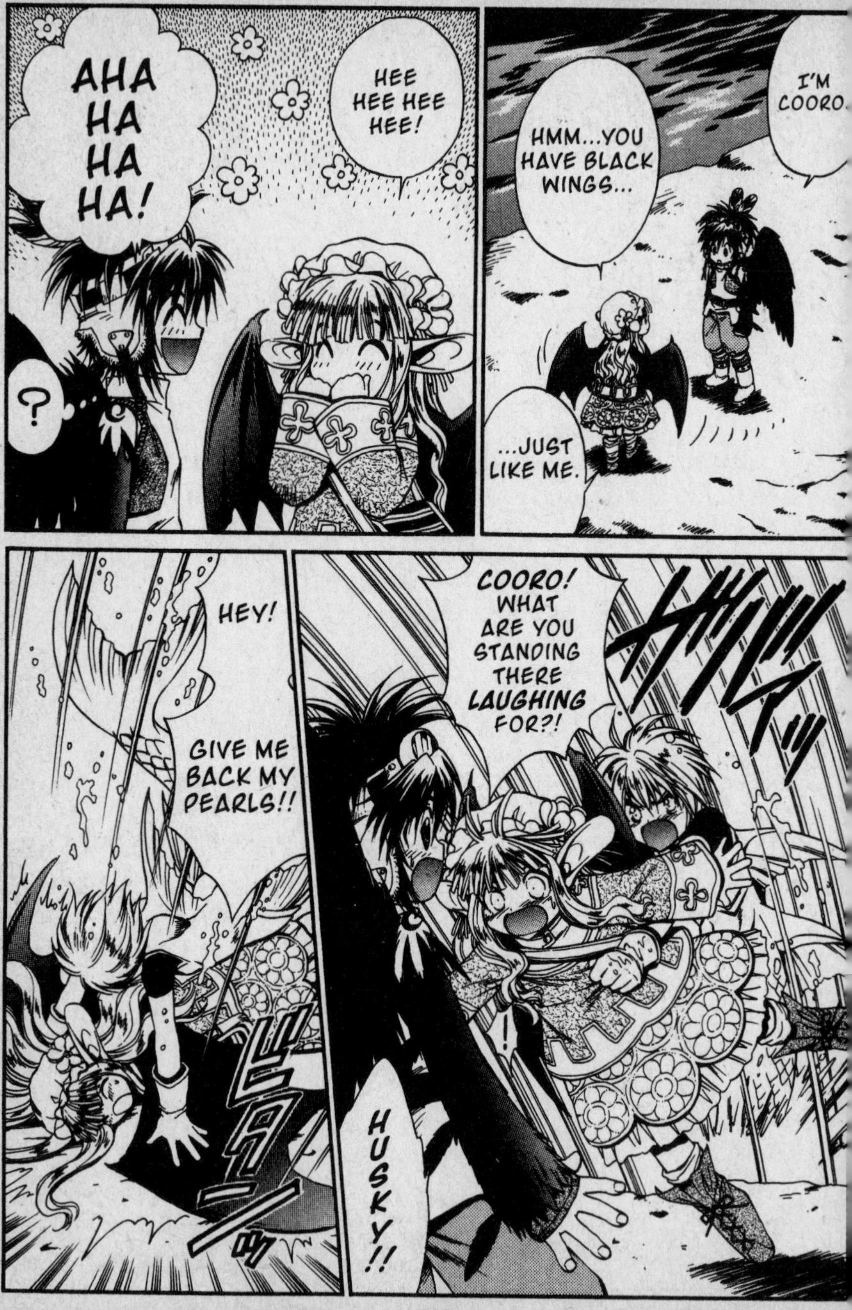
I'M COORO.
HMM...YOU HAVE BLACK WINGS...
...JUST LIKE ME.
HEE HEE HEE HEE!
AHA HA HA HA!
?
COORO! WHAT ARE YOU STANDING THERE LAUGHING FOR?!
!
HUSKY!!
HEY!
GIVE ME BACK MY PEARLS!!

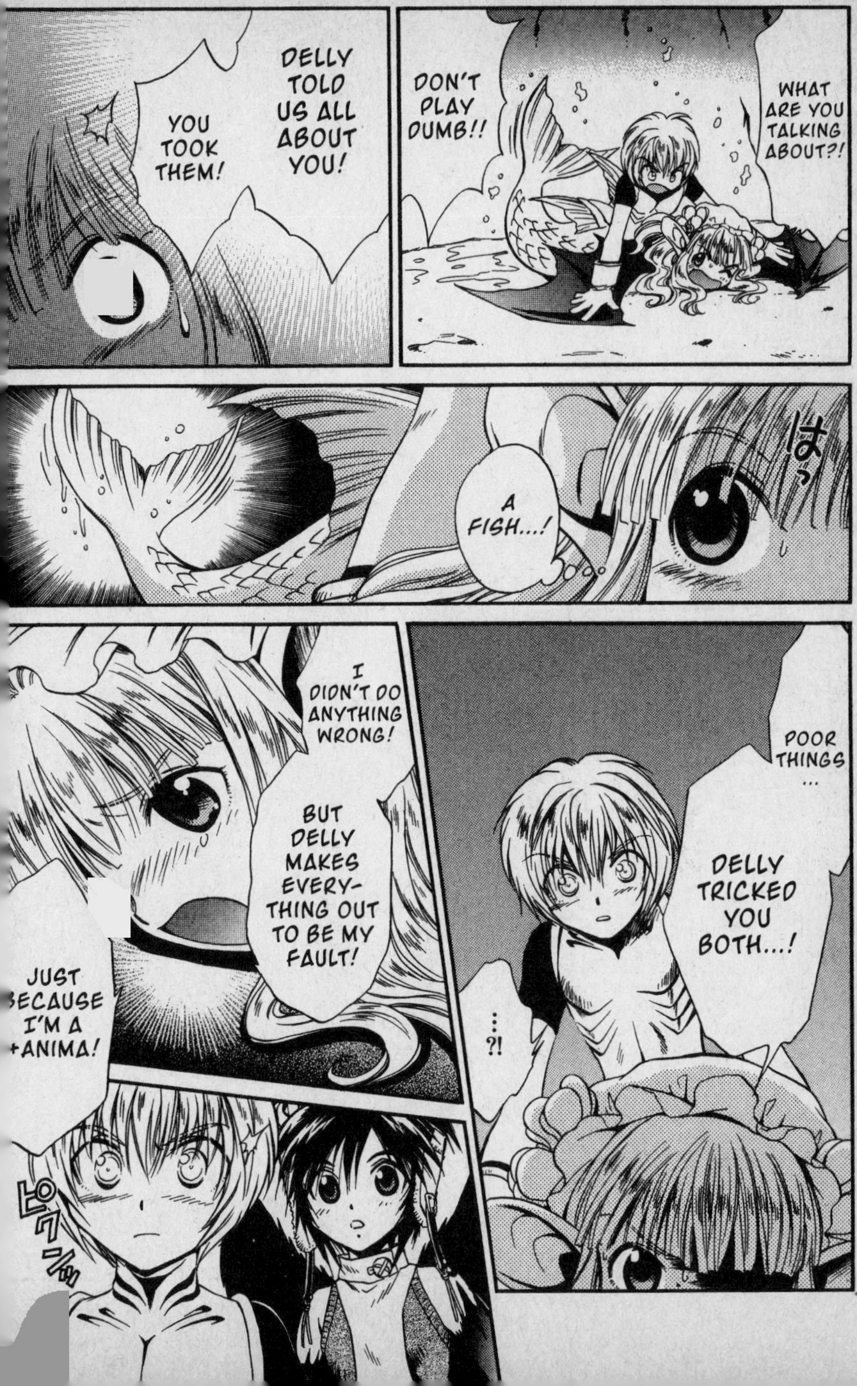
WHAT ARE YOU TALKING ABOUT?!
DON'T PLAY DUMB!!
DELLY TOLD US ALL ABOUT YOU!
YOU TOOK THEM!
は
A FISH...!
POOR THINGS ...
DELLY TRICKED YOU BOTH...!
...?!
I DIDN'T DO ANYTHING WRONG!
BUT DELLY MAKES EVERY-THING OUT TO BE MY FAULT!
JUST BECAUSE I'M A +ANIMA!

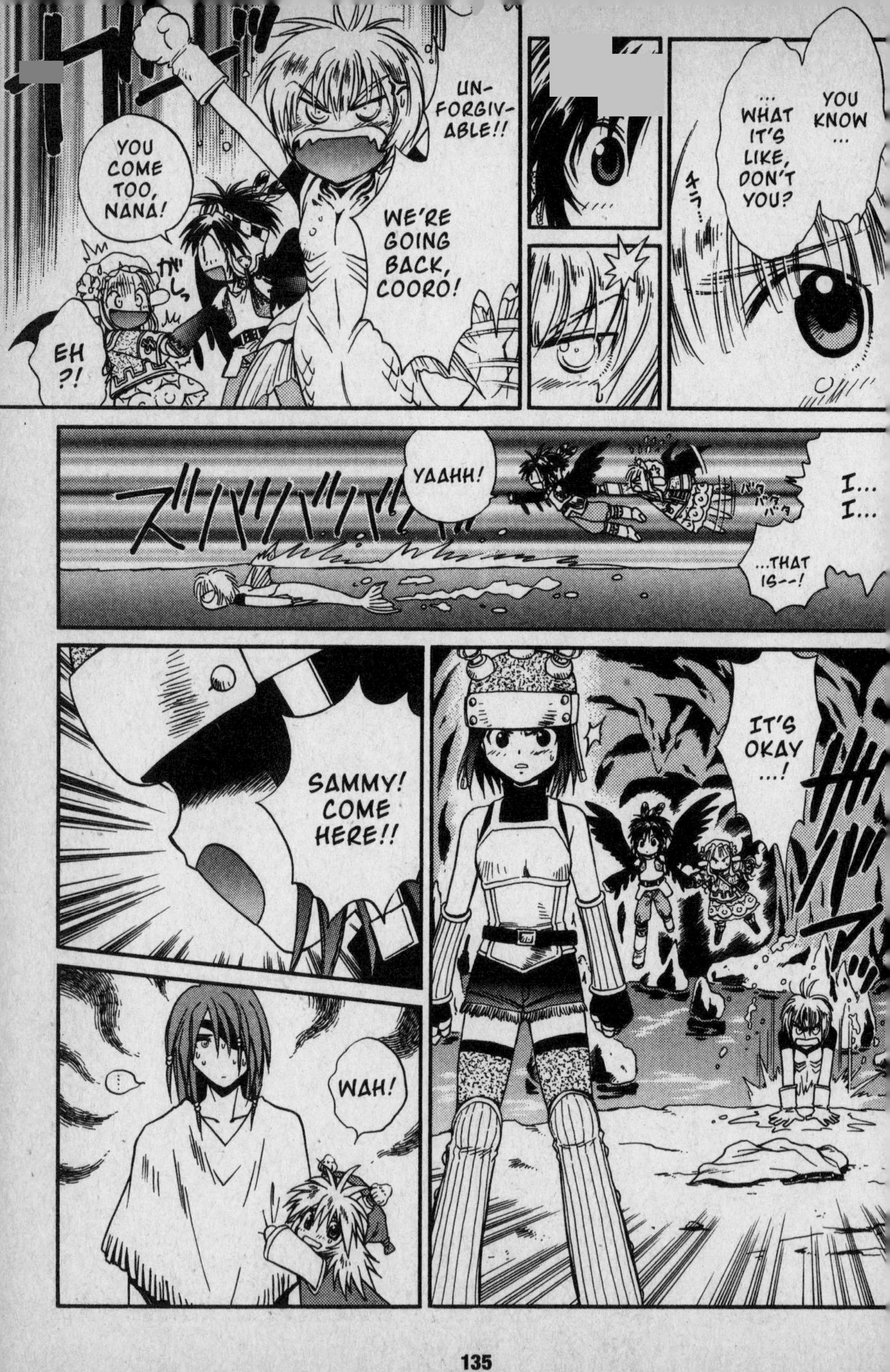
YOU KNOW ...
... WHAT IT'S LIKE, DON'T YOU?
UN-FORGIVABLE!!
WE'RE GOING BACK, COORO!
YOU COME TOO, NANA!
EH ?!
I... I...
...THAT IS--!
YAAHH!
IT'S OKAY ...!
SAMMY! COME HERE!!
WAH!
...

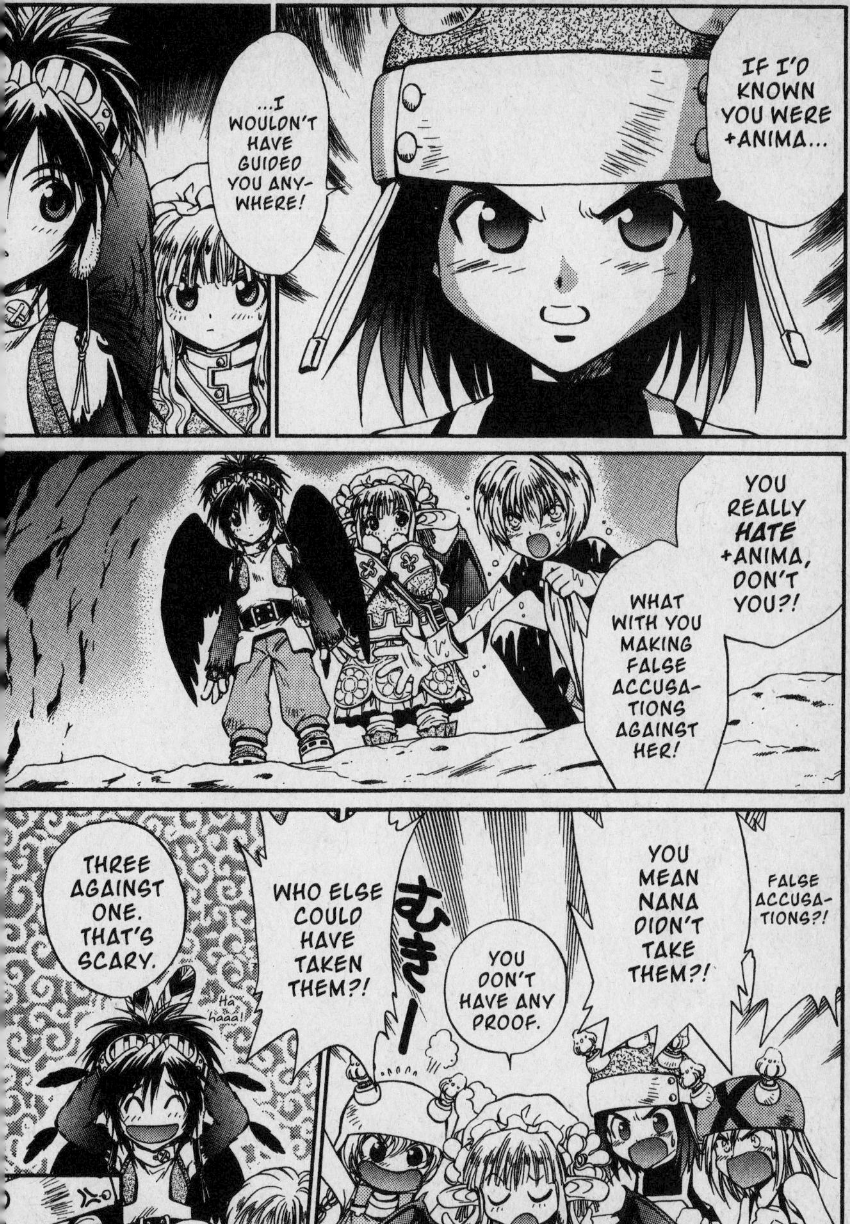
IF I'D KNOWN YOU WERE +ANIMA...
...I WOULDN'T HAVE GUIDED YOU ANYWHERE!
YOU REALLY **HATE** +ANIMA, DON'T YOU?!
WHAT WITH YOU MAKING FALSE ACCUSATIONS AGAINST HER!
FALSE ACCUSATIONS?!
YOU MEAN NANA DIDN'T TAKE THEM?!
YOU DON'T HAVE ANY PROOF.
むきー
WHO ELSE COULD HAVE TAKEN THEM?!
THREE AGAINST ONE. THAT'S SCARY.
Ha haaa!
OOH! IDIOT!

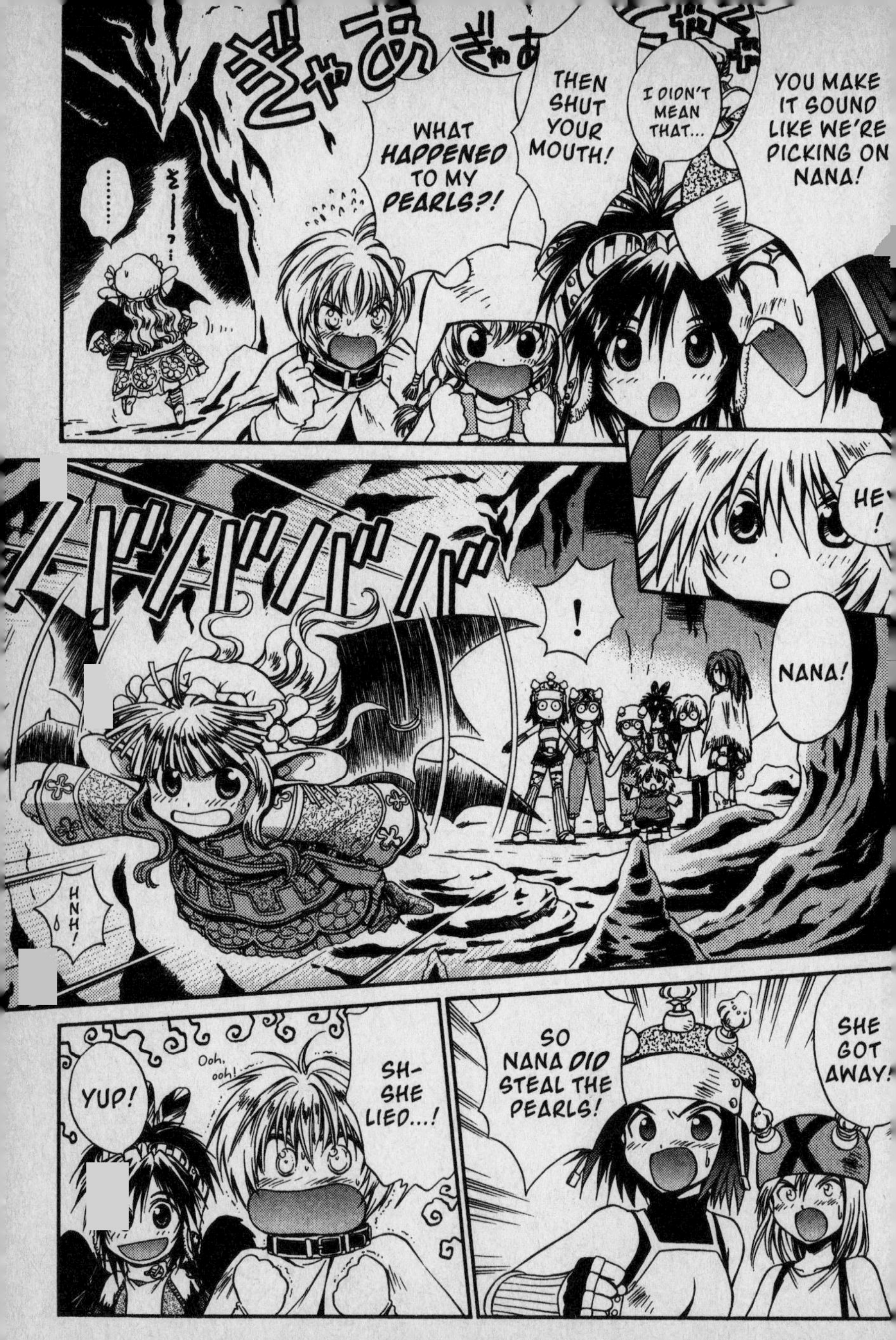
YOU MAKE IT SOUND LIKE WE'RE PICKING ON NANA!
I DIDN'T MEAN THAT...
THEN SHUT YOUR MOUTH!
WHAT HAPPENED TO MY PEARLS?!
......
HEY!
NANA!
!
HNH!
SHE GOT AWAY!
SO NANA DID STEAL THE PEARLS!
SH-SHE LIED...!
Ooh, ooh!
YUP!

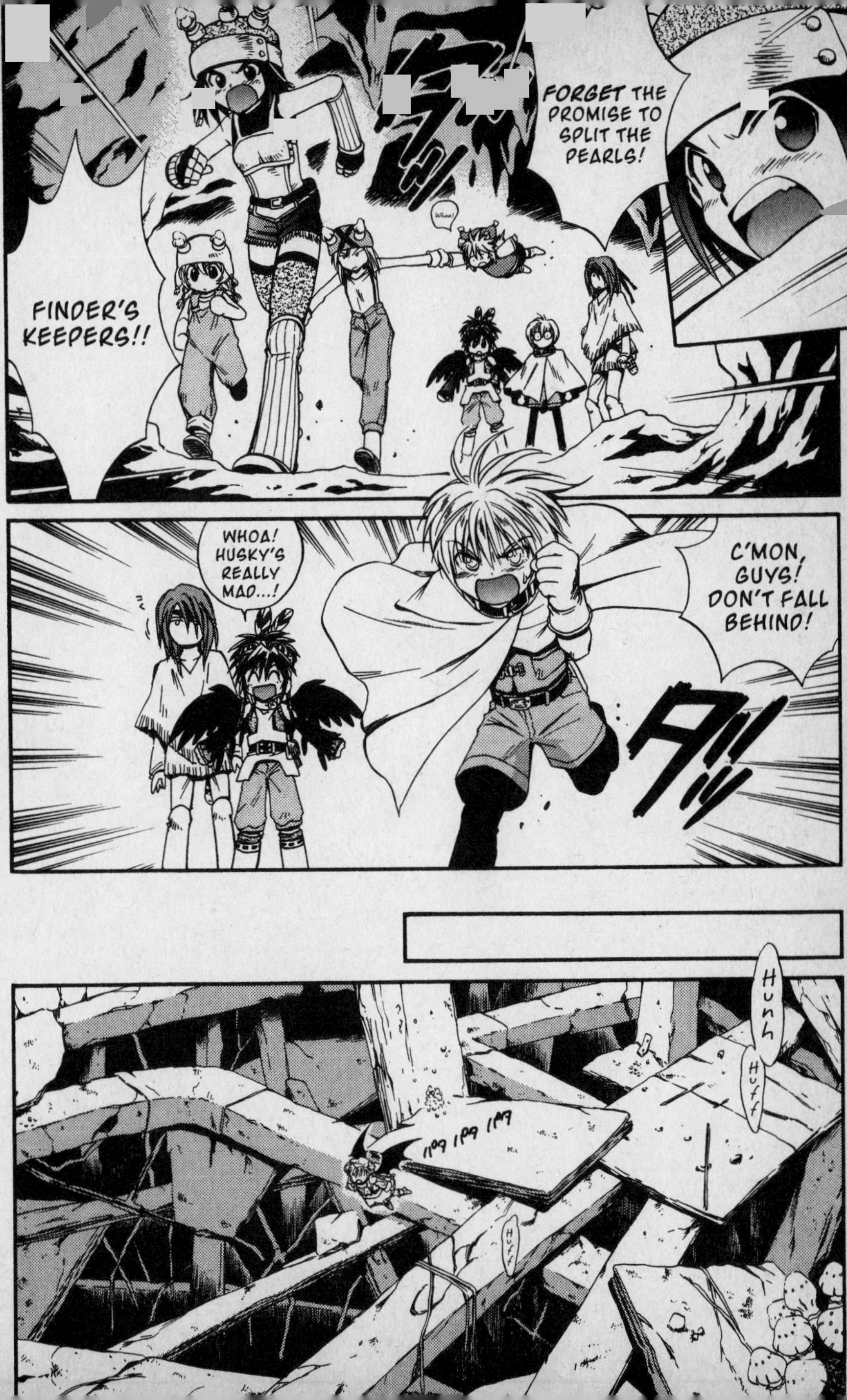
FORGET THE PROMISE TO SPLIT THE PEARLS!
Whoa!
FINDER'S KEEPERS!!
C'MON, GUYS! DON'T FALL BEHIND!
WHOA! HUSKY'S REALLY MAD...!
Hunh
Huff
Huff

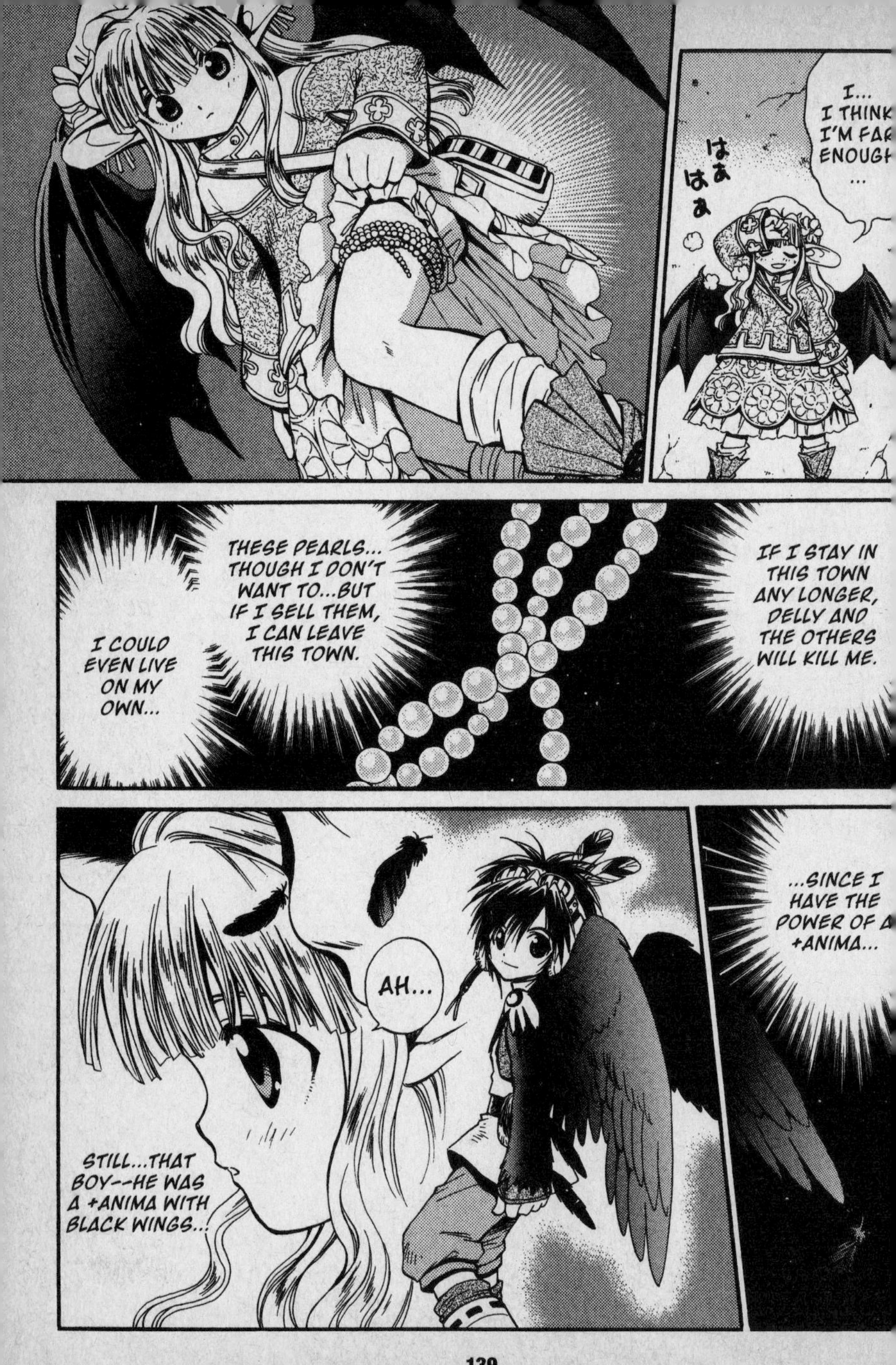
I... I THINK I'M FAR ENOUGH...
はぁ はぁ
IF I STAY IN THIS TOWN ANY LONGER, DELLY AND THE OTHERS WILL KILL ME.
THESE PEARLS... THOUGH I DON'T WANT TO...BUT IF I SELL THEM, I CAN LEAVE THIS TOWN.
I COULD EVEN LIVE ON MY OWN...
...SINCE I HAVE THE POWER OF A +ANIMA...
AH...
STILL...THAT BOY--HE WAS A +ANIMA WITH BLACK WINGS...

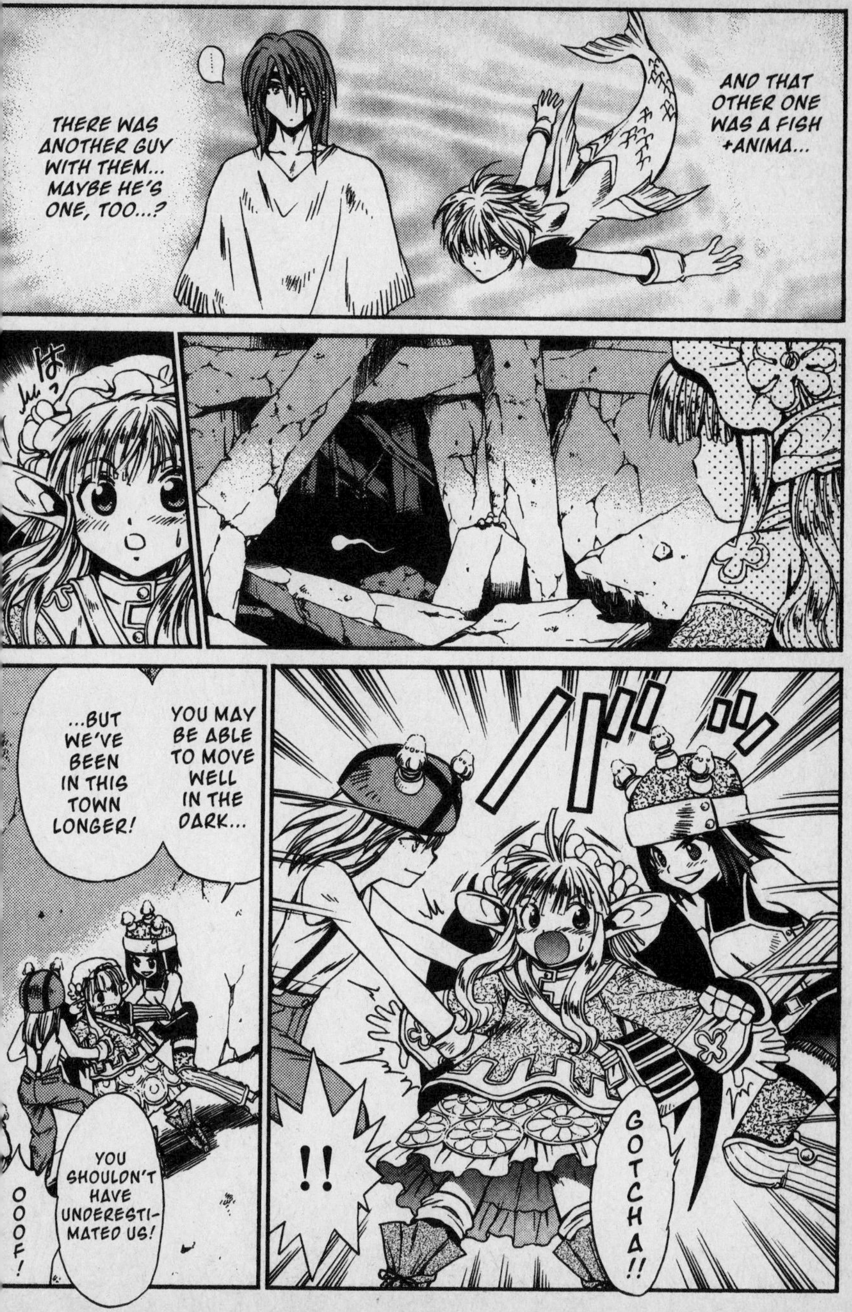

AND THAT OTHER ONE WAS A FISH +ANIMA...
...
THERE WAS ANOTHER GUY WITH THEM... MAYBE HE'S ONE, TOO...?
はっ
GOTCHA!!
!!
YOU MAY BE ABLE TO MOVE WELL IN THE DARK...
...BUT WE'VE BEEN IN THIS TOWN LONGER!
YOU SHOULDN'T HAVE UNDERESTI-MATED US!
OOOF!

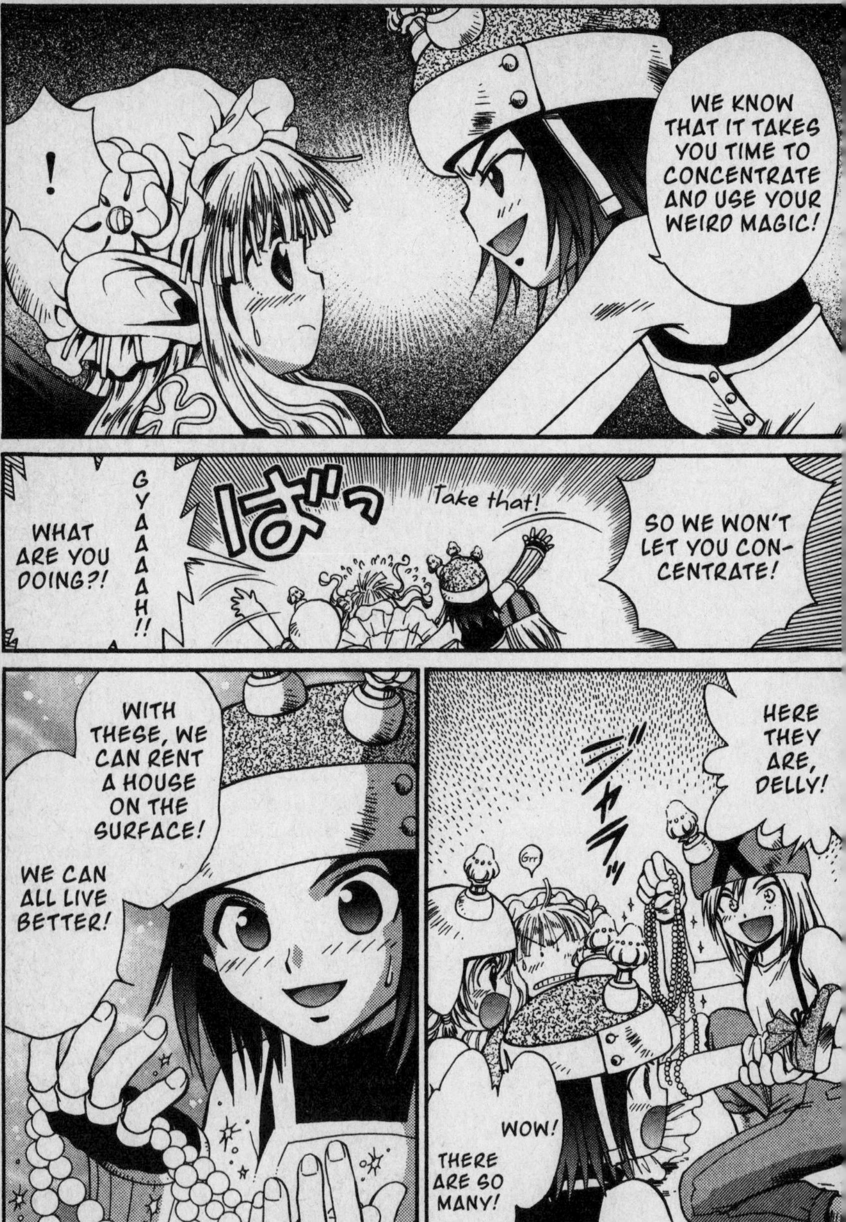
WE KNOW THAT IT TAKES YOU TIME TO CONCENTRATE AND USE YOUR WEIRD MAGIC!
!
SO WE WON'T LET YOU CON-CENTRATE!
Take that!
ばっ
GYAAAAAH!!
WHAT ARE YOU DOING?!
HERE THEY ARE, DELLY!
Grr!
WOW!
THERE ARE SO MANY!
WITH THESE, WE CAN RENT A HOUSE ON THE SURFACE!
WE CAN ALL LIVE BETTER!

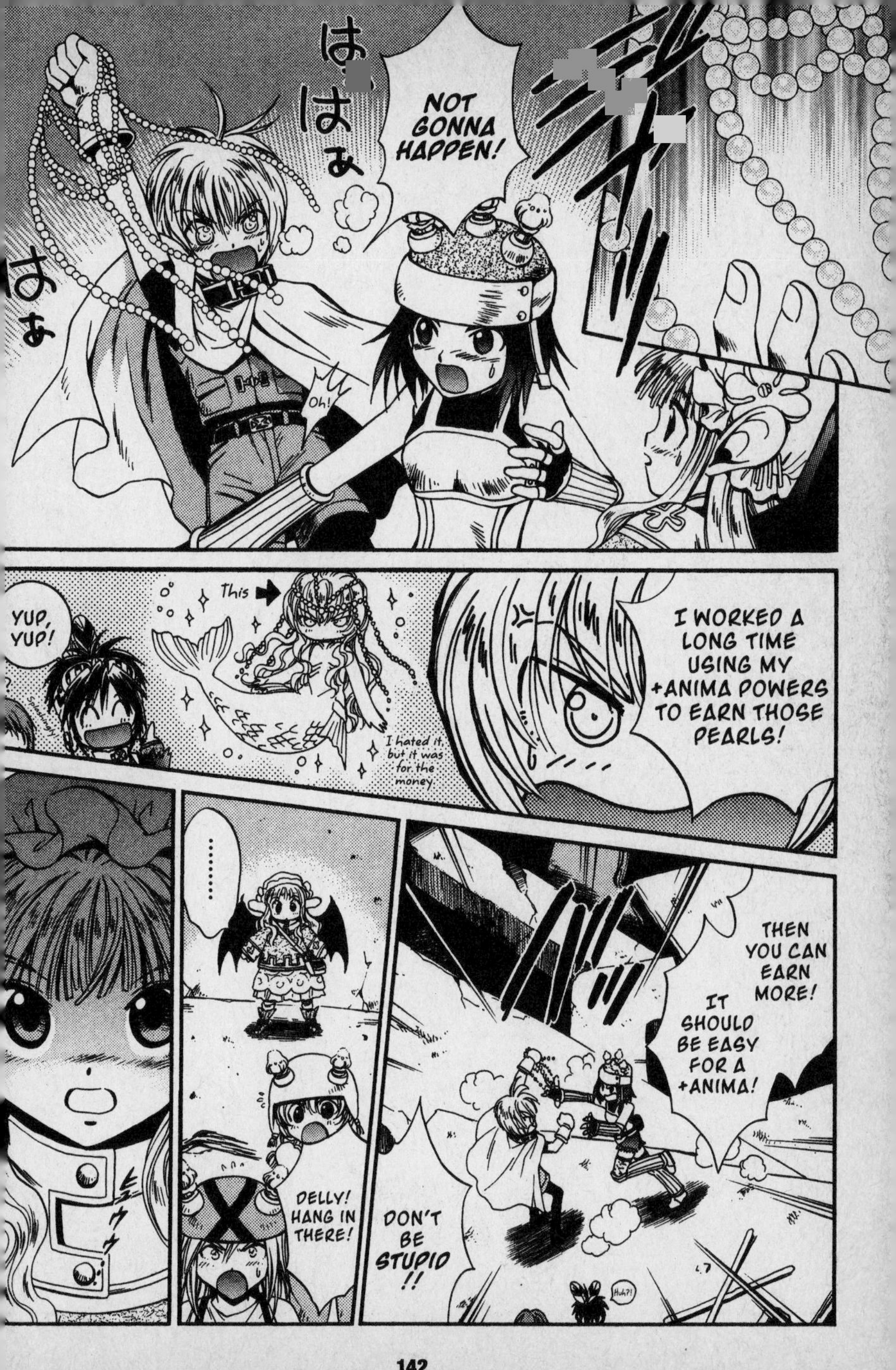
NOT GONNA HAPPEN!
はぁ はぁ
Oh!
I WORKED A LONG TIME USING MY +ANIMA POWERS TO EARN THOSE PEARLS!
This
I hated it, but it was for the money.
YUP, YUP!
THEN YOU CAN EARN MORE!
IT SHOULD BE EASY FOR A +ANIMA!
Huh?!
DON'T BE STUPID!!
DELLY! HANG IN THERE!
......

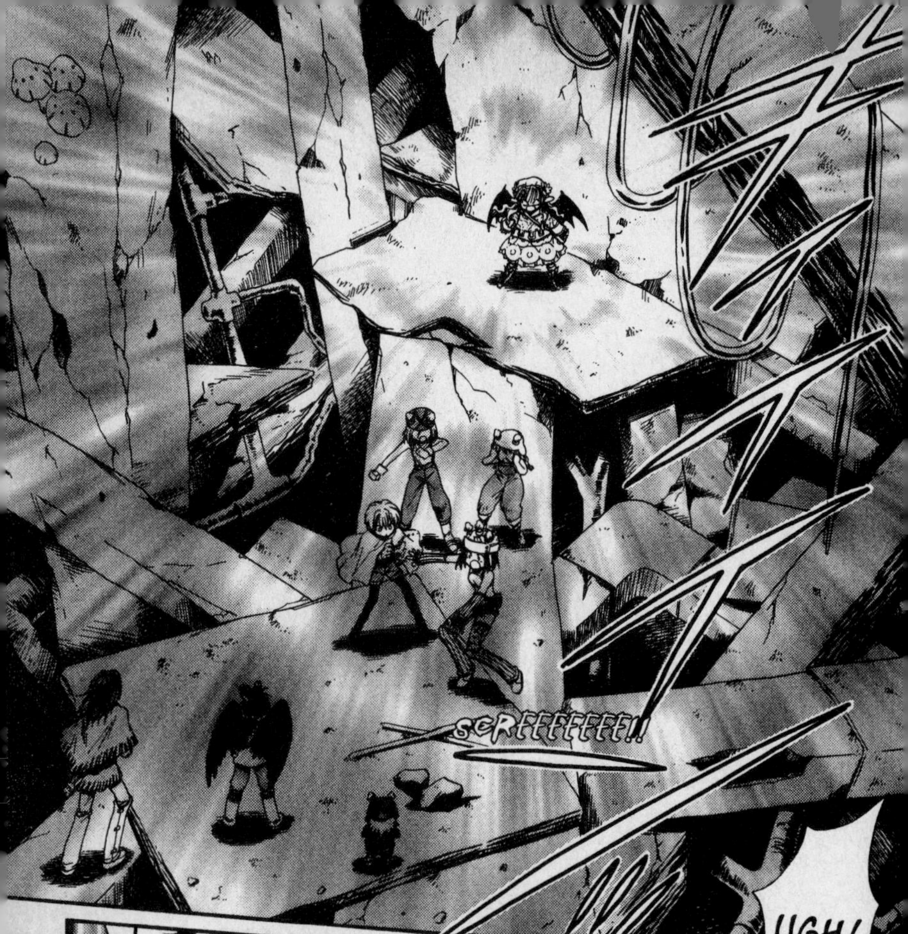
SCREEEEEEEE!!
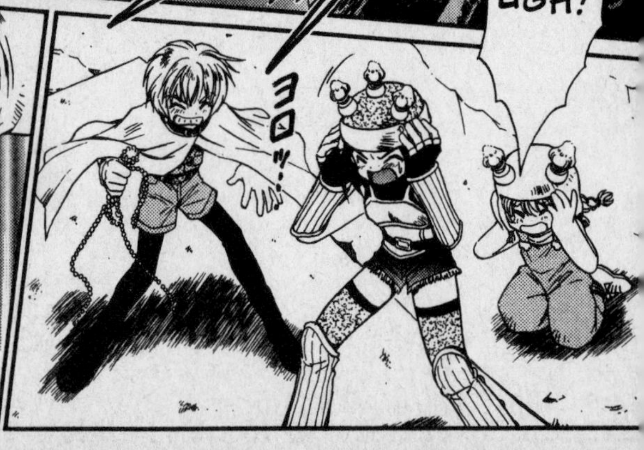
UGH!
ヨロッ!
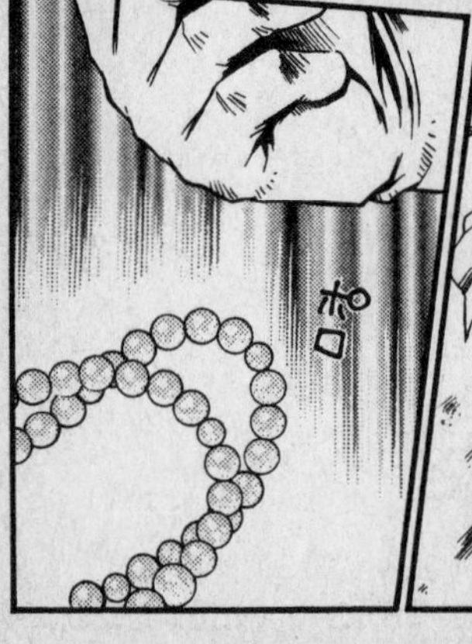
ポロ

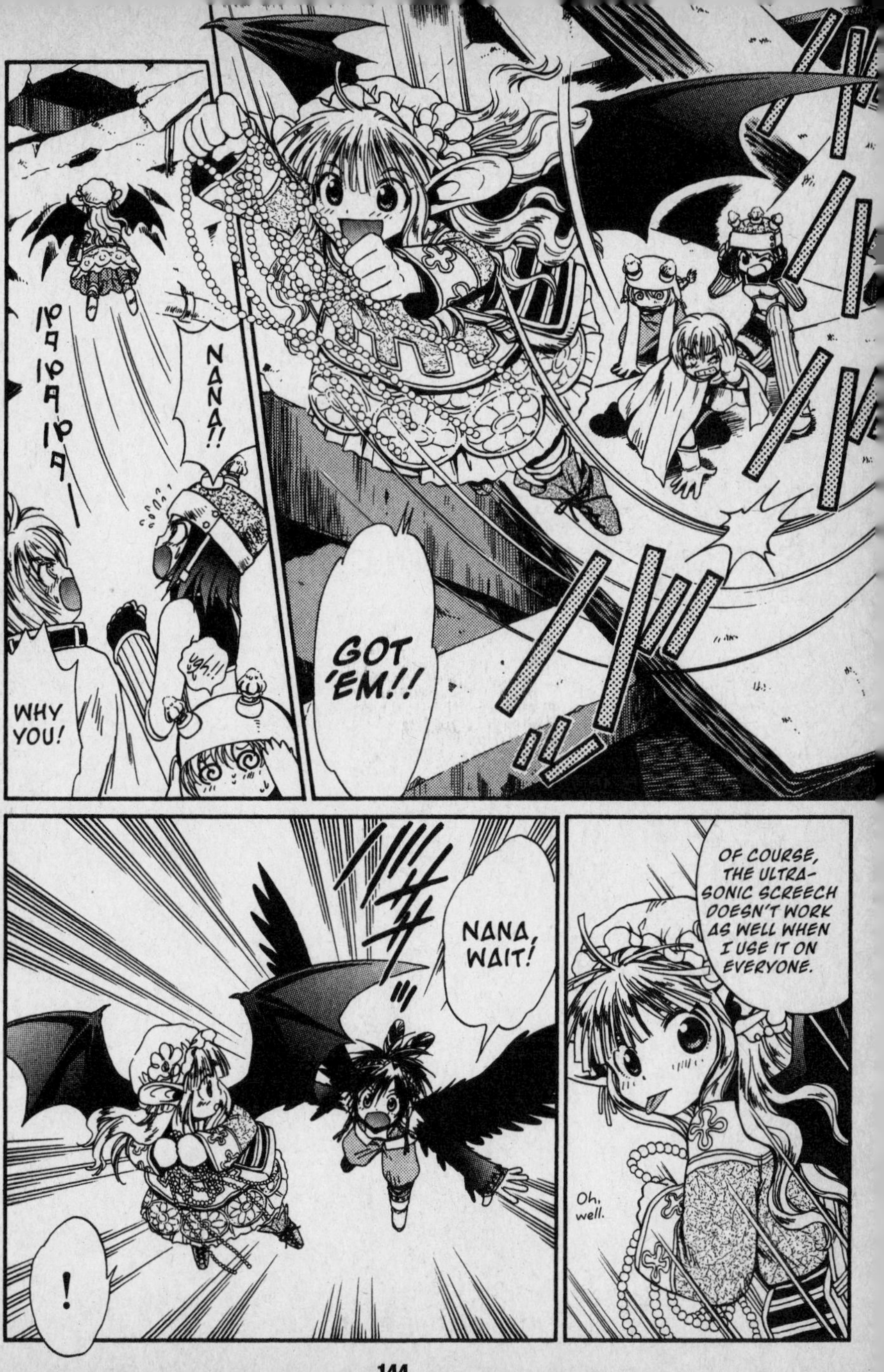
GOT 'EM!!
NANA!!
パタパタパタパタ—
ugh!!
WHY YOU!
OF COURSE, THE ULTRA-SONIC SCREECH DOESN'T WORK AS WELL WHEN I USE IT ON EVERYONE.
Oh, well.
NANA, WAIT!
!

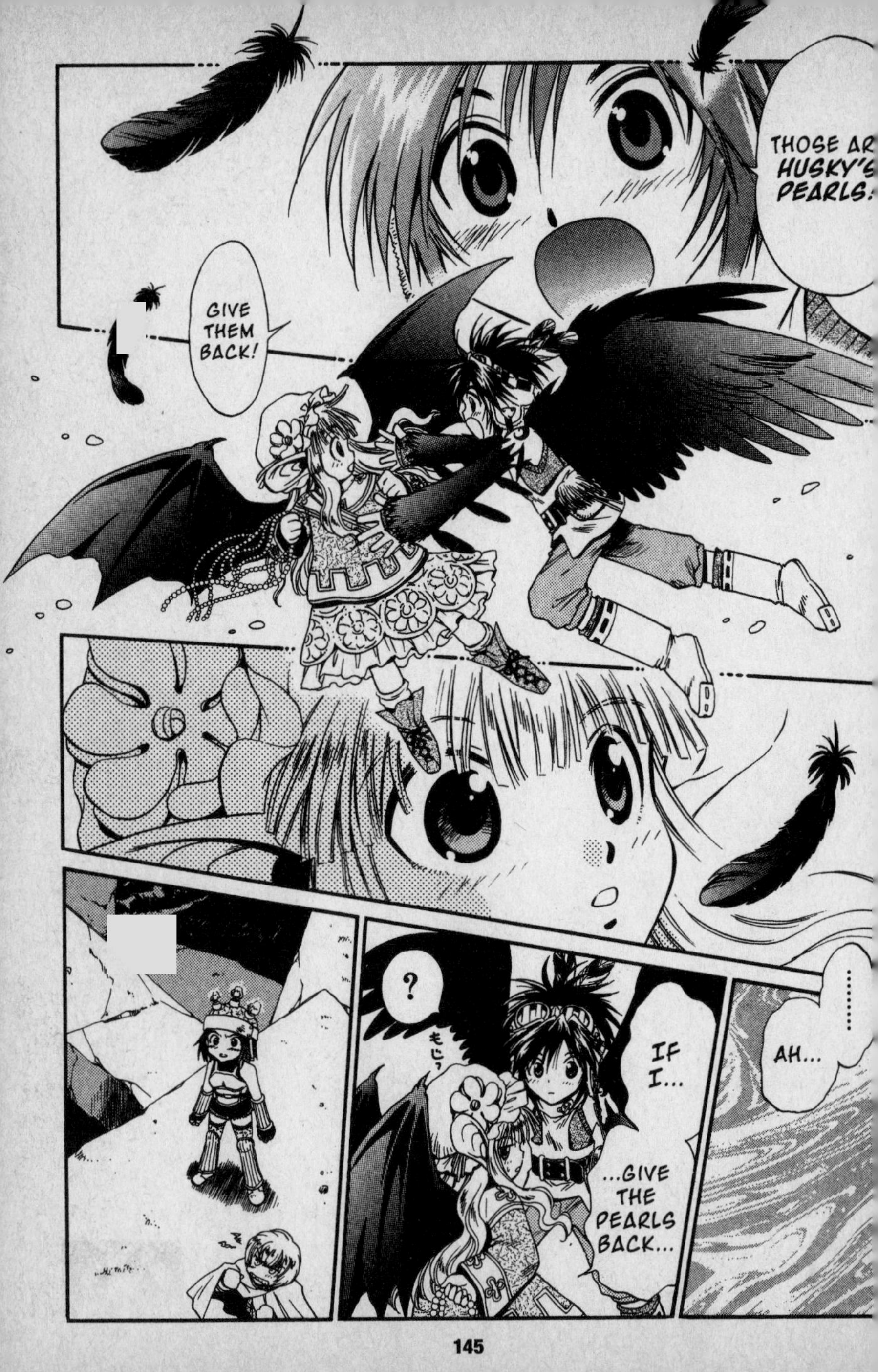
THOSE AR
HUSKY'S
PEARLS
GIVE THEM BACK!
......
AH...
?
IF I...
...GIVE THE PEARLS BACK...

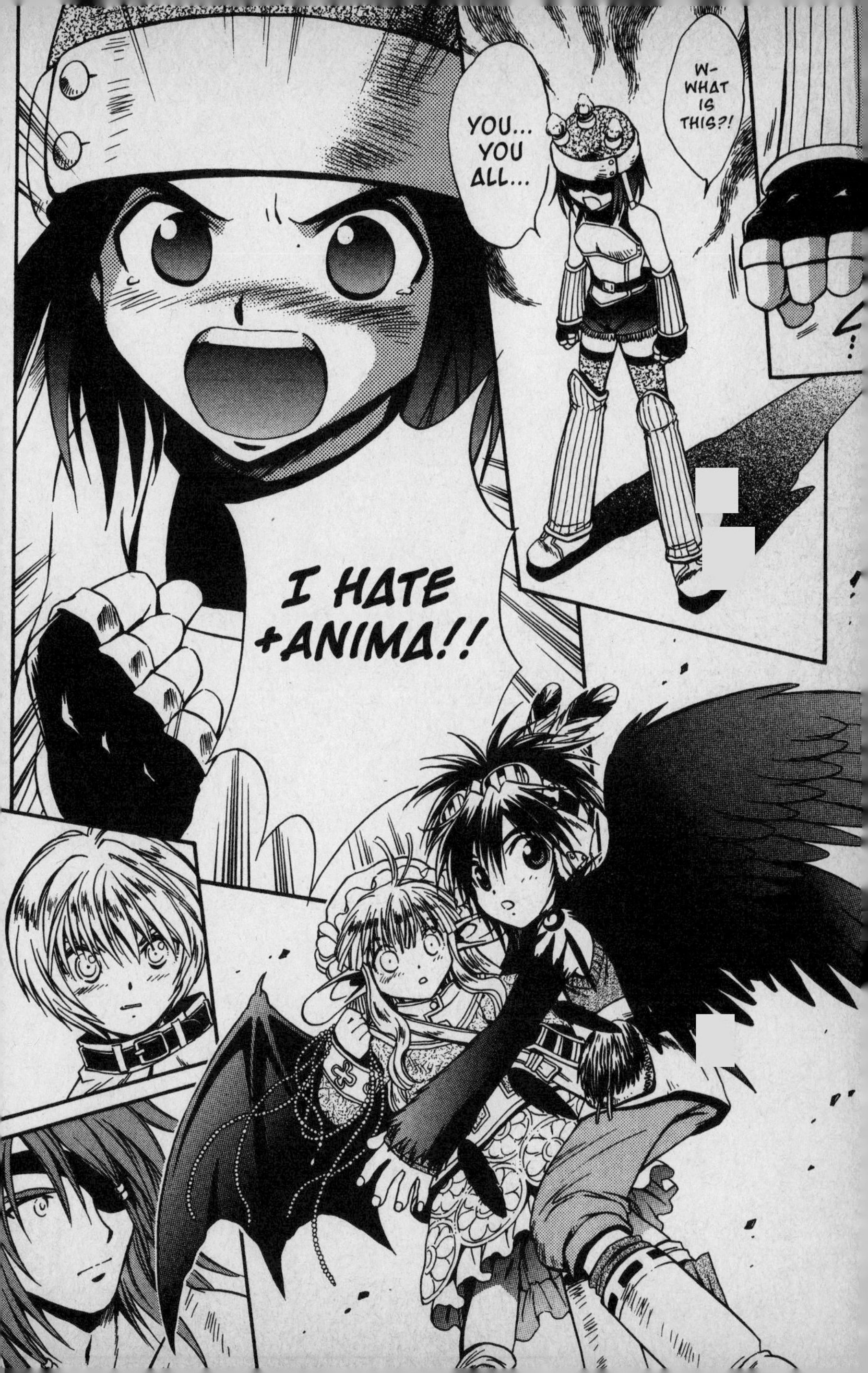
W-WHAT IS THIS?!
YOU... YOU ALL...
I HATE +ANIMA!!

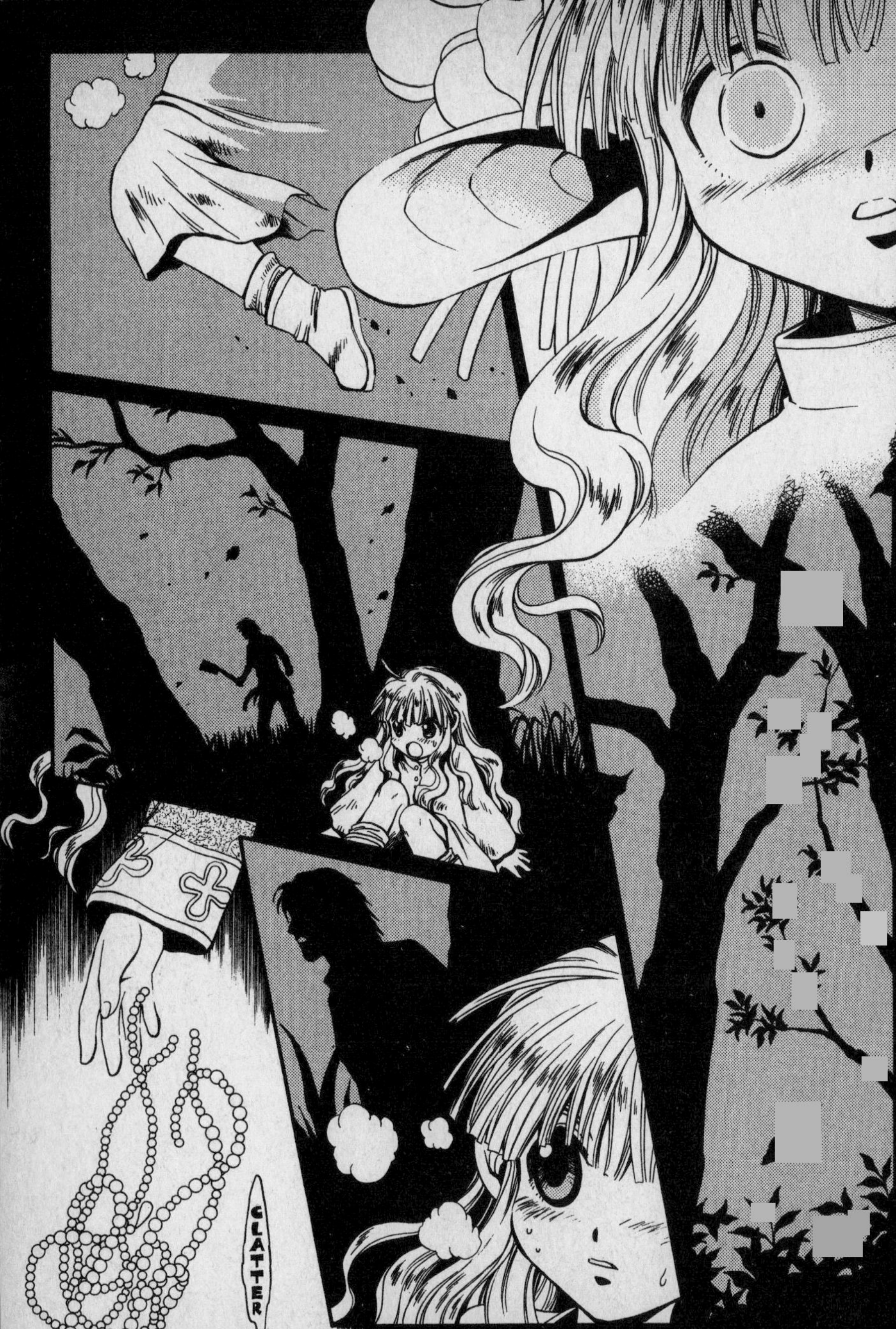
CLATTER

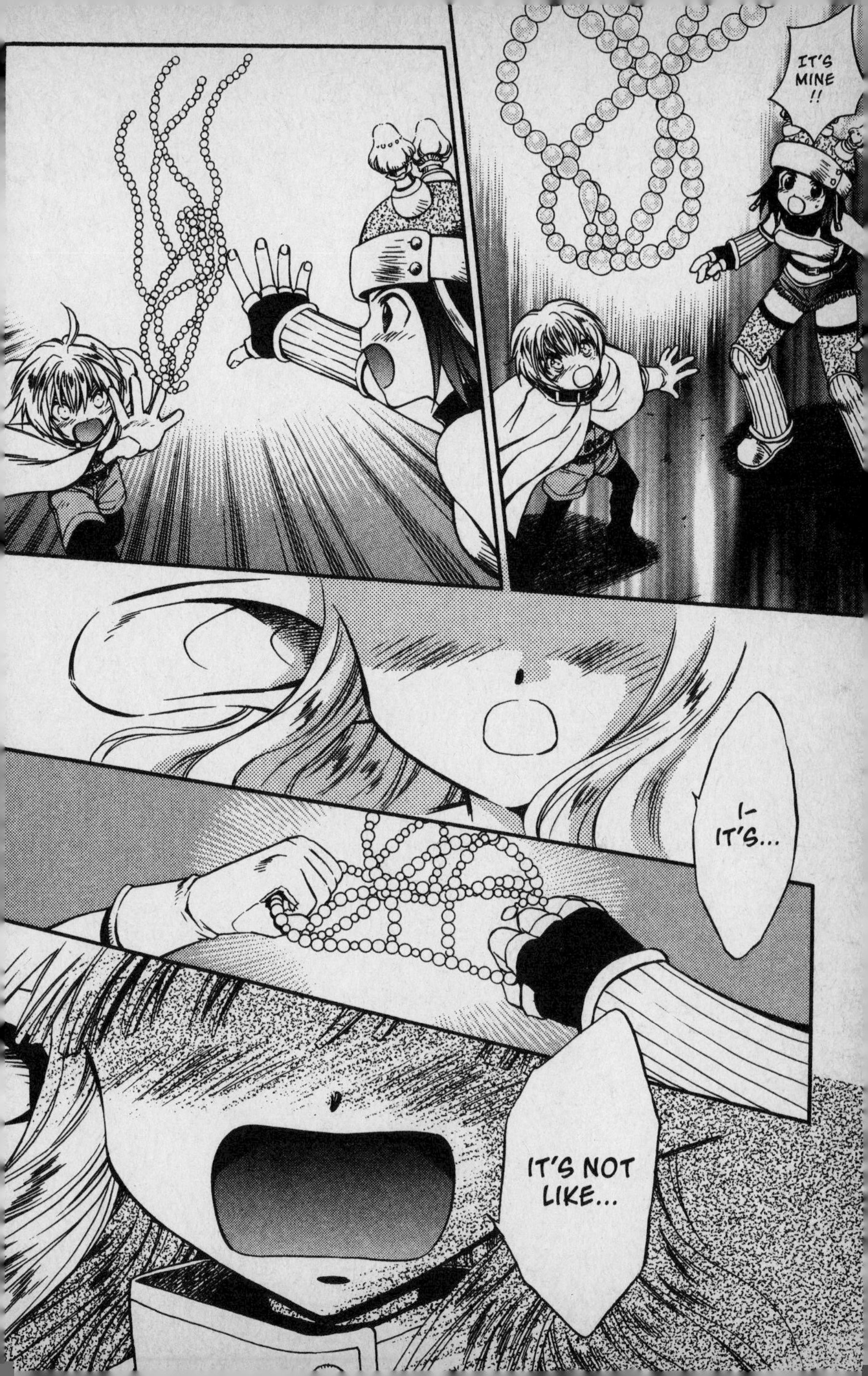
IT'S MINE !!
I- IT'S...
IT'S NOT LIKE...

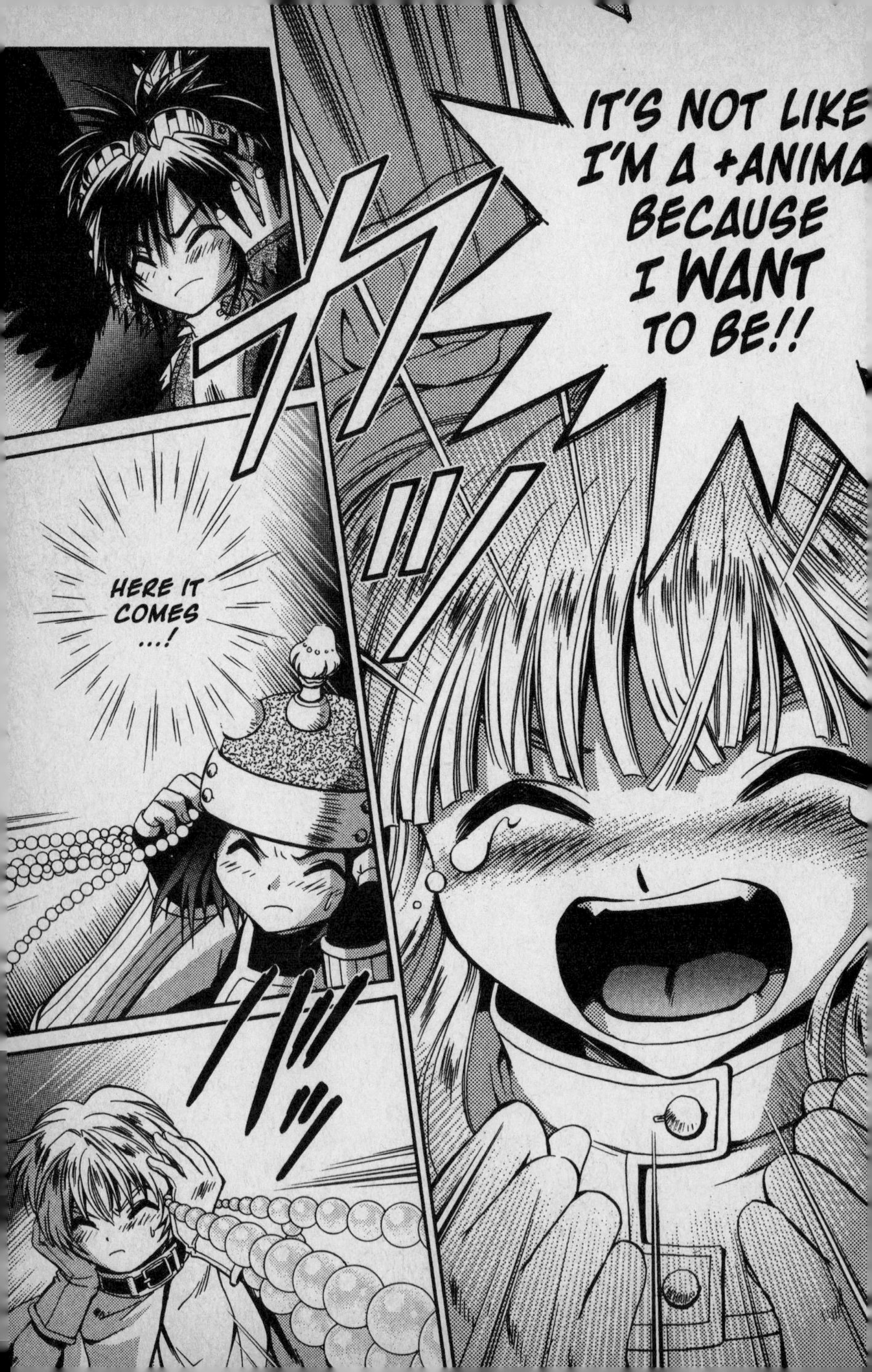
IT'S NOT LIKE I'M A +ANIMA BECAUSE I WANT TO BE!!
HERE IT COMES ...!

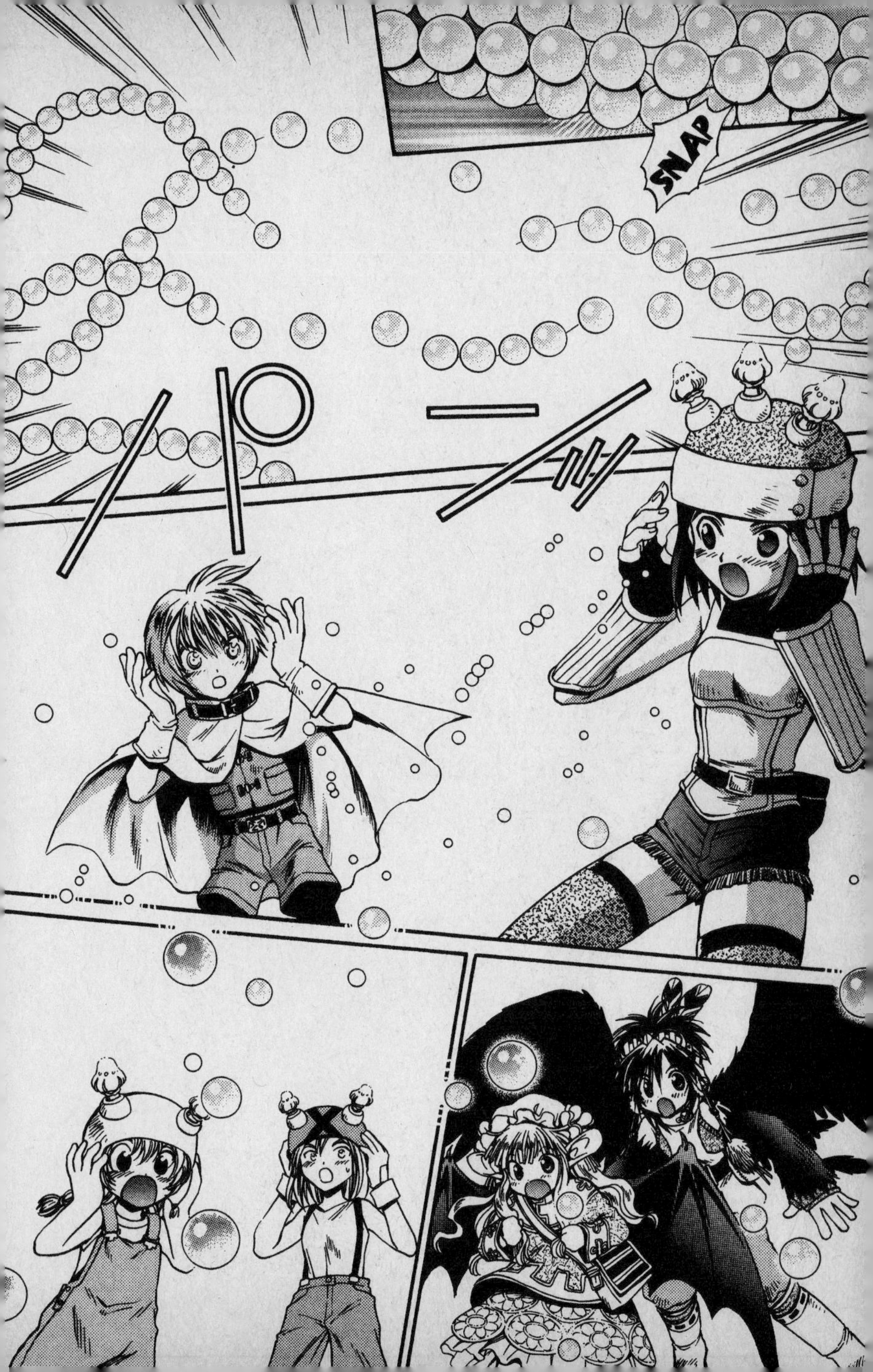
SNAP
パーン

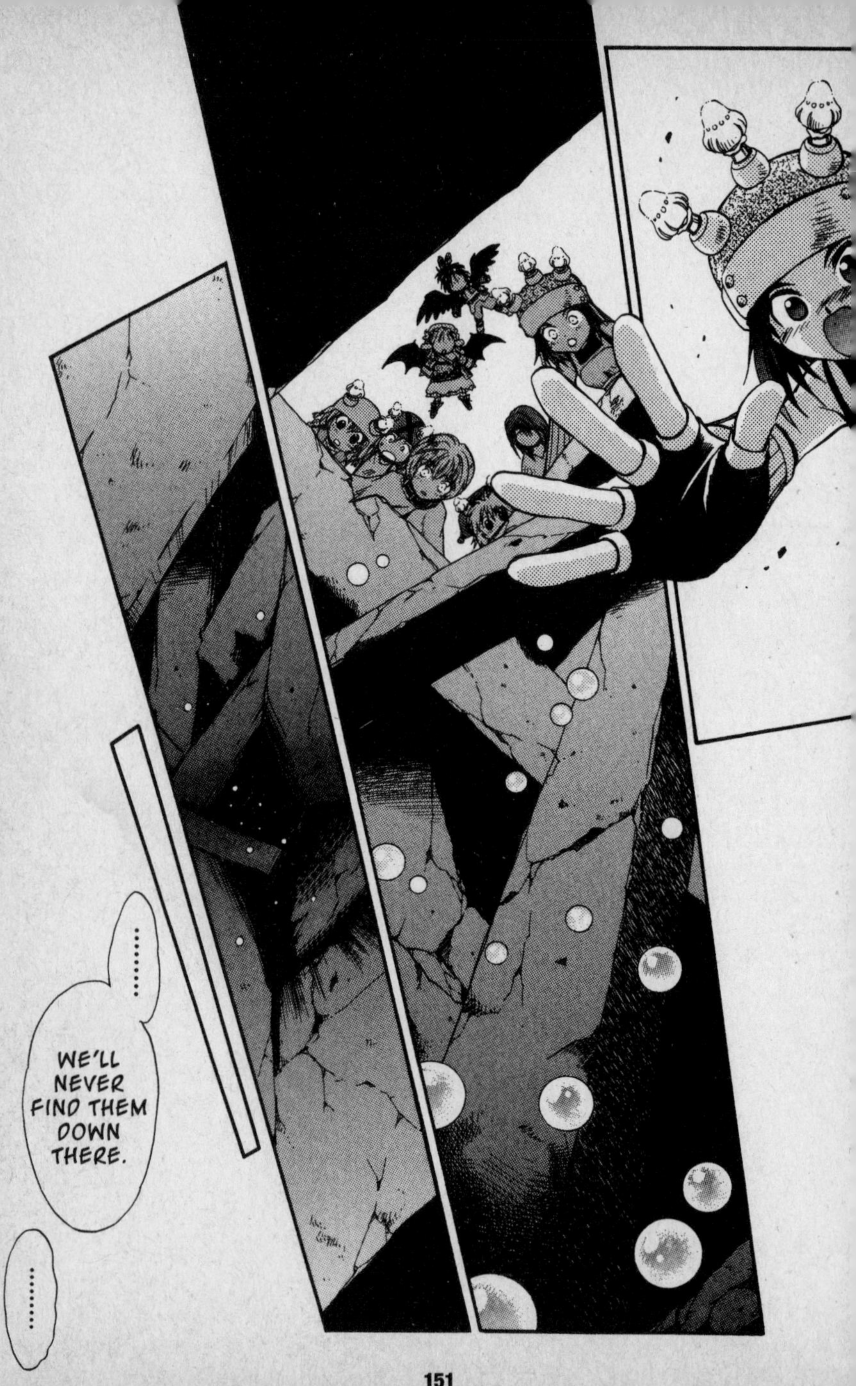
......
WE'LL NEVER FIND THEM DOWN THERE.
......

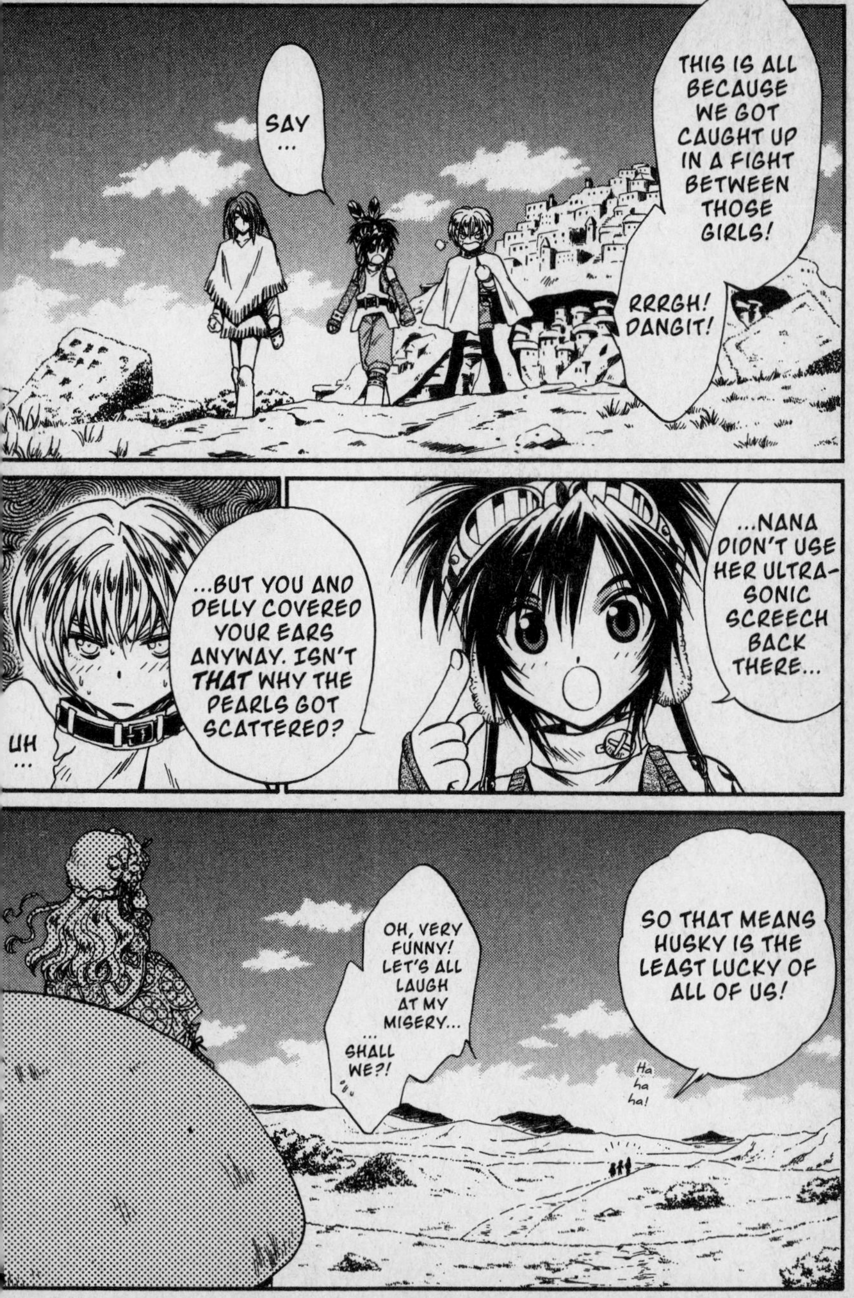
THIS IS ALL BECAUSE WE GOT CAUGHT UP IN A FIGHT BETWEEN THOSE GIRLS!
RRRGH! DANGIT!
SAY ...
...NANA DIDN'T USE HER ULTRA-SONIC SCREECH BACK THERE...
...BUT YOU AND DELLY COVERED YOUR EARS ANYWAY. ISN'T *THAT* WHY THE PEARLS GOT SCATTERED?
UH ...
SO THAT MEANS HUSKY IS THE LEAST LUCKY OF ALL OF US!
Ha ha ha!
OH, VERY FUNNY! LET'S ALL LAUGH AT MY MISERY... ...SHALL WE?!

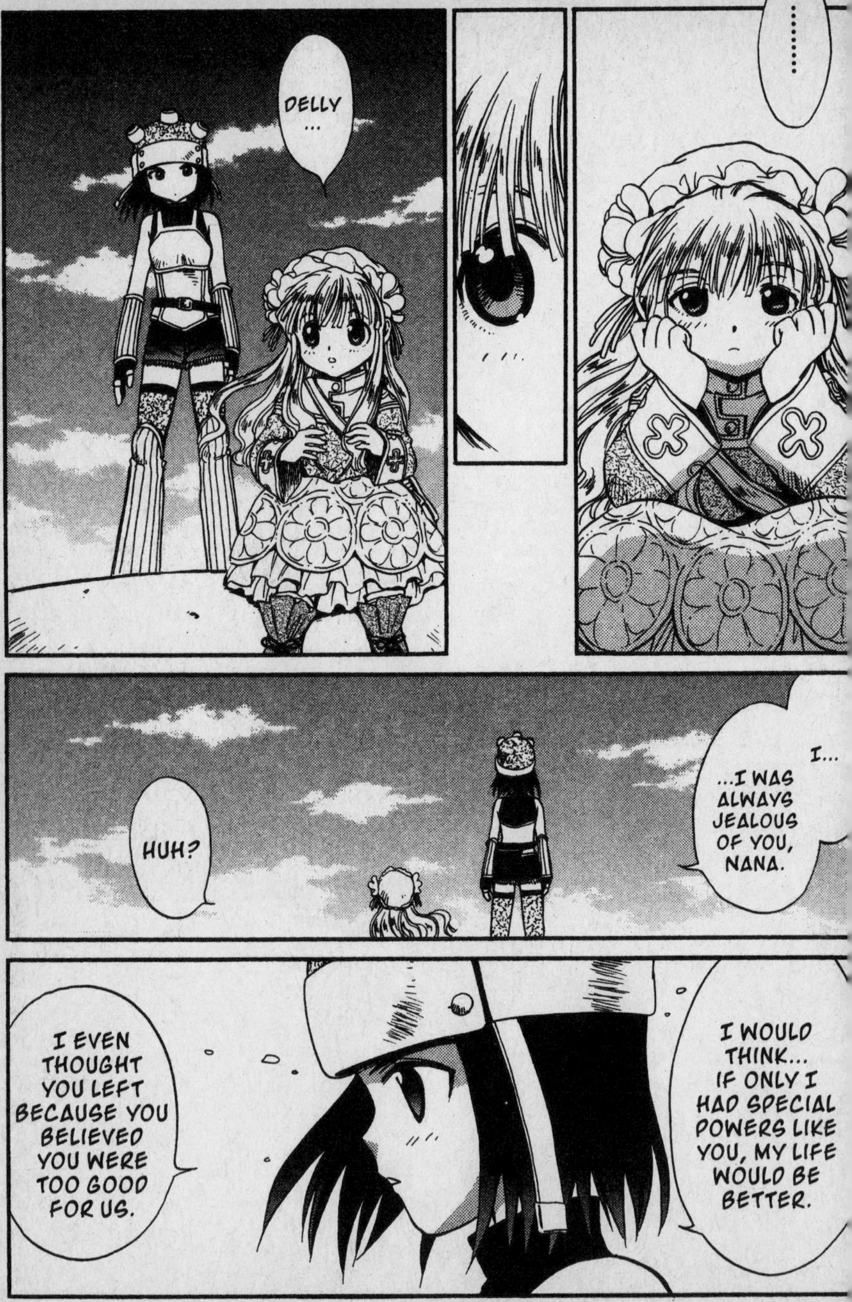
......
DELLY ...
I...
...I WAS ALWAYS JEALOUS OF YOU, NANA.
HUH?
I WOULD THINK... IF ONLY I HAD SPECIAL POWERS LIKE YOU, MY LIFE WOULD BE BETTER.
I EVEN THOUGHT YOU LEFT BECAUSE YOU BELIEVED YOU WERE TOO GOOD FOR US.

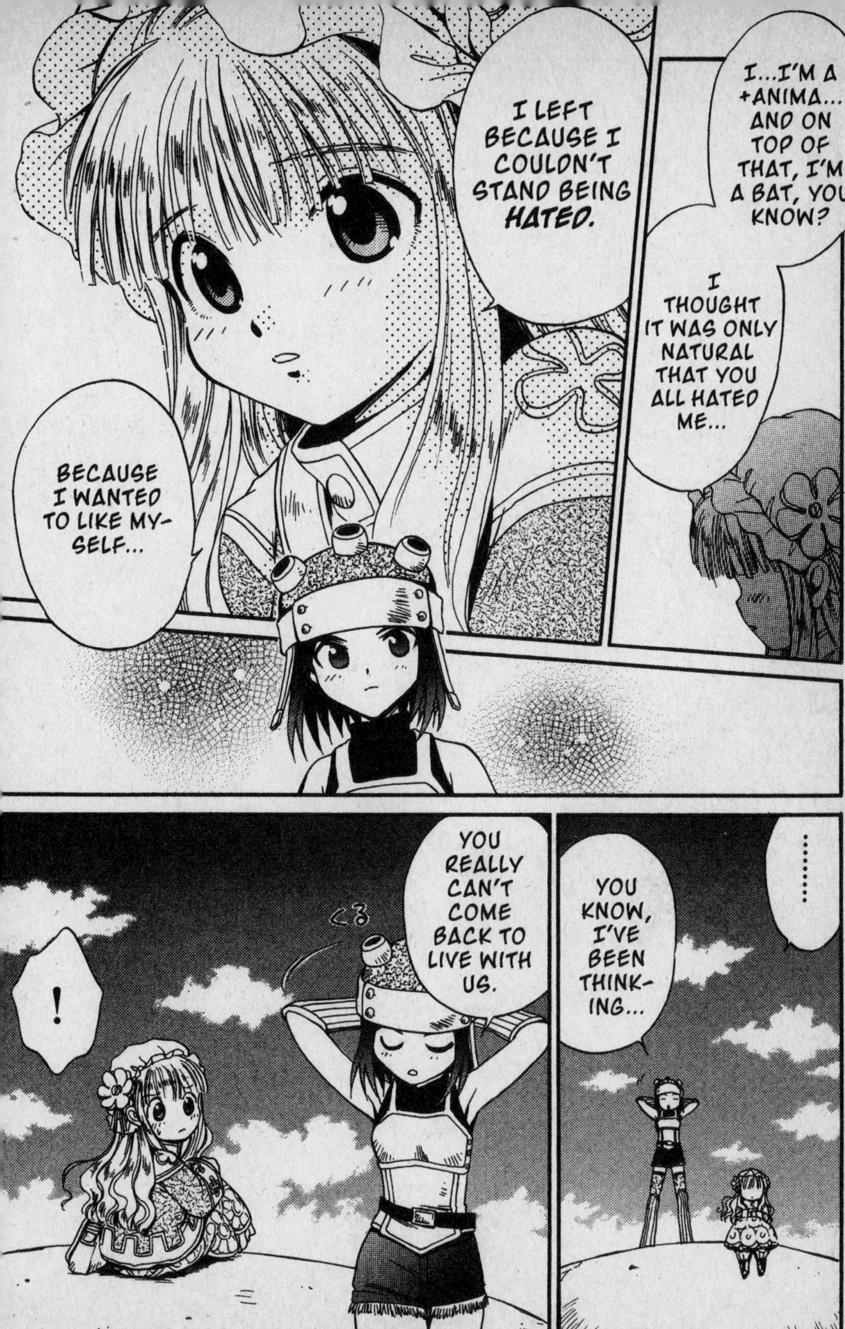
I...I'M A +ANIMA... AND ON TOP OF THAT, I'M A BAT, YOU KNOW?
I THOUGHT IT WAS ONLY NATURAL THAT YOU ALL HATED ME...
I LEFT BECAUSE I COULDN'T STAND BEING HATED.
BECAUSE I WANTED TO LIKE MY-SELF...
......
YOU KNOW, I'VE BEEN THINK-ING...
YOU REALLY CAN'T COME BACK TO LIVE WITH US.
くる
!

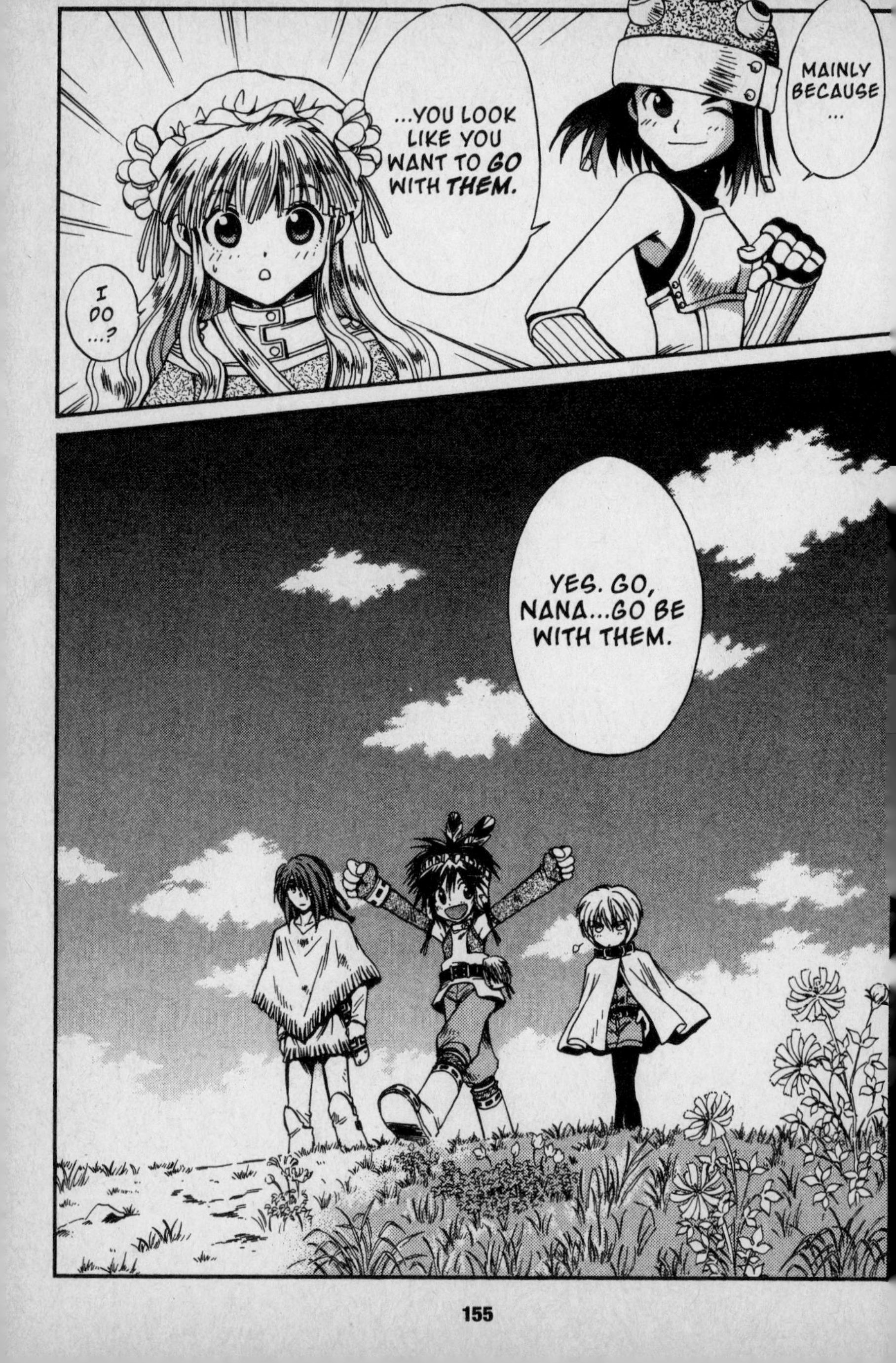
MAINLY BECAUSE ...
...YOU LOOK LIKE YOU WANT TO *GO* WITH *THEM.*
I DO ...?
YES. GO, NANA...GO BE WITH THEM.

Chapter 5
3 + 1 = ?

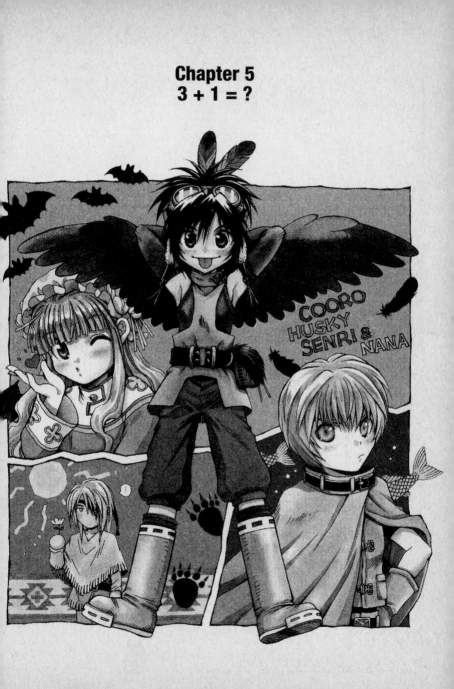

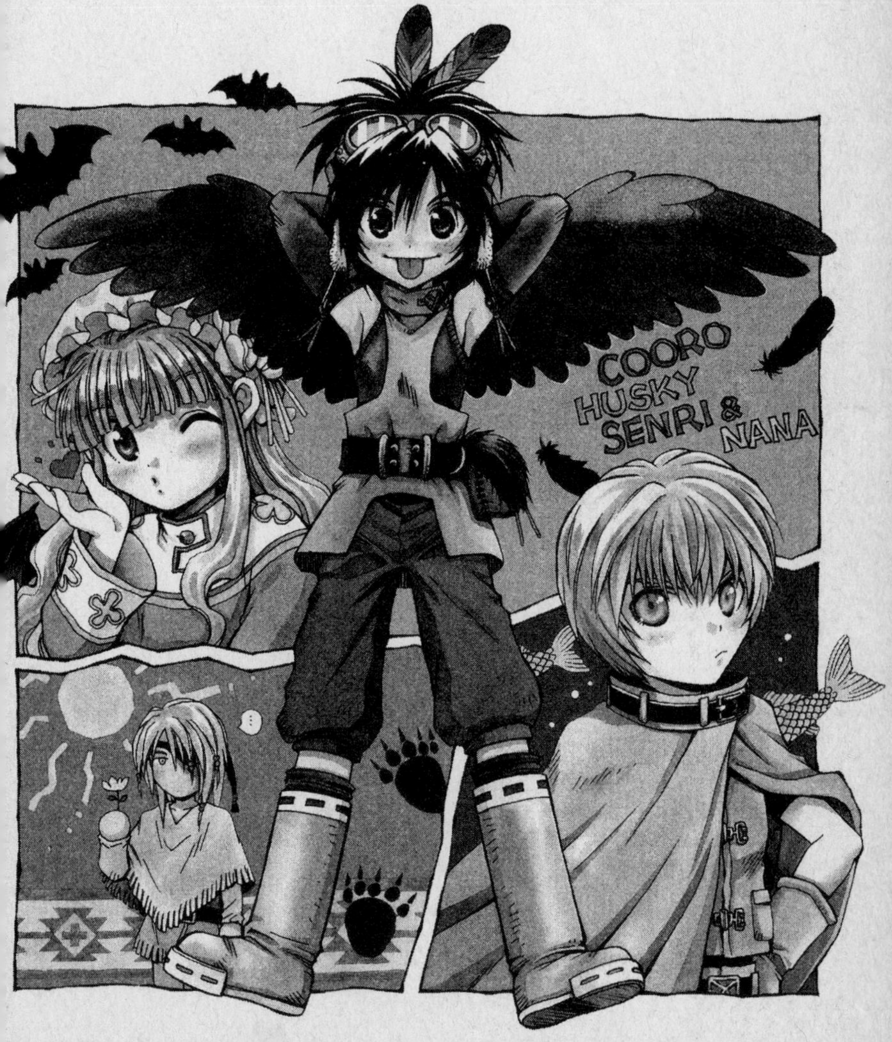
COORO
HUSKY
SENRI
&
NANA

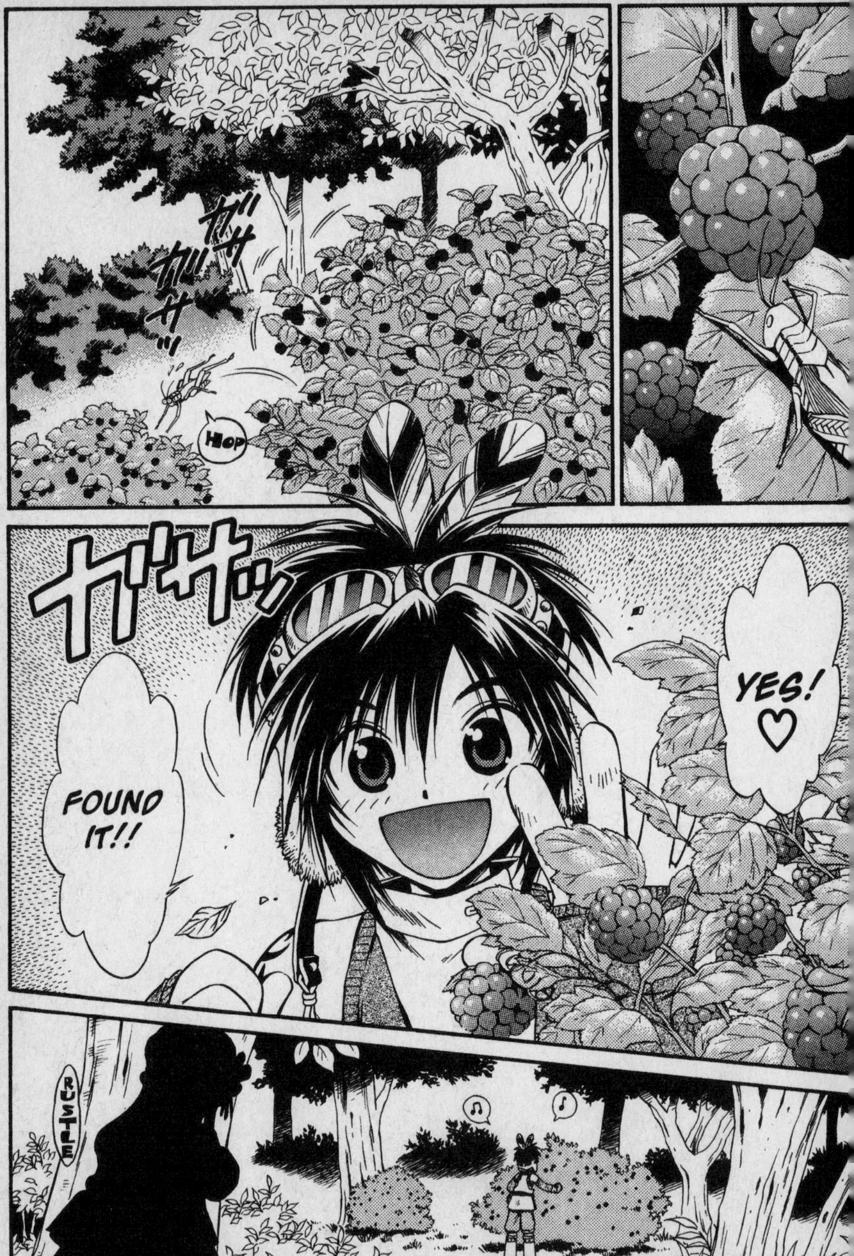
HOP
ガサッ
YES! ♥
FOUND IT!!
RUSTLE
♪
♪

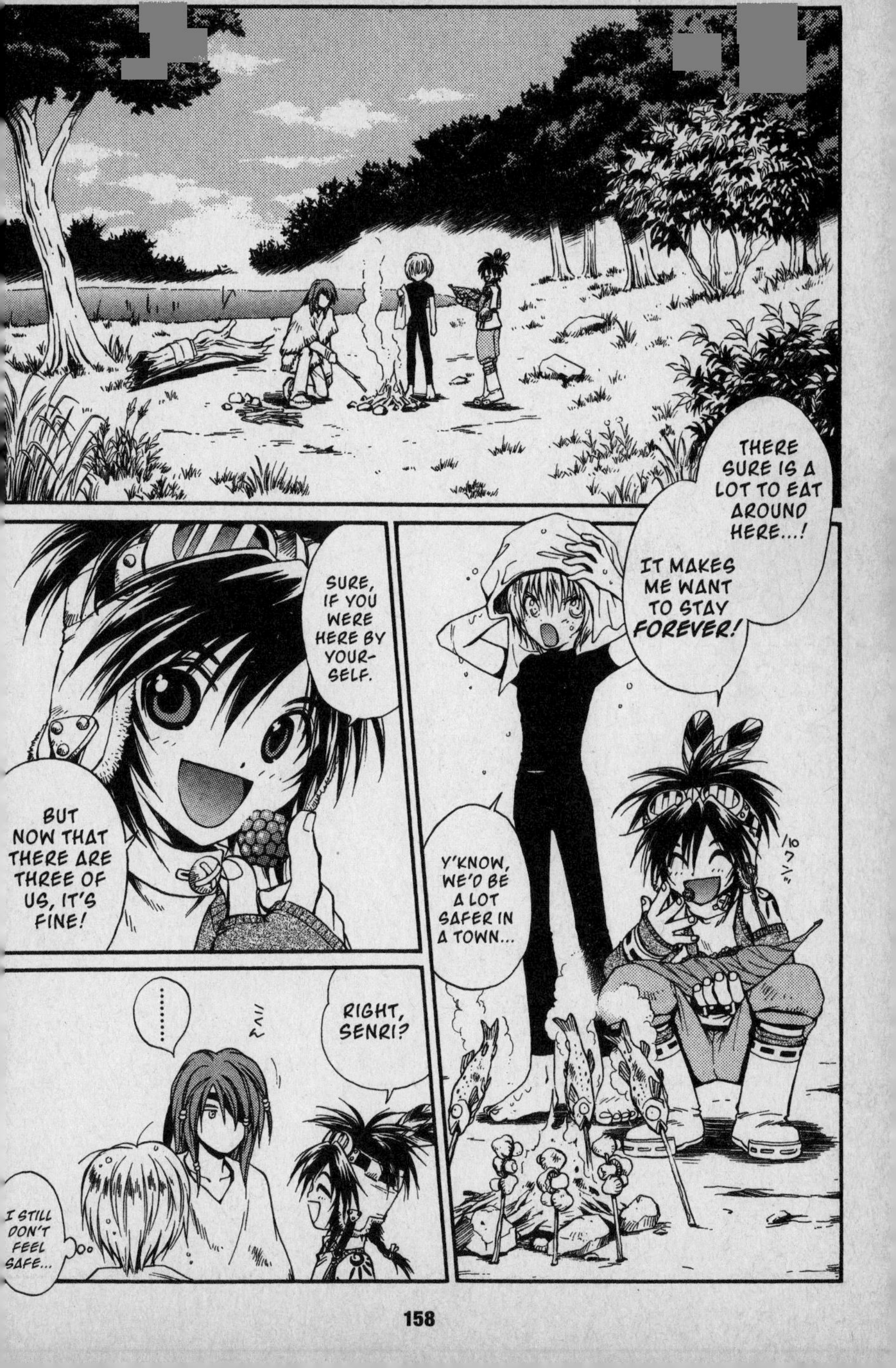
THERE SURE IS A LOT TO EAT AROUND HERE...!
IT MAKES ME WANT TO STAY FOREVER!
Y'KNOW, WE'D BE A LOT SAFER IN A TOWN...
SURE, IF YOU WERE HERE BY YOUR-SELF.
BUT NOW THAT THERE ARE THREE OF US, IT'S FINE!
RIGHT, SENRI?
......
I STILL DON'T FEEL SAFE...

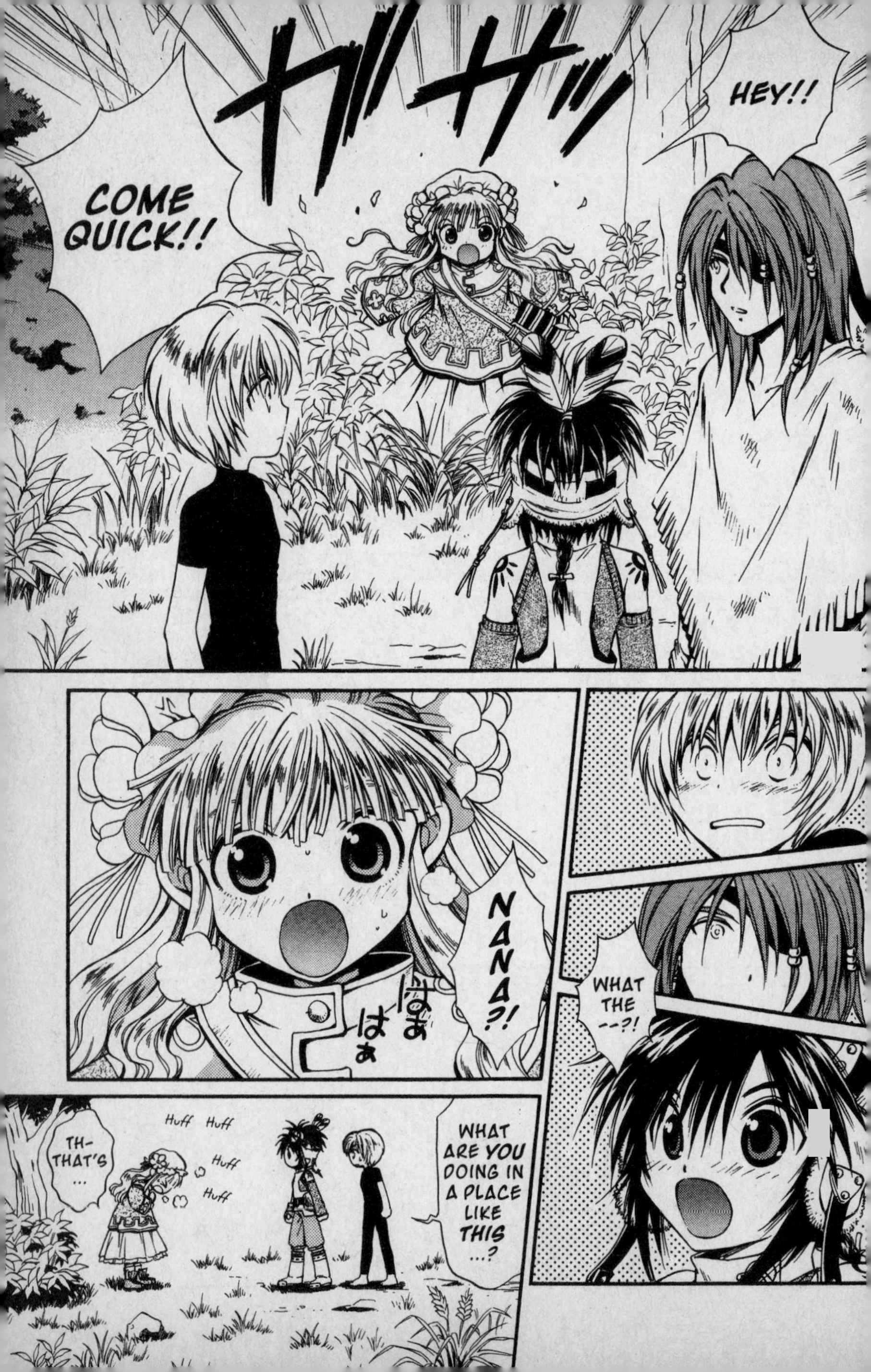
HEY!!
COME QUICK!!
WHAT THE --?!
NANA?!
はぁ はぁ
WHAT ARE YOU DOING IN A PLACE LIKE THIS ...?
Huff Huff
Huff
Huff
TH-THAT'S ...

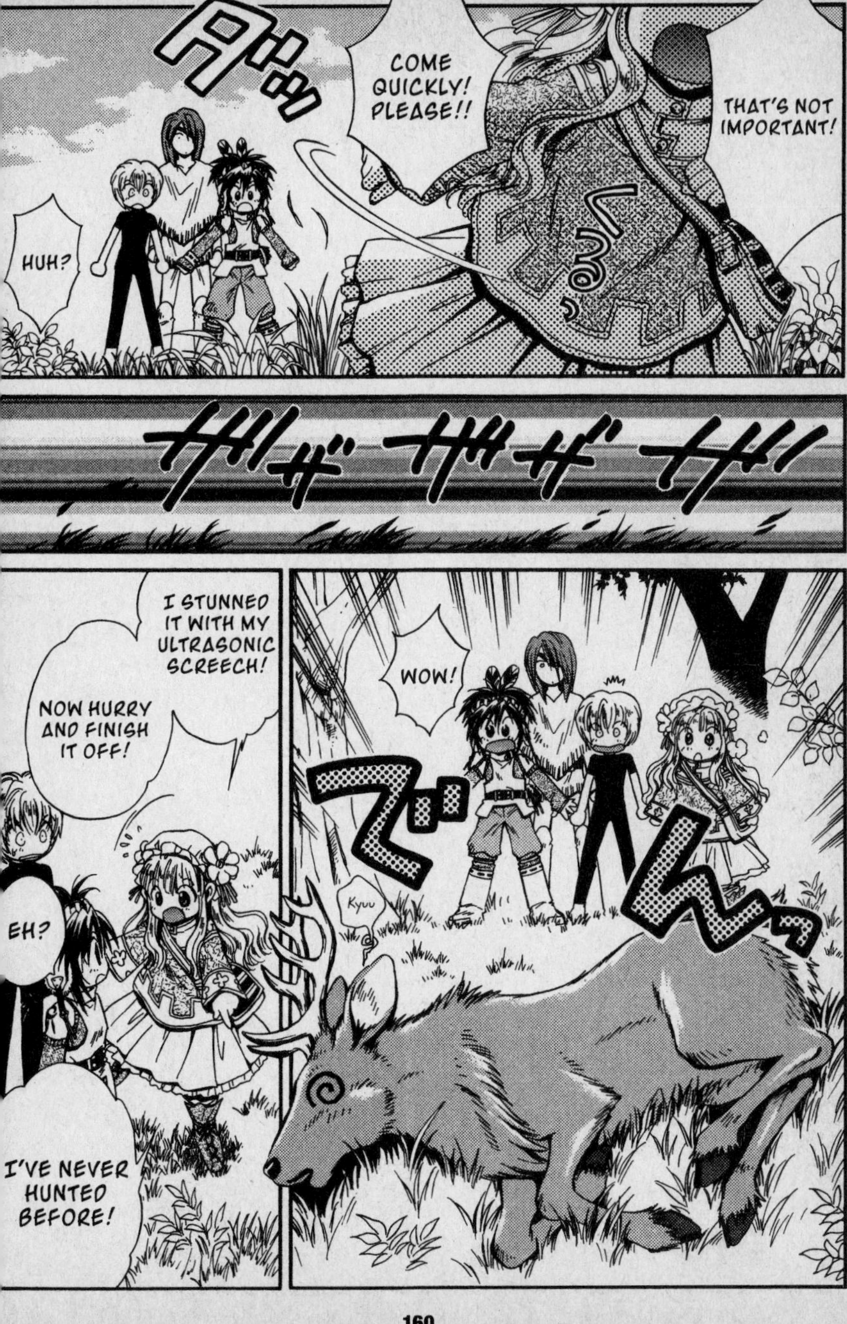
THAT'S NOT IMPORTANT!
COME QUICKLY! PLEASE!!
HUH?
WOW!
Kyuu
I STUNNED IT WITH MY ULTRASONIC SCREECH!
NOW HURRY AND FINISH IT OFF!
EH?
I'VE NEVER HUNTED BEFORE!

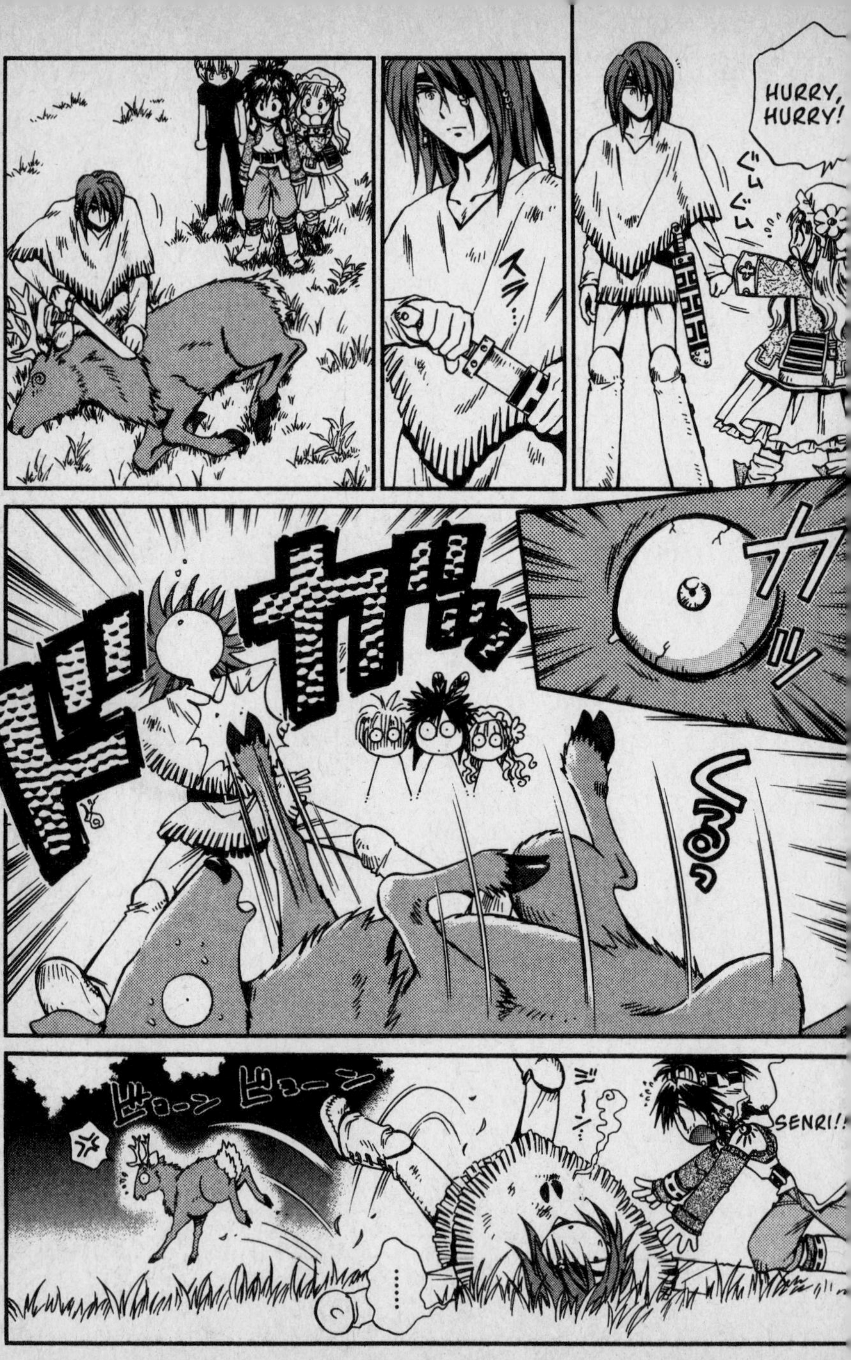
HURRY, HURRY!
ぐいぐい
スッ…
カッ
ビョーン ビョーン
SENRI!!
……

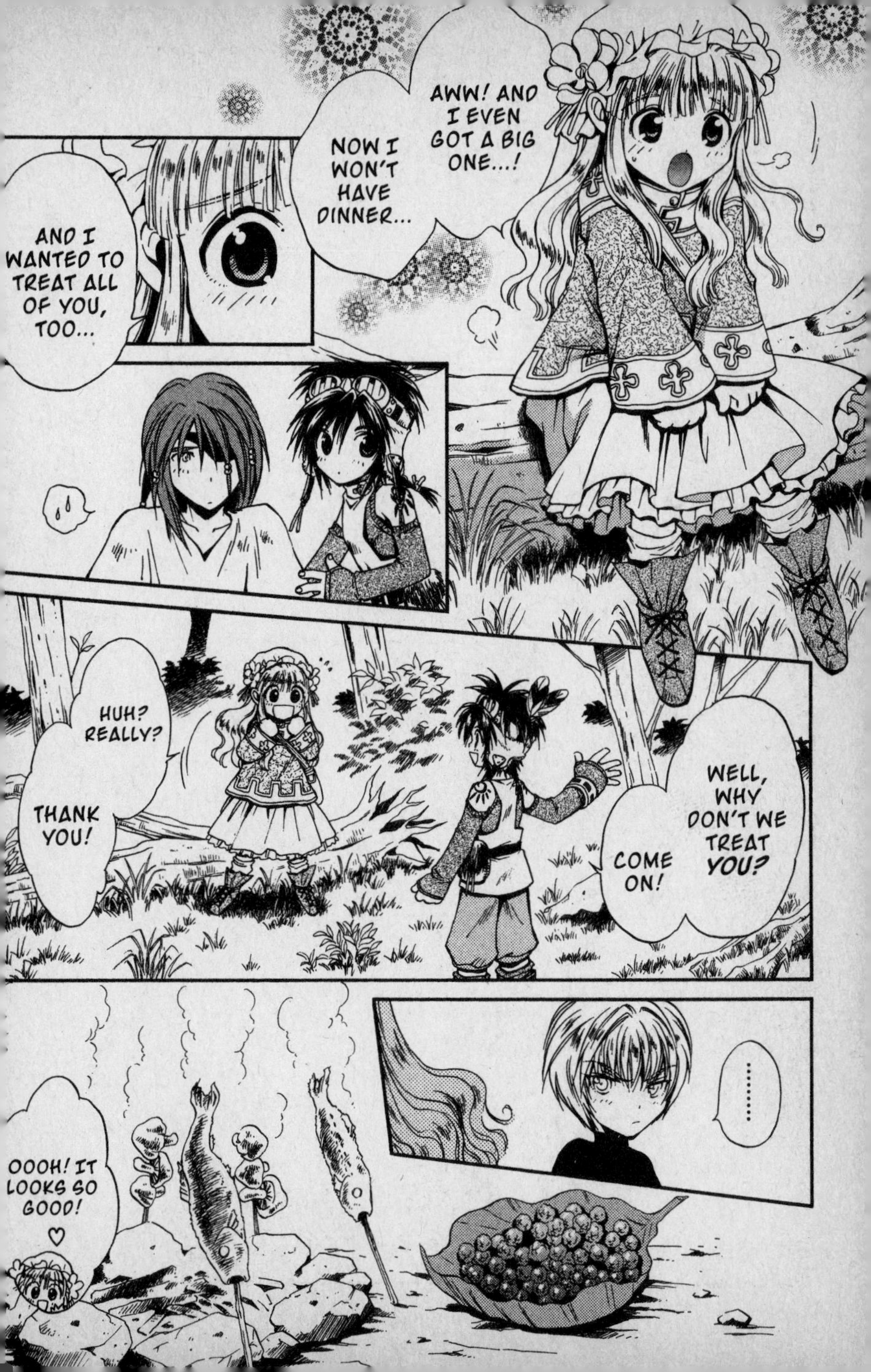
AWW! AND I EVEN GOT A BIG ONE...!
NOW I WON'T HAVE DINNER...
AND I WANTED TO TREAT ALL OF YOU, TOO...
WELL, WHY DON'T WE TREAT YOU?
COME ON!
HUH? REALLY?
THANK YOU!
......
OOOH! IT LOOKS SO GOOD! ♡

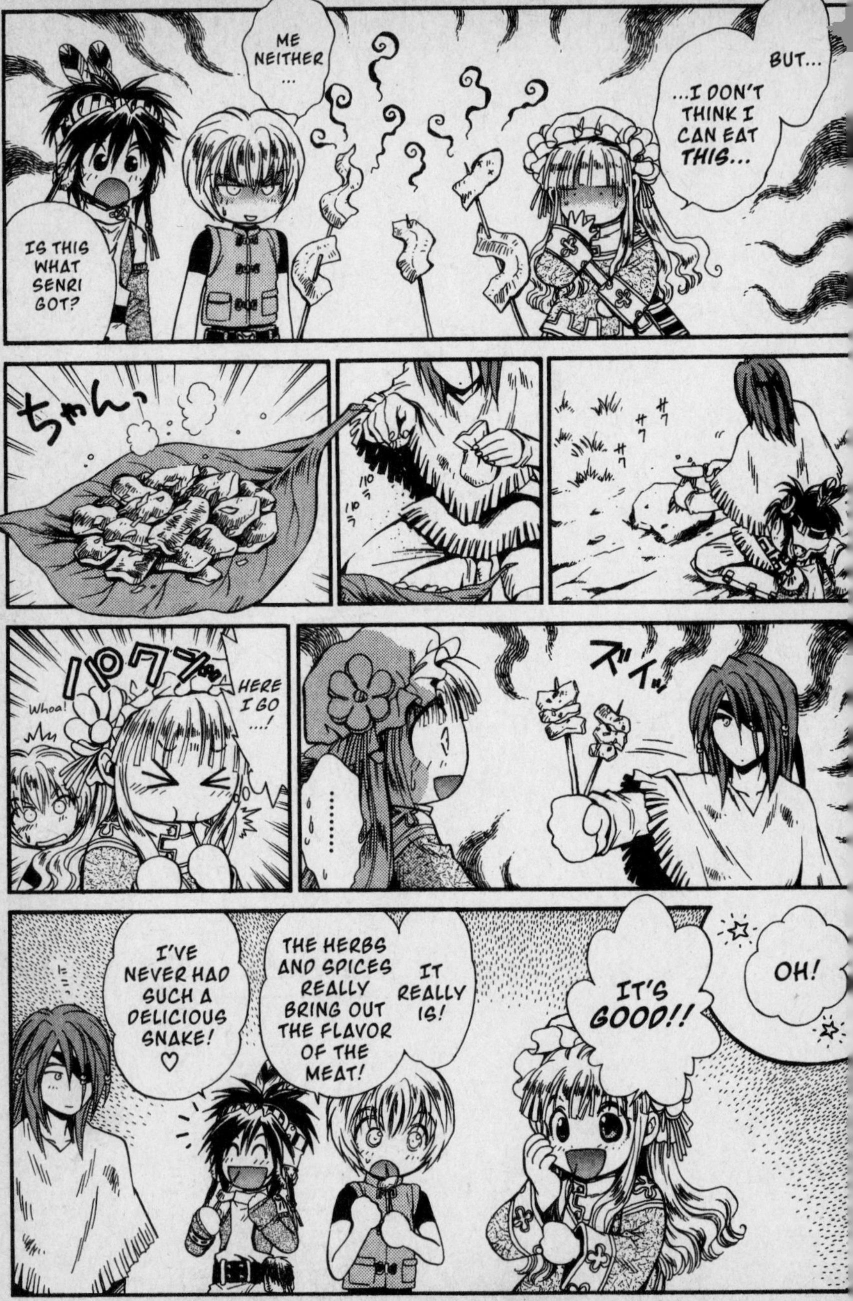

BUT...
...I DON'T THINK I CAN EAT THIS...
ME NEITHER ...
IS THIS WHAT SENRI GOT?
サク サク
ちゃんっ
ズイッ
......
パクッ
HERE I GO ...!
Whoa!
OH!
IT'S GOOD!!
IT REALLY IS!
THE HERBS AND SPICES REALLY BRING OUT THE FLAVOR OF THE MEAT!
I'VE NEVER HAD SUCH A DELICIOUS SNAKE! ♡

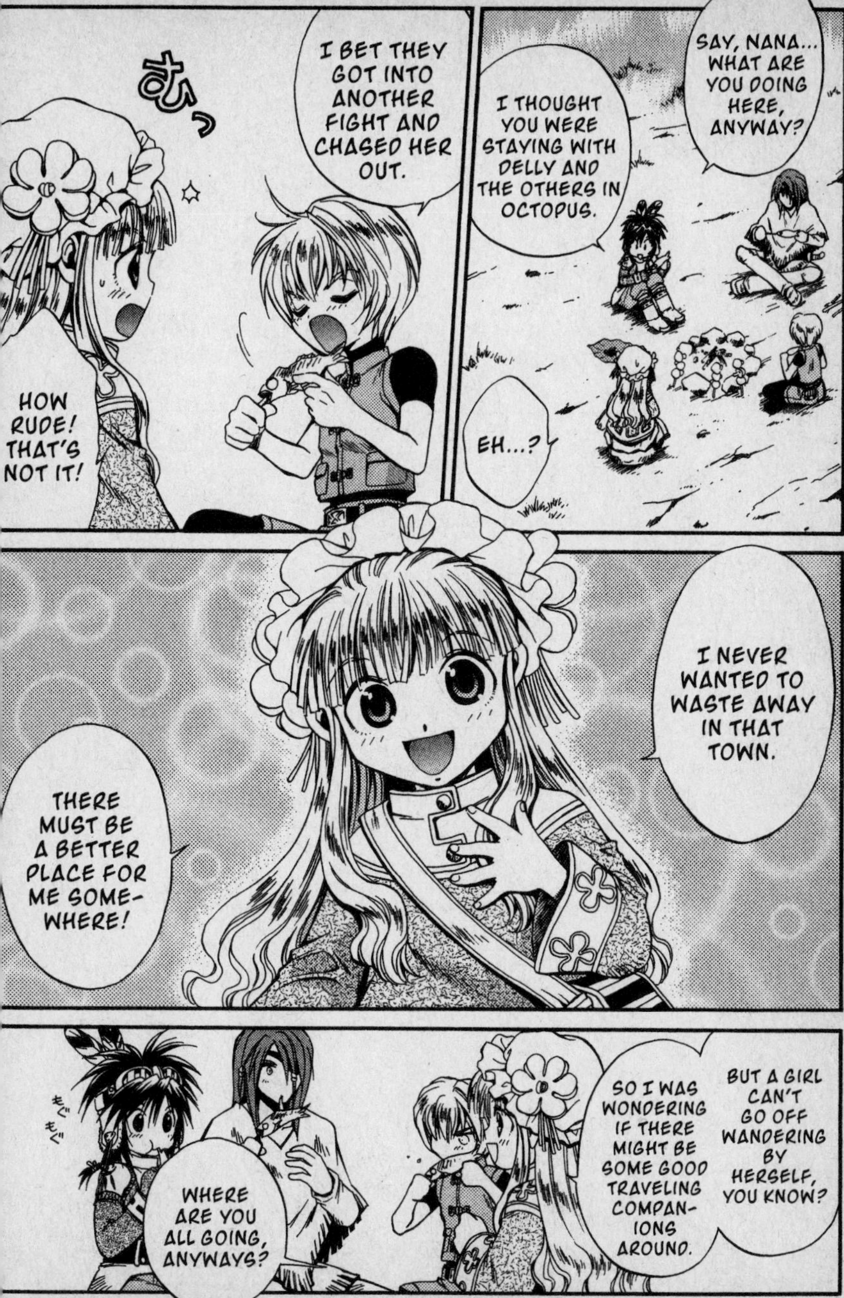
SAY, NANA... WHAT ARE YOU DOING HERE, ANYWAY?
I THOUGHT YOU WERE STAYING WITH DELLY AND THE OTHERS IN OCTOPUS.
EH...?
I BET THEY GOT INTO ANOTHER FIGHT AND CHASED HER OUT.
むっ
HOW RUDE! THAT'S NOT IT!
I NEVER WANTED TO WASTE AWAY IN THAT TOWN.
THERE MUST BE A BETTER PLACE FOR ME SOME-WHERE!
BUT A GIRL CAN'T GO OFF WANDERING BY HERSELF, YOU KNOW?
SO I WAS WONDERING IF THERE MIGHT BE SOME GOOD TRAVELING COMPAN-IONS AROUND.
もぐ もぐ
WHERE ARE YOU ALL GOING, ANYWAYS?

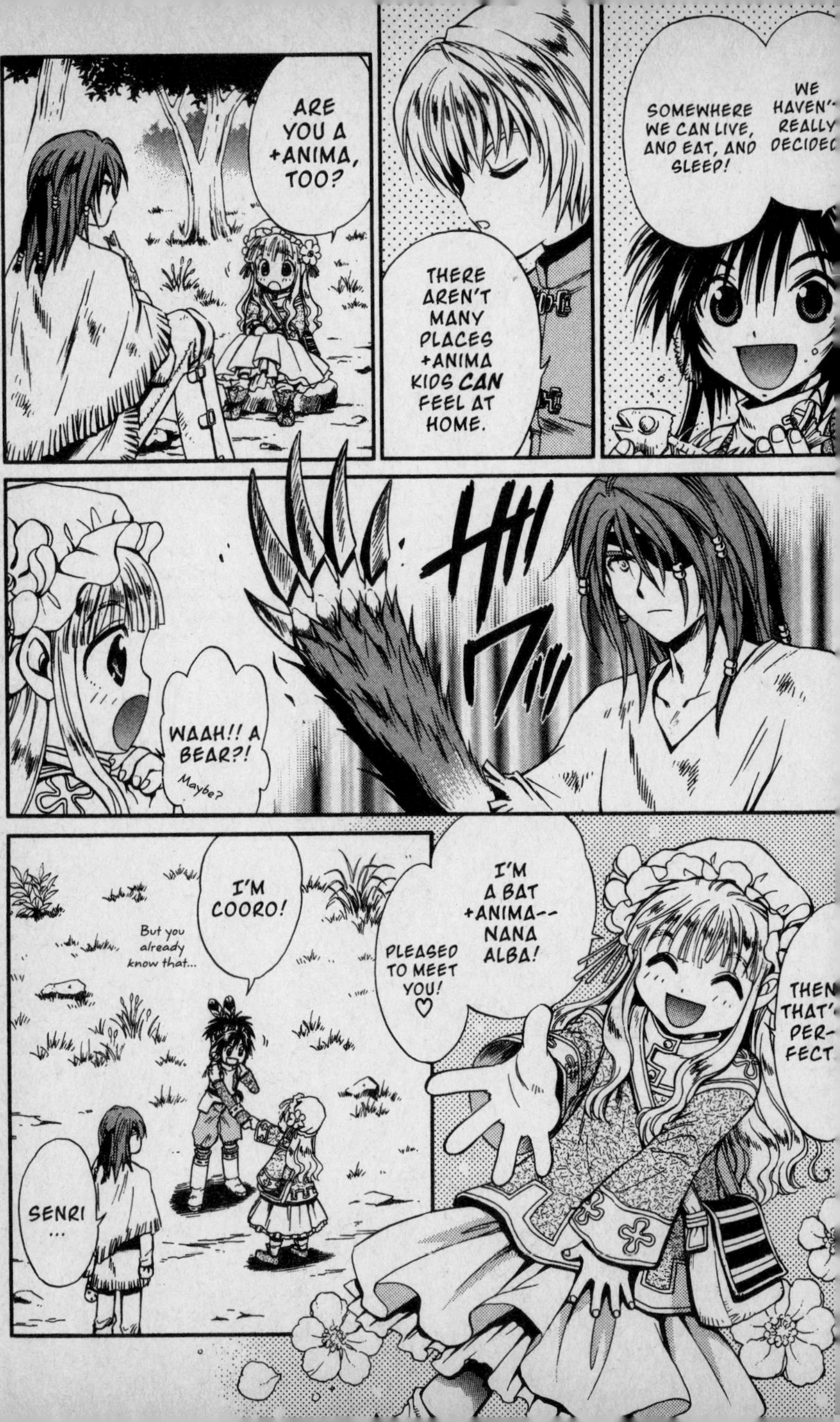
WE HAVEN' REALLY DECIDED
SOMEWHERE WE CAN LIVE, AND EAT, AND SLEEP!
THERE AREN'T MANY PLACES +ANIMA KIDS **CAN** FEEL AT HOME.
ARE YOU A +ANIMA, TOO?
WAAH!! A BEAR?!
Maybe?
THEN THAT' PER- FECT.
I'M A BAT +ANIMA-- NANA ALBA!
PLEASED TO MEET YOU! ♡
I'M COORO!
But you already know that...
SENRI ...

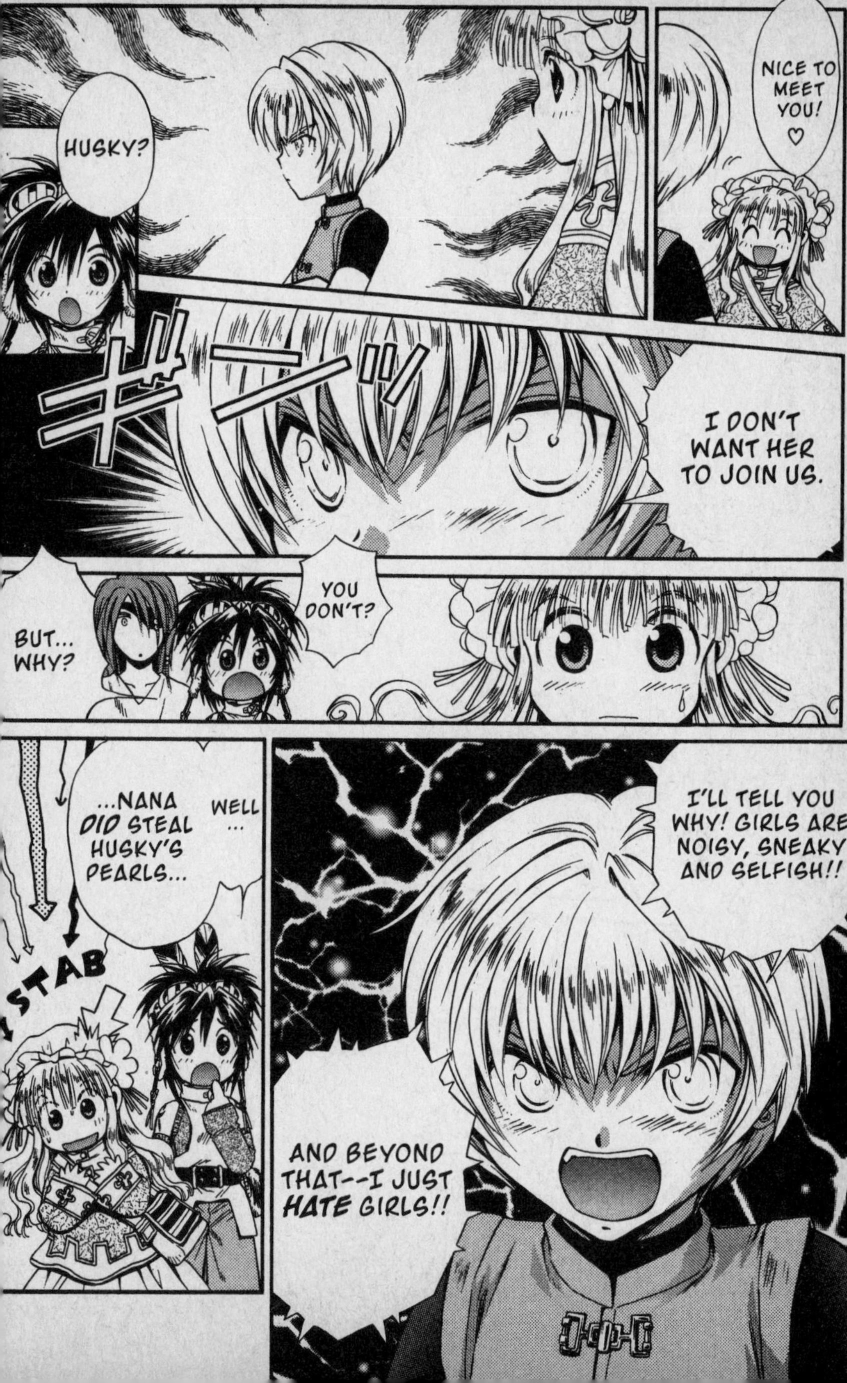
NICE TO MEET YOU! ♡
HUSKY?
I DON'T WANT HER TO JOIN US.
YOU DON'T?
BUT... WHY?
I'LL TELL YOU WHY! GIRLS ARE NOISY, SNEAKY AND SELFISH!!
AND BEYOND THAT--I JUST HATE GIRLS!!
WELL ...
...NANA DID STEAL HUSKY'S PEARLS...
STAB

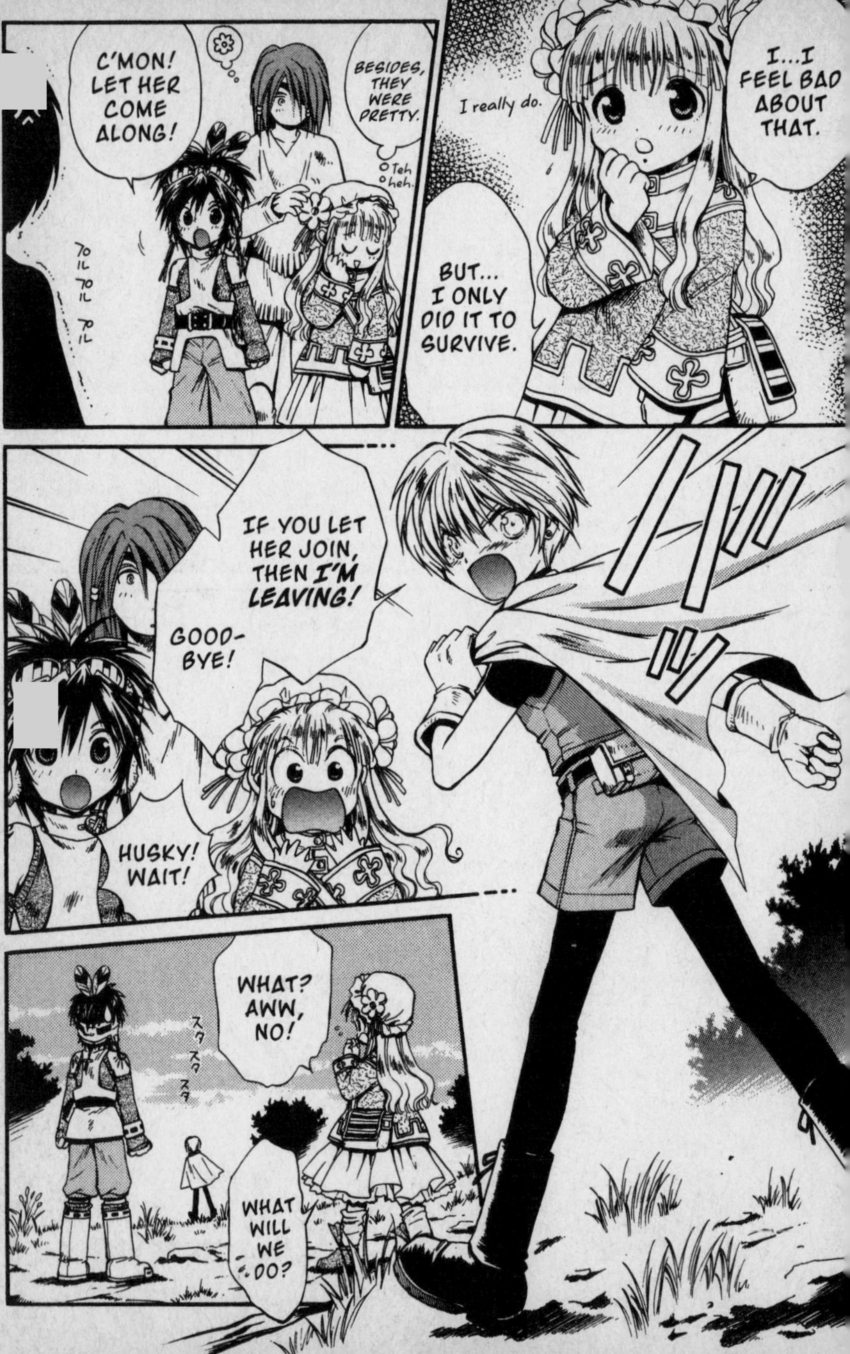
I...I FEEL BAD ABOUT THAT.
I really do.
BUT... I ONLY DID IT TO SURVIVE.
BESIDES, THEY WERE PRETTY.
Teh heh.
C'MON! LET HER COME ALONG!
フル フル フル
IF YOU LET HER JOIN, THEN ***I'M LEAVING!***
GOOD-BYE!
HUSKY! WAIT!
WHAT? AWW, NO!
スタ スタ スタ
WHAT WILL WE DO?

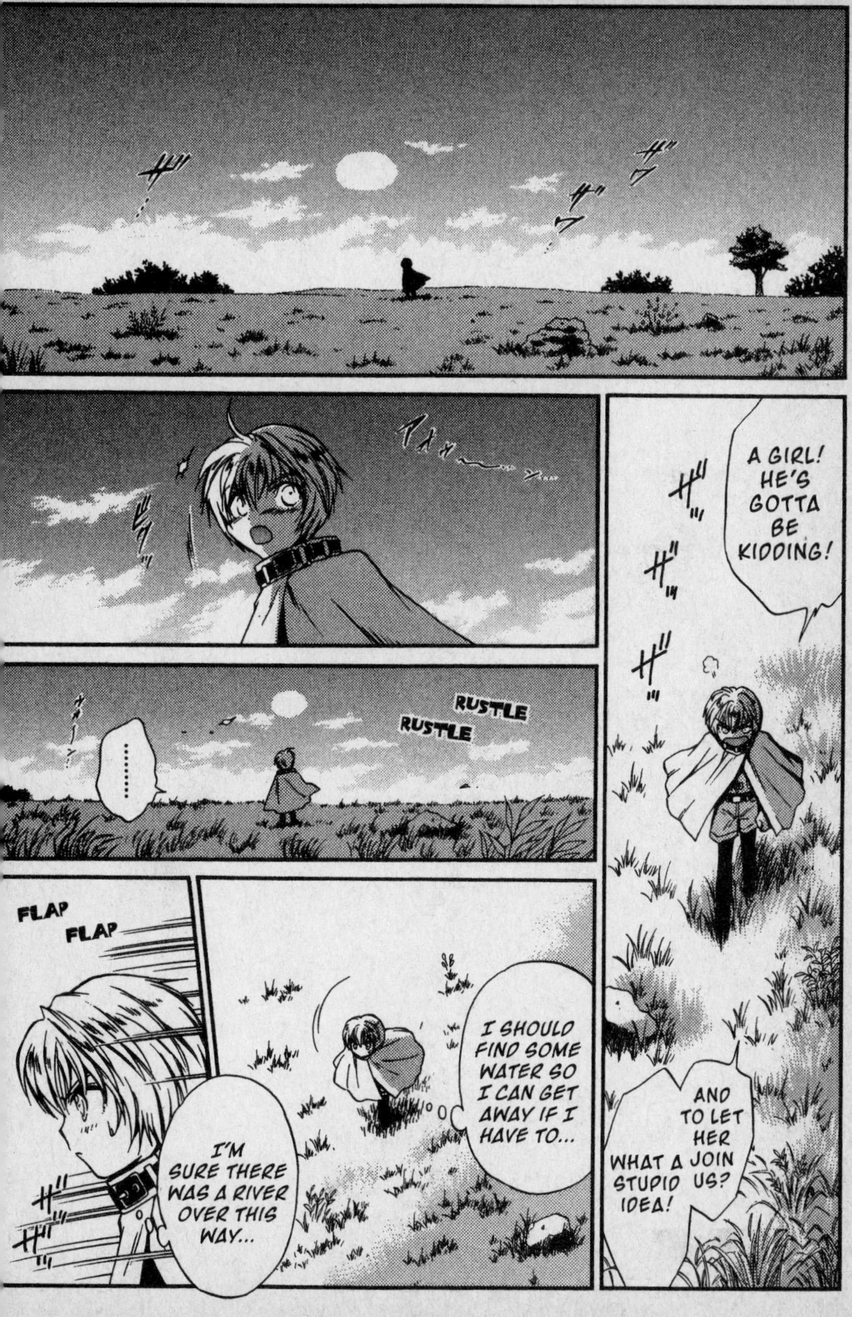
A GIRL! HE'S GOTTA BE KIDDING!
AND TO LET HER JOIN US?
WHAT A STUPID IDEA!
RUSTLE
RUSTLE
......
I SHOULD FIND SOME WATER SO I CAN GET AWAY IF I HAVE TO...
FLAP
FLAP
I'M SURE THERE WAS A RIVER OVER THIS WAY...

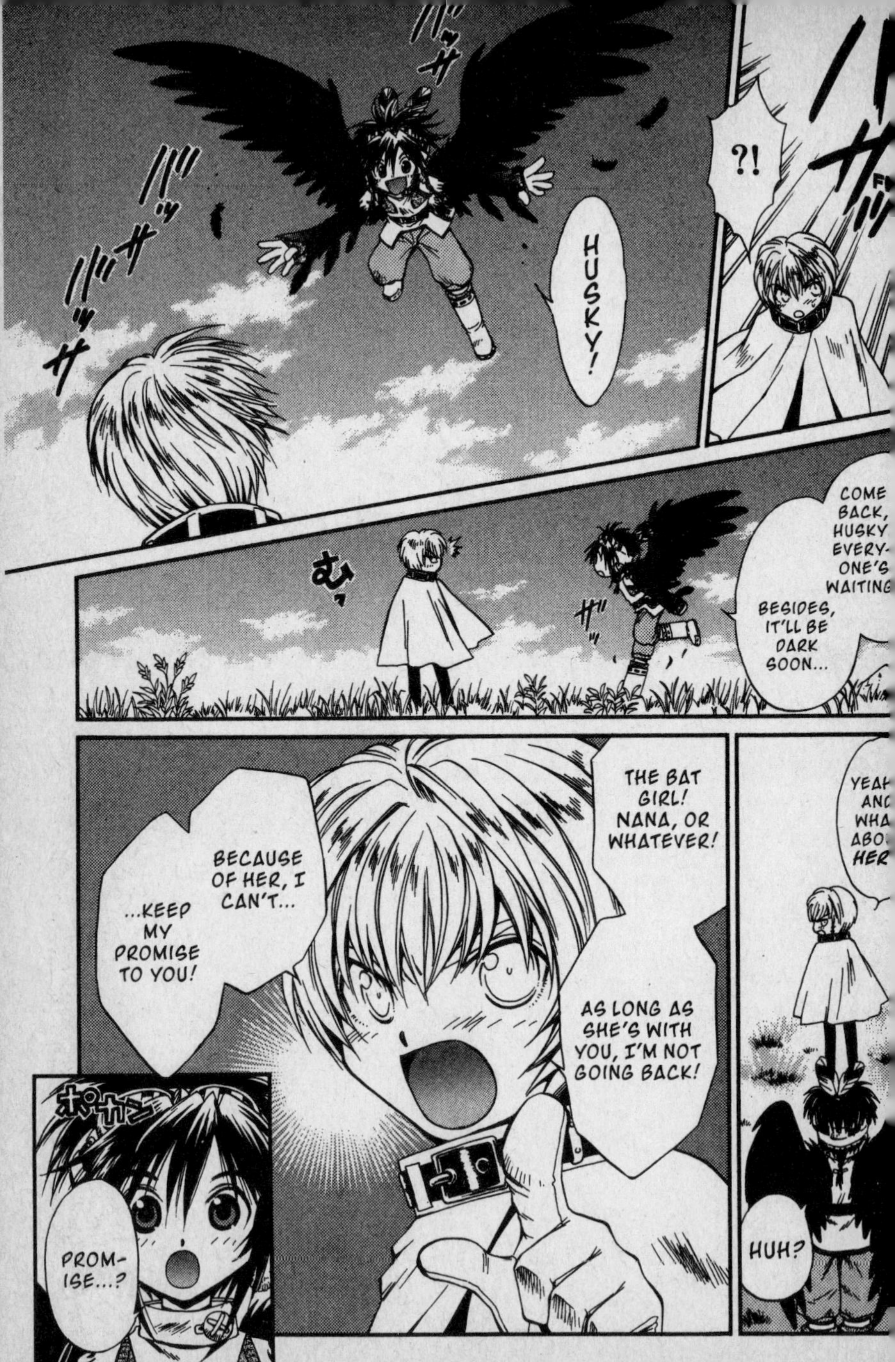
?!
HUSKY!
COME BACK, HUSKY EVERYONE'S WAITING
BESIDES, IT'LL BE DARK SOON...
YEAH AND WHA ABO HER
HUH?
THE BAT GIRL! NANA, OR WHATEVER!
AS LONG AS SHE'S WITH YOU, I'M NOT GOING BACK!
BECAUSE OF HER, I CAN'T...
...KEEP MY PROMISE TO YOU!
PROMISE...?

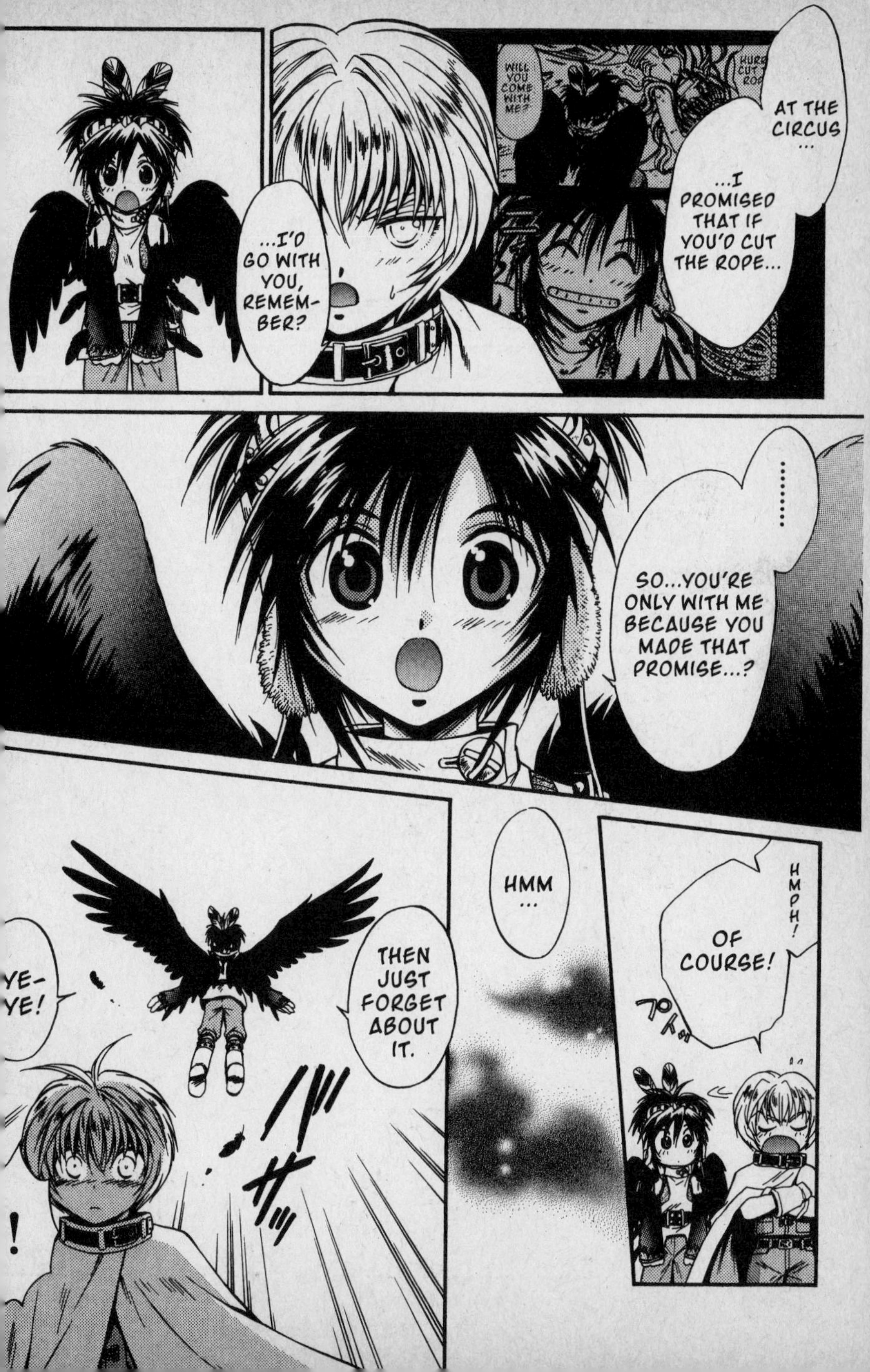
WILL YOU COME WITH ME?
AT THE CIRCUS...
...I PROMISED THAT IF YOU'D CUT THE ROPE...
...I'D GO WITH YOU, REMEMBER?
......
SO...YOU'RE ONLY WITH ME BECAUSE YOU MADE THAT PROMISE...?
HMPH!
OF COURSE!
HMM...
THEN JUST FORGET ABOUT IT.
YE-YE!
!

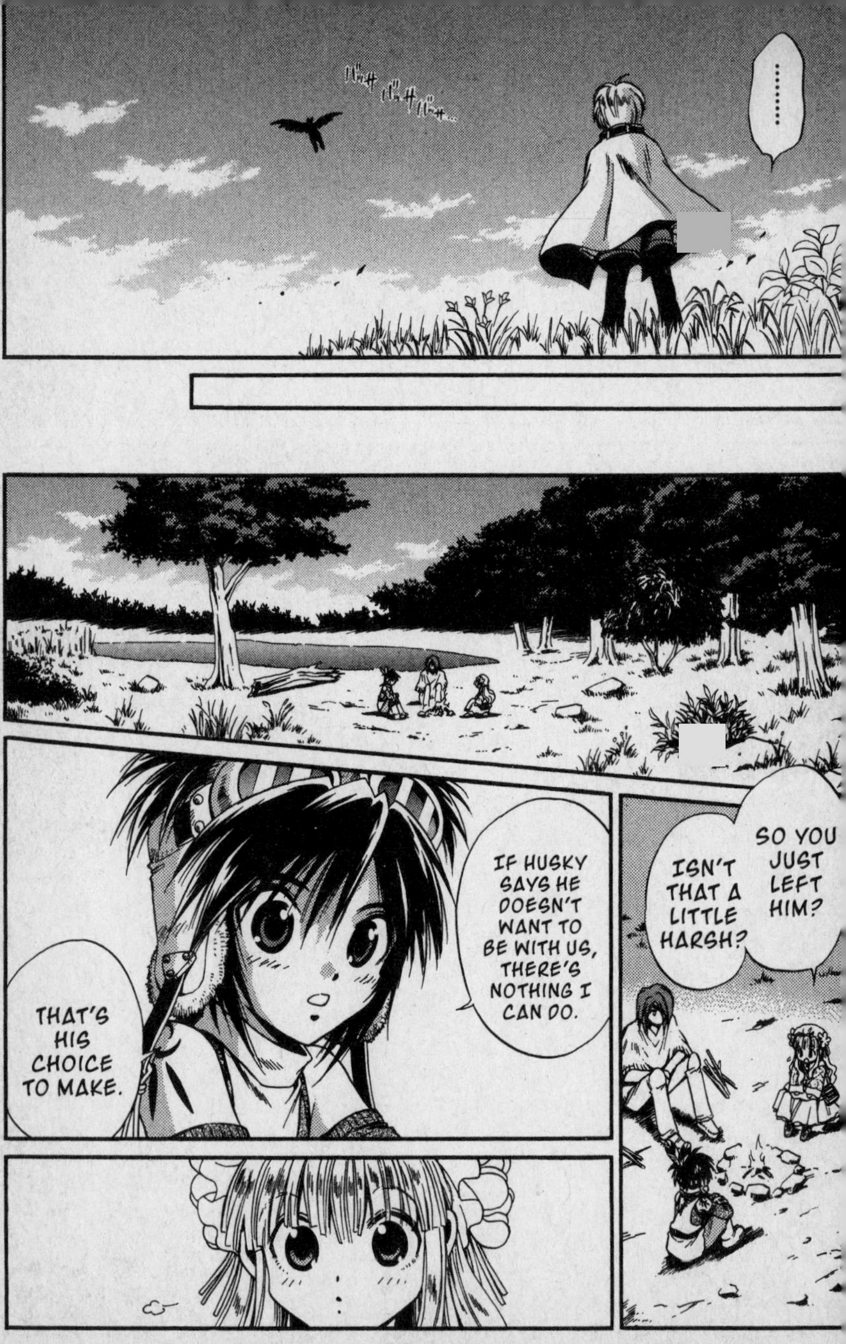
......
SO YOU JUST LEFT HIM?
ISN'T THAT A LITTLE HARSH?
IF HUSKY SAYS HE DOESN'T WANT TO BE WITH US, THERE'S NOTHING I CAN DO.
THAT'S HIS CHOICE TO MAKE.

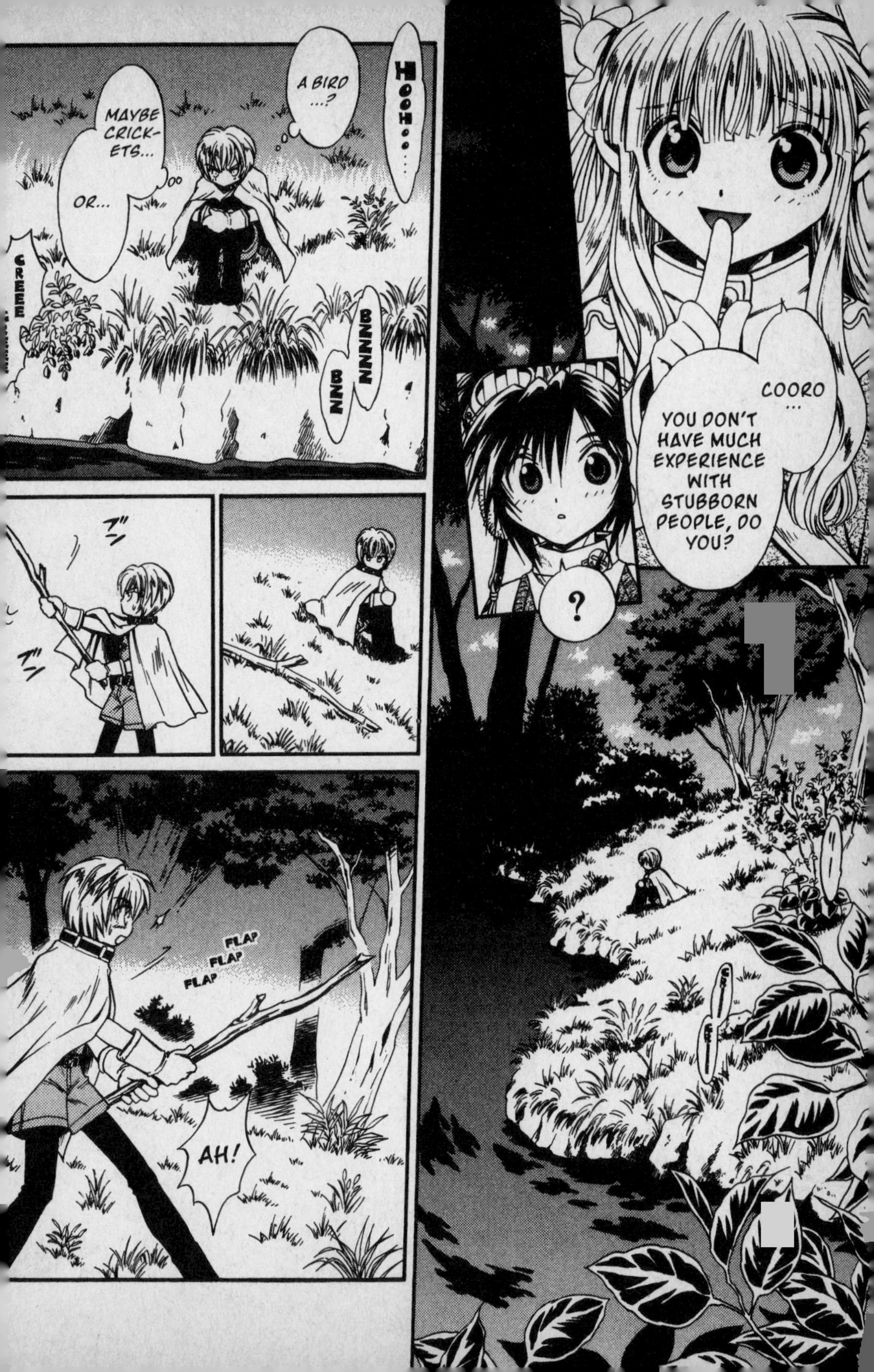
COORO ...
YOU DON'T HAVE MUCH EXPERIENCE WITH STUBBORN PEOPLE, DO YOU?
?
HOOHoo....
A BIRD ...?
MAYBE CRICK-ETS...
OR...
CREEE
BZZNNNNN
BZZ
FLAP FLAP FLAP
AH!

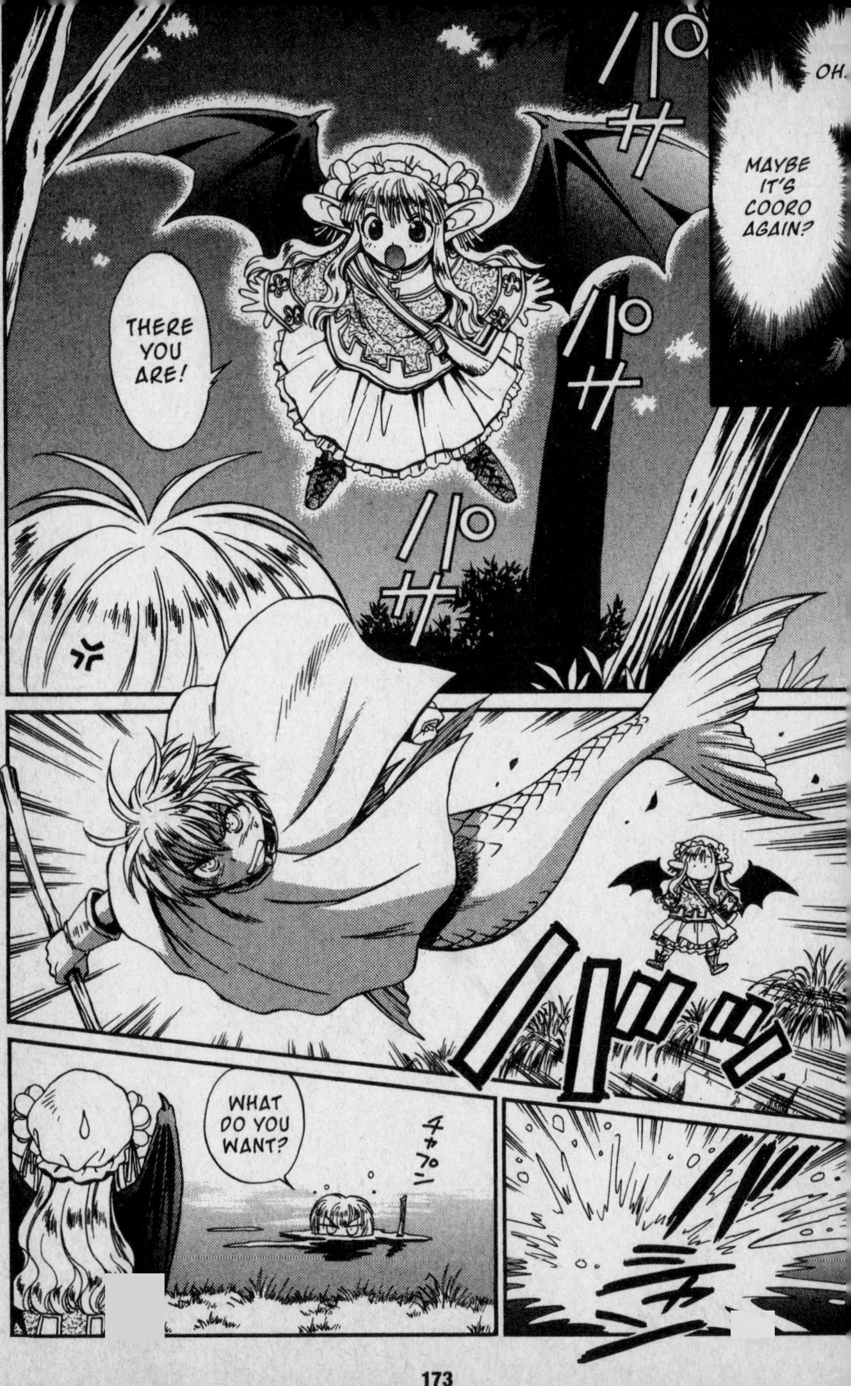
OH...
MAYBE IT'S COORO AGAIN?
パサ
パサ
THERE YOU ARE!
パサ
バッ
WHAT DO YOU WANT?
チャプン

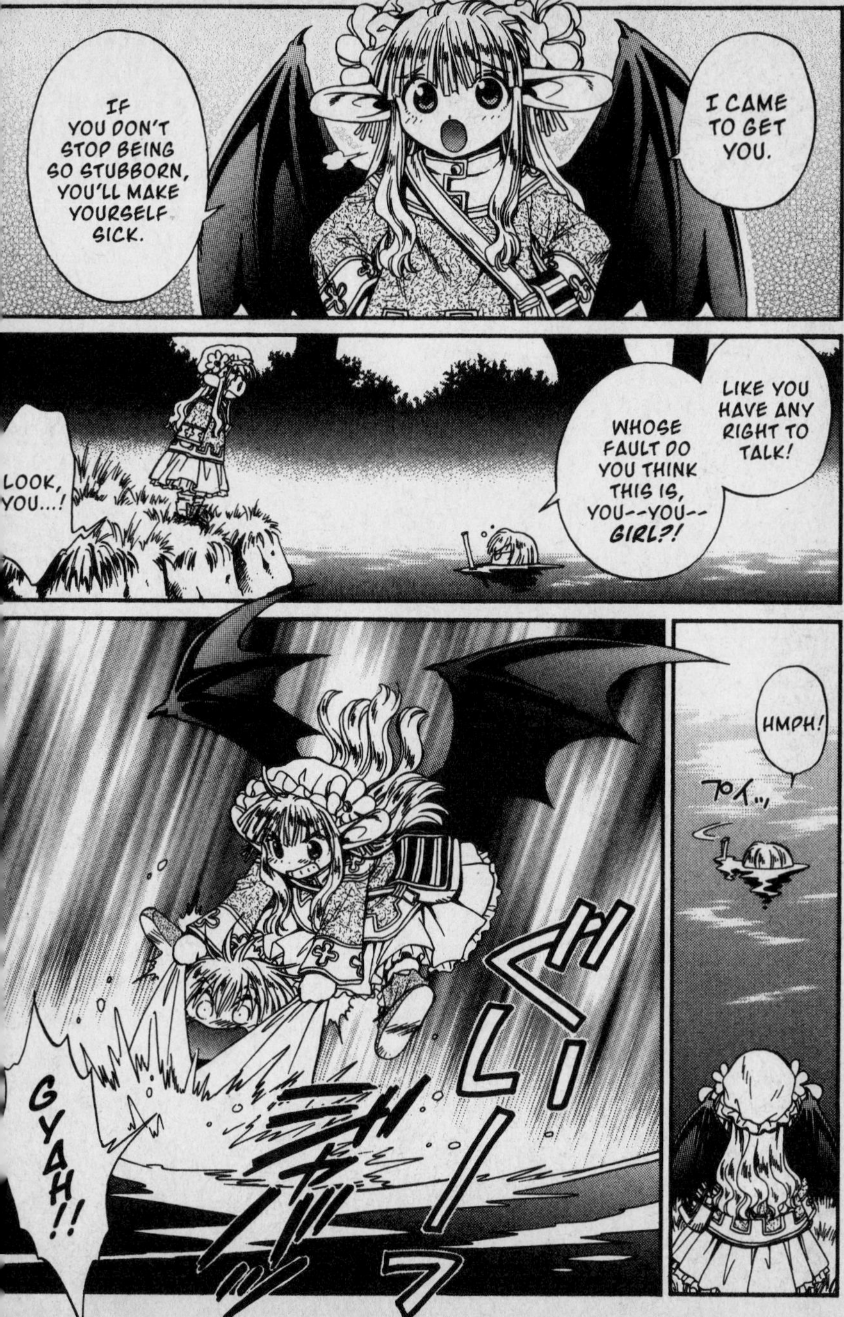
I CAME TO GET YOU.
IF YOU DON'T STOP BEING SO STUBBORN, YOU'LL MAKE YOURSELF SICK.
LIKE YOU HAVE ANY RIGHT TO TALK!
WHOSE FAULT DO YOU THINK THIS IS, YOU--YOU--GIRL?!
LOOK, YOU...!
HMPH!
GYAH!!

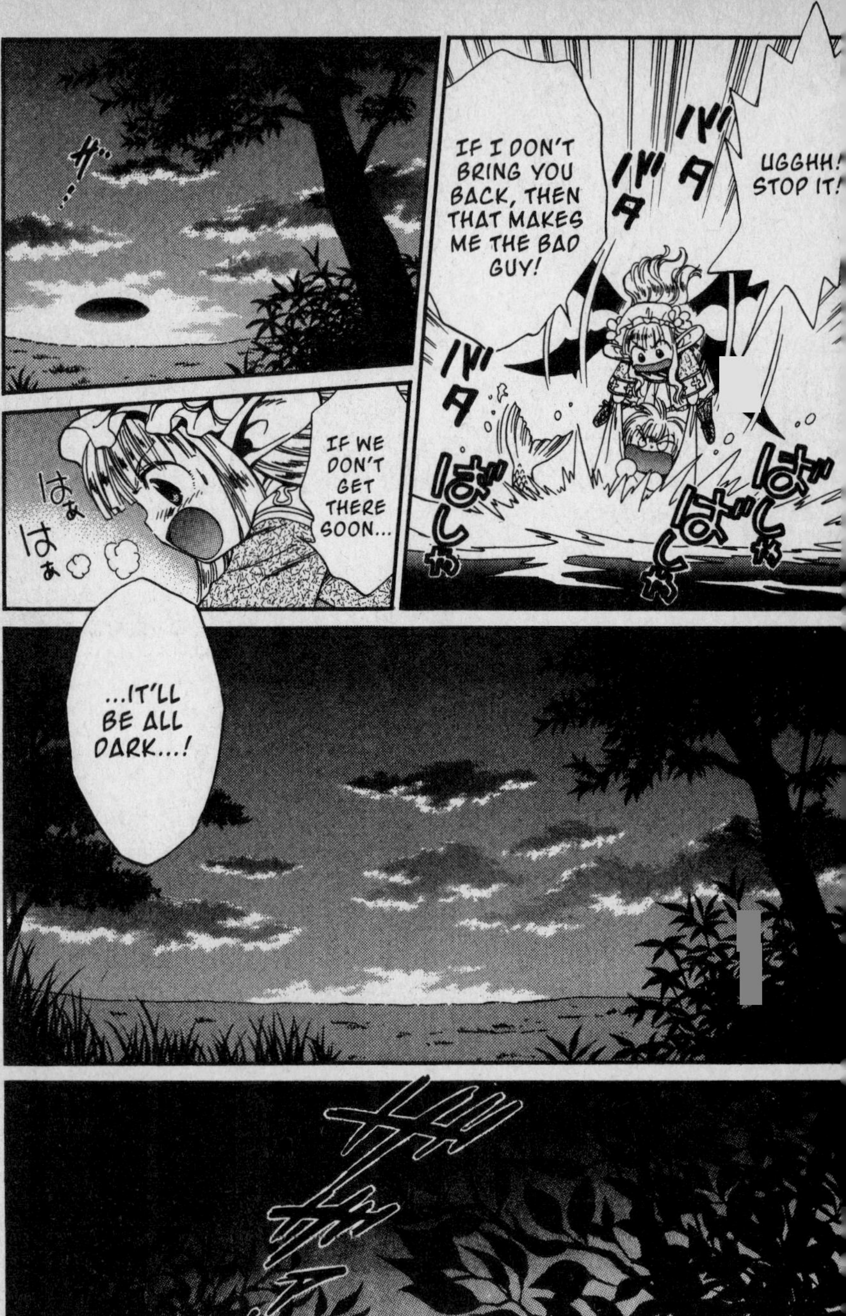
UGGHH! STOP IT!
IF I DON'T BRING YOU BACK, THEN THAT MAKES ME THE BAD GUY!
バタ
バタ
バタ
ばしゃ
ばしゃ
ばしゃ
ザ…
IF WE DON'T GET THERE SOON...
はぁはぁ
...IT'LL BE ALL DARK...!

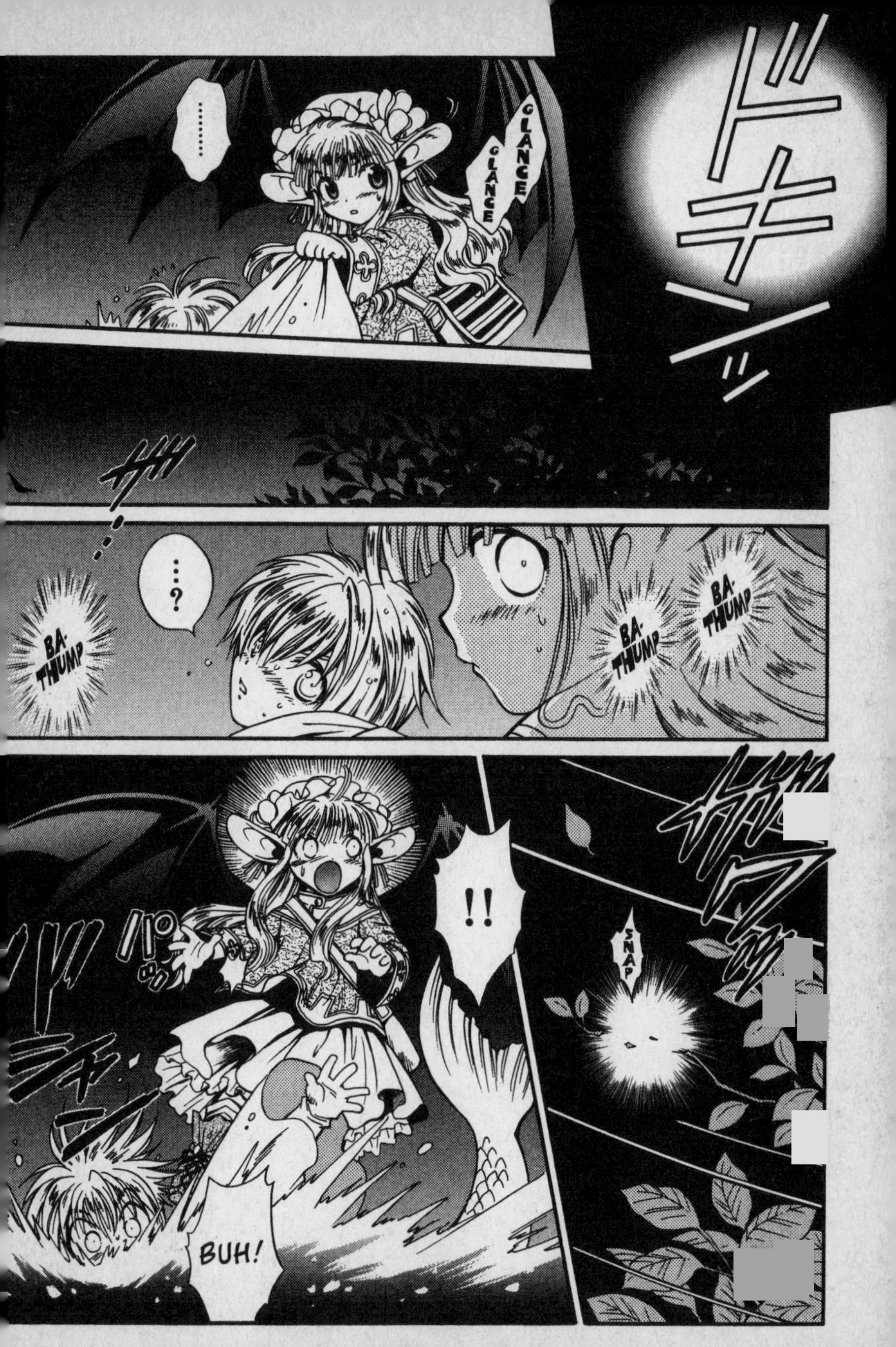
GLANCE
GLANCE
......
...?
BA-THUMP
BA-THUMP
BA-THUMP
SNAP
!!
BUH!

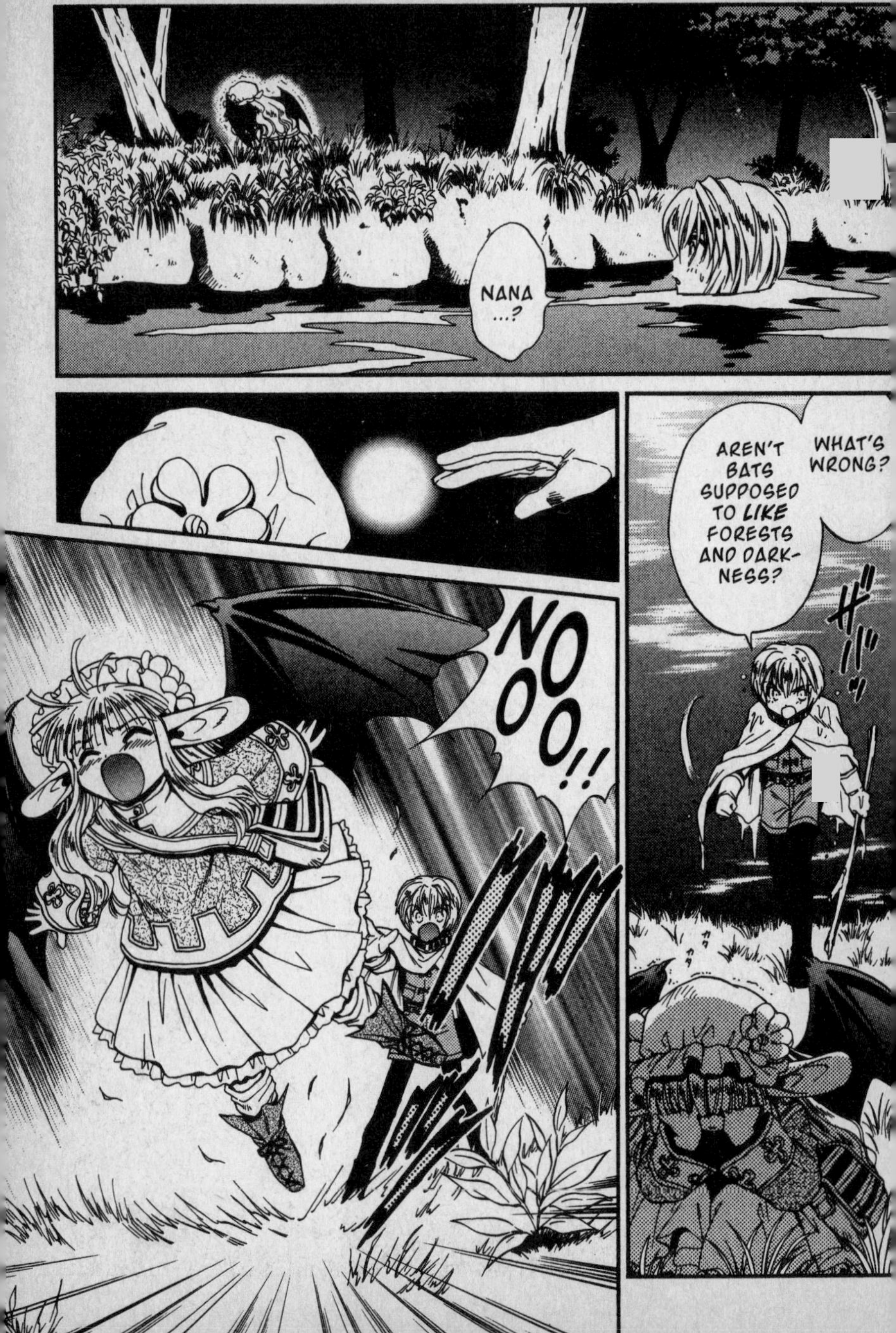
NANA ...?
WHAT'S WRONG?
AREN'T BATS SUPPOSED TO LIKE FORESTS AND DARKNESS?
NOOOO!!

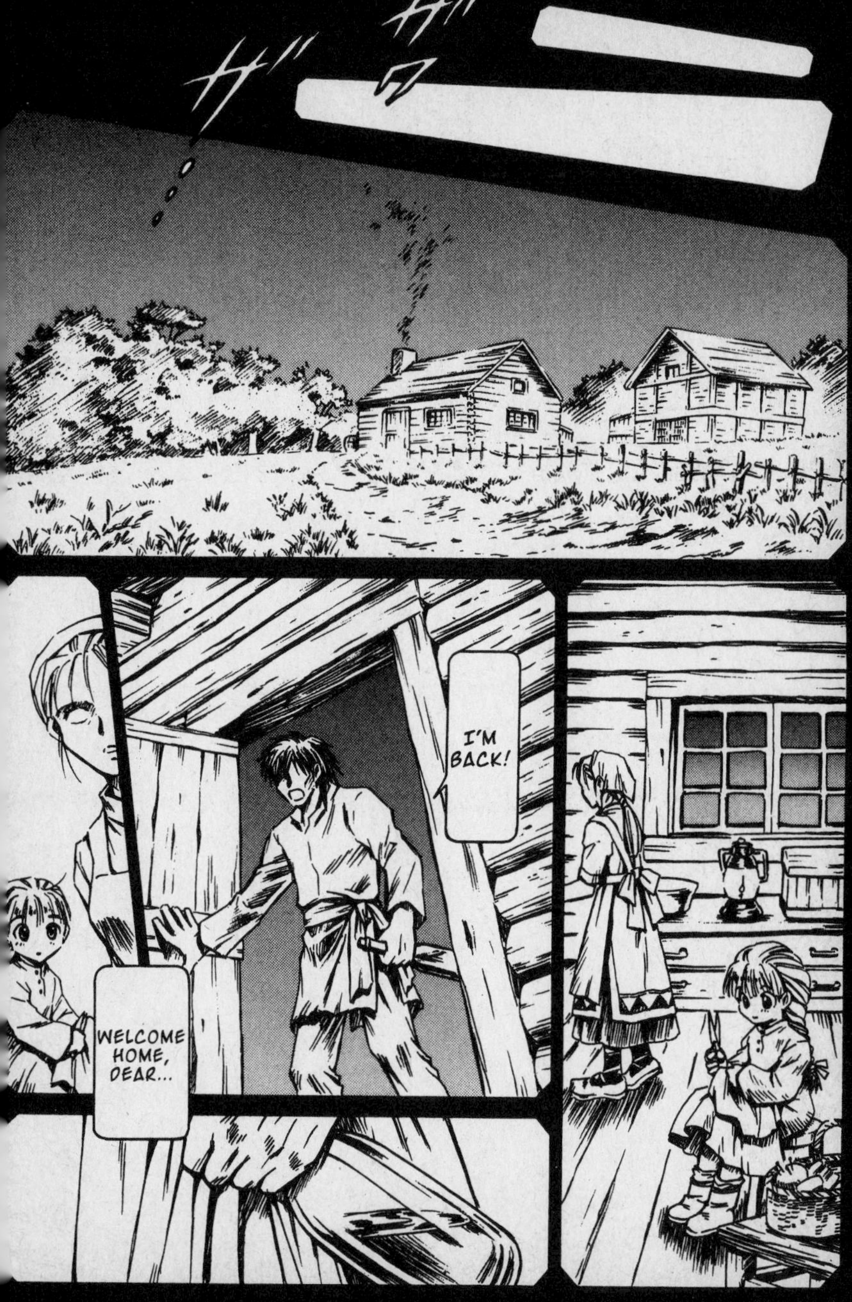
I'M BACK!
WELCOME HOME, DEAR...

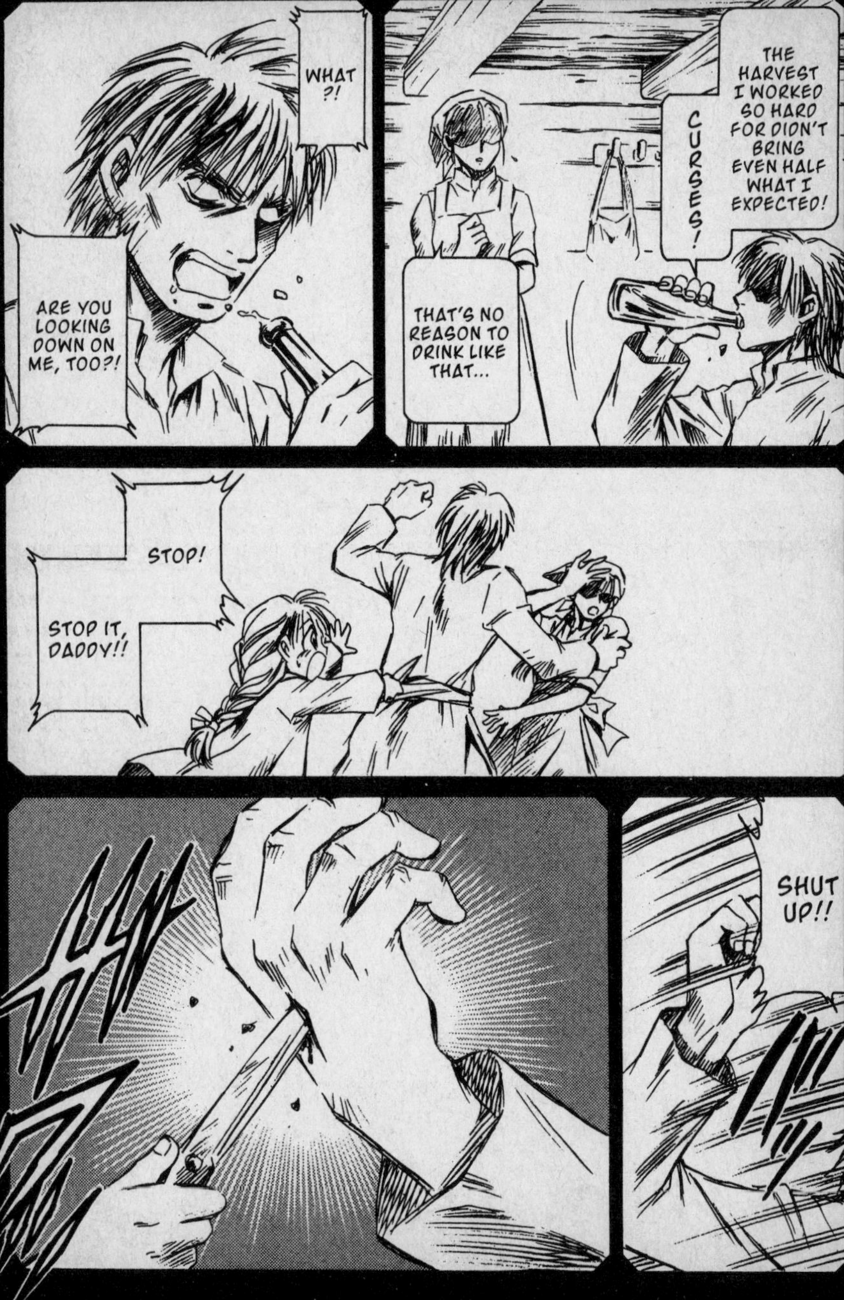
THE HARVEST I WORKED SO HARD FOR DIDN'T BRING EVEN HALF WHAT I EXPECTED!
CURSES!
THAT'S NO REASON TO DRINK LIKE THAT...
WHAT?!
ARE YOU LOOKING DOWN ON ME, TOO?!
STOP!
STOP IT, DADDY!!
SHUT UP!!

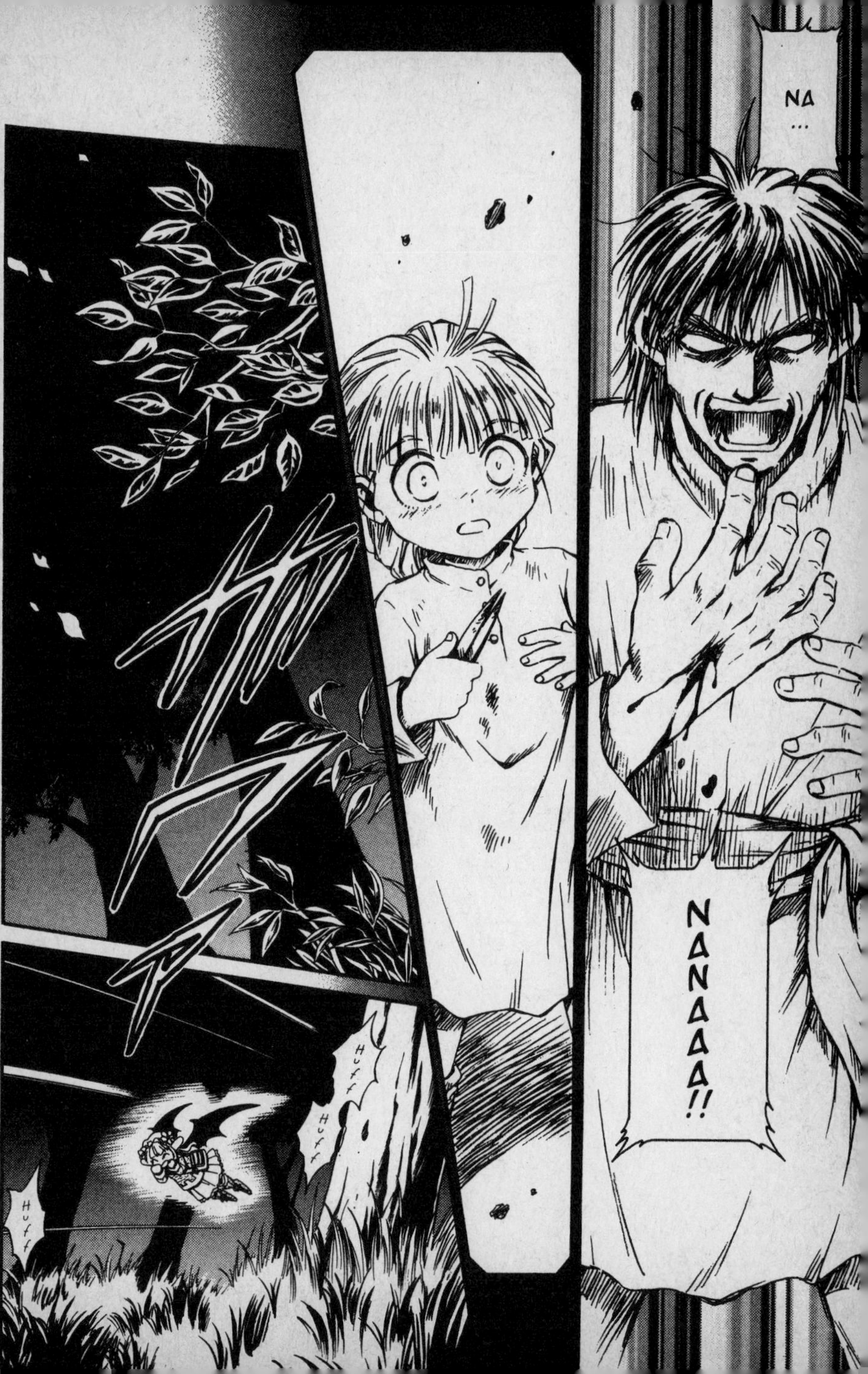
NA ...
NANAAAA!!
Huff
Huff
Huff

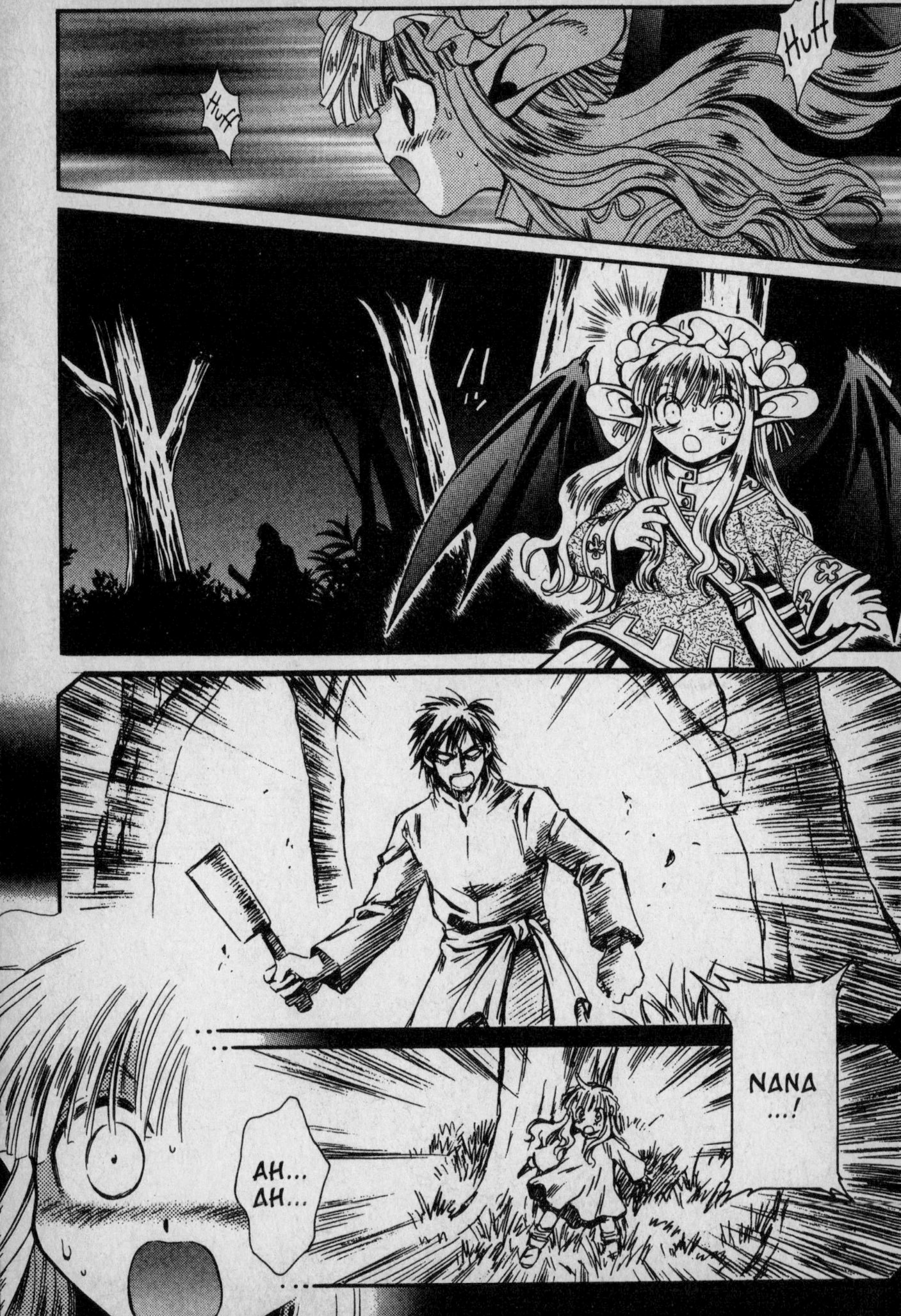
Huff
Huff
NANA ...!
AH... AH...

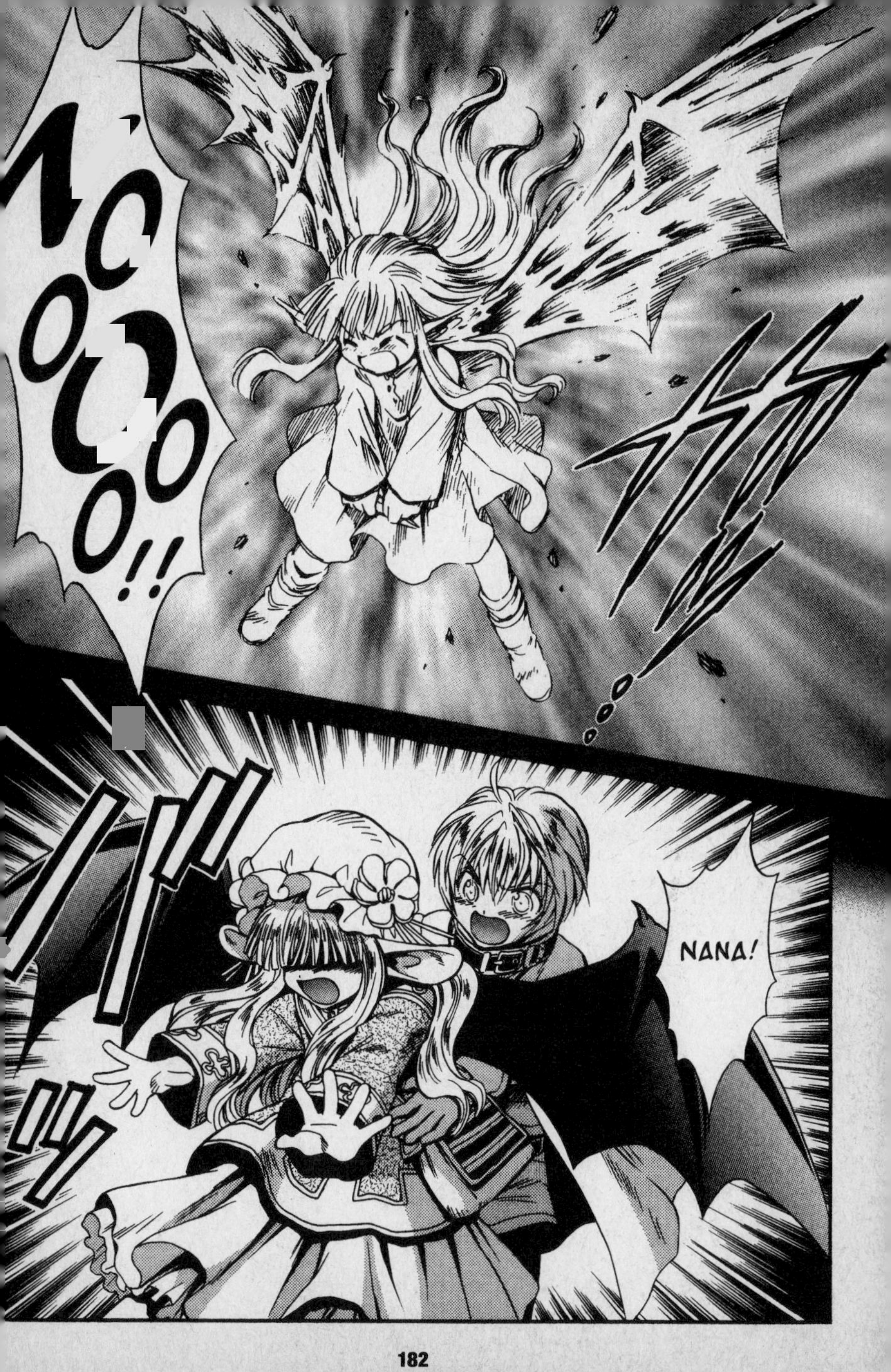
NOOOOO!!
NANA!

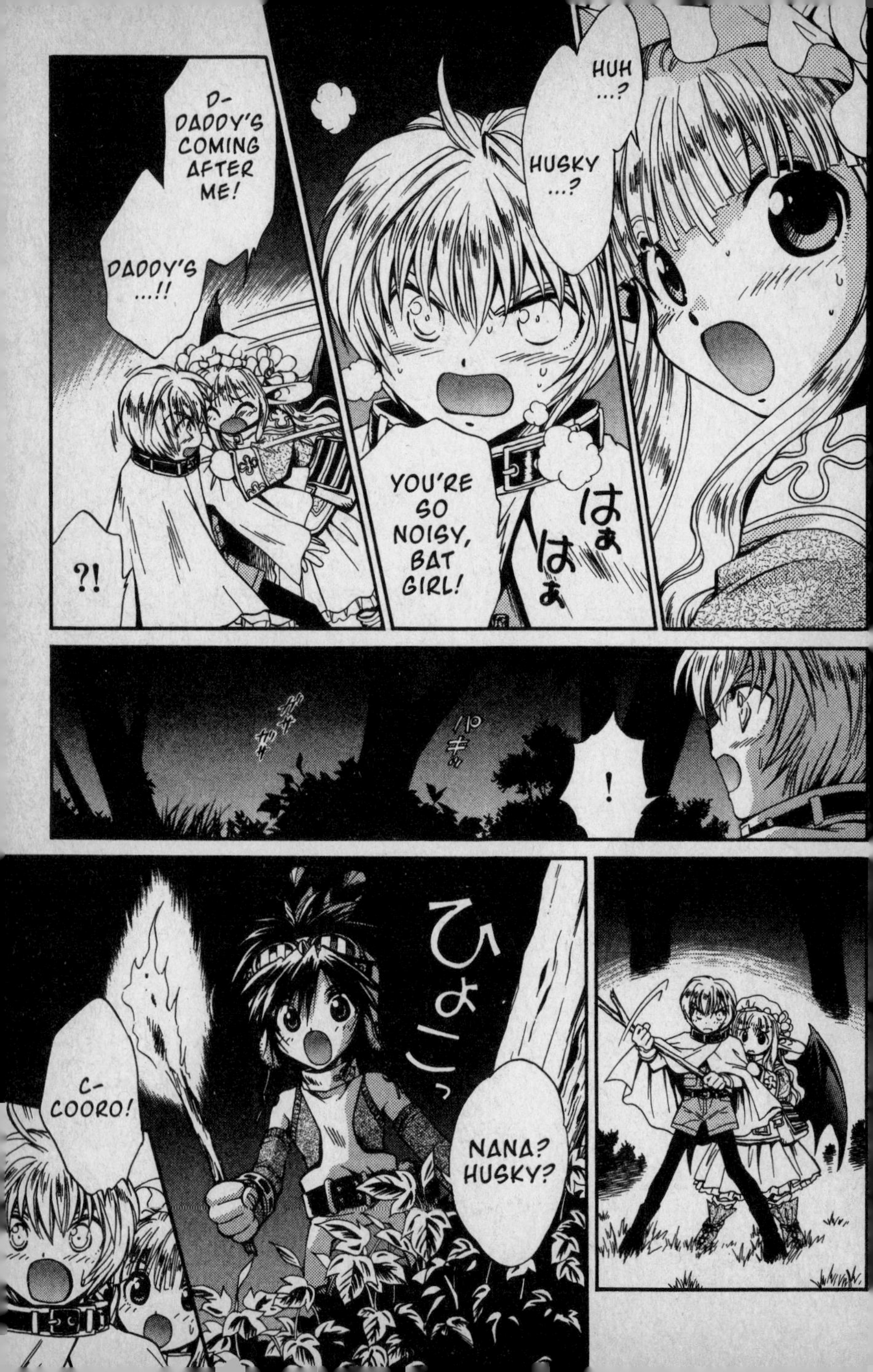
HUH ...?
HUSKY ...?
YOU'RE SO NOISY, BAT GIRL!
はぁ はぁ
D-DADDY'S COMING AFTER ME!
DADDY'S ...!!
?!
!
パキッ
ガサガサ
ひょこっ
NANA? HUSKY?
C-COORO!

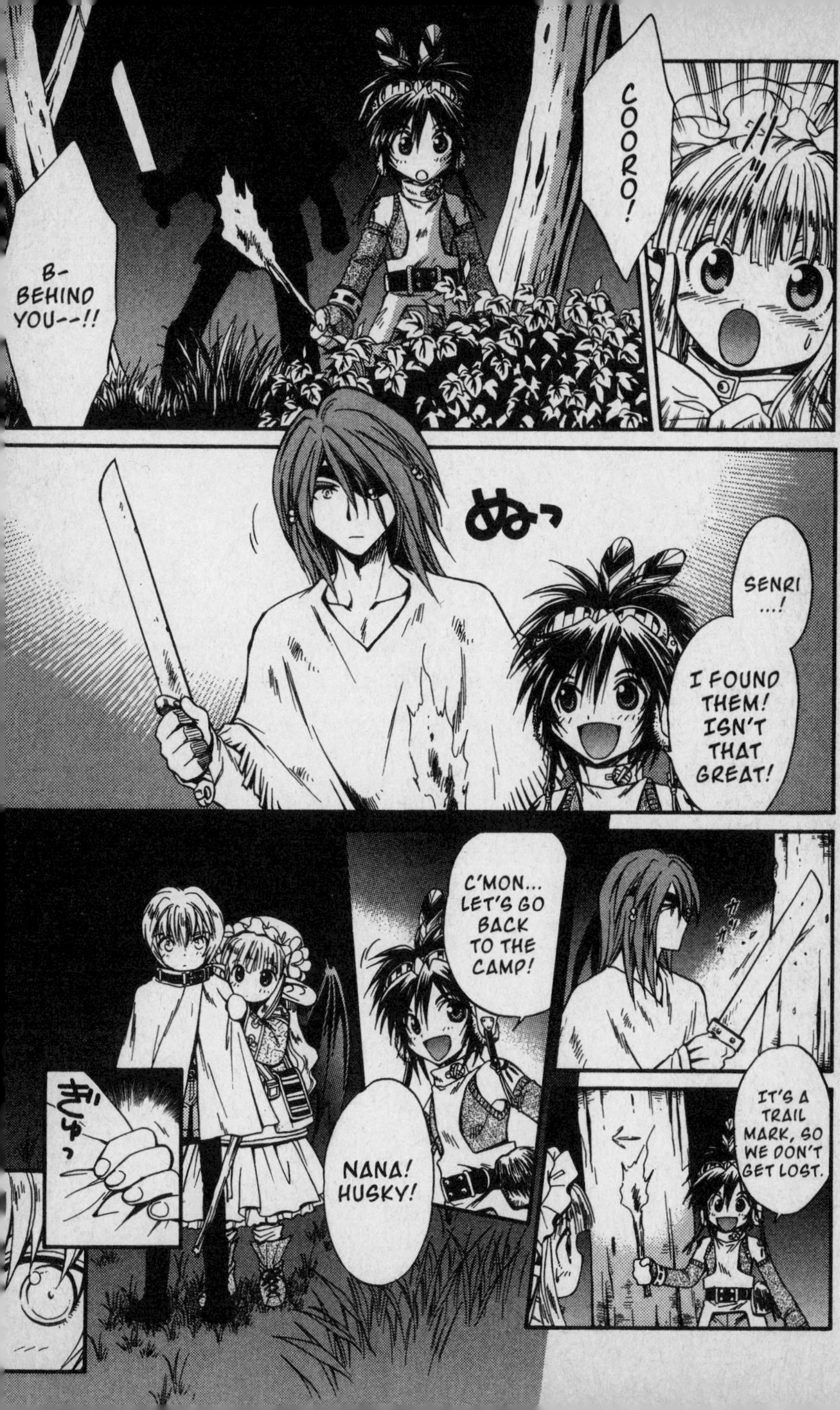
COORO!
B-BEHIND YOU--!!
ぬっ
SENRI ...!
I FOUND THEM! ISN'T THAT GREAT!
IT'S A TRAIL MARK, SO WE DON'T GET LOST.
C'MON... LET'S GO BACK TO THE CAMP!
NANA! HUSKY!
ぎゅっ

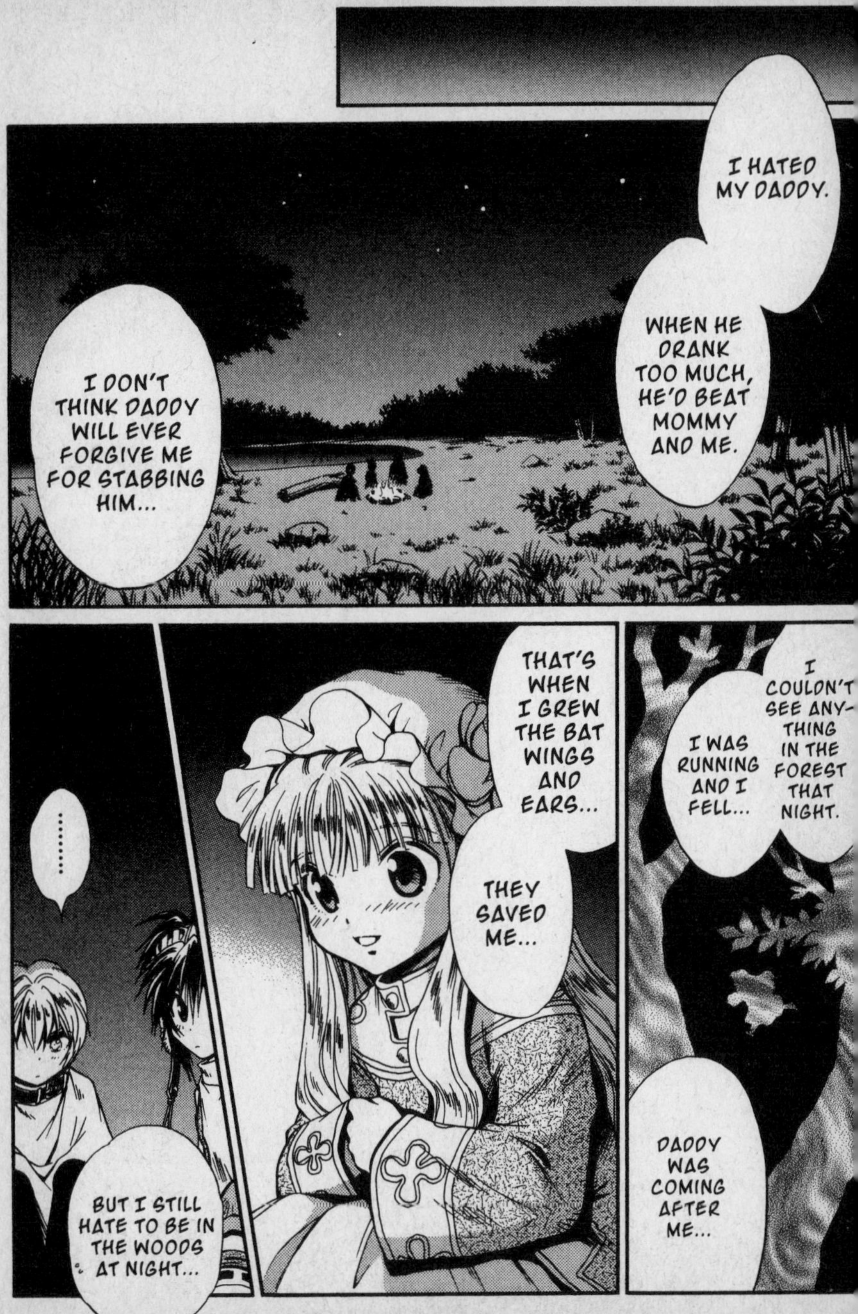
I HATED MY DADDY.
WHEN HE DRANK TOO MUCH, HE'D BEAT MOMMY AND ME.
I DON'T THINK DADDY WILL EVER FORGIVE ME FOR STABBING HIM...
I COULDN'T SEE ANY-THING IN THE FOREST THAT NIGHT.
I WAS RUNNING AND I FELL...
DADDY WAS COMING AFTER ME...
THAT'S WHEN I GREW THE BAT WINGS AND EARS...
THEY SAVED ME...
......
BUT I STILL HATE TO BE IN THE WOODS AT NIGHT...

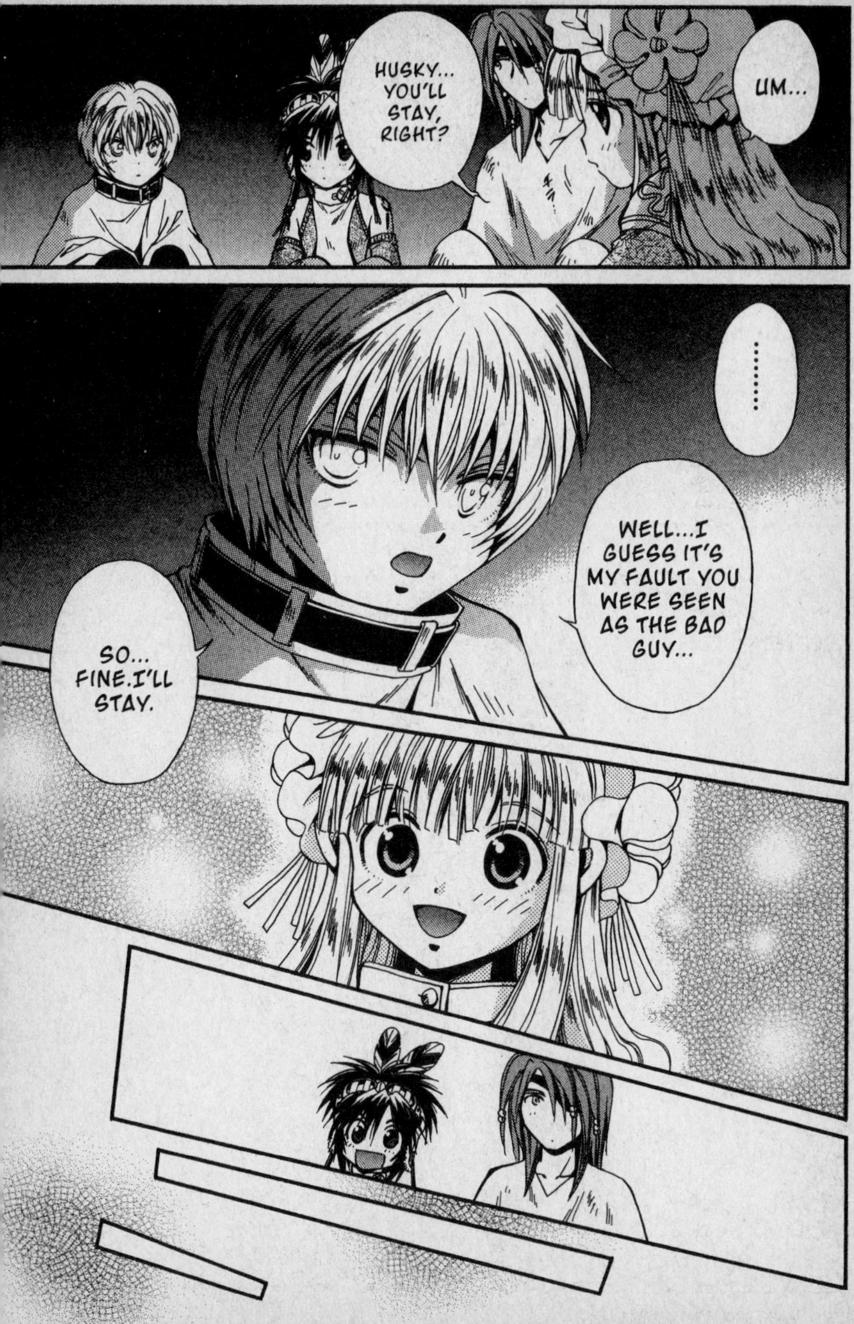
UM...
HUSKY... YOU'LL STAY, RIGHT?
......
WELL...I GUESS IT'S MY FAULT YOU WERE SEEN AS THE BAD GUY...
SO... FINE. I'LL STAY.

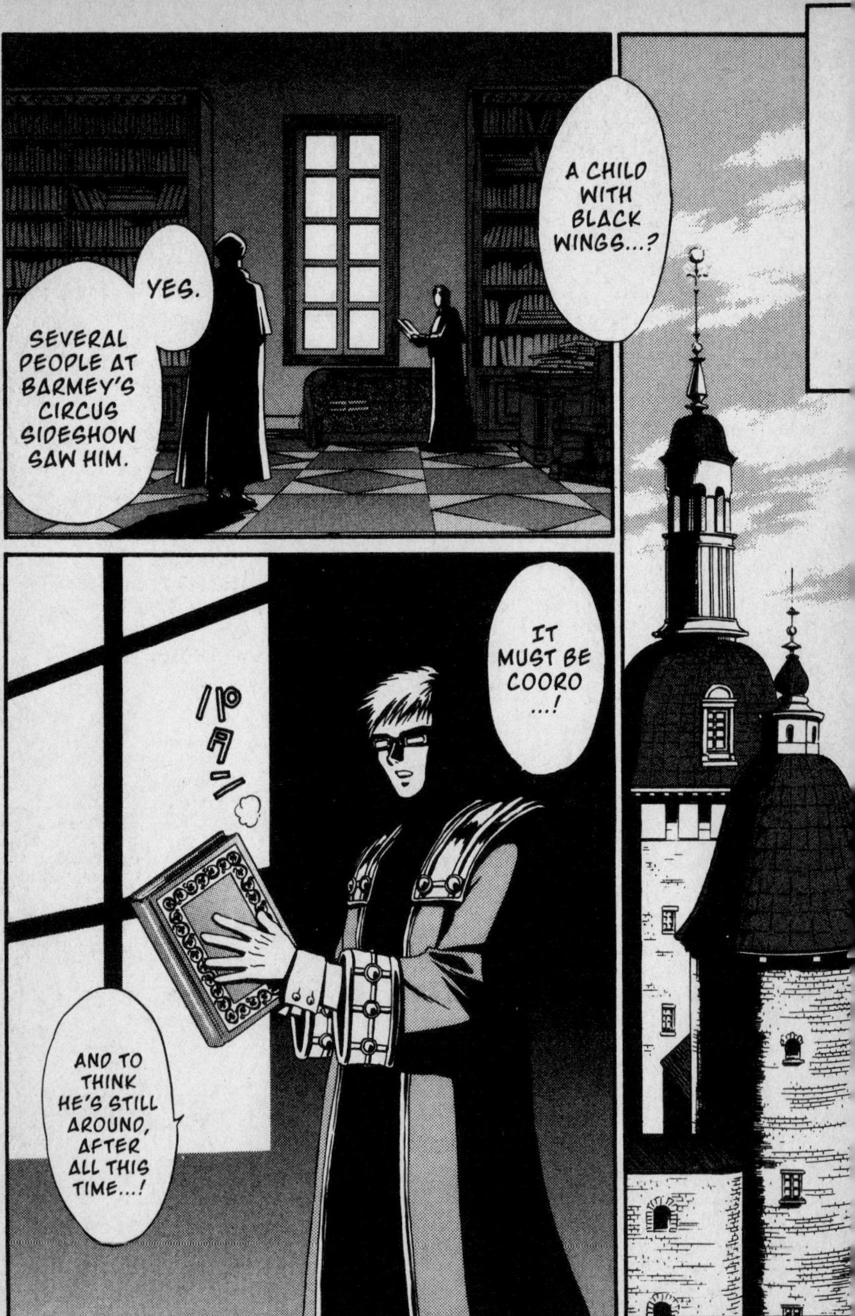
A CHILD WITH BLACK WINGS...?
YES.
SEVERAL PEOPLE AT BARMEY'S CIRCUS SIDESHOW SAW HIM.
IT MUST BE COORO ...!
パタン
AND TO THINK HE'S STILL AROUND, AFTER ALL THIS TIME...!

To be continued...

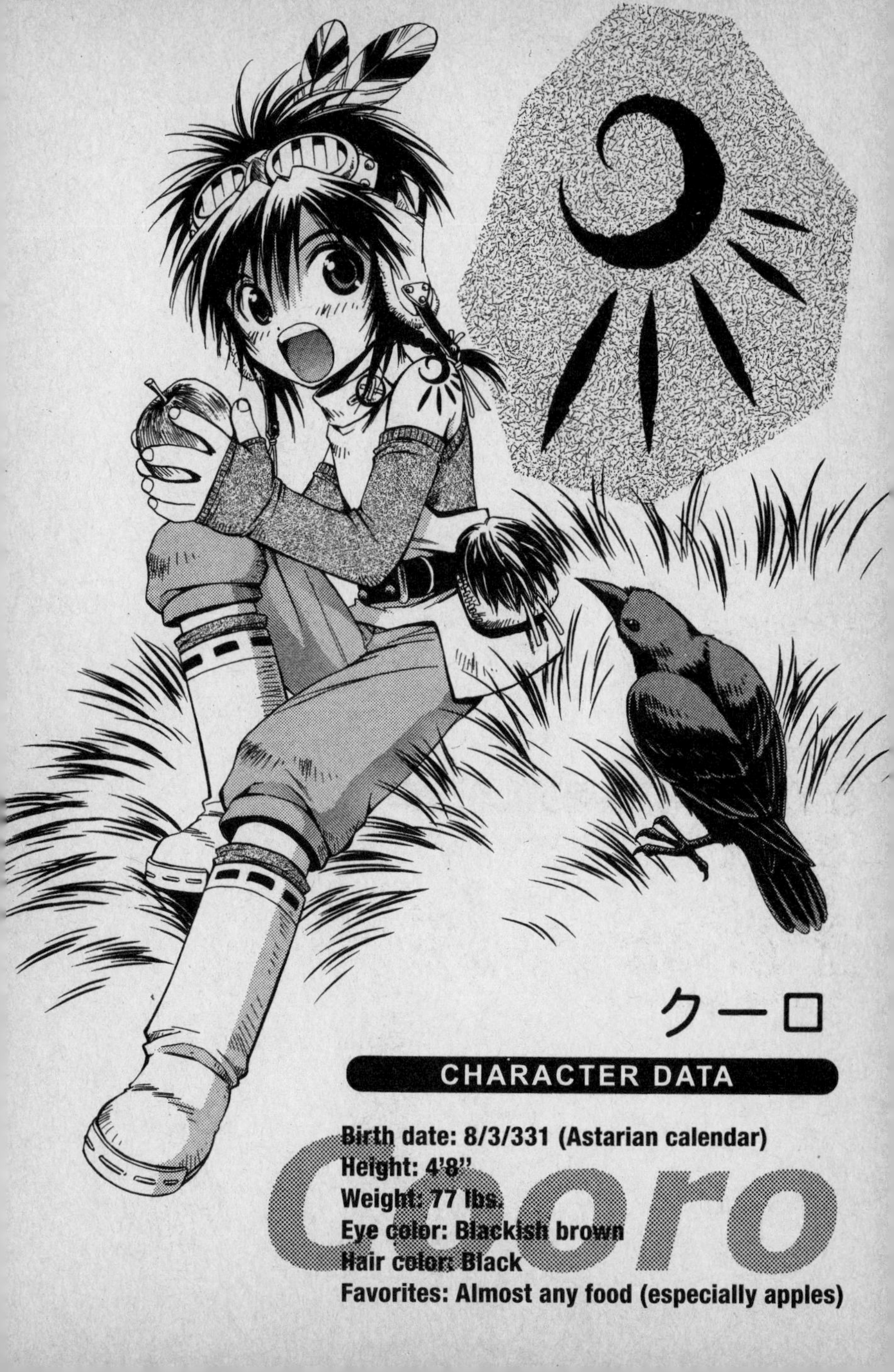

クーロ

CHARACTER DATA

Cooro

Birth date: 8/3/331 (Astarian calendar)
Height: 4'8"
Weight: 77 lbs.
Eye color: Blackish brown
Hair color: Black
Favorites: Almost any food (especially apples)

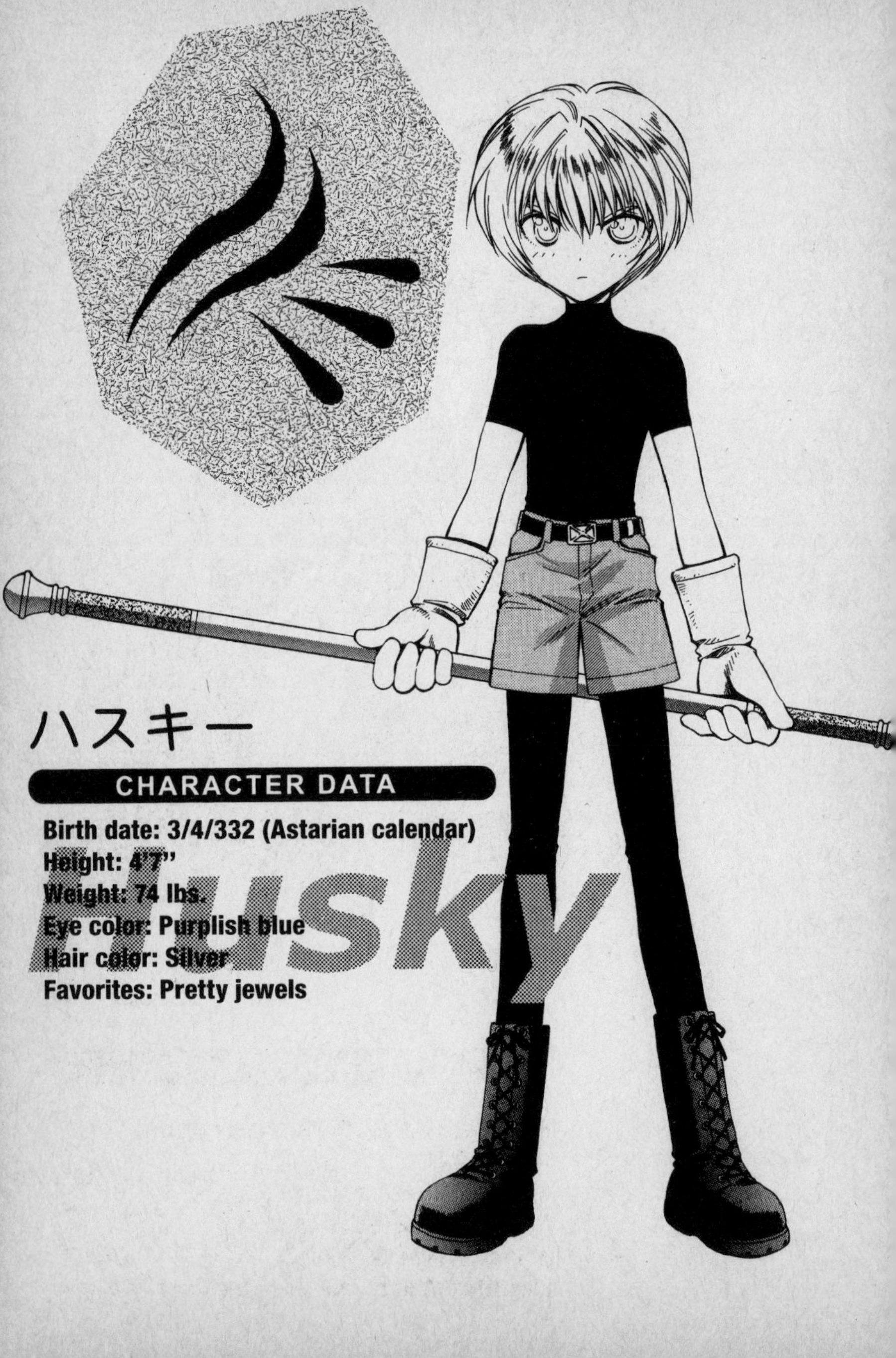

ハスキー

Husky

CHARACTER DATA

Birth date: 3/4/332 (Astarian calendar)
Height: 4'7"
Weight: 74 lbs.
Eye color: Purplish blue
Hair color: Silver
Favorites: Pretty jewels

センリ

CHARACTER DATA

Senri

Birth date: 4/30/327 (Astarian calendar)
Height: 5'8½"
Weight: 132 lbs.
Eye color: Gray
Hair color: Gray
Favorites: Small flowers

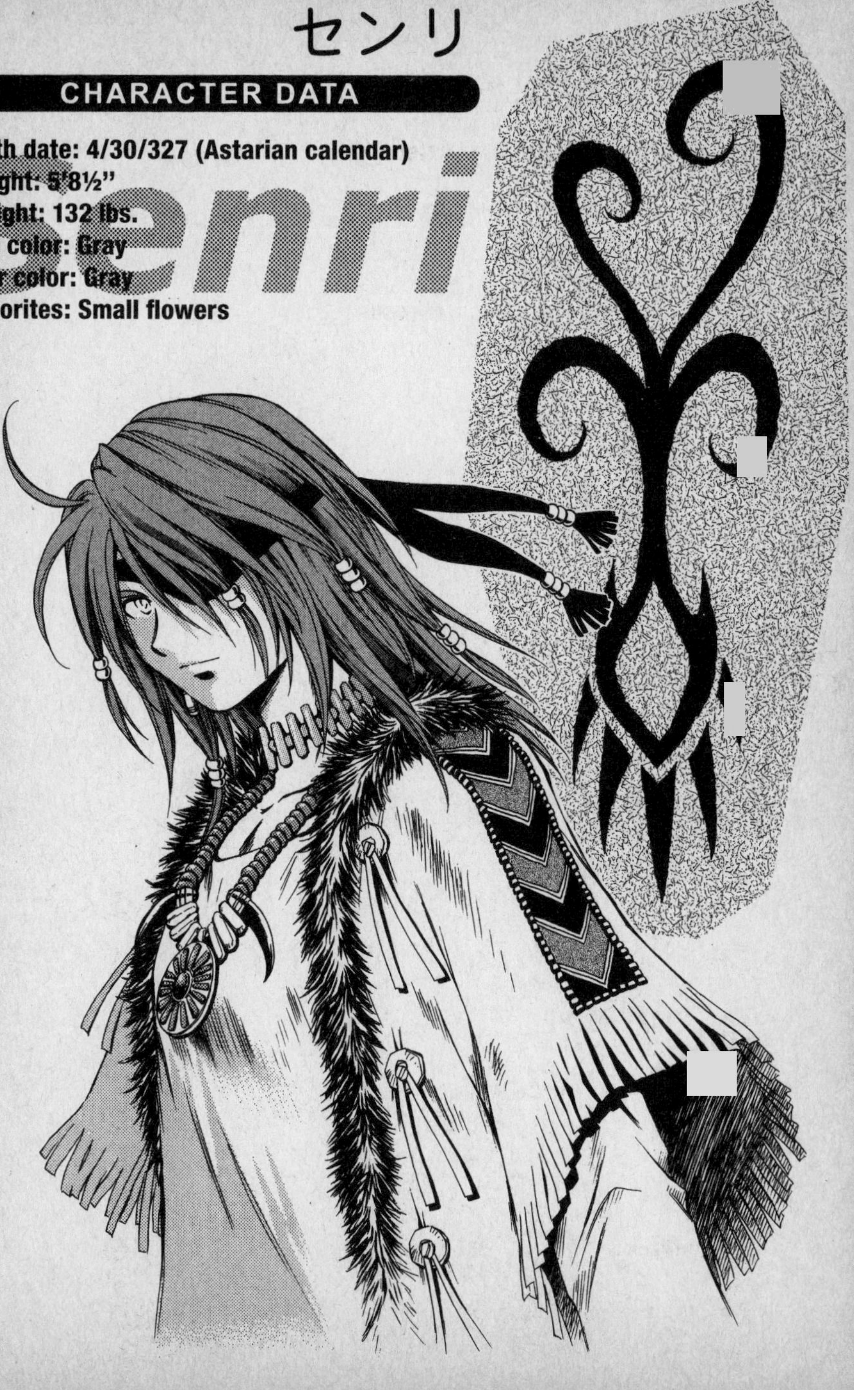

ナナ

CHARACTER DATA

Nana

Birth date: 10/12/332 (Astarian calendar)
Height: 4'5"
Weight: 65 lbs.
Eye color: Green
Hair color: Light brown
Favorites: Cute clothes, flowers, ribbons, etc.

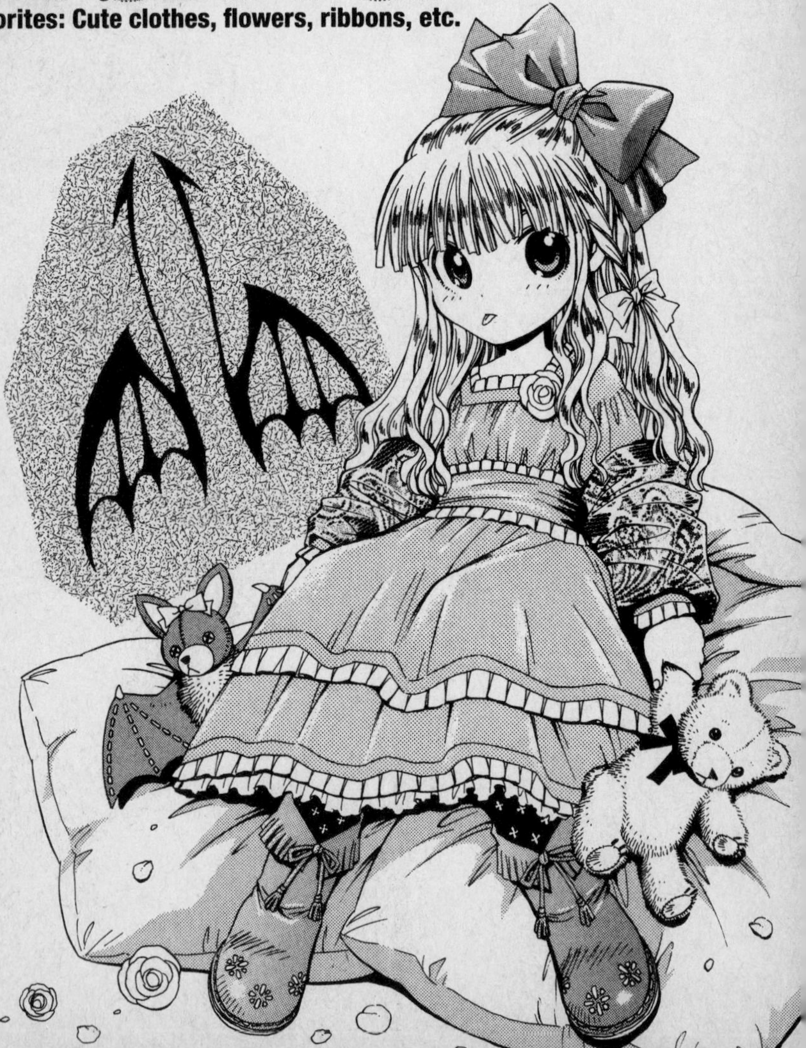

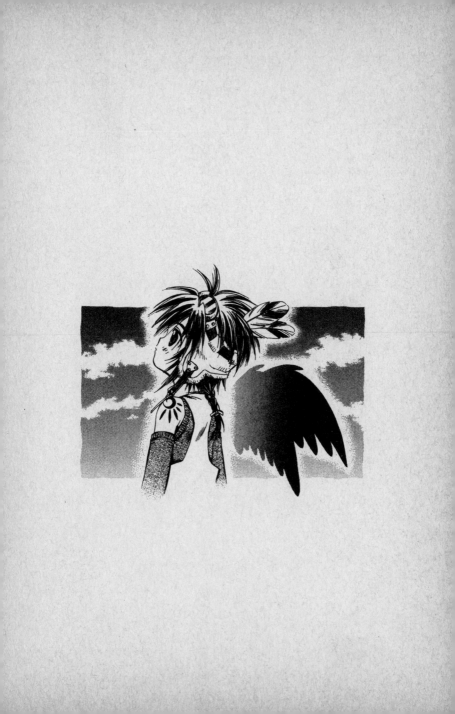

+ANIMA

COORO AND FRIENDS ENCOUNTER A TOWN LIVING IN FEAR OF A SUPPOSED "GIANT BEE" +ANIMA. BUT THE GROUP SOON DISCOVERS THAT LOOKS CAN SOMETIMES "BEE" DECEIVING... LATER, THEY BEFRIEND AN OLD WOMAN NAMED MARGOT AND HER TRAVELING COMPANION, ROSE. ROSE TAKES A SPECIAL INTEREST IN SENRI...AND WHEN GIANT BIRDS ATTACK COORO, SHE PROVES TO BE AN ALLY--WITH A SHOCKING SECRET. FINALLY, IN AN ALTERNATE +ANIMA STORYLINE, COORO BEFRIENDS A MAN WHO WISHES HE COULD BE A +ANIMA SO MUCH THAT HE TRIES TO USE COORO AS A RESEARCH SPECIMEN!

THE FEATHERS AND FUR WILL FLY IN THE NEXT THRILLING VOLUME!

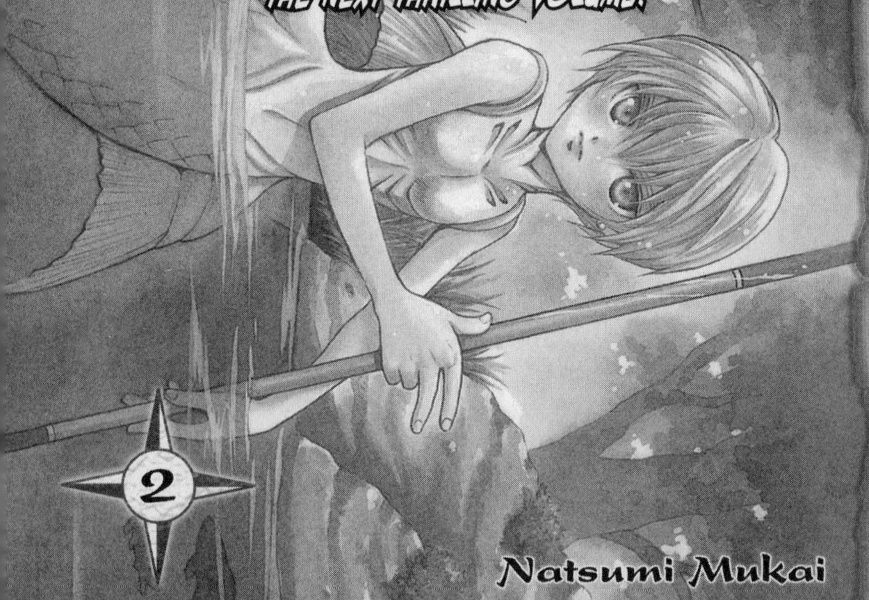
2

Natsumi Mukai

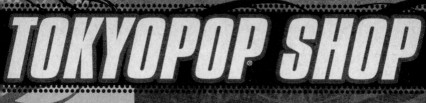
TOKYOPOP SHOP

WWW.TOKYOPOP.COM/SHOP

HOT NEWS!
Check out the
TOKYOPOP SHOP!
The world's best
collection of manga in
English is now available
online in one place!

BIZENGHAST POSTER

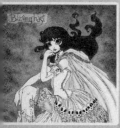

PRINCESS AI POSTCARDS

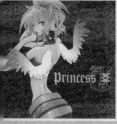

Check out all
the sizzling hot
merchandise and
your favorite manga
at the shop!

I Luv Halloween Glow-in-the-Dark STICKERS!

I LUV HALLOWEEN BUTTONS & STICKERS

- LOOK FOR SPECIAL OFFERS
- PRE-ORDER UPCOMING RELEASES
- COMPLETE YOUR COLLECTIONS

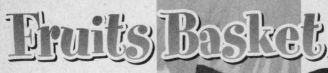
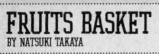

Ayumu struggles with her studies, and the all-important high school entrance exams are approaching. Fortunately, she has help from her best bud Shii-chan, who is at the top of the class. But when the test results come back, the friends are surprised: Ayumu surpasses Shii-chan's scores and gets into the school of her choice—without Shii-chan! Losing her friend is so painful for Ayumu that she starts cutting herself to ease her sorrow. Finally, Ayumu seeks comfort in a new friend, Manami. But will Manami prove to be the friend that Ayumu truly needs? Or will Ayumu continue down a dark path?

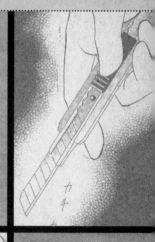

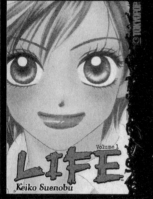

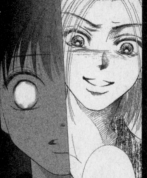

It's about real teenagers...

It's about real high school...

It's about real life.

Volume 1

LIFE

Keiko Suenobu

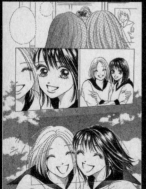

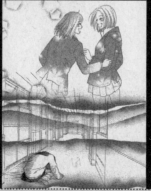

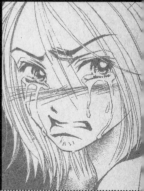

LIFE
BY KEIKO SUENOBU

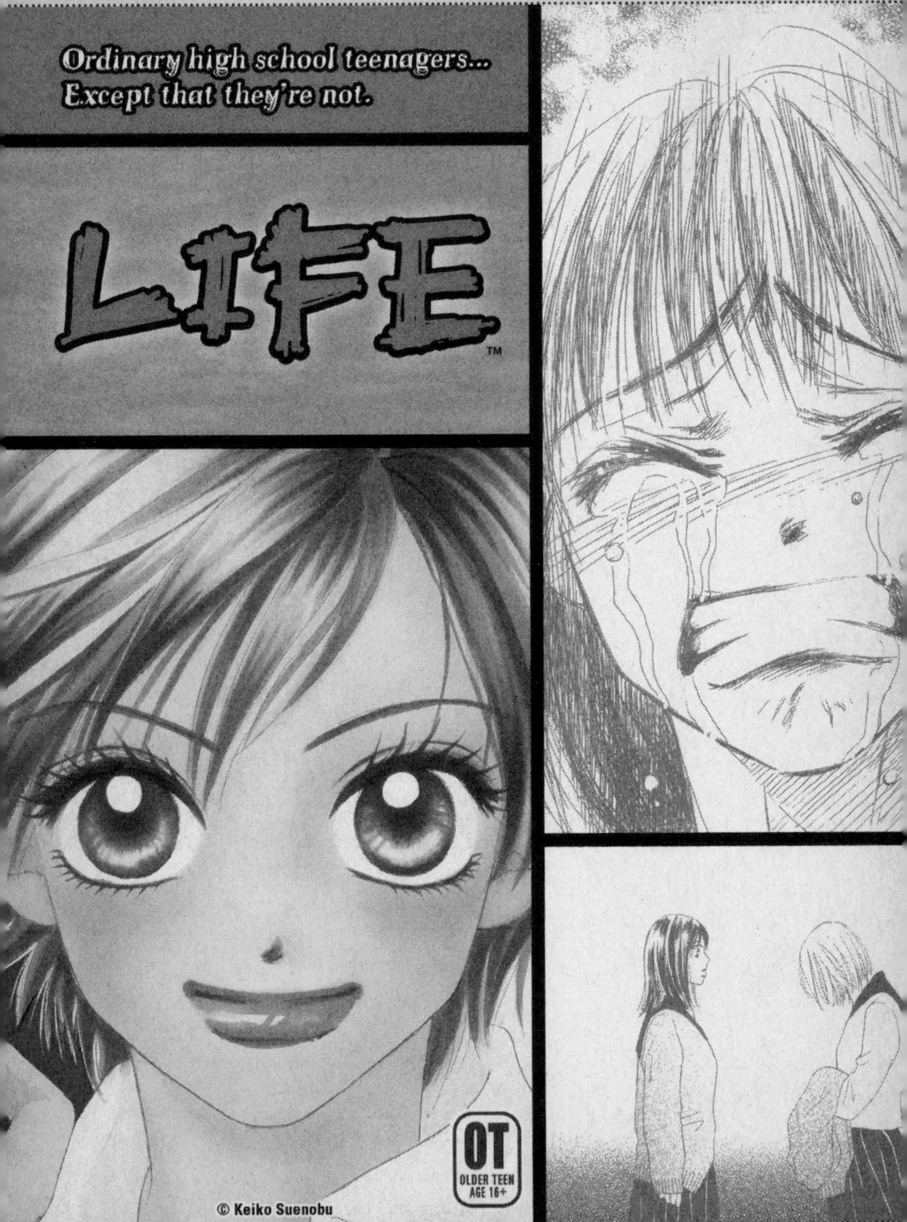
Ordinary high school teenagers...
Except that they're not.
LIFE™
OT
OLDER TEEN
AGE 16+
© Keiko Suenobu

READ THE ENTIRE FIRST CHAPTER ONLINE FOR FREE:

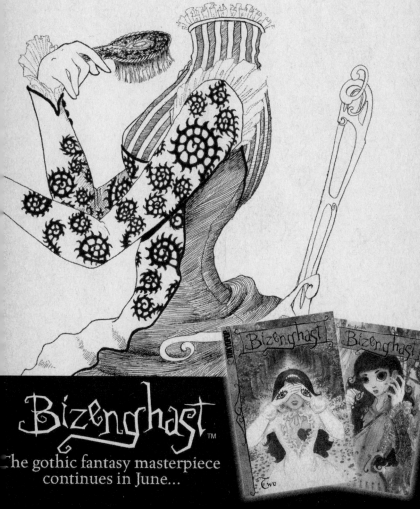

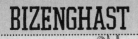

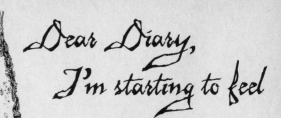

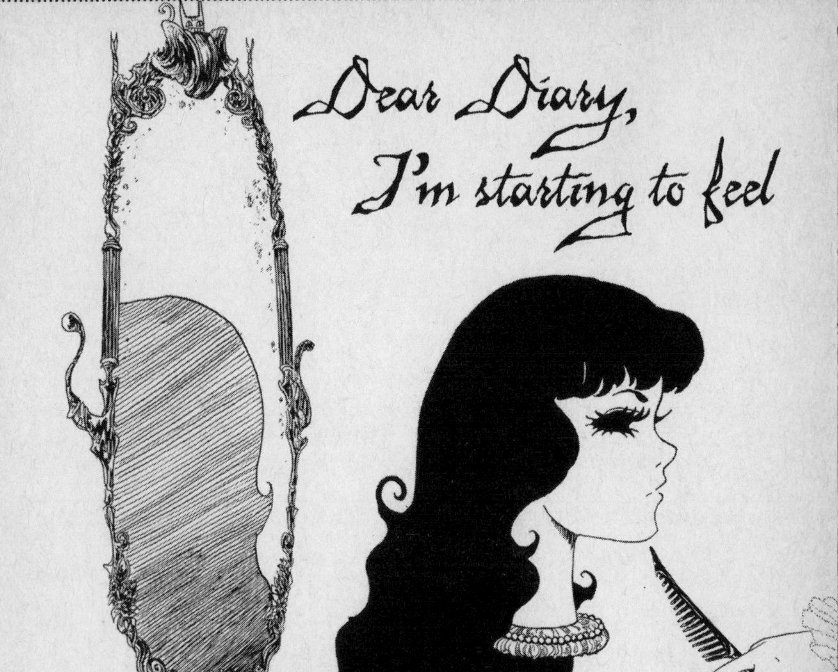

Dear Diary,
I'm starting to feel

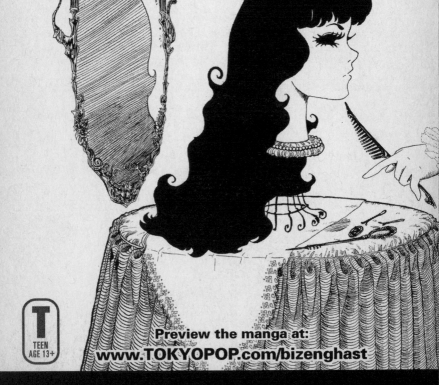

STO[P]

This is the back of the book.
You wouldn't want to spoil a great ending!

This book is printed "manga-style," in the authentic Japanese right-to-left format. Since none of the artwork has been flipped or altered, readers get to experience the story just as the creator intended. You've been asking for it, so TOKYOPOP® delivered: authentic, hot-off-the-press, and far more fun!

DIRECTIONS

If this is your first time reading manga-style, here's a quick guide to help you understand how it works.

It's easy... just start in the top right panel and follow the numbers. Have fun, and look for more 100% authentic manga from TOKYOPOP®!

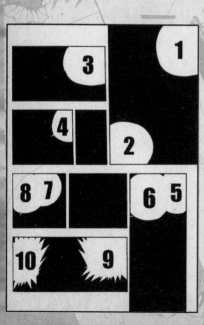

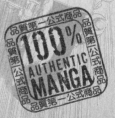